LAW AND DIPLOMACY IN COMMODITY ECONOMICS

LAW AND DIPLOMACY IN COMMODITY ECONOMICS

A Study of Techniques, Co-operation and Conflict in International Public Policy Issues

Emiko Atimomo

Preface by
Pierre Vellas

HM HOLMES & MEIER PUBLISHERS, INC.
IMPORT DIVISION
IUB Building
30 Irving Place, New York, N.Y. 10003

First published 1981 by
THE MACMILLAN PRESS LTD
London and Basingstoke
Companies and representatives throughout the world

ISBN 0 333 27745 7

Printed in Hong Kong

The book is dedicated to my late father Aboritsedueye Atimomo, in affectionate memory, for his industry and selflessness; and to the cause of international co-operation and world peace, in keeping with Article 55 of the United Nations Charter

Contents

Abbreviations

1 ORGANISATIONS

ADB	African Development Bank
AGC	African Groundnut Council
ANRPC	Association of Natural Rubber Producing Countries
AOPO	African Oilseeds Producers Organisation
BOAD	West African Development Bank
CEAO	Communauté Economique de l'Afrique de l'Ouest
CEBV	Meat and Cattle Interstate Committee (Ouagadougou)
CIEH	Inter-African Committee on Hydraulic Studies (Ouagadougou)
ECA	Economic Commission for Africa
ECOSOC	Economic and Social Council
ECOWAS	Economic Community of West African States
EEC	European Economic Community
EURATOM	European Atomic Commission
FAO	Food and Agriculture Organisation
GATT	General Agreement on Tariffs and Trade
GEPLACEA	Group of Latin American and Caribbean Sugar Exporting Countries
GSA	General Services Administration
GSP	Generalised System of Preferences
IBRD	International Bank for Reconstruction and Development
ICC	International Cocoa Council
ICJ	International Court of Justice
ICO	International Coffee Organisation
IFC	International Finance Corporation
ILO	International Labour Organisation
IMF	International Monetary Fund
ITC	International Tin Council
ITO	International Trade Organisation
IWC	International Wheat Council

MULPOC	Multinational Programming and Operational Centre
OAS	Organisation of American States
OAU	Organisation of African Unity
OCAM	African and Maurician Cameroon Organisation
OECD	Organisation for European Co-operation and Development
UAM	African and Malagasy Union
UAMCE	African and Malagasy Union for Economic Co-operation
UNICITRAL	United Nations Commission for International Trade Law
UNCTAD	United Nations Conference on Trade and Development
UNIDO	United Nations Industrial Development Organisation
UNO	United Nations Organisation
WARDA	West African Rice Development Agency

2 OTHER ABBREVIATIONS

JWTL	*Journal of World Trade Law*
AJIL	*American Journal of International Law*

Preface

Emiko Atimomo's work on 'Law and Diplomacy in Commodity Economics' makes a very useful contribution to the knowledge of some of the most important and most difficult contemporary problems of our times for the following reasons:

1) The application of the New International Economic Order cannot be envisaged without guaranteeing sufficiently stable prices for the raw materials exported by the third world, at a level which would put an end to the worsening terms of trade. Without this stability there could not be any social and economic development.

2) The supply of raw industrial and agricultural materials plays a significant role in the industries of the developed countries as regards their economic growth and their employment policy. That is, 'Commodity diplomacy' is fundamentally important not only for a stable economic growth and equitable distribution but also for the whole North-South relationship and international peace.

   Emiko Atimomo's work throws light with much pertinence on the diplomatic aspect of great international economic negotiations. These are difficult negotiations because, beyond the essential interests of the third world, the resources of the industrialised countries in raw materials and in food are considerable to the extent that the influence of 'food power' weighs on them. The search for solutions has been rendered so much more difficult that the diversity of raw materials and basic agricultural products implies, besides the diversity of interests, a very great imbalance in diplomatic means on either side.

   Atimomo has analysed the solutions proposed by the UNO and particularly the UNCTAD. His most important contribution is devoted to the legal analyses of commodity agreements, procedures of ratification, acceptance and approval as well as the chapter on legal provisions which forms the object of interesting developments.

   Atimomo has devoted the essential aspect of these developments to the analyses of the different markets of raw materials and to legal acts adopted for their stabilisation, and has brought in particularly useful elements of knowledge on the tin market which was a study previously carried out by him long before the present work. He has also included a study of coffee, tea and citrus fruits.

Emiko Atimomo concludes by opting for a flexible trade policy which uses subtle legal means adapted both to market realities and to the needs of the third world countries. Let us hope that these means will be the expression of fuller reciprocal interests. If they are it will therefore be necessary to determine their terms so that in a realistic diplomatic negotiation, evolutionary solutions can allow for an economic recovery under satisfactory equitable and stable conditions. This is the condition under which reciprocal interests between producers and consumers will generate social solidarity without which there cannot be a rule of law effectively respected.

PIERRE VELLAS
Professor, Faculty of Law, Toulouse.
Director, Institute of International Studies and Developing Countries

October 1980

Acknowledgements

This book, which was started in 1968 with case studies and which was only completed in manuscript form in 1979, shall first pay great homage to Professor Pierre Vellas of the University of Toulouse, France. It was under him that I studied International Law and Relations and it was he who eventually supervised my doctorate thesis, 'Nigeria and the International Agreements on Tin', some aspects of which have inspired the format of the section of this book dealing with legal techniques. I wish also to express gratitude to Professors L. Siorat and P. Ourliac, Director of the Institute of Political Sciences of the same University who taught me pure politics, which I have now found useful.

I taught International Affairs, Economic Development and Comparative Public Administration while at Ahmadu Bello University and not International Law; so that I did not have the opportunity of making my students participate more actively in the process of my growth in this discipline. Nevertheless, I still owe them a debt of gratitude for their stimulating contributions during our study of the politics and economics of raw materials at tutorials.

My unreserved indebtedness goes to Dr H. M. N. Onitiri, Director of the Nigerian Institute of Social and Economic Research, Ibadan, through whose instrumentality I was Adviser to the Ministry of Trade Delegation to the International Cocoa Conference in June 1968 in Geneva. Since then I have participated in subsequent meetings of the Cocoa Producers Alliance and have had several opportunities to participate at UNCTAD meetings and at several African Regional Organisations meetings which dealt with the problems of the Third World countries. My participation at both the European and African meetings has offered me greater insight into the problems of the Third and developed worlds, and a fuller understanding of the dimensions of the discipline of international economic law and diplomacy within the precincts of international economic co-operation. As most of the commodity negotiators, particularly of the developed countries, were regulars, it was easier for me to study and understand their general approach and thinking. While the consumers looked more offensive in their style and more knowledgeable in the problems under negotiation, the producers only until recently seemed to suffer from a general psychological malaise even when opportunities seemed bright for them to achieve meaningful results. I also owe my experiences to the Economic Community of West African States Institution, where I helped to set up the infrastructural facilities of its secretariat as a member of the Task Force.

Further indebtedness is acknowledged to the following persons who have read and criticised my manuscripts at every stage: Mr B. A. Clark, formerly Deputy Permanent Secretary, Ministry of External Affairs, Lagos, Nigerian Ambassador to Switzerland and to the United Nations Organisation in Geneva, Ambassador to Ethiopia and currently Nigeria's Permanent Representative to the United Nations Organisation; Mr Edward Martins, formerly Deputy Director, Africa Division of the Ministry and now Nigeria's Ambassador to Liberia; and Mr I. P. J. Obebe, formerly Deputy Director, International Organisations Division and now Consul-General of Nigeria, San Francisco, USA; Dr G. O. Ijewere, formerly Nigeria's Ambassador to Belgium and at present Director, International Economic Co-operation of the Ministry of External Affairs, Lagos; Chief S. L. S. Odili-Obi, Principal Secretary, Federal Ministry of Economic Development, who followed my research progress while in the Ministry of Trade since 1968 and Mr Olu Omonira, formerly Lecturer in the Department of Accounting of the Ahmadu Bello University and now General Consultant in Economic Matters in Lagos; Mr Emmanuel Ometan, a legal practitioner of the Supreme Court of Nigeria; and many other academics, too numerous to mention here.

I wish also to express gratitude to the following: (1) International organisations which provided me with documents and some of whose officials agreed to talk to me: international councils on tin, wheat, sugar, and coffee; UNCTAD; EEC; CEAO (Economic Community of West Africa, Ouagadougou); African Development Bank, Abidjan; Cocoa Producers Alliance, Lagos; African Groundnut Council with particularly reference to its Deputy Director, Alhaji Gani Issaka; and to Mr P. E. N. Malafa, Director of the United Nations Centre, Lagos. (2) National ministries and research centres in the West African sub-region: Ministries of Justice and Trade, Lagos; Institute of Administration's Zaria Library with particular reference to Mr Ita, its Chief Librarian and a lawyer; Nigerian Institute of Social and Economic Research and the University of Ibadan libraries; the Nigerian Institute of International Affairs Library, with particular reference to Mr A. O. Banjo

(Chief Librarian) and Mrs R. T. Okotore (Deputy Chief Librarian) who rendered invaluable services to me throughout my years of research. Outside Nigeria were the following ministries and research centres which I visited in my own capacity to find out about ECOWAS: the Ministry of Foreign Affairs, Cotonou (Republic of Benin); Ministry of Trade Lomé (Republic of Togo); Ivorian Centre for Foreign Trade with particular gratitude to Mr Bernard Douayere; Ministry of Foreign Affairs (International Co-operation Division, Abidjan) with particular reference to its Deputy Director, Mr Saidu Bamba; the Ministry of Economic Development, Abidjan ECOWAS/CEAO Division (with particular reference to Mr Tiebri Aka). This acknowledgement cannot be closed without mentioning some very important persons who carried out the secretarial jobs involved. First to Mr C. N. Aribana and Miss Taiwo Bakare, who typed most of the work in their leisure hours without financial reward as their contributions to my solo efforts in financing this project over the years. Finally, to my wife Aderonke, whose patience and resilience saw me through a determined period of over nine months of research fully consecrated to finalising this work, without earning any salary.

Lagos, 16 February 1979 E.A.

Introduction

In the present international systems of relations among states, the negotiation, conclusion and stabilisation of products arising from economic agreements or the establishment of economic regional markets like the EEC, ECOWAS and the East African Common Market and Community are carried out through the application of certain techniques which are not only traditional but also legal and institutional. These techniques involved in the raw material diplomacy, pose the problem of method within the specific discipline of International Economic Law. Also the study of the conflict and co-operation in this vast area of economic transactions must recognise the importance of the political and economic considerations involved, because they are vital to the proper understanding of economic diplomacy. This is to say that the study of international politics in our times will not be complete unless it is approached in an interdisciplinary manner. This factor cannot but motivate the thinking of scholars towards the need for a philosophy of action governing the relations between the rich and the poor nations of the world. This philosophy shall therefore be axed on international concepts already provided by the United Nations Charter but which are flagrantly ignored in international attempts at co-operation. For these reasons we shall first examine international politics within the Charter situation before finding out why traditional diplomacy has failed, in the field of international law, to satisfy the present international diplomatic approach to economic transactions. How this diplomacy is conducted within the precincts of law, politics and economics, and the techniques used in its conduct, will preoccupy our minds in a theoretical area. Hereafter we shall study the conflict and co-operation situations of commodity diplomacy within the United Nations and quasi-United Nations systems.

Part One

General Characteristics of International Economic Law and Diplomacy*

* This part makes clear the interdisciplinary nature of the volume as a whole, and it would therefore have defeated its purpose to have included here, in order to justify some of the assertions made, a full commodity-by-commodity study, which would have entailed description of the economics, politics and law of selected commodities. However, case studies of tin and coffee *are* presented here, and for the rest the reader is referred to sources and explanations given in the notes. For the purposes of this work, commodity agreements relating to tin, olive oil, coffee, sugar, cocoa and so on were examined.

Preliminary Considerations

Since the notion of international co-operation was embedded in Article 55 of the United Nations Charter, the world has witnessed a number of localised wars and crisis situations in the Third World: for instance Vietnam, the Middle East, the Congo, Cuba, Mozambique, etc. Some of these which arose from the desire of a people to assert their right to independence, have to some extent found solutions only at the mercy of reciprocal concessions between third or interested powers, while others, because of the diplomacy of distrust coupled with emergent nationalisms, have failed to find adequate solutions. This is to say that, within the field of international politics, international co-operation has not matured to a degree of sufficient solidarity. For example, the French and American military interventions in Gabon and in the Dominican Republic in 1964 and April 1965, respectively, the 'quarantine' or 'selective' blockade of Cuba in October 1962, meant to paralyse the construction and reinforcement of Soviet missile bases on Cuban territory, and various localised wars to which no concrete solutions have been found all suggest rightly that the political arena still has a long way to go to achieve a desired international co-operation and law. The Third World has also been characterised by a series of changes of government by violent means, particularly in Latin America and African countries. This fragility and instability reflects the dilemma in which these areas find themselves, the lack of functional co-operation among peoples of different creeds and races, and the inequalities in incomes among the haves and the have-nots. To bridge this gap, a moderating influence to international power politics has been provided by the notion of co-operation enunciated by Article 55 of the UN Charter which seeks, among other things, to promote peaceful and friendly relations among nations, based on respect for the principles of equal rights and self-determination of peoples. Article 55 also seeks to achieve 'a higher standard of living, full employment and conditions of economic and social progress and development . . .'. Consequently, the UN has for the past 34 years endeavoured to activate the basis for international co-operation through its specialised agencies and institutions, where multilateral consultations and plan formulations take place, for instance the United Nations Conference on Trade and Development (UNCTAD).[1] Working through these institutions, the UN has come to identify in conformity with the peaceful and friendly purposes of this Charter, economic development with the right to independence. But we know that there cannot be political independence without first achieving a certain standard of economic growth. In this respect historical evidences abound in the struggles for economic emancipation by the USSR, USA and China.

Another idea which Article 55 has brought out is the right to one's natural resources, which the Declaration on an International Economic Order, adopted in May 1974 in New York, has amplified. The idea emitted in this Declaration of Principles that the right to natural resources could give the right to nationalisation, met with the resistance of some Western countries, who shared the view that this right must be coupled with the right to adequate compensation according to international law.

In the face of all these conflict situations between the Third World and the rich of the globe, what approach would be adopted to achieve peace and friendliness among nations of the world as enumerated by the UN Charter? *First*, the UN holds the view that the answers could be found by encouraging the creation of institutions, for instance UNCTAD, where divergent interests of both the consumers and producers could be reconciled. Also for this purpose, the UNO has encouraged institutional arrangements for the stabilisation of the commodity market. *Secondly*, to the poor countries the immediate answer appears to be an imperative involvement in mechanisation of agriculture and industrialisation. Economic evidence justifies this position of the third world. For instance, it is well known that an increase in the demand for raw materials in the international market has not necessarily produced corresponding increase in the export earnings of the producer countries. For example, in 1954 the great demand for coffee exports led to further increase in production by Latin American and African farmers. But by 1962, when coffee exports had risen by 50 per cent more than the 1954 level, the total earnings amounted to 1·7 US billion dollars whereas in 1954, for a reduced export, the export earning was 2·5 US billion dollars.[2] In other words, the price for coffee had fallen, in spite of demand.

Furthermore, because of the rapid growth of organised trade unions in developing countries and the gradual evolution of these countries towards transformation of raw materials into finished products, industrial countries have intensified their research into discovering substitutes in synthetic form for many raw materials. Among the products for which synthetic substitutes exist are cocoa, rubber, cotton, wool, silk, sugar, vegetable oil, jutes and nitrates.[3] In these circumstances, the Third World has no other option than to research for alternative approaches for obtaining fair prices for their commodities. One of these options is that provided by the UN and regional systems which have brought about the establishment of commodity agreements and agreements arising from contractual relationship of a common market type as already mentioned. These areas of greater solidarity evolved within economic, social and technical fields offer tests to the application of law.

1 Characteristics

SECTION I. LEGAL NATURE AND SCOPE OF ECONOMIC DIPLOMACY

The laws which arise from a contractual relationship within a community of identified interests are usually supranational. They hurt the sovereignty of states less because of the gradual evolvement of a community of interests, which tend to override the fears of states and their sensitivities to sovereignty considerations. The solidarities created within these fields are motivated by the desire of heads of state or governments to satisfy the basic needs of the population under their jurisdiction, because in the present system of international affairs there is no single country, no matter how powerful, that is absolutely self-sufficient and independent of other countries. This notion of interdependence, which is the brainchild of Article 55 has found practical application in the establishment of international economic and social arrangements,[1] which are gradually creating laws applicable to states and which consequently limit their sovereignty. Within the field of international economic law, which is consequently created through economic diplomatic activities culminating in agreements, the failure of traditional law has become glaringly obvious, because of its voluntarist nature. This is to say that a modern international law has been evolved since the creation of the UN to stabilise International Commodity Market prices within specific international institutions embracing producer and consumer countries of raw materials. This community-oriented law arising from international economic transactions covers a wide variety of institutions: for instance, the International Bank for Reconstruction and Development (IBRD);[2] the International Monetary Fund (IMF); the International Finance Corporation (IFC);[3] the Convention on the Settlement of Investment Disputes between States and the Nationals of Other States, arising from the convention of 18 March 1965; the Treaty of Rome of 25 March 1957, which established the EEC, the Treaty of the West African Economic Community (ECOWAS) signed in Lagos on 25 May 1975; the General

Agreement on Tariffs and Trade (GATT) of 30 October 1947, and the international commodity agreements (e.g. tin, coffee, raisins, wheat, sugar). The evolution of an international economic law as a discipline would therefore pose problems of method of analysis and of reflexion in these areas of intensive economic activity, which gradually create laws that are supranational and which conform to the needs of governments and peoples.

To the developing world this law is very vital, not only because it poses a philosophy of international co-operation even for those in search of a world government, but also because it regulates the diplomatic activities of the poor versus rich countries. Whether it would attain its objectives will be dependent on how the notion of equity in a law that produces solidarity within a community of interests can be protected and encouraged in conformity with the 'principle of equal rights and self-determination' (Article 55 of the UN Charter) of peoples to raw materials and amenities. This is because, when we examine the movement of world commodity prices and their attendant contribution to the economic growth of the poor countries, which represent the producers, we shudder at the increasing gap created by the notion of international co-operation between the poor and the rich nations of the world. For, while the rate of economic growth of poor nations was 4·3 per cent – that is, less than 5 per cent earmarked for the first development decade up to 1970 – that of the developed world with liberal economy attained, between 1955 and 1960, 3·5 per cent; and 5·2 per cent between 1960 and 1964.[4] This is to say that international co-operation expressed in terms of trade and aid has made the poor nations poorer and the rich ones richer. But the objectives of Article 55 were to provide the poorer nations of the world with the necessary tools for development. This contradiction shows that the international society is still characterised, in its diplomatic activities, by mistrust and by the prominence which the developed world still gives to bilateral relations over multilateral relations expressed in terms of aid and trade.

SECTION II. TRADITIONAL INTERNATIONAL LAW AND MODERN ECONOMIC DIPLOMACY IN THE AREAS OF APPLICATION

Within the scope of all these economic international transactions, international economic law is trying to become a stabilising factor within economic agreements and treaties. This law is developing a peculiar nature and characteristics because of its method of analysis and the techniques used in creating a wider scope of application in conformity with our present-day, fast-moving changes in technological progress. Traditional international law is therefore found to be insufficient in respect of its application and adaptation to these rapidly changing situations. In the area of application, the subjects of international traditional law are limited and its analysis is based on political philosophies. It does not take sufficient account of empirical and analytical research methods, which are quite distinct from a general legal logic approach, which involves reasoning and the use of a common sense of justice.[5] While international economic law is not only applicable to states and persons as in traditional international law, it also extends to other moral and physical persons, like private national companies and international organisations. This supranational nature arises from the fact that decisions arrived at within economic institutions are immediately applicable to industries within the territories of member states. Such powers are more apparent within the European Coal and Steel Community than in the EEC and EURATOM where the power to decide resides with the Council of Ministers. This supranationality only exists at the moment within the framework of European economic integration, where the executives of the three European communities enjoy a real independence in respect of member states. They take decisions which are executory according to set provisions; so that in international economic law like in traditional international law, institutional authority over states is exercised in terms of decisions, control and sanctions. This is to say that international economic law still uses certain techniques of the traditional international law. For instance, decisions in international economic law, as in traditional international law, are expressed in terms of recommendations; the difference lies within the field of application. While a refusal to carry out these recommendations in economic institutions could lead to the compulsory withdrawal of a member state with a two-thirds distributed majority of producers and consumers,[6] recommendations or resolutions in political organisations have no force of law. For instance, the General Assembly resolution of 20 November 1959 requesting France to abstain from testing atomic bombs in the Sahara was simply an invitation to abstain.[7] France ignored this recommendation without having infringed her obligations as a member of UNO with a consequent sanction.

Within the fields of adaptation, traditional international law is less suited to a more complex international society that has evolved since the creation of the UN. Nationalism in its various forms, which tend to cripple solutions to international crises, such as the Vietnam war, Cyprus and the Middle East conflicts, are living testimonies to the failure of traditional international laws to adapt to present requirements. This is why commodity institutions have evolved their own methods of conflict settlement as distinct from the procedures of the International Court of Justice. This will be examined in Chapter VI, Section 1, of this book. These procedures not only border on the panel system, 'consultation and co-operation', as with specific commodity institutions, but also on consultation[8] and conciliation as with GATT and UNCTAD respectively. All these procedures require profound knowledge of the subject matter to be settled – for instance collection of adequate facts that could bring about an equitable settlement. The procedures used in economic institutions are therefore subtle and flexible but effective, as we shall see in the case studies. It is therefore a non-judiciary approach where there is often no 'victor or vanquished'. As an illustration, there was a controversy in the International Wheat Agreement[9] by which the United Kingdom government wanted a system of arbitrage in the agreement during a renewal exercise, but the USA was opposed to this on the grounds that an external organ was not competent to exercise competence in complex economic problems. The American delegate held that there was need for conciliation of interests which would satisfy everybody without hurting anyone. She therefore preferred the competence of the Wheat Council in the settlement of conflicts.

The development of these methods only took root after the Second World War within international organisations. Before this time, there was the Committee of the League of Nations, which created a group of 14 experts for this purpose. We can therefore now say that in international economic law and diplomacy the method chosen for conflict settlement in the first instance is that of negotiation, consultation, conciliation and the panel system as a first instance, before further binding decisions are taken. A solution is consequently found within the organisation itself without recourse to an outside judge or a third party.

Furthermore, this discipline has destroyed the notion of equality among states prevalent in traditional law, although, curiously enough, ECOWAS and its sister organisation, CEAO, situated at Ouagadougou, employ the rules of unanimity. Nowhere in the ECOWAS Treaty or in its Rules of Procedure of the Council of Ministers is mention made of a voting procedure which is being tacitly agreed upon by the Council of Ministers and the Authority as the unanimity rule prevalent in political organisations, although Rule 27 (Miscellaneous) of Rules of Procedure of the Council of Ministers mentions that 'If there is any doubt as to the procedure to be followed in any particular case, or if no procedure is prescribed by or under the Treaty or these Rules, the procedure to be followed may be determined by the Council.' In practice the procedures used so far at meetings are those of negotiation, conciliation and, above all, consensus (i.e. unanimity) which is really meant. This is also true of the meetings of the Authority. On the other hand, the CEAO Treaty in its Articles 31 and 32 specifically mentions that the *Acts* and *Decisions* of the Authority and Council of Ministers, respectively, shall be taken by the unanimity rule. These are exceptions rather than the rule, and an innovation in African community law and diplomacy, based on voluntarist law which is traditional and which is bound to raise unforeseen problems in the future, more at ECOWAS level than at the CEAO level, whose culture and linguistic affinity are Francophone.[10]

However, the notion of equality of states has become unworkable in other economic institutions and has been replaced by the weighted system which put into consideration the financial contributions of a Member State and the amount of tonnages allotted to it.

International commodity agreements have encouraged the group system – for instance, producers and consumers – while in the UNCTAD, there is the Group of 77 (made up of Groups A and C) and the rich world (made up of Groups B and D). In all these group formations the techniques of negotiation and the functioning of the mechanisms in commodity agreements and institutions have become new sources of legal obligations. Furthermore, because of the provision of periodical renewal in these agreements, the provision of amendment now questions *pacta sunt servanda* since *rebus sic stantibus* allows any state to question the validity of any previous engagement, particularly when such an engagement threatens or jeopardises the interests of a given state.

We can now see from the foregoing analysis that if the world must survive and tensions lessen, a new type of law must be evolved and encouraged for international relations; this has found expression in the areas of economic and social international arrangements which are bound to bring the people of the world together within a community of interests for the purpose of world peace and order. Thus we have now seen why traditional law is unsuited and inadaptable to the increasing needs of our contemporary international society, because the law itself is based on the goodwill of states. International economic law is therefore a flexible law because it is easy of adaptation to international economic relations. It is a law by which the exercise of power contributes to a gradual limitation of sovereignty in multinational economic and social arrangements and to the gradual evolution of a legislative authority. It recognises equity as a basis for functioning in conformity with Article 55 of the UN Charter and the need in various economic institutions to prevent discriminatory trade practices, and to establish quota systems in the production and exportation of commodities.

SECTION III. METHODOLOGY IN INTERNATIONAL ECONOMIC LAW AND DIPLOMACY

This discipline is young in the sense that it dates from the creation of the UN whose organs are deliberately provided with set provisions in order to promote its rapid evolution. The League of Nations had no direct control over international technical institutions which were independent of it, so that jurists could not preoccupy themselves to a great extent with the task of evolving a theory based on a progressive methodology. Since it covers a wide variety of fields of human activity, the international jurist is confronted with a new approach to legal analysis – an approach which requires an interdisciplinary knowledge or what Rosenthal and Rosnow call 'boundary-melting disciplines',[11] because he is now also confronted with the politics and economics of this great field of international transactions. In other words, the international jurist of the present day is expected, in addition to the study of law, to have a sufficient knowledge of economics, politics, history and sociology. He must therefore be a technocrat with good knowledge of the surroundings to which this law is applicable. Strict adherence to the study of law would make the jurist conservative and insufficiently open-minded to new social realities and techniques. He is therefore as rigid as traditional international law, so that if this discipline is still not properly known and well understood, it is because of the non-exposure of our jurists to interdisciplinary studies during their university training period. Unless the jurist acquires the mind of a technician, he cannot translate, with sufficient realism, the solutions and findings of economists into precise rules of law. It is therefore not surprising to find most delegations of the developing world during international negotiations on commodities losing grip and in fact ignoring legal battles involved to the advantage of developed nations who, however, either do not seem to, or refuse to, understand the philosophy arising from this discipline. This observation on the developed nations is necessary because they still encourage the use of vague and imprecise terminologies in economic negotiations where the solidarity which is born from a concluded agreement is based upon the notion of a new community of interest. It is discouraging to note how well-known negotiators of developed nations argue interminably or childishly because their draft proposals have not been accepted in general imprecise terms.[12] No doubt this is still due to the precarious nature of the international society and also to the age-groups and conservative academic background of the negotiators who have not yet understood, or have refused to understand, the modern concept of international co-operation as a doctrine based on equity enunciated in Article 55 of the UN Charter. Or perhaps for simple purposes of power-display they have decided to regard 'man as wolf to man' by throwing smaller eager nations into further possible confusion, because they are either helpless or unable to use to advantage certain favourable instruments at their disposal.

Thus we have seen that terminological imprecision characteristic of traditional international law is still unfortunately highly encouraged in international economic law, and even in community law, for the purpose of legal politics. It would, however, be greatly appreciated if international texts of economic and social nature discourage the use of vague terminologies not only for the purpose of clarity and international co-operation but also because producer nations, very sensitive to the desire to sell their products rapidly, most willingly hasten to append their signatures to legal texts without great consideration of depth. This attitude is naturally most rampant with mono-producers. Much more so that such legal texts in a generality of cases[13] go into effect on signature provisionally while awaiting the accomplishment of diverse constitutional methods of ratification. There is also the problem which official languages pose to the developing world, whose mother tongues are not often used in texts. The use of imprecise and meaningless terminologies could produce certain difficulties in understanding, interpretation and translation.

All the factors enumerated above pose the problem of further precise methodology because, as we have seen, the international jurist still possesses the tendency to use the hypothesis which is typical of traditional international law, and still bases his approach on the voluntarist law where states sovereignty is absolute and 'laissez-faire' is based upon an established order. But this is no more true of the contemporary international society where the notion of interdependence has grown considerably. This is to say that traditional international law does not offer adequate rules of law for the purpose of encouraging a new system of progress based upon the need to satisfy certain economic and sociological needs. A law must be made to conform to the evolutionary needs of a people for whom it is made, because it is expected to fashion them towards a desired goal. This is the direction which international economic law is gradually paving for itself.

Consequently, its method poses many research difficulties arising from the fact that states which do not belong to a legal community of interest scarcely want to divulge their national policies to the inquisitive research student. The student therefore must make great use of his personal contact not only to the secretariat of the organisations concerned, but also to national appropriate ministries where he could have fruitful discussions with their functionaries. His ability to achieve some satisfaction from his visit would depend on his personal charm and approach. Apart from the oral method, his other sources which are material conform to those established by traditional international law, with slight but important differences. These differences conform to those between the requirements of the International Court of Justice and traditional international law.[14] With the International Court of Justice, 'International Conventions whether general or particular, establishing rules expressly recognised by the contesting states' plays a more important role than international custom to which traditional international law gives a primary role. The role played by international economic law therefore conforms to the order established by the International Court of Justice, except that its other major sources apart from treaties, are decisions of international institutions, conference papers, jurisprudence and doctrine. To these are added national commercial policies because they determine commodity prices and government attitudes to trade. Custom in international economic law plays a negligible role because it is confined to old customary laws of international communications, particularly maritime, and to some principles of traditional commercial relations.[15] So that the international economic jurist is now expected to possess a firm knowledge of these added factors to enable him to interpret laws emanating from contractual communities of interest. Doctrine is also a material source in international economic law because of the nature of Article 55 of the UN Charter which enunciates not only the notion of equality of access to raw materials but also that of the right to independence of peoples. This doctrine has become necessary because of the need to protect growing foreign investments within national boundaries and to recognise the right to compensation for the nationalisation of properties.

International economic law is therefore a boundary-melting discipline; that is, a meeting point for various disciplinaries (economist, moralist, jurist, political scientist and sociologist). This is why, in analysing a legal economic text, we must examine it from several angles: politics, economics, law and diplomacy and institutional framework within which function the administrative and law-making processes. This peculiar nature arises from its use of techniques which are not only traditional (negotiations, adoption, ratification and entry into force) but are also institutional and legal. These techniques help to facilitate the provisional entry into force of an agreement from signature[16] with a promise of intention to ratify the agreement within a given period. For instance the International Coffee Agreement of 1968 in its Article 62, paragraph 2, stipulates that the agreement shall enter into force provisionally for any signatory government on 1 October 1968, provided that this government notifies its intention or 'undertaking to apply the agreement provisionally', to the Secretary General of the United Nations not later than 30 September 1968, while awaiting the accomplishment of its constitutional procedure of ratification. Thus in international economic law, a simple notification of intention to ratify has the same effect in law as an instrument of ratification, approval or acceptance. In traditional international law, signature has no immediate legal effect except with executive agreements[17] or on express provision as with the Japanese–Australian Trade Treaty of 6 July 1957 which operated on provisional basis as from the date of signature.[18] In this discipline sanction depends on economic and psychological pressure because any country that violates the provisions of an agreement could be suspended or excluded or be asked to withdraw compulsorily, thus making sanction reside in its non-participation.[19]

SECTION IV. THE ROLE OF TRADITIONAL DIPLOMACY IN THE MODERN WORLD OF ECONOMIC TRANSACTIONS

(I) DIPLOMACY AND LAW

Diplomacy between states with the view to concluding commodity agreements starts to play a role from the stage when preliminary negotiations begin. In classical law there cannot be said to be diplomacy between states at war, until the first peace negotiations emerge either through bilateral or multilateral discussions. This notion also extends to economic and technical negotiations. In traditional diplomacy, negotiations could take place within any agreed traditional institutions, either in a diplomatic mission or in a Ministry of Foreign Affairs, among heads of states or their agents. In modern times, if it is a multilateral diplomacy, the locus could be in an international organisation or in a specialised institution. This is typical of modern economic diplomacy where negotiations are conducted within specialised institutions like UNCTAD, the EEC and in UNO, as we shall see in Part 2 of this book. From these meetings emerges law in diplomacy when negotiations lead to acceptable legal texts which set out rules and conduct for participating countries to adhere to. This is the case of international commodity agreements which set out to establish rules of law on how a commodity is to achieve stabilisation. This in itself constitutes diplomatic law, defined by Philippe Cahier in his work, *Le Droit Diplomatique Contemporaine* as: 'L'ensemble des normes juridiques destinés à régler les rapports qui se forment entre les différents organes des sujets de droit international chargés de manière permanente ou temporaire des relations extérieures de ces sujets.' These rules of law which determine the conduct of relationship between different subjects of international law establish the notion of diplomacy within institutions and between the states.

(II) THE ROLE OF TRADITIONAL DIPLOMACY IN THE MODERN INTERNATIONAL ECONOMIC DIPLOMACY

(A) Decadence of traditional diplomacy

Secret diplomacy became open after the First and Second World Wars with the rapid development of communication facilities. Diplomacy which was conducted in the secrecy of chancelleries was rendered *ouverte* after President Woodrow Wilson of the USA had presented his 14-point peace programme, after the First World War period, during the Treaty of Versailles negotiations. He believed in rendering diplomacy public rather than having it secret. Although there are advantages and disadvantages in open diplomacy, we are here more concerned with the disadvantages of open diplomacy where, certainly, reciprocal concessions cannot adequately be made since its openness might destroy the entire objective of attaining peace or achieving useful results. This is why in modern economic diplomacy there is still a certain amount of diplomatic secrecy required so as to maximise the advantages that might accrue to contractual parties of an international agreement. This explains why there are closed sessions after an opening session, and even within an already established institution working sessions are not open to the press and to the public, although political institutions like UNO, OAU and OAS at a certain level have almost completely rendered modern diplomacy, which is essentially multilateral, open.

The decadence of traditional diplomacy, which was essentially political and military, has given place to modern diplomacy which has extended its tentacles to the areas of economics. *First*, this has been due to greater interdependence among states with the advent of more rapid communication systems. This is to say that no one country is self-sufficient as of today. *Secondly*, political struggles of the old diplomacy have made a place for ideological struggles which have found fertile terrain in the areas of economics, commerce, culture and even technology. *Thirdly*, the creation of UNO, whose Economic and Social Council (ECOSOC), and United Nations Conference on Trade and Development (UNCTAD) furnish the world with a locus for economic negotiations and planning. Modern diplomacy, whether political or economic, is therefore today characterised more in terms of bloc, for example, 'group of 77' in UNCTAD; the third world; the Western or Socialist alignments at the UN. This bloc diplomacy limits the liberty of action of individual states since they have submerged their specific national policies within the group system. This is also the case of contractual members of an international commodity agreement. We therefore can say that the development of international organisations has greatly led to the decadence of traditional diplomacy characteristic of *ad hoc* meetings and absolute respect for state sovereignty. In this modern type, negotiation is no more the exclusive prerogative of career diplomats because the development of rapid communication systems now makes it possible for even heads of state, prime ministers or ministers of foreign affairs to concern themselves directly with negotiations taking place within international organisations. In the technical and economic areas, diplomats are no more essential figures of negotiations because technicians of various disciplines from ministries other than the Foreign Ministry, now participate in the art.

(B) Modernity in diplomacy

Modern diplomacy is expressed in two ways: through negotiations in international organisations and through direct contacts between political heads of state and not sovereigns, as of old. The turning-point in multilateral negotiations was reached with the creation of the League of Nations and then UNO after the First and Second World Wars.

The League was not as successful as UNO has grown to be, because the greater part of multilateral diplomacy was carried out outside the League. On the other hand, UNO has since provided the forum for the expression of modern diplomacy with its specialised agencies like UNCTAD, ILO, WHO, UNESCO, etc. Although it could be said that within UNO the Great Powers get away very easily with their actions in the security council, because of their veto power, UNO has been a magnificent forum for small nations which need international public opinion to survive, as will be demonstrated in Part 2, during the examination of the role of the UN General Assembly on the debate on the New International Economic Order.

Meetings held within specialised institutions eventually produce decisions often afterwards implemented by states because of their anxiety to contribute to national growth. On the African continent, modern diplomacy has been expressed in terms of what classical diplomacy called itinerant diplomacy because of the contact which this has generated among heads of state, e.g. OAU and ECOWAS. This type of African diplomacy has helped to solve certain thorny problems or made them better understood without necessarily achieving success, e.g.: (i) attitudes to liberation movements have since been modified although with little financial participation from members of OAU; (ii) the idea of a continental defence system is generally accepted as desirable and understood but not entirely accepted yet, because of the divergent national interests and the problems of logistics involved.

Modern diplomacy still keeps the triple function of representation, observation and negotiation. The techniques involved in this diplomacy are principally still those of the traditional, although it is gradually evolving its own peculiarities and characteristics as will be seen in Chapter 2: 'Diplomatic Techniques'. We shall subsequently see that through this triple function, a continuous communication is established between states and international organisations. In this continuous communication, the diplomat has not lost his complete status because diplomacy as an art is better carried out by a career diplomat since it requires some flexibility and finesse which technicians do not possess.

This is why a diplomat in modern diplomacy still plays the role of adviser in the art of, and approach to, negotiations. The technicians of diplomacy and the diplomat are therefore complementary, in spite of the diminishing role of the latter in economic and technical negotiations. In economic conference diplomacy, the diplomat still furnishes essential political information required by the technician for on-the-spot assessment of negotiation position. This role is also true if an ambassador is the chief negotiator or head of a delegation. In itinerant diplomacy or diplomacy of contact, the diplomat prepares the groundwork necessary for discussions between heads of state who are supposed to take decisions. In economic negotiations, the technical requirements are prepared by relevant ministries as we shall see later in this book, while in political conferences heads of state take with them essentially career diplomats as advisers. However, in this book we are most concerned with economic negotiations and agreements, the techniques of which will be discussed in subsequent chapters.

2 Diplomatic Techniques

SECTION I. TECHNIQUES OF NEGOTIATION IN INTERNATIONAL ECONOMIC LAW AND DIPLOMACY

The negotiation of multilateral treaties stems from the initiative of states in traditional international law and the adoption of a draft text is carried out by an *ad hoc* conference of negotiators representing the interests of their states. The initiative of convening such a conference remains the onus of a state which undertakes the preparation of a draft agreement or convention, which to a very great extent reflects its interests and policies. The practice in modern international law is identified with the growth of multilateral economic and social treaties in recent years. Thus in international economic law, the initiative of convening a conference is with an international organisation (that is, the Secretary General of UNO) even when there is a specific institution created for the product for which stabilisation is envisaged. This was the case of the preparatory conference on tin convened at the initiative of the Secretary General of UNO in 1953 which later produced the 1st International Agreement on Tin in 1956. When there is an existing institution, the initiative is still that of the Secretary General of UNO or UN Conference on Trade and Development since its creation in 1964, under the invitation of the Institution.[1] The importance of UNO or UNCTAD as a convening power can be attributed to their fairly universalist nature and the immense contribution which their highly qualified administrative personnel could make to the materialisation of an agreement. Most of them are highly skilled in treaty-drafting and on the various problems posed to raw materials.

When the Secretary of UNCTAD convenes, he sends out copies of a draft agreement[2] to all the interested state governments and relevant specialised agencies. This draft contains the general framework on which the negotiations should be based. In the case of governments, it is the Ministry of External Affairs that first receives it or in some cases the Ministry of Trade. The ideal practice in such a case, would be for the

External or Trade Ministry depending on the practice in a given country, to convene all interested bodies (corporations, producers and consumers association or marketing boards) to a national preliminary consultation meeting where the intentions of UNCTAD are exposed and discussed at length. This should be the practice for a product for which there is yet no existing international agreement. The Trade Ministry, as a technical administrative body of experts on commodities, then co-ordinates their views and draws up a general policy. This preliminary meeting is very informative because it could expose other sociological and technical problems posed by the exploitation of the product in question on which the ministry could base its modification or an addition to the draft agreement; for instance, the need to pressurise private exploiting national companies to create social facilities for their workers. It is this type of information that led to the inclusion of Article 16 in the 3rd International Tin Agreement which promises to promote fair labour standards. In co-ordinating the views of the interest groups, the government is reducing the unforeseen frictions that could in the future arise between it and private interest national groups. In the case where a general policy has been formulated because they had assembled all relevant data, the primary and very important duty of the Trade Ministry would be to convene another meeting of possible negotiators of the product.[3] In the Nigerian practice,[4] negotiators are drawn from extra-ministerial departments like marketing boards, producers and consumers association, chambers of commerce, universities and other relevant interested bodies including officials of the Trade Ministry itself. The purpose of the above meeting is to plan out, through further discussions, a common strategy and to allot assignments so that the burden of the negotiations could be lessened by specialisation of duties among the various advisers. This would eventually lead to co-ordination of techniques at the conference table.

With increasing involvement of the international society in commodity agreements, negotiations are no more the exclusive prerogatives of Foreign Ministry officials or diplomats. The diplomat in economic and social negotiation is now simply a co-ordinator. He is chairman of the preliminary meeting of interested bodies mentioned above, with the view to arriving at conclusions as to whether it would be advisable to accept the invitation of UNCTAD on behalf of the home government before the appropriate ministry takes over direct communications with UNCTAD or its trade representative in Geneva.[5] During active negotiations in Geneva, or at any chosen capital, it is the trade attaché or diplomat to the embassy or high commission that leads a national delegation in the absence of its ambassador who is a political representative. Before the negotiations start, the Secretary General of UNCTAD, or his representative, opens the conference before a chairman is appointed. During these negotiations, the chairman is free to apply techniques which to him would bring about a quick solution to the problems posed. Often, he resorts to meeting consumers and producers separately, with a view to conciliating their divergent viewpoints because in most cases when both sides meet in direct confrontation, they arrive at no concrete solutions.[6] He then finally communicates his findings to a full house of both interest groups. At other times, he resorts to forming special working groups to study knotty problems and then makes recommendations to the plenary session. At any of these periods, the secretarial contributions of UNCTAD are highly appreciated because the chairman would want to have the results of their findings printed out for circulation in the working languages quickly before he re-assembles the negotiators in a plenary session.

Negotiations are carried out in two ways: either certain articles of the draft agreement are negotiated in a 'package deal' or they negotiate article by article. The 'package deal' approach is very thorny in the sense that it is a strategy not unconnected with another, although it could be interpreted to mean a desire to hurry up the negotiations. However, in any of these methods, reciprocal compromises and concessions[7] are never ruled out and the advantages which accrue to each side depend on diplomatic prowess based on depth of knowledge of the product in question, moment of price opportunity and finesse in the use of language and in the expression of emotion.[8] At the end of a successful negotiation, the draft text is adopted by a majority vote[9] or by unanimity of the final plenary session. Final adoption, which is an expression of the general will of the negotiators, can be taken as having a certain force of law in international economic law because it precedes signature which authenticates it. For instance, on 24 June 1960, at the International Tin Preparatory Conference, the Japanese and German delegates expressed their reservations to the adopted draft text of the agreement because they felt that if they adopted the text, it would be tantamount to 'acceptance'. What strikes the student of this discipline is the increasing divergence in methodology employed in the adoption of texts. Sometimes it is the chairman of the conference who makes the proposal for adoption, and at other times it is a delegate that proposes it in the name of his group of interest. This innovation arises from the need to achieve rapidity in the adoption of economic texts and this often depends on the personal diplomacy of the chairman.

SECTION II. INSTITUTIONAL AND ADMINISTRATIVE TECHNIQUES

Apart from legal and negotiation techniques, international economic law also makes use of institutional and administrative techniques. These institutions carry out permanent administrative duties under a titular secretary and his personnel. All the commodity agreements which have come into existence since UNO have made use of *travaux préparatoires* or preparatory conferences which have semi-institutional and diplomatic characters. It is within this pro-tem institution that all negotiations are carried out until a text is adopted. Within the permanent institution created to administer agreements, laws are gradually being made. These laws are supranational because of the nature of the solidarity arising from the signatory members of the agreement. For instance in the 3rd International Tin Agreement, Article VII, paragraph 4, the council is empowered, among other measures, to reduce the percentage of any producer country which fails to export an authorised total, unless the country had renounced a part of the total permissible exports 'not later than one calendar month after the date upon which such permissible export amount has become effective' (Article VII, paragraph 8[a]). Voting is by a simple majority unless otherwise expressly stated. In deliberating organs a qualified distributed majority of two-thirds or three-quarters, also based on a weighted system of votes, are often required for important matters. This system is based upon the strength of financial contribution of contracting parties. In diplomatic practice, the rule of unanimity conforms to the principle of legal equality of states prevalent in political organisations, although this rule does also exist in OECD and in the three European communities (EURATOM, EEC and Coal and Steel) where it is being used in some cases. This system requires a very tedious negotiation before a compromise could be reached. Recommendations in international economic law are not compulsory but they are often carried out by states, as a refusal to carry them out could lead to executory sanctions, as we have already seen. It goes without saying that these permanent institutions play a great role because they carry out diplomatic functions, study the market trends of products, find compromises to divergent national policies of states and co-ordinate decisions. In addition we must also realise that since economic institutions have come to stay as an answer to the need for international co-operation after the Second World War, secretariats have developed in function and powers. These secretariats are headed by a titular secretary and his technical personnel. The secretariat is an administrative organ whose functions are those of information, co-ordination and execution. Its personnel are expected to be independent of their home governments although in the past conflicts had arisen between secretariats and governments. For instance the period of McCarthyism witnessed the witch-hunt, in international institutions, of American personnel suspected of communist tendencies, in the secretariats of UNO and its specialised agencies. The USA demanded and obtained the dismissal of suspects. But when the Administrative Tribunal of UNO and the International Court of Justice recognised the illegality of such actions, compensations were paid and such actions were stopped. Another example of an abuse of the independence of a secretariat was when Mr Etienne Hirsch, President of the Commission of EURATOM, was withdrawn by the French government from exercising his functions because he was thought to be too inclined to the cause of European integration. These pose the question as to whether economic institutions established for the purpose of stabilising raw materials have given thought to solving these problems. The question also asked in evolving a new system, is whether in strict law, secretariats should influence state decisions or remain neutral? In answering these questions it must be realised that secretariats of technical institutions have grown considerably in strength and technical expertise since 1945 and that their influence over state decisions is unquestionable in many aspects, even though decisions are taken by government delegates. This is because they possess the diplomatic capacity to consult, inform and make opinions on available statistical materials, on which states themselves could base their final decisions. In order therefore to lend credence to the findings of these commodity institutions, their personnel are internationally recruited, with preference given to the nationals of the participating countries. As in many other institutions, the staff are expected to keep professional secrecy unless authorised by the council.

Another type of institution in which there is intense diplomatic activity is the *travail préparatoire* or preparatory conference. These are temporary institutions in which all negotiations are carried out until the adoption of the text of a draft agreement. Here the delegations of all participating countries meet as producers and consumers. These include those whose intention is to accede at a later date but who are primarily actively participating, e.g. the USA vis-à-vis the tin agreements. Such delegations contribute towards the orientation of the conference and drafting of an agreement for adoption. There are also those who express their reservations by remaining as observers with a right to sit in specialised committees. At this juncture, it is important to appreciate the increasing role which International Institutions like FAO, GATT, IBRD, and IMF are playing in the process of treaty-drafting and negotiation. This is because they possess adequate financial and diplomatic capacity which could later be expressed in terms of loans and the formulation of certain conventions necessary to aid the execution of the agreement. During these negotiations it is observed that the nature and composition of each delegation are determined by the importance which it attaches to the product under negotiation. If the country is a big producer or consumer, it sends in a large delegation of experts. A close examination of the delegations shows that most of the producer delegates are of ambassadorial rank, while those of the consumers of developed countries are technicians and experts. This feature is very true of all the tin and cocoa conferences held under the aegis of UNO/UNCTAD. These ambassadorial representations, which normally contribute very little to a technical negotiation, show the importance which these countries give to politics rather than to technical expertise. However, it must be accepted that they do not all stay throughout the conference, since they sometimes leave the onus of negotiations to experts. Among these are states with small delegations having no direct interest in the product in question, but who are simply interested in gaining experience or preparing themselves towards a possible accession. For instance the case of Guinea and Turkey which are negligible or small consumers of tin (Turkey's consumption in 1963 was 750 tons) or Togo in cocoa negotiations although she is a small producer. Guinea is neither a producer nor consumer of tin.

SECTION III. STABILISATION TECHNIQUES

All commodity agreements have mechanisms for the stabilisation of market forces within given price ranges. This need for stabilisation has arisen because of incessant price fluctuations of raw materials in the international market. On the other hand there has not been any attempt to create international mechanisms for stabilising industrial products whose prices are arbitrarily fixed by consumer manufacturing countries and which are not subjected to price fluctuations. The dilemma of the African world can therefore be found in their heavy dependence on primary commodities for their foreign exchange earnings. For instance, 77·8 per cent of Chad's export earnings are from cotton; 57 per cent of Senegal's come from groundnuts; 66 per cent of Ghana's come from cocoa; 48 per cent of Uganda's come from coffee; 46 per cent of Egypt's come from cotton. Coffee, cocoa and timber account for 73·1 per cent of Ivory Coast's exports.[10] This heavy dependence on raw materials for exchange earnings has motivated the provision of stabilisation techniques in commodity agreements.

The methods usually explored are the following: export quota system (coffee, sugar); buffer stocks (tin); multilateral contracts (sugar, wheat); supervision of the marketing of surpluses and reserve stocks; commodity agreements.

(I) EXPORT QUOTA SYSTEM

This system is called into application during periods of overproduction of the commodity (e.g. coffee, tin, 1968 sugar agreement). Quotas are fixed for each contracting party of the agreement. If some countries are unable to fulfil their contractual obligations (that is, supply their quotas), a redistribution takes place among other exporters.[11]

(II) BUFFER STOCK[12]

This often combines the export control and quota systems with the buffer stock system e.g. the tin agreements. The operations of the buffer stock by a manager fall within a margin of prices between a ceiling or maximum price and a floor or minimum price. The manager of the buffer stock must sell tin when there is a shortage in the world market in order to force down prices within the maximum and minimum price ranges. He buys when the price falls below the minimum, in order to raise up the price within the contractual ranges. When stocks are exhausted, prices often shoot beyond the ceiling price. The commodities for which there is a buffer stock are cocoa and tin. Because some consumer countries sell their surplus stocks, prices often fall.

(III) MULTILATERAL CONTRACTS

This operates among contracting parties. Each exporter agrees to supply a stipulated quantity of the product at a given price not above the maximum contractual price, and the importer buys at an agreed quantity not less than the minimum price. This operates for identical products.

(IV) MARKET SITUATION AND STABILISATION ATTEMPTS OF SELECTED AFRICAN COMMODITY EXPORTS

(a) Coffee

(i) Market situation

This is an extremely important market, for certain African countries. Ivory Coast, Columbia and Brazil export about the annual volume sold. Between 1967 and 1971 the percentages of the earnings of African producers were as follows: 31·6 per cent for Ivory Coast; 51·3 per cent for Ethiopia; 48·2 per cent for Uganda; 24 per cent for Cameroun; 15·6 per cent for Togo; 28 per cent for Madagascar; 18·9 per cent for Central African Republic; 14·3 per cent for Tanzania and 18·2 per cent for Kenya. For developing countries in 1974 the value of exports amounted to US $4189 million, which represented about 13·4 per cent of the unit value of their total commodity exports for that period.[13]

(ii) Stabilisation attempts

The first stabilisation attempt was made in 1962 when an international agreement was signed during a period of overproduction (also true for tin in 1953). In addition to other measures, a diversification programme was drawn up for coffee-producing countries. This agreement was renewed in 1968, but in 1971 the need for a pricing policy led to conflict situations among producers. It is also noteworthy that when Brazil lowered its prices by 12 cents/lb in February 1971, prices drastically dropped below the minimum fixed prices, consequently leading to reduction of quota for all types of Arabica.

(b) Cocoa

(i) Market situation

This is a commodity for which speculation causes fluctuation in prices. Between 1967 and 1971, the proportion of export earnings was high for African countries. For example, for Ghana, 66·2 per cent; Togo, 32·5 per cent; Cameroun, 24·1 per cent; Ivory Coast, 19·2 per cent; Nigeria, 18·1 per cent. About 70 per cent of world production comes from Africa while exports of Nigeria and Ghana alone represent 52 per cent of the quantities exported in 1968. The main importers of cocoa are the EEC and the USA, then the UK, Denmark, Norway and Ireland according to the order of importance. The main producers are: Ghana, Nigeria, Brazil, Ivory Coast, Cameroun and Togo. The associated African and Malagasy members of the EEC supply nearly half of the EEC imports, while Italy buys more than half of its imports from Commonwealth countries.

(ii) Stabilisation

An agreement came into force on 30 June 1973 after many years of negotiations between the producers and consumers. It was not signed by the USA, which is the second largest importer of cocoa after the EEC (218,000 tons in 1969 as against 334,000 tons by the EEC in the same year).

(c) Oil products

(i) Market situation

Some of the oil products exported by developing countries are: copra and coconut oil, palm oil, palm-kernel and palm-kernel oil, groundnut oil, and olive oil. Those from developed countries are: soya bean, rape-seed and sunflower-seed oil, cotton oil, butter, marine oil (whale, fish and seal). In the areas of soya beans, rape-seed and sunflower-seed oils, there has been increased trade between industrialised countries to the detriment of developing countries. The share of groundnuts in world oil-seed exports has decreased considerably over the years from an average of 28·2 per cent between 1961 and 1963 to 16·7 per cent in 1969. The EEC imports, which represent 80 per cent of world total, have been drastically affected by the drought, particularly in Senegal. This has led to a reduction in imports. If one goes by FAO reports and UNCTAD studies, the palm-oil market appears more encouraging because of its increase in demand over supply. However the EEC has now encouraged the growth of palm plantations in some African and Latin American countries, Indonesia and Malaysia. This means that a future increase in world exports could pose marketing difficulties in the long run unless demand equals production. The production from the Associated and Associable African countries of copra and copra oil is insufficient to cope with EEC demands. The Philippines dominates the copra market because it provides 51 per cent of the world's supply. There will be problems posed to African countries when generalised preferences and non-tariff barriers become applied. Although oil seeds are in principle not affected by customs duties within the EEC, there is some protection for edible oils. In the UK duties were quite high, as much as 10–15 per cent, before her association to the EEC.

In Francophone Africa, production of quality oil represented two-thirds of the total production in 1954, while the pre-war production level of quality oil was at one-third. Nigeria was the first world producer of palm oil with 420,000 metric tons approximately, before 1967, followed by Zaïre whose production between 1955 and 1956 was 196,000 tons, and 240,000 tons in 1960–61. Her immediate post-independence political problems subsequently reduced her production. Indonesia, which has good quality oil, comes third with 165,000 tons in 1953–56. The three world producers represent 75 per cent of world production. Other producers are: Malaysia, Dahomey and Cameroun who appears to give greater prominence to cocoa and coffee because of profit motive. The centres of production are therefore principally in Africa and South East Asia.

(ii) Stabilisation of oil products[14]

There are no special international agreements but attempts have been made by France, Great Britain and the EEC to establish preferential treatments of a long- and short-term nature. The FAO has also established inter-governmental procedures of consultation, and it is struggling to get agreements concluded for butter and milk products.

(1) Long-term agreements

This type of agreement was concluded by Great Britain, for a period of 3–9 years, for the purpose of guaranteeing favourable prices to producers. She concluded such agreements with Nigeria and Sierra Leone between 1952 and 1955. While the agreement with Nigeria absorbed all she produced except those exported to Ghana, Sierra Leone and the Gambia, that concluded with Sierra Leone concerned a percentage of her production except the quantity exported to Nigeria, Ghana and the Gambia. These agreements have not been renewed since 1958 because of Great Britain's deficit situation in the face of price degradation in the world market. However this policy did not in any way contribute to stabilising world prices. They were politically motivated by cultural and linguistic affinity. Africa is also finding ways of creating a stabilisation organisation for oil seeds. To this effect, a meeting of African oil seeds producers was held in Lagos 8–11 August 1974.[15] After a detailed analysis of the world market of oil seeds and considering Resolution CM/RES.225(XV) of the Council of Ministers of the OAU adopted during its 15th Ordinary Session in August 1970, the meeting recommended the creation of an organisation of African oil seeds producing countries. To this effect a working group of seven countries was set up to study this possibility.

Subsequently, a convention creating the African Oilseeds Producers Organisation (AOPO) was adopted at its first Ministerial Meeting in Lagos 11–13 April 1978. Delegates were drawn from twenty-one African countries[16] and the African Groundnut Council (AGC) was represented as an observer. This convention, which was unanimously adopted, is subject to ratification by its signatories according to their respective constitutional procedures. The instruments of ratification shall be deposited with the depository government (the Federal Republic of Nigeria). The convention shall enter into force one month after at least eight member countries shall have deposited their instruments of ratification with the depository government which shall 'supply on request to any state qualified to accede to this Convention, certified copies thereof'. Production figures for liquid edible and lauric acid oils are shown in Table 2.1.

The African Groundnut Council at a subsequent meeting, held in Lagos from 29 August to 7 September 1978, decided that its Council should remain a separate body from the AOPO[17] and the membership of this organisation remained the absolute prerogative of any member state. The African Groundnut Council, founded in January 1963, is

TABLE 2.1. Liquid edible and lauric oil production figures 1963–67 (expressed in thousand metric tons)

Product	*1963*	*1964*	*1965*	*1966*	*1967*
Liquid edible oils					
Soya bean	3,314	3,424	3,659	4,032	4,260
Groundnut oil	2,371	2,408	2,629	2,448	2,510
Cotton-seed oil	2,228	2,159	2,377	2,269	2,000
Olive oil	1,003	1,933	1,024	1,362	1,440
Others	1,510	1,525	1,981	1,823	1,980
TOTAL	10,425	11,449	11,670	11,934	12,190
Lauric acid oils					
Coconut oil	2,129	2,138	2,112	2,207	2;050
Babassu oil	64	65	65	65	65
Palm-kernel oil	405	412	421	401	320
Palm oil	1,307	1,320	1,315	1,318	1,280
TOTAL	3,905	3,935	3,913	3,991	3,715

Source: Cracknel, in *JWTL*, Vol. 2, No. 4 (July/August 1968) and FAO Doc. CCP: OF/WP/68/WP.1.

made up of six countries: Niger, Nigeria, Senegal, Sudan, the Gambia and Mali. Zaïre and Upper Volta, who were original members, later withdrew. Its council of representatives meets twice yearly in ordinary sessions in April/May and October/November respectively,[18] while its council of ministers meets once yearly. Decisions are taken by consensus in practice although voting is done by simple majority for procedural matters and a two-thirds majority for important matters. Of the financial contributions to its budget 50 per cent is divided between Nigeria and Senegal while the remaining 50 per cent is divided according to production levels. Mali contributes 7·5 per cent; Sudan 15 per cent; Ghana 10·5 per cent; and Niger 17 per cent.

While in 1966–67 the total budgetary contribution was £4,000,[19] that is, about N8000*; in 1977–8 it increased to N568,750 and to N585,850 for 1978–9.[20] For the production and marketing of groundnut and oil in 1977–8 see Table 2.2.

* N = Naira.

TABLE 2.2 Production and marketing of groundnut and oil – November 1978 (effective figures for 1977/78 recapitulation)

1	*Information* *2*	*Nigeria* *3*	*Senegal* *4*	*Niger* *5*	*Sudan* *6*	*Gambia* *7*	*Mali* *8*
A	Quantity of groundnut exported	Nil	Nil	Nil	155,600 MT	24,832 MT	5,400 T
B	Average export price of groundnut	Nil	Nil	Nil	$550 FAQ $720 HPS	D1,136·52 $568·26	250,000 FM FOB $595·23
C	Quantity of oil exported	Nil	15,000 T	1,953·5 T	43,000 MT	13,386 MT	Nil
D	Average export price for oil	Nil	450 FF CIF/CAF/MT $1,071·4	225,000 F Tonne $1,071·43	$1,000 T.FOB	D2,119·80 $1,059·90	Nil Nil
E	Quantity of cake exported	Nil	55,000 MT	2917 T	60,000 MT	14,426 MT	Nil
F	Average export price for cake	Nil	FF.1,000/T $238·09	42,855 F $204·07	$200 CIF T	D422·36 $211·18	Nil

Source: Appendix II, Doc. AGC/CR/30/225 of 3 December 1978.
Draft Report of 30th Ordinary Session of the Council of Representatives.

Abbreviations: MT = metric ton
FAQ = fair average quality
CAF/CIF = cost insurance freight
HPS = hand-picked selected
T.FOB = ton freight on board
FM = million francs
D = delasie (Gambian currency)

Compensation Fund of the African Groundnut Council

At a meeting of the AGC in Lagos from 28 August to 7 September 1978, a proposal to establish a Compensation Fund failed to materialise for a lack of consensus. But at the 30th Ordinary Session in Banjul (the Gambia) in December 1978, a consensus was reached in a prevailing spirit of co-operation and solidarity on the creation of the fund. It was decided among others that an *ad hoc* committee should meet in Bamako (Mali) before April/May 1979 in order to draw up a list of priorities submitted by member states and to prepare a draft statute and draft rules of procedure of the fund for use of the *ad hoc* committee.

Objectives of the fund

The fund is established to contribute to the solution of transport problems involved in the marketing of groundnut and its derivatives by the AGC members. In the first phase the intervention of the fund will be limited to a number of these problems which shall be identified after a thorough study of a list of priorities furnished by member countries.

Financing

Its resources shall come from contributions from AGC member states, subsidies and other contributions from all sources, grants from bilateral and multilateral sources including foreign sources, incomes derived from loans made or from guarantees given by the fund and borrowing.

Operation

Its accounts are separated from those of the AGC Secretariat and shall have the following:

(a) an administrative account for running costs;
(b) compensation account for payment of compensation to member states for extra transportation costs and the charges involved in other possible constraints to be defined;
(c) a special operations account for loans, investments, guarantees, commissions and interest charges.

The meeting generally agreed that payments should be for exceptional transportation costs incurred in the normal transportation of groundnut and its derivatives in the AGC countries. In respect of the organisation and procedure of the fund, it was agreed that it should be separated from the AGC secretariat and should be headed by a Managing Director. Its governing body is made up of a Board of Directors consisting of one representative per AGC member state answerable and reporting to the AGC Council of Ministers. The voting procedure is that of the equality principle of one vote per country. The general management and organisation of the fund shall be based on international public law similar to that governing regional or international funds. The executive secretary of the AGC shall be a non-voting *ex-officio* member.

(II) Short-term agreements

This type was contracted by France with her overseas territories and Francophone African states. It was a one-year type of agreement meant to guarantee prices well above the world price. It consequently was not production-oriented. With the establishment of the EEC, a law was presented by the Commission on 2 December 1964 by which African associated states were to have a preferential market in the areas of oil products. The purpose was to progressively reduce customs duties on importation into the EEC countries. It also established a system of aid to render production profitable in the producer countries of the associated states.

3 Diplomatic Prerequisites for Legal Techniques

INTRODUCTION

The study of Credentials and Full Powers and the role of jurists in modern economic diplomacy as a prelude to the study of legal techniques (from the act of signature to ratification, territorial application and conflict resolution) stems from the following facts:

(i) without proper Credentials and Full Powers, a delegate cannot be allowed to participate in the negotiation and signing of an adopted agreement. But the entry into force of an agreement starts from signature or adoption of an agreement, as we shall see later in subsequent chapters; for as soon as an agreement is signed it could go into force provisionally or definitively for the signatories according to certain conditions as may be stipulated in the agreement.

(ii) The drafting of an agreement precedes the adoption of a concluded agreement and adoption could be taken in economic international law and diplomacy as having a certain force of law, as we shall see later in subsequent chapters. It is in the light of the above that we shall first examine 'Credentials and Full Powers' in Section I, before 'Drafting' in Section II.

SECTION I. VERIFICATION OF CREDENTIALS AND FULL POWERS

There was a time in the past when it took a diplomatic envoy several weeks to get to his destination, either for the purpose of accreditation or negotiations of some sort of peace treaties. Because of this, the envoy was invested with Full Powers (Pleins Pouvoirs) to negotiate a treaty which was considered as binding to the principal (sovereign).[1] Today, because of the rapidity in communication systems, the previous practice whereby a treaty was binding on the sovereign has to a great extent been modified. This is because the act of ratification is now the prerogative of Parliament or heads of state. The modern practice in multilateral economic agreements in the verification of Credentials, is that when a country intends to participate actively in the negotiations and conclusion of an agreement its accredited representatives are issued with Credentials and Full Powers, which they present to the secretariats or headquarters governments of the convening institution.

In spite of this, economic negotiations of commodity types still require at the end of the concluded text of the agreement the authentification of their powers thus: 'In witness whereof the undersigned, having been duly authorised to this effect by their respective Governments, have signed this Agreement on the dates appearing opposite their signature.'[2] At the end of the negotiations the plenipotentiaries sign on behalf of their respective governments.

As a general rule, and in the Nigerian practice, Credentials are issued by the head of state, the head of government or the Minister or Commissioner for External Affairs or by an appropriate authority duly appointed by one of the above-named. Where Credentials are issued by an authority external to the head of state, head of government or Minister/Commissioner for External Affairs, it is clearly stated or specified that the necessary authority has been accredited to the person issuing the Credentials and this includes the source from which this authority has been given. In addition Full Powers are required of representatives or their alternates authorised to sign any convention, protocol, agreement or similar instrument which may be drawn up by the conference and opened for signature. Wherever applicable, the Full Powers state that the representative is empowered to sign subject to ratification, approval or acceptance or whatever expression is appropriate in accordance with the constitution and practice of the state in question. Full Powers are only issued by the the head of state, head of government or Minister/Commissioner for External Affairs. Wherever these are required in advance by the convening body, it is to facilitate the work of the conference, and it is necessary to stress that the form each country adopts depends on its laws and practice. However, it is often appreciated by international institutions if governments adhere to the prototype models 1–3 as established at the end of this section, particularly because of the information necessary to be furnished in these instruments. Often, cabled communications are treated as provisional as they require to be authenticated by the appropriate instruments in due form.

Before the negotiations begin, the Full Powers and Credentials are submitted or have been submitted for verification by the headquarters government of the convening institution, in multilateral negotiations. But in the modern practice in UN system sponsored negotiations on commodity agreements, the onus of verification lies with the secretariat of the convening institution or in the absence of one, the secretariat of UNCTAD or UNO, assisted by a committee of plenipotentiaries or credentials committee. In the case of the UN conferences on olive oil, for instance that of the 1967 conference in New York,[3] the Credentials of delegates[4] were verified by an *ad hoc* specialised committee called the Credential Committee consisting of the following countries: Belgium, Greece, Portugal, Tunisia and the UK (Great Britain and Northern Ireland). Mr F. de Alcambar Pereira (Portugal) was elected chairman of this committee. In the case of the above conference, it was Mr Choussudovsky (secretary of the conference) who read out a draft resolution providing for the appointment of a Credentials Committee. During this conference, Mr Mahbouli (Tunisia) drew attention to the fact that Greece was not represented at the conference, but after Mr Choussudovsky, the secretary of the conference, indicated the intention of Greece to participate in the work of the conference, Mr Janton (France) proposed that consideration of the item on Credentials be postponed until the arrival of the Greek representative, and it was so adopted. When the session met again on Thursday 3 March 1967, Mr de Alcambar Pereira (Portugal), speaking as chairman of the committee after the arrival of the Greek representative, presented their report, which was adopted. This procedure is typical of commodity negotiations because the 1960 United Nations Tin Conference at its 2nd session also set up a Credentials Committee comprising Spain, Nigeria, the Federal Republic of Germany and the UK (Great Britain and Northern Ireland). The report of this committee was adopted on 7 June 1960 at the UN headquarters in New York.

MODEL ONE: *To be signed by the Head of State, Head of Government or Minister of Foreign or External Affairs or another authority duly empowered by one of them for this purpose.*

CREDENTIALS

Sir,

This is to certify that I, ...
(full name)
of . . . . , have appointed
(name of state)
. . . .
full name(s) and title(s)
as the Representative(s) of. . . . .
(name of State)
to the International Conference on. . . . .
(name of the Conference)
to be held in . . . . from . . . .
(place) (duration)
and have also designated. . . . .
(full name(s) and Title(s) of Alternates)
. . . .
as Alternate Representative(s) to the Same Conference*

OR

I have the honour, acting upon instructions from the . . . .
. . . . of. . . . .
(Title) (name of state)
to inform you that . . . .
(full name(s) and title(s))
has (have) been appointed as the Representative(s) of . . . .
to the Conference on . . . .
to be held in . . . . from . . . .
and have also designated. . . . .
. . . .
(full name(s) and title(s) of Alternate(s))
as Alternate Representative(s) to the same Conference†
The said . . . .
(name(s) of Representative(s) and Alternate(s))
is (are) authorized fully to take part in the Conference, to transact all such matters as appertain to its work, and to vote with other Representatives in accordance with the agreed procedures. The delegation . . . .
(name of state)
assisted in its mission by . . . .
. . . .
(full name(s) and title(s) of Adviser(s))

Please accept Sir, the assurance of my highest consideration.

(Signature)

(full name and title)

---

* For Credentials signed by Head of State, Head of Government or Minister for Foreign/External Affairs.

† For Credentials signed by another authority empowered to do so by one of the above.

MODEL TWO: *Letter Conferring Full Powers. To be signed by the Head of State, Head of Government or Minister/Commissioner for External/Foreign Affairs*

I, ...
(full name and title)
of . . . . hereby certify that
(name of state)

. . . .
(full name(s) and title(s) of Representative(s))
Representative(s) of . . . . and
(name of state)

. . . .
(full name(s) and title(s) of Alternate(s))
is (are) designated to do and transact all matters on behalf of . . . .
. . . . at the Conference
(name of state)
on . . . . , to be held in . . . .
(title of Conference) (place)
from . . . .
(duration of Conference)
and is (are) vested with Full Powers and authority to sign any Convention or other International Instrument which may be adopted by the said Conference.*

IN WITNESS WHEREOF I have affixed my signature to the Full Powers at . . . . on . . . .
(place) (date)

(signature)

(full name and title)

---

* *N.B.* If it is intended that the signature of the Representative(s)/Alternate(s) should not suffice to bind the state unconditionally, the words "subject to Acceptance" or other appropriate expression should be inserted here.

MODEL THREE: *Letter of Credentials combined with Full Powers. To be signed by the Head of State, Head of Government or Minister/Commissioner for External/Foreign Affairs.*

Sir,

This is to certify that I, ...
(full names)

of . . . . have appointed
(name of state)

. . . .
(full name(s) and title(s))

as the Representative(s) of . . . . to the
(name of state)

International Conference on . . . .
(title of the Conference)

to be held in . . . . from . . . .
(name of Capital) (duration of Conference)

and have designated. . . . .
(full name(s) and titles of Alternates)

as Alternate Representative(s) to the same Conference.

The said . . . .
(name(s) of Representative(s) and/or Alternates)

is (are) authorised fully to take part in the Conference, to transact all such matters as may appertain to its work, to vote with other Representatives in accordance with agreed procedures.

The said . . . .
Name(s) of Representatives or Alternate(s)

is (are) authorised to sign any Convention or other International Instrument which may be adopted by the Conference.*

The delegation of--
(name of state)

will be assisted in its mission by: --

(full name(s) and titles of Adviser(s)

as adviser(s).

Please accept, Sir, the assurance of my highest consideration.

(signed)

(full name and title)

---

* If it is intended that the signature of the Representative(s) or Alternate(s) should not suffice to bind the state unconditionally, the words "subject to Acceptance" or other appropriate expression should be inserted here.

SECTION II. DRAFTING AND THE JURIST IN INTERNATIONAL ECONOMIC NEGOTIATIONS

(A) THE ROLE OF THE JURIST IN INTERNATIONAL DRAFTING PROCESSES

The jurist plays very significant roles in the drafting of commodity agreements and other economic arrangements particularly in the early stages of negotiation within study groups and specialised committees. These are meant to study specific problems arising from interpretation in the use of the words, for instance, 'floor price in force' and liquidation of the buffer stock in tin agreements. The most important of these committees in the tin agreements is the Technical Committee on Renewal of the Agreement.

When a UN Conference on Renewal of the Tin Agreement was scheduled for 1960, a committee of experts was created in November 1958. This committee, composed of several experts[5] of national and international reputation, was set up to prepare the draft of the second international agreement which was submitted to the UN preparatory conference which prepared and adopted the new agreement. This committee presented the 'Draft International Agreement on Tin' in three official languages: English, French and Spanish, as was the case in 1960 and 1965. The practice of incorporating international experts and jurists lends more weight to the draft document. For further example, the draft treaty of ECOWAS was prepared by the Accra Meeting of Jurists and Experts which met 11–15 February 1974.[6] This prepared draft was thereafter sent to the states for their comments and from there commenced the negotiation as each state studied it and made comments for further study before the formal meeting took place for the signature of the agreement on 28 May 1975 in Lagos between member heads of state. This is to say that in economic agreements of international nature, the initiative of preparing a draft emanates from an international body of jurists and experts, while for political or bilateral agreements, the initiative comes from states themselves.

As a general rule, small developing countries with little interest in a given commodity do not include jurists in their delegations. On the other hand, large delegations of producer and consumer countries, depending on the importance of a commodity to them, pay great attention to legal matters. For instance, at the 1962 Coffee Conference, the countries that included jurists in their delegations were: the UK, USA, Brazil, Germany, Colombia, and Ethiopia. However the legal advisers in the

UN or UNCTAD secretariat are often made available to conference negotiations. Their contributions are highly appreciated because of their special skills and acquired experiences in the field of economic negotiations. From the experience of the author in commodity negotiations, legal issues are not taken up frequently in debates by developing countries, probably because of the enormous discussions that have taken place in the specialised committees or because of the neglect by them of legal issues since they lack sufficient expertise in economic international law. The result is that most concessions which the consumers make in the economic provisions they tend to withdraw in legal provisions. Or what could explain the participation of consumer countries in the law-making processes of commodity agreements when they do not contribute financially to the administration of a buffer stock? Yet the advantages that accrue go to both sides of the contracting parties. However, the gradual introduction of voluntary contributions to the buffer stock coffers is an indication of a gradual awareness of the developing countries in the areas of legal economics. For example during the 1968 Cocoa Negotiations in Geneva, a situation arose which was contrary to the logic and spirit of the functioning of any equitable agreement. This conflict situation arose from the desire of the US delegation to restore quota cuts at less than the minimum price range being negotiated when prices fall below this minimum. Accepting this mode of functioning by the producers would have meant the defeat of the purpose of an agreement itself, which is to permit prices to fluctuate between the minimum and maximum price ranges[7] and this would be permitting the effect of law at a level contrary to the purpose of the agreement. No wonder most producers rejected it, except Ghana. The skill or expertise of the lawyer in drafting can best be appreciated in such matters on the examination of draft proposals which may conflict with national policies and laws and any other issue that could arise during the negotiations. The jurist in delegations also helps in lobbying activities and by so doing is able to help in such legal matters that may arise before the negotiations begin. For instance:

> in the preparation of a negotiating position consistent with national law, securing any necessary negotiating authority or credentials, assisting in the technical aspects of signature and ratification and preparing and bringing into effect any necessary implementing legislation or regulation.[8]

His presence is mostly felt as a member of a conference legal and drafting committee and when he prepares the draft which forms the basis of conference negotiations. He is responsible for drafting the most important areas of any economic agreement. For example, the 'final clauses' which is made up of: entry in force; application of the agreement; duration of the agreement; amendment; and settlement of conflicts. Final clauses often raise

> complex and interesting legal and legal policy questions, but also political questions of great importance, particularly in the context of the 'cold war'. Thus, the clauses in multilateral agreements relating to signature and accession – that is, which countries can become members – raised serious problems as regards regimes unrecognised by the USA, such as East Germany, Communist China, North Korea and North Vietnam.[9]

The ability of the jurist to judiciously interpret an economic agreement would depend upon his competence in the area of legal economics, better still if he is interdisciplinary. However, an important aspect of international drafting is that most international jurists with a municipal law background tend to introduce the ambiguity characteristic of municipal terminology into international economic relations. We have already seen the example of the author's experiences at the 1968 Cocoa Conference where they argued interminably on minor issues and over simple words or expressions. To reduce this tendency, it will be advisable to encourage the study of international law as distinct from municipal law so that we can evolve terminologies that could reflect the spirit of co-operation in economic matters. However there is a dissenting opinion which states that, because the 1962 Coffee Study Group draft was not done with the help of Foreign Office legal experts, the text was ambiguous and out of accord with internationally accepted drafting practice. It lacked standard terminology already in existence in commodity agreements.[10]

Finally it is important to note that a draft agreement has no standard parts into which it is divided, but as a general practice it is divided into Parts and Chapters, into which Articles are negotiated and adopted one after the other. The final division of a draft text agreement depends on the problems posed to the commodity. For instance, the 1968 Coffee Agreement is divided into 22 Chapters with 72 Articles while the 1962 Wheat Agreement is divided into 7 Parts of 37 Articles, and the 1972 Cocoa Agreement into 26 Chapters of 77 Articles. However, as a general rule, the provisions of a draft submitted for ratification after adoption and signature are often divided into several areas: the general, which contains the objectives, definitions; rights and obligations; membership; adjustment regulations on quotas, exports, buffer stock and prices etc; administration and organisation; privileges and immunities and final clauses or provisions. The present difficulty in arriving at general and acceptable drafting techniques in the light of the above description stems from the peculiarity of the problems posed to agriculture as distinct from metal and energy diplomacy, as will be seen from the case studies in subsequent chapters of this book. This is not to say that a case-by-case study is most suitable, but to underline the importance of establishing agreements according to the following groups: agriculture, metals and energy. In this way, general drafting techniques could be developed for each group until the solidarity of the world is comparable to those of economic regional groupings where general techniques will be easier to establish. For instance, the ECOWAS Treaty, although highly simplified, was inspired by, and fairly similar to, the EEC Agreement.

(B) NATIONAL DRAFTING PROCESSES

On the national levels, governments are often concerned with the initial preparation which usually precedes any international conference. For instance they are concerned with the choice of delegations and the overhead costs of their strength. This is most usual with small, poor countries which have very little commitment to the outcome of the conference. For a negotiation to be effectively carried out, strategies and divergent positions have to be worked out, and if there are problems arising therefrom they have to find advance solutions to them at very high policy-making echelons. It is in this consideration that we shall examine two cases of treaty drafting techniques – USA and Nigeria – which are both interesting to study for the peculiarities which both display, as will be seen below.

(I) The United States of America

The drafting procedure of the US administration could be categorised into five stages, with each stage having specialised functions to perform.

First Stage This consists in appointing its delegates to the conference and preparing all necessary Credentials. If the commodity is of particular political or strategic importance, its delegation is large. For instance, the coffee agreement which the USA holds in great esteem, not only because of its role as the biggest consumer but also for its policy to co-operate with the countries of the Third World, particularly Latin America. The Tin Agreement is also important for the USA because of its importance as a strategic material. It is, however, regrettable that it is not yet a contracting party to the Tin Agreement although it sends very large delegations to its preparatory conferences, as we shall see in Chapter 7. To the 1962 Coffee Negotiations, its delegation consisted of eleven government officials from the State Department, Commerce and Agriculture and eight advisers from private industry.[11] The US alternate delegates were Mr Henry Brodie and Mr Paul E. Callanon, both of the State Department's Office of International Resources. A greater number of private advisers were from the National Coffee Association and its Foreign Affairs Advisory Committee; Mr Jerome Jacobson of International Economic Consultants Incorporated played a significant role in the negotiations. He had once served as a consultant on contract basis with the Agency for International Development. Mr W. Michael Blumenthal, Deputy Assistant Secretary of State for Economic Affairs, who had played an important part in the work of the Coffee Study Group, was appointed Chairman of the United States Delegation.

Stage II A series of meetings between government officials and private-interest groups take place. It is here that the US basic position and objectives, as well as the strategies to be adopted, are tabled for discussion. These positions are incorporated in a formal confidential negotiating instruction issued to the delegation. For the 1962 Coffee Negotiations, the US basic position was as follows: since the Coffee Agreement is a long-term one, it should be based upon realistic export quotas not exceeding available estimates of probable world demand. The quota system should be extended to all types of coffee exported to all destinations for all purposes, and no loopholes must be left. No ex-quota shipments to 'new markets' must be allowed. No specific price margins must be indicated in the agreement because prices should be determined by market forces under the quota system. Specific provisions should be included in the agreement to protect consumer interest against unwarranted price rises. The agreement should provide for free movement of coffee on a non-discriminatory basis and should attempt to eliminate obstacles to trade and fiscal burdens which prevent consumption. It should also encourage diversification of the economy of a coffee-producing area, and provide means for the systematic reduction of production and stocks.[12]

Stage III Several categories of lawyers examine the draft agreement usually prepared either by the preparatory conference drafting committee or the UNCTAD secretariat. Those who examine this draft are drawn from the office of the legal adviser in the State Department and from other agencies, and their role is to examine the draft from a legal angle with the greatest attention being paid to the possible obligations which the USA might be called upon to assume. During this discussion it could be discovered that before the USA could join an agreement a new legislation would be necessary and it could also be discovered, as was the case in the 1962 Coffee Agreement, that such a legislation for all practical purposes could not be secured before the adjournment of Congress.[13]

Stage IV This is the stage for action. The US government officials hold several meetings with foreign embassy officials in Washington and, through American embassies abroad, inform foreign governments of the 'importance which the US government attaches to the success of the conference, the need for thorough and timely preparation'. It also requests them to view the problems or issues realistically, and also stresses the importance of compromises as an act of diplomacy in order to accomplish the objectives of the conference.

Another method often employed is that the US government officials meet with foreign officials to examine whether their views correspond. If they correspond they could then establish plans for a concerted action at the conference. When all these have been accomplished important personalities of the US Congress are then advised of the coming negotiation in terms of the US position and objectives. The purpose of this is to facilitate the eventual ratification of the agreement after all formalities have been completed.

Stage V In accordance with the practice and procedures[14] of the US State Department, permission is then sought and received from the Secretary of State for the US delegation to enter into formal negotiations because:

> the customary process of negotiating a multilateral agreement and in some cases a bilateral agreement, involves the designation of a US delegation specifically authorised and appointed for that purpose.

> The office frequently assists in the preparation and clearance of delegation instructions, which in the case of more important negotiations, provide guidance to such delegations as to the positions and actions they should or may take on the various issues involved. These instructions may be very detailed or precise, or may give the delegation considerable discretion. Frequently, as the negotiation develops, it is necessary for the delegation to request a change in its instructions in order to meet an unanticipated situation or effect a compromise. The delegation cannot, however, properly exceed the terms of its instructions without authorisation from the Department.[15]

The lawyer who is attached or assigned to a delegation is expected to participate actively in the negotiations, thus putting his legal knowledge or skills to the service of his delegation in matters pertaining to interpretation of its instructions, the drafting of proposals and statements. He also undertakes the analyses of proposals put forward by other delegations so as to ascertain whether there are conflicts between them and US internal legislation or practice. During the process of the negotiation, he serves as his delegation member of the drafting committee. If the negotiations prove successful, it is the responsibility of the office of the legal adviser to prepare the agreement for signature, and if a treaty, for the ratification of the Senate and the eventual deposit of its instrument of ratification.

(II) The Federal Republic of Nigeria

Although Nigeria's drafting techniques conform to acceptable international standards, they present an interesting study because of the differences which occur in the process as compared to that of the USA, as we shall see later. We shall therefore examine these in their various stages and also examine her practice in the formulation of her Letters of Credence and Full Powers because these naturally follow at the end of the drafting processes, particularly with regard to participation at negotiations and signing of an agreed document.

(A) Bilateral and multilateral drafting and ancillary process

In bilateral economic relations, more so in political relations, the initiative of drafting an agreement lies with one of the states involved in the negotiations although agreement could be reached by both parties to produce drafts for mutual consideration and reconciliation. If Nigeria takes the initiative, for instance, she sends a draft copy of the proposed agreement prepared by the Federal Ministry of Justice in conjunction with the relevant or appropriate ministry, to the other party for consideration. As a general rule, the content of a draft reflects the objectives, goals and national interest of the initiating country. For example, the Ghana/Nigeria agreement on the use of Ghana's port facilities for off-loading Nigerian goods was drafted by the legal advisers of the Federal Ministry of Justice, Lagos and, thereafter, sent to the Ghanaian government for comments. What came out of the revised draft was the result of reconciled interests between the two contracting parties. The agreement was executed on mere initialling in August 1975 by the Federal Commissioner for Transport, Lt Col. Shehu Musa Yar' Adua for the Federal Republic of Nigeria and Col. J. K. Agyerkum, the Ghanaian Commissioner for Transport and Communications for the Republic of Ghana. Its entry into force before formal signature or exchange of instruments of ratification was a testimony to the new spirit of co-operation resulting from the ECOWAS Treaty signed on 28 May 1975 by fifteen West African heads of state of the sub-region.

In multilateral economic relations, the drafting procedure is quite different. The initiative lies with a group of experts or an international organisation, as we have already seen. However, when the draft proposal gets to the Ministry of External Affairs, the processes of its consideration take the following stages:

Stage I This draft proposal now at the appropriate department (which could be International Organisations Department or Economic Department) of the Ministry of External Affairs, is sent to the Ministry of Trade if it concerns questions of international regulation of a proposed commodity. Here it is again studied and sent to the Federal Ministry of Justice for legal advice and comments. The legal advisers try to examine it as in the American practice, in the light of its consistency with national practice, policies and laws.

Stage II This draft is then returned to the Federal Ministry of Trade with comments and thereafter an inter-ministerial meeting composed of all relevant ministries is held. At this meeting, each ministerial representative who must have read this draft, because he is directly concerned schedule-wise with the subject-matter, submits the observations of his ministry. At the end of these deliberations, decisions are then taken as to which position or strategy should be adopted at the negotiating conference. The outcome of this meeting constitutes the negotiating position of the Nigerian delegation. However, these representatives could still report back to their respective ministries to examine whether further modifications could occur. Outsiders are not admitted to this meeting, as in the American practice, but they could be invited to participate as advisers to the Nigerian delegation. For instance, the Nigerian delegation to the 1968 Cocoa Conference and the 1960 and 1965 Tin Conferences were composed of ministry officials, and advisers outside the ministry, for instance, the university, the private sector of the tin industry and the Cocoa Marketing Board. The ECOWAS negotiations included, among others, members of the Nigerian Chamber of Commerce. Nigeria therefore, in her practice, does not divulge or discuss her negotiating positions with outsiders until the delegates are about to leave for the conference, when they are then briefed.

Stage III The Nigerian delegation is also drawn from the various interested or relevant ministries that took part in discussing the draft. They are normally very conversant with the subject-matter, which they usually handle as their schedules. In some cases, the same administrators with a previous experience on the negotiation in question continue until the conclusion of an agreement, but it is significant to note that Nigeria does not, as a matter of practice, constitute a group of permanent commodity negotiators.

Stage IV Before the departure of the said delegates to the conference, the Ministry of External Affairs issues Credentials and/or Full Powers to the delegation in which are stated their names, official status, departments and roles at the negotiations. For instance, Mr A., Deputy Permanent Secretary, Federal Ministry of Trade, Leader; *or* Mr B., Principal Assistant Secretary, Federal Ministry of Finance, Member; *or* Mr D., Senior State Counsel, Federal Ministry of Justice, Adviser. The Credential is addressed to the secretary of the convening body and signed by the head of state, head of government or Commissioner for External Affairs or another authority duly authorised for this purpose. The prototype of the Nigerian practice takes the following format:[16]

Sir,

I have the honour, on the instructions of the Honourable Commisioner for External Affairs, to inform you that the Nigerian delegation to the International Conference on . . . .
scheduled to be held in London from 23rd of April to the 9th of May, 1975, will comprise the following:

1. Mr. A. O. O.
Acting Deputy Permanent Secretary
Federal Ministry of Trade
Lagos. – Leader
2. Mr. F. H. O.
Senior Assistant Secretary
Federal Ministry of Finance
Lagos. – Member

I shall be grateful if you will accord the above-mentioned persons all necessary assistance to enable them to participate effectively in all aspects of the meeting and give them due regard as accredited Nigerian representatives at the said meeting. Accept, Sir, the assurances of my highest consideration.

Signed . . . .

Permanent Secretary
Ministry of External Affairs
Federal Republic of Nigeria.

Nigeria does not usually issue Credentials in bilateral negotiations because of the exchange of departmental notes which normally precedes such negotiations. For instance the negotiations which preceded the signing of a long-term bilateral trade agreement between the Federal Military Government of the Federal Republic of Nigeria and Bulgaria in September 1975. The Federal Commissioner for Trade, Brigadier M. Shuwa signed on behalf of the Federal Republic of Nigeria, while Mr Ivan Nedev, the Bulgarian Minister of Foreign Trade, was co-signatory with the Bulgarian Minister of External Affairs, Mr Peter Mladevov.[17] In bilateral trade negotiations, it is the Federal Executive Council or Parliament that gives the authority to negotiate, and the signature is effected by the Trade Commissioner.

In multilateral negotiations, it is the Minister/Commissioner for External Affairs or head of state or government that signs the Full Powers authorising an official to sign or negotiate on behalf of the federal government. This is to say that the authorised official could sign any convention, protocol or similar instrument which has been drawn up by the conference and opened for signature.

Wherever applicable the Full Powers always state that the representative or official authorised to sign, does so subject to our constitutional requirements of ratification, approval or acceptance. This means that a resident ambassador leading a delegation or a *chargé d'affaires* could sign the resultant agreement or protocol of agreement or a convention. For instance, the Full Powers and authority to sign the protocol for the extension of the 1962 International Wheat Agreement on behalf of the Federal Republic of Nigeria until 31 July 1966, was given to a *Chargé d'Affaires Ad Interim* by the Minister of State for External Affairs who signed the Full Powers. The authority may be to participate in negotiations alone and not to sign any resultant convention or agreement. For instance, at the United Nations Commission for Internal Trade Law (UNCITRAL) at which the convention for the limitation period in the international sale of goods was discussed, the Credentials issued to the Nigerian delegation was for participation only and not for signing. Brazil, apart from taking part at the conference, had powers to sign on the date of adoption. The Nigerian attitude was simply that of a country willing to participate in order to contribute to its outcome with a view probably to acceding in the future. This has also always been the attitude of the US government to the Tin Conferences in which she participates actively but whose agreements she has persistently refused to sign.

FIGURE 3.1 Prototype of Nigerian Full Powers

Whereas it is expedient that a fit and proper person should be invested with Full Powers and authority to sign the protocol for the extension of the International Wheat Agreement, 1962 until 31 July 1966, on behalf of the Government of the Federal Republic of Nigeria.

Now, THEREFORE I, ...
Minister of State for External Affairs, do hereby name, make, constitute and invest . . . .
Chargé d'Affaires Ad Interim with Full Powers and Authority to sign on behalf of the Federal Military Government of the Federal Republic of Nigeria, the protocol for the extension of the Wheat Agreement as recommended by the International Wheat Council on 4 February, 1965.

Further, I do hereby certify that the said protocol shall be subject to any necessary approval by the Federal Military Government of the Federal Republic of Nigeria, be agreed to, acknowledged and accepted by the said Federal Military Government of the Federal Republic of Nigeria.

In WITNESS WHEREOF I have signed these Presents, and affixed hereto my Seal.
Signed at the Ministry of External Affairs, Lagos
the . . . . day of . . . . 19 .

Minister of State
for External Affairs.

Stage V If it is intended that Nigeria should become a contracting party to a concluded agreement, the following procedure applies: the constitutionally responsible ministry, which for the purpose of our discussion is the Trade Ministry, takes a memorandum to the Federal Executive Council in a military regime or Parliament in a civilian regime, stating the history of the subject matter and the reasons Nigeria should become party to the agreement. At the conclusion of the memorandum the Federal Executive Council or Parliament is invited to authorise that Nigeria becomes party:

1. By the appropriate Commissioner/Minister signing the agreement on behalf of the Federal Military Government who could however delegate his Powers either to an ambassador or *Chargé d'Affaires* as we have already seen.
2. By authorising the Attorney General and Commissioner / Minister of Justice to prepare the instrument of ratification for the signature of the head of state after going through necessary constitutional forms of ratification. In the Nigerian practice, ratification of all types of agreements, is the act of the Federal Executive Council in a military regime and Parliament in a civilian regime.
3. By authorising the Ministry of External Affairs to deposit the executed instrument of ratification, with the depository government or in the case of bilateral agreement to exchange instruments of ratification, acceptance or approval.

FIGURE 3.2 Prototype of a Nigerian Instrument of Ratification

FEDERAL REPUBLIC OF NIGERIA
INSTRUMENT OF RATIFICATION OF THE PROTOCOL FOR THE CONTINUATION IN FORCE OF THE INTERNATIONAL COFFEE AGREEMENT 1968 AS EXTENDED

WHEREAS the International Coffee Council approved in London on 26 September 1974 the Protocol for the continuation in force of the International Coffee Agreement 1968 as extended;

AND WHEREAS it is provided in Article 4 of the said Protocol that in cases in which approval, ratification or acceptance is required, the appropriate instruments shall be deposited with the Secretary-General of the United Nations not later than 30 September 1975;

AND WHEREAS the Federal Military Government of the Federal Republic of Nigeria has by a decision duly reached in accordance with its constitutional processes agreed to ratify the aforesaid Protocol;

NOW, THEREFORE, I, ... HEAD OF THE FEDERAL MILITARY GOVERNMENT, COMMANDER-IN-CHIEF OF THE ARMED FORCES, FEDERAL REPUBLIC OF NIGERIA, on behalf of the Federal Military Government of the Federal Republic of Nigeria, hereby confirm and ratify the Protocol for the continuation in force of the International Coffee Agreement 1968 as extended.

IN WITNESS WHEREOF I have hereunto set my hand and caused the seal of the Federal Republic of Nigeria to be affixed to these presents.

DONE at Lagos this . . . . day of . . . . in the year of Our Lord one thousand nine hundred and seventy-five.

Head of the Federal Military Government,
Commander-in-Chief of the Armed Forces
of the Federal Republic of Nigeria.

4 Legal Techniques: Conclusion and Entry into Force

INTRODUCTION

The study of the legal techniques used in the stabilisation of commodity agreements and common market arrangements, stems from what is usually termed in such agreements as 'final clauses' or 'formal provisions'. The preceding chapter has examined the legal prerequisites for the techniques which we are about to study here. This is because the signature of a concluded agreement cannot be done by an unaccredited representative. The scope of this examination will therefore cover two important areas:

I. The conclusion and entry into force of an agreement; that is, signature and its effects in terms of application of a concluded agreement; ratification, acceptance, approval. These form the elements of treatment for this chapter. The next chapter, which is a continuation of the study of legal techniques, will treat:
II. The scope of application of the legal obligation of an agreement, that is duration, termination and renewal; suspension, techniques of dispute settlement or conflict resolution.

The final clauses of all commodity agreements or arrangements are made sufficiently flexible to allow 'provisional entry into force'[1] after a prescribed number of contracting parties have signed. This is because an agreement of an economic nature requires rapidity in its execution and in this way, responds to the aspirations of a world in search of functional cooperation and to precise legal techniques of commodity stabilisation. These legal provisions are formal and similarly possess force of law because of the coercive powers which they have. A law is said to be effective not only at a point where it is able to impose respected sanctions but also where the laws are respected for fear of possible sanctions.

This is the technique which economic agreements truly apprehensive of the desire of governments to satisfy the basic needs of their societies employ. Consequently these governments try to avoid sanctions or withdrawals with similar effects. The formal provisions of all international commodity agreements or arrangements contain articles which state the conditions for their conclusion and entry into force. They are contained in the Articles of the following international agreements: 3rd and 4th Tin Agreements (Articles XXIV and 46–47 respectively); 1968 Coffee Agreement (Article 62); 1972 Cocoa Agreement (Article 67). These legal conditions are those of signature, and its effect on the eventual entry into force and the category of states entitled to sign an agreement. These conform to the requirements of international economic agreements. In bilateral economic agreements, their provisions do not go into effect immediately unless expressly stated and they go through the slow rigour of constitutional procedures respectful of sovereignty. We shall see this later. But the most recent in the Nigerian bilateral practice is that between particular ministries and the other state agencies or departments of other countries or private companies. We have already referred to the Ghana/Nigeria agreement on the use of port facilities. The interdepartmental agreements concluded directly between government departments of different states are *stricto senso* arrangements which pertain to matters of private law rather than international law. For instance, the purchase or sales of goods or the bilateral agreements between a government department and the nationalised interests of other states, which can be regarded as government departments or corporations of government. These types of bilateral trade agreements are not registrable under the requirements of Article 102 of the UN Charter. For example:

(i) Agreement of 29 August 1949 between the United Kingdom Minister of Food and the Norwegian Director of Fisheries in connection with the landings of fresh white fish in the UK from Norwegian fishing vessels.[2]

(ii) The Peugeot Assembly Agreement signed in Lagos on 11 August 1972 on behalf of the Federal Military Government of Nigeria by Dr J. E. Adetoro, the Federal Commissioner for Industries and on behalf of Messrs Automobiles Peugeot of France by its Director, Mr Gerard de Pins. This agreement provided for 10,000 Peugeot passenger cars annually on completion of the assembly plant.[3] This agreement has now been executed since the plant has started production.

SECTION I. SIGNATURE OF AN AGREEMENT

While signature in international economic law plays a very important role because of its possibility of immediate binding effect, in traditional international law it has no immediate force of law except in executive agreements. This is also to say that signature in certain political agreements could have immediate effect of law in spite of the fact that not all signatories have signed. These are exceptions rather than the rule; for instance, the Treaty of 22 May 1926 recording that Belgium's neutralisation had come to an end and the Trustee Agreement of 5 October 1954 known as Memorandum of Understanding, which did not receive the signature of the USSR.[4] Signature plays an important role also when a need occurs for a time lapse between the date of adoption of the draft agreement and the actual signature. This signature at adoption while awaiting a formal act is known as signature *ne varietur*. But where a time lapse is given between dates, it is known as signature *ad referendum* or deferred signature. Signature *ne varietur* often takes the form of initialling, and in international economic law it has no legal value for it is simply a guarantee of the authenticity of the text.

We shall therefore examine the deferred signature as a technique used in international economic law and diplomacy.

(1) SIGNATURE *AD REFERENDUM* OR DEFERRED SIGNATURE

Commodity agreements as a general rule provide for a period of signature. This is true of coffee, tin, wheat and cocoa agreements. For instance, Article 44 of the 4th International Tin Agreement declares as follows:

> The agreement shall be open for signature in London with the government of the United Kingdom of Great Britain and Northern Ireland (hereinafter referred to as depository government) from 1 July 1970 to 29 January 1971 inclusive, on behalf of countries participating in the 3rd International Tin Agreement and on behalf of governments of independent states, those represented at the United Nations Tin Conference, 1970.

While the 1968 Coffee Agreement was open for signature from 18 March to 31 March 1968, the 1962 Wheat Agreement and its rules of procedure from 19 April 1962 until and including 15 May 1962 (Article 35, paragraph 1), the 1972 Cocoa Agreement adopted on 20 October 1972 was open for signature at the United Nations headquarters from 15 November 1972 until and including 15 January 1973 by any government to the 1972 UN Cocoa Conference (Article 63). These tin provisions which are similar to other texts therefore deliberately extend their binding force of law to two categories of signatories, depending on whether there had been a previous agreement or not. First, to those governments who were contracting parties of a previous agreement; otherwise not. Secondly, those governments which participated in the adoption of the current agreement, that is those invited to a UN preparatory conference and which include observers who have no voting rights. The flexibility of these agreements is demonstrated in this way as a technique of adherence by as great a number of states as possible. This is why a deferred signature has specific characteristics. First, from the general adoption of a draft text of an agreement to the day of its signature, there is a period of grace. In the 3rd Tin Agreement, this period totalled 47 days; in the 1972 Cocoa Agreement it was 26 days, while on the contrary, the international Olive Oil Agreement adopted on 23 April 1963 received signatures from this day until 30 June 1965. Where there is a period of grace, it simply corresponds to a period of reflexion at the disposal of delegates who would normally wish to consult with their home governments before they sign; it has no legal value. However, because of its regular use, a period of grace has become an important feature of international community agreements and it is an indicator of reservations which must be ironed out before signature. From a study of the above-mentioned commodities (coffee, wheat, cocoa, olive oil and tin), the period of the deferred signature ranges from 13 days to 6 months. The length of the period required for signature is indicative of the difficulties envisaged for the act of signature and eventual ratification. *The second characteristic* of a deferred signature is that of its advantages. A deferred signature presents specific advantages because it provokes not only the provisional entry into force of an agreement but also gives participating countries a breathing space for consultation among themselves on some unsettled vital issues. For example, they could consult on certain reservations which have emerged at signature and which may arise at ratification although international economic law limits its scope through amendment and withdrawal clauses. On the part of the commodity institution itself, it is able to thus consult with certain governments which proved difficult during the negotiations so as to facilitate the eventual entry into force of the agreement at the scheduled time. For instance, when Malaysia expressed the desire that it would not sign the 3rd International Tin Agreement because it contained certain restrictive measures militating against her, as producer of two-thirds of world tin supply, a Tin Council delegation led by Mr H. W. Allen, Chairman of the Council, left for Malaysia on 25 December 1965 before the expiry date of the deferred signature, 31 December 1965. It was during this meeting that he was able to convince the Prime Minister of Malaysia, Mr Tunku Abdul Rahman, to sign the agreement 'in the interest of international co-operation and good will',[5] when on the previous day, 24 December 1965, his Finance Minister had declared: 'We said it was not in Malaysia's best interests to join the agreement. We made it clear we could not accept even for compromise or if modifications were made. The cabinet had reached a firm decision after very careful consideration of all aspects of the case. We will stick to that decision.'[6] The refusal of Malaysia to sign the agreement would have been detrimental to the organisation of the tin market since she is the greatest world producer.[7] This is why we cannot ignore or underestimate the legal effects which a deferred signature could have on the eventual entry into force of an agreement. *The third characteristic* is that of states entitled to sign an agreement. These states could be classified into two categories:

(i) *Participating countries*: this comprises those countries who were signatory to a previous agreement of the same type and those who were invited to participate actively in a UN preparatory conference. This second group are specifically invited for the role they could eventually play in the stabilisation of a product by their membership. The most notable examples are the USA and the USSR as regards tin agreements. While the latter has now joined the international tin agreement, the former has persistently refused to join in spite of its active participation in preparatory conferences.

(ii) *The governments of independent states*: represented at a previous UN preparatory conference. This group includes observers and other invitees. If commodity agreements provide for a wider range of signatories, this is because they are desirous of extending their binding force of law to other states. It is important to note that the observer status of any state ends immediately it signs the agreement and that the fact of this status indicates a type of expression of reservation which denies the holder voting rights in

> the decision-making processes of preparatory conferences. If Articles 44 of the 4th Tin Agreements and 62 of the International Coffee Agreement like other commodity agreements with precedents, employ the term 'participating countries' to mean those who were actively engaged in the negotiations and 'governments of independent states', this is because the first expression recognises that the agreement would eventually be binding to individuals, while the second expression recognises that governments are exclusive signatories. This is to say that 'country' carries with it a sociological notion which 'government' does not.

The fourth characteristic of signature is unravelled when we examine the seat of the act of signature. This act takes place at the UN headquarters in New York which is the depository of most commodity agreements with some exceptions. For example, the act of signature in the International Coffee Agreement (1968),[8] the International Cocoa Agreement (1972), and Olive Oil (1963) took place at the UN headquarters in New York while for tin agreements it takes place in London where the International Tin Council has its headquarters. For the Tin Council, whose headquarters is in London, this appears logical, although the coffee, olive oil and cocoa councils are not in New York.[9] By this signature, the depository authorities, whether governments or UN, are expected to notify all participating governments of any ratification, signatures, approvals or acceptances and other requirements established in the formal provisions of agreements which includes reservations expressed at signature. That most commodity agreements provide that signatures be made at the UN headquarters and instruments of ratification deposited with the Secretary General of the UN, is enough justification to recommend this as desirable practice for all commodity agreements. This is the more desirable when we realise that the authentic text of any international agreement, once printed, must be registered with the UN Secretariat in accordance with the provisions of Article 102 of the UN Charter. This approach will not only help to 'denationalise' and 'depoliticise' the secretariat of the various commodity councils, but will also increase the prestige and position of the UN by according it a universalist orientation. We refer here to the Tin Council, to which USA and China are not yet members. This is also to say that the London and Madrid governments should no more be depository to the tin and the current olive oil agreements.

(2) PROVISIONAL EFFECTS OF SIGNATURE

There are two ways by which provisional effects are produced in commodity agreements by the act of signature: first, in terms of bringing about a provisional application; secondly, by creating continuity among signatory or contractual members of an agreement.

(i) Signature provokes a provisional application of the agreement

Each commodity agreement provides for the conditions under which it could enter into force provisionally. For instance, the 1968 International Coffee Agreement stipulates in Article 62, paragraph 2:

> The agreement may enter into force provisionally on 1 October 1968. For this purpose a notification by a signatory government or by any other contracting party to the International Coffee Agreement 1962, containing an undertaking to apply the agreement provisionally and to seek approval, ratification or acceptance in accordance with its constitutional procedures, as rapidly as possible, that is received by the Secretary General of the United Nations Organisation not later than 30 September 1968, shall be regarded as equal in effect to an instrument of approval, ratification or acceptance and shall be provisionally regarded as a party thereto until either it deposits its instrument of approval, ratification or acceptance or up to and including 31 December 1968, whichever is the earlier.[10]

This provision, and similar ones of this nature contained in commodity agreements, show that a simple notification of intention or an undertaking to ratify, approve or accept an agreement has the same effect of law as an instrument of ratification provided normal constitutional procedures are accomplished. Consequently, notification by a signatory government produces, in the same way as an instrument of ratification, a provisional entry into force of an agreement provided that such instruments or notifications have been deposited with a depository authority by a stipulated date.[11] If we refer here to the case-study on coffee, we can understand why the USA found it difficult to ratify the 1962 agreement. With the Senate having voted on the ratification of the 1962 coffee text on 21 May 1963, carried by roll-call vote of 69 to 20 with 11 senators absenting, the motion to notify the President was also carried without objection. But the problem arose when what was left was to obtain the implementing legislation. Brought before the Congress, it was evident that it would be delayed because of the two-thirds majority vote required, so that the US government had to notify its intention to ratify the Coffee Agreement on 24 March 1963. While the 1962 Coffee Agreement entered into force provisionally on 1 July 1963, that of 1968 entered into effect provisionally on 1 October 1968. For the protocol modifying and extending the Wheat Trade Convention (part of the International Wheat Agreement) 1971, done at Washington on 2 April 1974, Nigeria declared a provisional application on 20 June 1974; Brazil on 30 June 1974; and Egypt on 7 May 1974.

The above examination shows that the entry into force of a commodity agreement can be brought about by two categories of signatory governments:

(i) those who have ratified, approved or accepted the agreement;
(ii) those who have undertaken to 'apply the Agreement provisionally and to seek approval, ratification or acceptance in accordance with its constitutional procedures as rapidly as possible' (Article 62, paragraph 2 of the 1968 Coffee Agreement). Thus a notification of intention to apply could be considered an undertaking with a binding force of law and an act of promise.[12]

The purpose of the agreement therefore is to extend its binding force of law to as many states as possible and to create a legal continuity among signatory states even after the date of termination of an agreement has expired. This is usually done by extending the agreement. The provisional nature of signature explains why an institutional action could be taken should an agreement not go into effect definitively. For instance, in the 1968 Coffee Agreement, Article 62, paragraph 3 provides that if the agreement has not entered into force definitively or provisionally by 1 October 1968, those governments which have deposited their instruments of ratification, approval or acceptance . . . or notifications with a promise of intention could consult together on what action the situation requires. They either could decide by mutual consent that the agreement could go into force among themselves, or if it had entered into force provisionally, but not definitively by 31 December 1968, the said governments could also by mutual consent decide that it should go into force definitively or continue provisionally. In the 1966 and subsequent tin agreements, the Chairman of the Council could intervene after a period of six months from the date which follows the termination of a previous agreement. The Executive Chairman could thus convene an urgent meeting of the council 'to consider the position'. The flexibility of action displayed here is an indication of a need to take into account certain economic and diplomatic factors that militate against ratification. This flexibility is displayed in two ways by the Council; either:

(i) by terminating the agreement at a date which it is only competent to fix; or
(ii) by reviewing on any date convenient to it whether the agreement shall be terminated.[13] The competence of the council here as regards its ability to take a binding decision is unquestionable, yet if it could hesitate on the date on which such a decision could be taken, it is at the same time limited within a given period of time. For instance, if within twelve months, that is, on 30 June 1967 (for the 3rd Agreement) or 30 June 1971 for the 4th Agreement, counting from the date of provisional entry into force of the agreement, the agreement does not enter into force definitively, it must be terminated.

(ii) Signature allows for an extension of an expired agreement

Article XXIII paragraphs 1b and 53b of the 3rd and 4th Tin Agreements respectively, provide that the council could by a two-thirds distributed majority vote of consumers and producers extend the duration or life of the agreement by a period not exceeding twelve months. Article 69, paragraph 2 of the 1968 Coffee Agreement states that the council could also by a two-thirds distributed majority 'either negotiate or extend the agreement with or without modification for such period as the council shall determine'. Article 74, paragraphs 3 and 4 of the 1972 Cocoa Agreement stipulate that the council could by a special vote (two-thirds) decide the extension of the Agreement for another twelve months, if:

(i) before the end of the third quota year, negotiations for a new agreement to replace the existing one have not been concluded;
(ii) if an agreement has been negotiated, concluded and signed but has not gone into effect provisionally or definitively.

Although the Coffee Agreement does not state the period of possible extension, we could imagine that this could be twelve months like the others since this is a sufficient time to await ratification. It is significant to note that all the above-mentioned agreements provide for possible extension by a two-thirds distributed vote. It therefore follows that once an agreement has been signed, an extension of the life of a previous agreement is possible provided the renegotiated and signed one has not entered into effect provisionally or definitively. These provisions are not new since they do exist also in another agreement. For example, Article 37, paragraph 4 of the 1956 International Agreement on Olive Oil. Therefore signature in international economic law and diplomacy has the role of establishing continuity of interests while an agreement awaits the accomplishment or fulfilment of the conditions of provisional and definitive entry into force. As soon as these conditions are fulfilled we could consider the provisional effects of signature as having come to an end.

SECTION II. RATIFICATION, ACCEPTANCE OR APPROVAL OF AN AGREEMENT

INTRODUCTION

All commodity agreements contain specific provisions for the act of ratification, acceptance or approval depending on the choice of procedure required. For example, ratification, approval, acceptance are provided for in Articles XXIV and 45 of the 3rd and 4th Tin Agreements. In the 1968 Coffee Agreement, Article 61 provides for only ratification or acceptance while in the 1972 Cocoa Agreement, Article 64 provides[14] for ratification, acceptance or approval. The Agreement Revising and Renewing the International Wheat Agreement adopted at Washington on 13 April 1953 and the protocol modifying and extending the food aid convention (part of the International Wheat Agreement 1971) provide for ratification and acceptance alone.

The above variations in the usage of these procedures show a measure of flexibility accorded governments with different methods of constitutional procedures. And indeed this flexibility gives them room to manoeuvre because the traditional method of parliamentary ratification alone is not often as rapid as would demand an agreement of an economic nature which thrives on conjunctional evolution of world market forces.

A constitutional requirement for ratification often insists upon two main things: first the scope and purpose of a treaty; secondly, the organ and procedure of ratification for example:

1. *The French Constitution* of 1958 (Article 58) requires that the Parliament only is competent to ratify important treaties, for example:

   . . . les traités de paix, les traités de commerce, les traités ou accords relatifs à l'organisation internationale, ceux qui engagent les finances de l'état, ceux qui modifient les dispositions de nature legislative, ceux qui sont relatifs à l'état des personnes, ceux qui comportent cession, échange ou adjonction de territoire. Les autres traités sont ratifiés par le President de la République seul: les précédents devant être également ratifié par lui, après autorisation parlementaire.[15]

2. *The United States of America*: Article 11 Section 2 of the American Constitution entrusts the power of ratification on the President, who shall exercise it by and with the advice and consent of the senate. In this way he makes treaties provided two-thirds of the senators present concur.
3. *Nigeria*: Nigeria's ratification procedure can be categorised into two parts – the civilian or Parliamentary and military era. The 1963 Constitution in its Chapter V, Part 4, Section 74, reads:

   Parliament may make laws for Nigeria or any part thereof with respect to matters not included in the legislative list for the purpose of implementing any treaty, convention or agreement between the Federation and any other country or any arrangement with or decision of the international organisation of which the Federation is a member . . .

   Section 60 (2) '. . . for the purpose of determining any question the required vote is by simple majority of members present and voting'. The procedure is less cumbersome under the military regime, for the agreement is ratified by an act of the Federal Executive Council.

The diversities in the procedures examined above are such that economic agreements must receive the blessing of a flexible approach to make ratification possible and rapid. This is why commodity agreements provide a wide range of choice – some of which require legislative and others administrative procedures as the case may be. For this reason, we shall examine the following procedures:
– Procedure of ratification, acceptance or approval

– Reservation in ratification, approval or acceptance
– Notification of the Depository Authority

(I) PROCEDURE OF RATIFICATION, ACCEPTANCE OR APPROVAL

Article 45 of the 4th International Tin Agreement stipulates:

> This agreement shall be subject to ratification, approval or acceptance by the signatory governments in accordance with their respective constitutional procedures. Instruments of ratification, approval or acceptance shall be deposited with the depository government.[16]

Although these procedures are very respectful of state sovereignty because they concede a choice of constitutional procedures, they limit this sovereignty at the same time by this flexibility of choice, since they induce states willing to contribute to economic co-operation into committing their governments more rapidly. This measure of surrender of sovereignty would therefore require a study of the various techniques used in these procedures and the problems involved.

(a) Ratification procedure

The traditional procedure of ratification through parliaments is very respectful of sovereignty and therefore little suited to a fast-moving international society where intrinsic co-operation is needed quickly to assuage food shortages and provide higher living standards for the poor nations which characterise the majority of the international society. An economic agreement such as would emanate from commodity agreements is expected to take cognisance of the evolution of international economic conjunctures. As this evolution is usually very unpredictable, a basic solidarity among signatory members desirous of stabilising the commodity world market is above all welcome. This type of solidarity is slow to achieve through traditional ratification methods. Ratification no doubt taken from municipal law terminology was meant to confirm an act of promise (an intention to ratify) or an act of international engagement. It was a *quondam* usage by sovereigns to confirm the authority by which their accredited representatives concluded a treaty. This gradually evolved to ratification through senate as in the USA. In

France doctrine and practice interpret the role of Parliament as merely that of authorising the President of the Republic to ratify. Thus ratification has become the discretionary competence of the President. This is also true of Belgium where ratification is a mere executive act with Parliamentary approval. This process of Parliamentary approval is often too long for a treaty of an economic nature which requires its application on signature. This is why other rapid and more effective methods have been evolved in order to facilitate the entry into force of an agreement, through acceptance or approval procedure. In military regimes, however, ratification is often the act of a small body, called the Federal Executive Council in Nigeria, and the instrument of ratification is signed by the head of state, as we have already seen in the preceding chapter.

(b) Acceptance procedure

By the present international practice, this procedure is not left to commodity agreements alone. It is largely used in some post-war constitutive texts. For example, Article 21 of the Constitutive Convention of the FAO, prepared in July 1943; Article 17 of the Provisional Agreement on International Civil Aviation of 7 December 1944; and also Article 15 of the Constitutive text of the UNESCO Convention. The purpose of this procedure is to shorten the ratification procedure which is often too long and which requires the fulfilment of certain difficult constitutional conditions: for example, in the USA, where a two-thirds majority of senate is a prerequisite for the ratification of a treaty by the President. This was why other methods of by-passing this condition have been developed in the USA, and this takes the form of executive agreements or agreements in a simplified form and legislation by act or joint resolution of the Congress.[17] In 1911 President Taft drew up an agreement with Canada on the reciprocal lowering of tariffs which was expected to be ratified by the concurrent legislation of the Congress and the Canadian Parliament. The Congress passed it but the Canadian Parliament failed to do so.

Because of the difficulties in ratification by parliamentary approval, many countries have grown to prefer the acceptance procedure because it permits a signatory government of an agreement, the right of immediate membership as soon as certain internal legal acts or procedures are accomplished. For example, a written declaration or notification of intention by a head of state or government or by an authorised Minister of Foreign Affairs, accepting the agreement already signed. This procedure could also emanate from legislative financial decisions taken within budgetary provisions permitting the execution of the agreement without having to pass through the crucible of a formal parliamentary approval. This type of procedure is then purely administrative. Apart from executive agreements which are binding only to governments, and which require a great deal of diplomatic secrecy (such as the Munich Agreements of 29 September 1938 ceding the Sudeten territory of Germany and the Yalta Agreement of 1945 consecrating the division of the world into zones of influence), and which are all political agreements[18] the procedure of acceptance in economic international agreements is as binding to an entire population, and by extension to the individual who draws direct benefit from the Agreement and who is also direct subject of international law. Consequently, the acceptance procedure produces the same effect of law as that of ratification by way of an eventual entry into force of an agreement.

(c) Approval procedure and vague terminologies

Although the approval procedure seems very ambiguous and not yet well defined, commodity agreements alternate its usage with the acceptance procedure. An approval is done by an executive or legislative authority and in which case, it appears similar to the acceptance procedure. Its ambiguity and vagueness must have been responsible for its omission in the 2nd International Tin Agreement of 1961, the 1956 International Olive Oil Agreement and the 1962 International Coffee Agreement which only incorporated the acceptance and ratification procedures in their texts. Frankly speaking, the use of the word 'approval' is not undesirable, but if we examine the problem from another angle (that of a vague and imprecise terminology), we cannot help wishing that approval be completely stricken off legal documents for three reasons:

(i) We must avoid as much as possible the use of vocabularies which have no precise meaning in international law in order to avoid errors in interpretation.
(ii) The final objective of a commodity agreement is not only to stabilise market forces but also to attract the accession of as many states as possible with relevant interest in the commodity under regulation. Thus if an imprecise and vague terminology

could make states accede to agreements because it gives them the possibility of manoeuvring their interests at short term, its long-term implications could engender unpleasant interpretation that could lead a signatory government into withdrawing from an agreement if the action of another member leads to its interests being jeopardised. In such a case the purpose of an agreement is defeated. It is, however, not surprising to observe the recurrent use of this method in the process of treaty-making in international negotiations[19] where states are expected to be more sensitive to their reciprocal needs because of the modern concept of international co-operation expressed in Article 55 of the UN Charter. This is to say that solidarity among nations has not yet reached the stage where nations negotiate without suspecting the intentions of the other.

(iii) Another reason commodity negotiations must work towards avoiding or eliminating the use of vague terminologies is the problem which official languages pose to developing countries whose national languages are not used in international organisations.

There is often a great difficulty in understanding certain texts and this is again worsened by bad translations and improper interpretations. Thus we have seen that for the purpose of legal politics, international commodity texts still find it more convenient to employ imprecise terminologies which must be discouraged, however, for the purpose of clarity and international co-operation within the areas of international economic law and diplomacy where producer nations very desirous of selling their products very quickly want to append their signatures to legal texts without great considerations of depth, particularly when they are mono-producers.

(II) THE SCOPE OF RESERVATIONS MADE AT RATIFICATION, APPROVAL OR ACCEPTANCE

Under traditional international law, reservations are allowed in ratification, approval or acceptance, but international economic law, which is modern, tries to limit the scope of its usage so as to facilitate entry into force in this area of precise solidarity.[20] This is why most commodity agreements have provided for the right of either voluntary or compulsory withdrawals or both in order to limit the scope of the use of reservations during ratification, approval or acceptance. For example, the tin agreements (and for this purpose the 4th one) provide not only for amendment in Article 51 but also for the right of withdrawal of any contracting government which fails to ratify, approve or accept an amendment by the date it goes into effect (Article 52, paragraph (ii)).

A 'deferred signature' which is a type of reservation, also tries to limit the scope of application of its use in economic agreements.[21] Since most commodity agreements only limit the scope of the use of reservation by their various techniques contained in the right of withdrawals and amendments they can be termed 'imperfect treaties'[22] when in fact, they do not expressly forbid the right to express reservations. There are certain multilateral treaties in traditional international law which forbid the right to express reservations such as the Naval Declaration of London of 26 February 1909; Article I of the Covenant of the League of Nations or conventions drawn up by the International Labour Organisation Conferences.[23] Reservations made during the process of negotiations pose no problems, because if accepted and modified they become integral parts of the agreements. This is also true of those made at signature except in the case of multilateral treaties opened for signature, which pose some difficulties arising from the need to enter into force provisionally. This is why there is a deferred signature granted to enable states to consult among themselves and reflect on the issues involved in the negotiations before appending their signatures. The type of difficulties which reservations made at signature pose to technical or economic agreements come up when they are already provisionally in force and when modifications have already been accepted by a number of states. Reservations are generally not accepted while a state is acceding to a commodity agreement because the acceding state is admitted 'upon conditions to be determined by the Council' (Article 48, paragraph (a) of the 4th Tin Agreement). This is a general feature of all commodity agreements. A question therefore arises as to whether reservations made at signature could be withdrawn on final acceptance or accession. Here opinion is still divided. However, since reservations have only a limiting effect, particularly at signature and acceptance, we could expect that, in economic agreements, reservations would be withdrawn before acceptance; this could not arise at accession since it is determined on conditions established by the council. Finally, at signature, there should be no need for reservations to be made because ample opportunity or time lapse is often given between adoption and date of signature for further negotiations to take place on possible reservations unless there is need for more time.

(III) THE ROLE OF THE DEPOSITORY AUTHORITY IN NOTIFICATION

There is as yet no uniformity in the practice of notification by depository authorities. However, in direct application of the principles of traditional international law, governments and international organisations are depositories of instruments of ratification, acceptance or approval. For instance, while the Secretary-General of the UN is the depository authority for the cocoa and coffee agreements, the governments of Great Britain, Spain and the USA remain depositories of the tin, olive oil and wheat agreements respectively. Before examining the role and scope of depository authorities in respect of notifications, let us in the first instance examine the legal persons entitled to receive them, and the extent of the powers of the depository authority.

(a) Legal persons entitled to receive notifications

In traditional international law, usually only governments receive notifications and are depositories of ratifications, acceptances or approvals. This practice has been greatly modified since the birth of modern economic international law arising from commodity transactions. Consequently the legal persons to whom notifications could now be sent are the UNO and governments. But the categories of other legal persons to whom they must in turn send notifications are of different types. First, it is in recognition of the principles of traditional international law that governments or the UN Secretariat must in the first instance notify all the governments represented at a preparatory conference before member governments of a previous agreement, and those who have acceded in accordance with the set provision of an agreement. For instance, Article 54 of the 4th Tin Agreement states:

> The depository government[24] shall notify all governments represented at the United Nations Tin Conference, 1970, all governments members of the 3rd Tin Conference Agreement, all governments which have acceded to this agreement in accordance with the provisions of Article 48, the Secretary of the Council and the Secretary-General of the United Nations of the following.[25]

For notification by the UN, Article 71 of the International Coffee Agreement (1968) states:

> the Secretary General of the United Nations shall notify all contracting Parties to the International Coffee Agreement, 1962, and other governments of states, members of the United Nations or of any of its specialised agencies of each deposit of any instrument of approval, ratification, acceptance or accession and of the dates on which the agreement becomes provisionally and definitively into force . . .[26]

This is to say that member states of the UN and its specialised agencies which were not even represented at the preparatory conferences, but which had acceded to an agreement, must be notified. The depository authority must also notify all governments with the right of 'separate participation' and the secretary of the commodity council. Although the Tin Agreements are silent with regard to specialised agencies, they could be included as legal persons entitled to receive notifications for three reasons:

(i) because specialised agencies were represented at the preparatory UN conferences, e.g. GATT; ILO; IBRD; IMF;
(ii) because the Secretary General of the UN is one of those whom the UK government is expected to notify;
(iii) because some commodity agreements specifically request that they be notified; e.g. Article 71 of the International Cocoa Agreement (1972).

(b) The scope of the powers of the depository authority as regards notifications

(i) Powers of the depository authority

Although these notifications do not produce any legal effect, they help to strengthen the politico-diplomatic prestige of the depository authority whether this be the UN Secretariat or the headquarters government of the commodity agreement or the capitals of the host governments. The nature of the international society could justify the UN as the best depository of the instruments of ratification, acceptance or approval which should in turn notify all interested governments and institutions. Alternatively, the secretariats of the commodity councils could undertake this themselves so that the administrative psychology of the seat of the agreement could be more relaxed. This transfer of power to the UN Secretariat would have no particular legal effect but it could help to portray the UN as the chief organiser of international instruments of co-operation and thus increase its prestige and nobility. For after all, the Cocoa and Coffee Agreements with seats in London recognise the UN Secretariat as their depository authority. This method was originally adopted by the 1st International Agreement on Olive Oil (1956) which provided that all instruments of ratification, acceptance or approval be deposited with the UN Secretariat before this competence was later transferred to the government of Madrid. This method appears more satisfactory; much more so that all treaties are required to be registered with the UN according to Article 102 of its charter.

(ii) Areas where those powers can be exercised by the depository authority

The areas where a depository authority can exercise its powers as regards notifications can be classified into six. The 4th International Tin Agreement drawn up at Geneva on 15 May 1970 provides the prototype classification which could go for the other agreements. Article 54 classifies them as follows:

(i) signatures, ratifications, approvals, acceptance and notifications of intention to ratify, approve or accept;
(ii) the entry into force of the agreement, both definitive and provisional;
(iii) accessions and notification of separate participation;
(iv) notifications of ratification, approval or acceptance of amendments and dates of their entry into force;
(v) notification of withdrawal and cessation of participation; and
(vi) notifications of the termination of this agreement.

Some salient comments on the above areas

(i) Signatures, ratifications, approvals, acceptances and notifications of intention to ratify, approve or accept

As soon as all participating governments have signed and accomplished their respective internal procedures of ratification, they proceed to deposit their conventional instruments of ratification before the depository authority who in turn notifies all the countries involved in the agreement. This administrative procedure simply aims at establishing a legal chronology of events as they arise within the commodity council.

(ii) Provisional and definitive entry into force

This conforms to the conditions of entry into force which we shall discuss later in greater detail.

(iii) Accession and notification of 'separate participation'

Article 49 of the 4th Tin Agreement states:

> A contracting government may at the time of depositing its instruments of ratification, approval, acceptance or accession or giving notification of intention to ratify, approve or accept or at any time thereafter, propose the separate participation as a producing or as a consuming country, as may be appropriate of any territory or territories interested in the production or consumption of tin, for whose international relations the contracting government is responsible and to which the agreement applies or will apply when the agreement enters into force. Such separate participation shall be subject to the consent of the council and to the conditions which the council may determine.

This is to say that a contracting government declaring the separate participation of any country could do so while notifying the depository authority or could notify this authority appropriately when it decides to declare the separate participation of a territory still under its sovereignty. In this case, it is only logical that the notification be made between the contracting government and the depository authority which could be the UN or a government. This is true of the 1968 International Coffee Agreement (Article 65, paragraph 1) and the 1972 International Cocoa Agreement (Article 76) where the depository authority is the UN Secretariat which in turn, like any depository government, notifies all contracting parties of each instrument deposited. Article 65, paragraphs 1–3 of the 1972 Cocoa Agreement on notification by an acceding government, stipulates that any government which has been accepted by the council for accession would remain in observer status if it does not give a notice of intention to accede at least two months after the depository authority has notified it of the council's decision. If its delay is attributed to constitutional procedures, the date of its accession could be extended and it, however, remains an observer.

(iv) Notifications of termination of an agreement

This is a new element in the 4th International Tin Agreement which was absent in the previous agreements. Although most other texts are expressly silent with regard to this competence of a depository authority in respect of termination, it could be assumed proper that when an agreement comes to its contractual end, it is incumbent on the depository authority to notify all contracting parties and relevant bodies. For instance Article 69 of the 1968 Coffee Agreement, in stipulating that the agreement could be terminated by a two-thirds distributed majority of the total votes, requires that such termination takes effect on the date which the council only was competent to decide. Such a date must also be notified.

5 Legal Techniques: the Scope of Application of the Legal Obligations in Commodity Agreements

The study of the scope of the legal obligations in commodity agreements is an area of study which concerns the following: duration of application; renewal; date of entry into force; rationae personae to whom the agreements are binding; territorial application; procedure of amendments; techniques of conflict resolution and headquarters agreement. These areas will form the object of our analysis.

SECTION I. DURATION OF APPLICATION

Commodity agreements are generally flexible because they provide for what may be called normal and exceptional durations. The latter arises from the fact of the possibility of extending an agreement. This is why it would appear proper to examine, in the process of our analysis, the different procedures of extending an agreement before those of the legal effects of terminating it.

The normal life of a commodity agreement ranges between three and five years, depending to a very great extent on its cyclical nature. This is to say that there is yet no standard duration for all agreements. While a commodity like tin is stockable for a long time and non-perishable and therefore kept at five years, the cocoa agreement is three years[1] because of its attendant planting and harvesting problems. The duration of an agreement can therefore be studied under two headings: its Normal and Exceptional life. That the latter comes before its termination, is to say that the normal life can be modified by extending the Agreement before it expires, through a council recommendation.

(1) THE NORMAL LIFE

The normal life of an agreement is between three and five years. This is in direct application of the general principles enunciated in the Havana Charter[2] in matters pertaining to commodity agreements. For tin agreements, the period of 5 years does not consider any production cycle because it is non-perishable, while other agricultural products do.[3] However this length of time facilitates a systematic and evolutionary study of all market forces from which subsequent agreements could draw experiences. This normal life could be modified in two ways: First, before an agreement expires through a council recommendation; and secondly by extension which is considered the exceptional duration.

(i) Before the termination or expiration of an agreement

Any contracting government 'may at any time give notice in writing to the Executive Chairman that it intends to propose at the next meeting of the council the termination of thc agreement' (Article 53 paragraph d(i) of the 4th Tin Agreement). The conditions for achieving this proposal are established in texts. For example, the 1968 Coffee Agreement in its Article 69, paragraph 3 and the 1972 Cocoa Agreement in its Article 74, paragraph 5, like in the Tin Agreement also provide for a two-thirds distributed majority if they have to be terminated. But adoption of a decision to terminate is insufficient to execute the recommendation of the council to terminate unless the contracting parties (consumers and producers) have notified the council of their acceptance of the recommendation or proposal. This is the point at which a recommendation or a proposal produces an effect of law. Thereafter, the council must decide the date[4] at which an agreement will be terminated, which in most cases must not go beyond six months after the last instrument of notification of acceptance of the recommendation has been deposited.

(ii) By extension of an existing agreement

All commodity agreements grant their councils the power to extend their lives over a given period. For instance, while the 4th Tin Agreement grants a period of twelve months, the Coffee (1968) does not specify any time lapse. In the 1972 Cocoa Agreement, the right to extension of its existing life comes up during the period of renegotiation which is 'before the end of the third quota year' and the extension period must not exceed twelve months. We could then recommend that a period of twelve months is also sufficient for the 1968 Coffee Agreement. The power to extend the life of an agreement depends on a two-thirds distributed majority of the contracting parties to the agreement. Although these agreements do not specify what would become of them if the conditions of extension are not satisfied, we could assume that the council could proceed to slight liquidations as provided in Article 53, paragraph (e) of the 4th Tin Agreement and Article 69, paragraph 4 of the 1968 Coffee Agreement. They stipulate that the 'council shall remain in being as long as necessary' for the carrying out of the operations of liquidation. This period would then permit the council to await either the provisional or definitive entry into force of the agreement.

(2) LEGAL CONSEQUENCES OF TERMINATION

The legal consequences of terminating an agreement could be examined from what obtains within the domains of liquidation and the procedure of liquidation itself. Although the coffee and cocoa agreements are silent on the details of the operation, they both give some indication as to the obligations that must be fulfilled. Only the tin agreement appears to be detailed and provides the distinct procedures.

(a) Within the domain of liquidations

In the tin agreements, liquidations are carried out depending on whether the council will have a successor or whether it will continue on termination of the agreement. If the council is continued or if it is succeeded by another body, all archival and statistical materials must be transferred accordingly. In the case of a successor body, the council could transfer all other assets to it upon a two-thirds distributed majority. In the absence of a successor body, the council must transfer all its statistical and archival materials to the Secretary General of the UN or to any international organisation nominated by him. But if he fails to do so, the council is empowered to make its own nominee (Article XXIII, paragraph 4a–d of the 3rd Tin Agreement and Article 53, paragraph f(i) of the 4th). All monetary assets of the council must be sold or liquidated as directed by the council and the total sum realised shared among contracting parties in proportion to their contributions to the Administrative Account. Article 74, paragraph 5 of the 1972 Cocoa

Agreement recognises that an end to the agreement would be said to have been achieved only on condition that the 'obligations of members under Article 37 shall continue until the financial liabilities relating to the buffer stock have been discharged . . .'. Although it goes further, in paragraph 6, to say that the council could 'remain in being for as long as it is necessary' to carry out the liquidation of the organisation, settlements of its accounts and disposal of its assets, it does not specify which assets or which procedure should be used in the liquidation. This is also true of the 1968 Coffee Agreement (Article 69, paragraph 4). We could then assume that if its council is empowered to liquidate, it could apply the procedure in the Tin Agreement as established below.

(b) Procedure of liquidation

In order to determine the share of each country by virtue of its contributions in the tin agreements, the buffer stock manager has to follow some definite procedures, which are the following:

(i) The contributions of each contracting party except those emanating from voluntary contributors, are evaluated.
(ii) The contributions in tin metal calculated at the floor price of the day of entry into force of the agreement shall be added to the total contributions of each country made in monetary value.
(iii) The tin metal held by the buffer stock manager at the termination of the agreement shall be valued at the London market price of the date of termination. To this value shall be added the total sum of money held at this date after subtracting a sum sufficient to cover the total expenses of liquidating the buffer stock.
(iv) If the total evaluation is more than the contributions made, the contributions of member countries will be integrally reimbursed and the surplus proportionally divided, according to their respective contributions, multiplied by the number of days that these contributions have been made to the buffer stock manager up to the date of termination of the agreement. In calculating the number of days, the day when the contributions were received by the manager and the day of termination are not taken into consideration.
(v) On the other hand, if the contributions referred to above are superior to the total evaluation, the deficit shall be proportionately divided among the contributing countries.

(vi) After these operations, the manager could then repay to each contributing country the cash allocated to it. As regards tin metal, the manager could transfer it in twelve instalments except when a contributing country makes her request in monetary value; in such a case her instalments are sold and the proceeds paid to her.

SECTION II. RENEWAL OF AN AGREEMENT

The renewal of any commodity agreement is often a matter of joy to the international society and particularly to contracting parties of an agreement. This is because it is taken as a concrete manifestation of solidarity and co-operation in the area of international regulation and stabilisation of the commodity trade. Therefore, in order that an agreement might continue after normal termination, commodity agreements provide for renewal clauses. These clauses impose upon their councils the duty to make recommendations on a two-thirds distributed majority to contracting governments 'not later than four years after the entry into force of this agreement . . . whether it is necessary and appropriate that the agreement should be renewed' (Article 53, paragraph C of the 4th Tin Agreement).[5] The ideas[6] expressed here are similar in all commodity agreements. However, before a recommendation, usually made before the last year of an agreement, the commodity institution is expected to have studied the market situation of supply and demand of the commodity. The purpose of this is to enable it to determine the form and content of the next agreement if the recommendation to renew it is adopted. In the practice of all commodity agreements, their councils nominate a committee of experts[7] which prepares a draft agreement neither binding to it nor to the members of the council. This draft, properly prepared and studied, is submitted for adoption to a UN preparatory conference,[8] convened for that purpose. This conference convened by both the Secretary General of the UN and a commodity council, presents an interesting character because an invitation to attend produces an eventual legal effect, in the sense that only invited states could sign the adopted draft of an agreement or accede to it before it enters into effect. Article XXII, paragraph 2 of the Agreement Revising and Renewing the International Wheat Agreement, Washington, 13 April 1953, provides that the council could recommend renewal or replacement of the agreement both to exporting and importing countries at any time of its choice. On the other hand, the council could also invite any government not party to the agreement, but with a substantial interest in the international trade in wheat, to participate in its discussions in connection with such renewal or replacement (Article XXII, paragraph 2b). This provision, which was not in the text of the 1953 main agreement, was meant to attract new membership. At its 38th session of the International Wheat Council in November 1963, the council gave to the executive committee the task of arranging the renegotiation of the 1962 Wheat Agreement which was to expire on 31 July 1965. It then requested the committee to submit its recommendations to the 39th session in June 1967. The opinion of the committee was based on the attendant problems that affected the wheat trade; for instance, the discussions in the GATT Cereals Group as part of the Kennedy Round negotiations and in UNCTAD which were feared might raise issues of great significance for the scope and content of a future agreement.[9]

SECTION III. DATE OF ENTRY INTO FORCE

The date of entry into force of an agreement is the normal climax of all the administrative and constitutional procedures employed in the process of ratification, acceptance or approval. An entry into force could either be provisional or definitive depending on whether certain stipulated conditions in the text of an agreement have been fulfilled. Let us then proceed to examine these two types of entry into force.

(1) DATE OF DEFINITIVE ENTRY INTO FORCE

As soon as an agreement has been ratified, accepted or approved by a stipulated number of consumer and producer countries of an agreement, holding a prescribed amount of votes, it enters into force definitively for them. For example, Article 46, paragraph (a) of the 4th Tin Agreement stipulates that:

> This agreement shall, for the governments which have deposited instruments of ratification, approval or acceptance, enter into force definitively as soon after 30 June 1971 as such instruments have been deposited on behalf of governments representing at least six producing countries as set out in Annex A holding together at least 950 of the votes set out in that annex and at least nine consuming countries as

set out in Annex B holding together at least 300 of the votes set out in that annex.[10]

Certain parts of an agreement could also go into force separately, because they satisfy certain specific problems. For instance, the 1962 International Wheat Agreement and rules of procedure stipulates in Article 35, paragraph 5, that Parts I and Parts II–VII shall enter into force on February 1962 and Part II on 1 August 1962 for governments which have deposited their instruments of accession and acceptance by those dates (provided that such governments hold not less than two-thirds of the votes of exporting countries and not less than two-thirds of votes of importing countries) in accordance with the distribution of votes in Annexes B and C.[11] An agreement could also provide that if it enters into force provisionally according to stipulated conditions, it shall enter into force definitively as soon as conditions for definitive entry are fulfilled. This was the case of the 2nd International Tin Agreement which, after having entered into force provisionally on 1 July 1961 because five consuming countries and two producing countries had deposited their instruments of ratification before this date, it was sufficient for Spain, a consumer country, and Bolivia, a producer country, to deposit their instruments of ratification on 27 January 1962 and 21 February 1962 respectively, for the conditions of definitive entry into force to be fulfilled.[12] Thus while the 2nd International Tin Agreement entered into force definitively on 21 February 1962, the 3rd entered into force definitively on 21 March 1967 after the Spanish government had deposited its instrument of ratification with the UK government. It is worth noting here that the Federal Republic of Nigeria deposited its instrument of ratification, in the case of the 3rd Agreement, with the UK government on 3 September 1966. For the 1968 International Coffee Agreement, amending and extending its texts approved by the International Coffee Council at London on 14 April 1973, and which entered into force on 1 October 1973, Nigeria deposited its instrument of accession on 28 May1974.[13] It is then noteworthy that Nigeria's appurtenance to these agreements vindicates her willingness to honour all her international obligations and, in this way, she contributes to the legal continuity of the community of signatory governments.

Let us consider other aspects of this discussion. There is the problem of the legal status of a signatory government which, after having notified its intention to ratify, accept or approve an agreement, has not yet deposited its instrument of ratification within a given number of days after the date of the definitive entry into force. Article 67, paragraph 3 of the 1972 International Cocoa Agreement states that if the requirements for the definitive entry into force[14] are not met on 30 April 1973 or by 30 June 1973 (that is, in two months as extended), the Secretary General of the UN could invite, at a convenient date after June 1973, those governments that have deposited instruments of ratification, acceptance or approval or those which have indicated their intention to apply provisionally, to meet and decide whether this agreement could enter into force provisionally or definitively among themselves in part or in whole. Those which had indicated a provisional application are admitted as observers in this meeting. Article 67 does not pose the problem of those governments that have not ratified after definitive entry into force while Article 62, paragraph 1 of the 1968 Coffee Agreement simply states that:

> the agreement shall enter into force definitively for any government that deposits an instrument of approval, ratification, acceptance or accession subsequent to the definitive entry into force of the agreement for other governments, on the date of such deposit.

This does not give a time limit within which the Secretary General of the UN would convene a meeting if it has not entered into force definitively. Article 67, paragraph 4 of the 1972 Cocoa Agreement goes further here to authorise the Secretary General of the UN to convene the first session of its council not later than 90 days after the provisional or definitive entry into force.

This means that if the agreement has entered into force as indicated in paragraph 3, for a group of countries, this meeting could decide the fate of those who have not ratified but who have given a notice of intention, after a given period of 90 days. This period appears similar to that given in Article 46, paragraph (d) of the 4th Tin Agreement, but dissimilar in the sense that the Tin Agreement specifies the consequences of a non-ratification while the Coffee Agreement is satisfied with authorising the Secretary General of the UN to convene a meeting. The Tin Agreement therefore solves the dilemma of the legal consequences of non-ratification as examined above. Its Article 46 states that a government which has notified its intention to ratify but which has not deposited its instrument of ratification, approval or acceptance within a period of 90 days, from the date of definitive entry into force of the agreement, will cease to participate in the agreement unless the council extends the above period on the request of that government. But if this government wishes to cease to participate in the agreement before this period expires, or before an extension of the expiry date, it must give at least 30 days notice to the depository authority which is the UK government. Since this government could cease to participate in the agreement unless under the above conditions, it follows that it could be allowed to remain as an observer since it had provisionally applied the agreement. Although this could be considered a discretionary power of the council, it could be assumed proper, since Article 67, paragraph 3 of the 1972 International Cocoa Agreement provides this status for such a country during the meetings convened by the Secretary General of the UN, as we have already examined above. However, if this government was unable to ratify the agreement because of its internal constitutional difficulties, the council could extend the 90-day period. This was why the council was able to extend this period up to the end of 1962 during its April 1962 meeting in the 2nd Tin Agreement, for those countries that had not yet ratified, accepted or approved the agreement. On the other hand, if the government has decided to cease participation before the 90 days or as extended, it is obliged to give 30 days notice. This notice is devised to provide opportunity for negotiations between this government and the council with a view to finding out a solution to the problem necessitating cessation. If this government is ceasing participation because its interests have been injured or if this had been due to constitutional difficulties in ratification, this period of 30 days could be extended. This is also a discretionary power of the council.

(2) DATE OF PROVISIONAL ENTRY INTO FORCE

In order to bring about a provisional effect of signature in international economic law and diplomacy, commodity agreements are provided in their texts, with conditions[15] for provisional entry into force. For instance, the 1968 Coffee Agreement states:

> The agreement may enter into force provisionally on 1 October 1968. For this purpose, a notification by a signatory government or by any other contracting party to the International Coffee Agreement, 1962, containing an undertaking to apply the agreement provisionally and to seek approval, ratification or acceptance in accordance with its constitutional procedures, as rapidly as possible, that is received by the Secretary General of the UN not later than 30 September 1968, shall be regarded as equal in effect to an instrument of approval, ratification or acceptance. A government that undertakes to apply the

agreement provisionally will be permitted to deposit an instrument of approval, ratification or acceptance and shall be provisionally regarded as a party thereto until either it deposits its instrument of approval, ratification or acceptance or up to and including 31 December 1968, which ever is earlier.

A similar provision exists in all commodity agreements. This type of provision is meant to facilitate the application of an agreement while awaiting the accomplishment of constitutional procedures of ratification, approval or acceptance and also to establish a continuity of the legal community of signatory states. For instance within the 2nd International Tin Agreement of 1961, notifications of intention to ratify, accept or approve the agreement, having been deposited on 30 June 1961, the agreement entered into force provisionally on 1 July 1961 after seven consumer and four producer countries had deposited their conventional instrument of ratification. Seven other consumer countries and six producers finally notified their intention to ratify.[16]

SECTION IV. *RATIONAE PERSONAE* EFFECTS OF COMMODITY AGREEMENTS

The effects of the various provisions in commodity agreements, on private and public persons, will be treated here under three headings:

I The effects of commodity agreements on states.
II The effects of commodity agreements on persons of civil or private law.
III The effects of commodity agreements on international organisations.

(I) THE EFFECTS OF COMMODITY AGREEMENTS ON STATES

Two acts determine the legal status of states: the act of inviting them to preparatory conferences and their appurtenance to these agreements. This is why the legal effects of an agreement are extended to several categories of states depending on whether they are signatory to an agreement or not. We shall therefore treat these effects under the two following categories:

(A) *Contracting states of an agreement*: these are of three sub-categories:

(i) *Signatory states of an agreement*: these are states that have fulfilled all requirements for entry into force, such as the deposition of instruments of ratification, acceptance or approval. For these states, an agreement has a full legal effect or value.

(ii) *States that are provisionally parties to an agreement*: these are states that have signed an agreement but are unable to accomplish their constitutional procedures of ratification, acceptance or approval, and have consequently pledged application of an agreement by notifying their intention to ratify, accept or approve it. Their legal status is that of temporary members, who would cease to be so as soon as they deposit their instruments of ratification, acceptance or approval.

(iii) *States acceding to an agreement*: the accession procedure of commodity agreements is sufficiently flexible because it takes into consideration several categories of states seeking to accede. They are either states invited to a preparatory conference of the UN or states not invited but which are members of UNO and its specialised agencies. *First, a state invited to a UN conference*: This is a state that has not signed an agreement but is allowed to accede because it was not only invited to the UN preparatory conference but also was a contracting party of a previous agreement. To such a state, the commodity council 'shall as appropriate, establish a basic quota . . .' (Article 68, paragraph 1 of the 1972 Cocoa Agreement and Article 63, paragraph 1 of the 1968 Coffee Agreement). Such a state must deposit an instrument of accession with the depository authority. In this way, the Tin Council approved the accession of the Republic of Korea which deposited its instrument of accession in December 1961. Such accessions are usually done without expecting any reservations from the acceding state. This instrument of accession produces the same legal effect as an instrument of ratification, acceptance or approval because it does bring about an entry into force of an agreement. But where an accession is made after the entry into force of an agreement, its legal value is limited to the participatory nature of the state. Such an accession must be approved by the council on a two-thirds distributed majority provided that the state was invited to a preparatory conference (Article 35, paragraph 4 of the International Wheat Agreement and Rules of Procedure 1962) and that it sought accession under conditions established by the council. As soon as instruments of accession are deposited with the depository authority, it must proceed to notify all interested governments including the commodity council.[17]

Secondly, states not invited to a preparatory conference of the UN but which are members of UNO and its specialised agencies: The accession of such states is done on consent of the commodity council which is empowered to determine the conditions of their accessions. One of such conditions is that it is only possible to accede after the definitive entry into force of an agreement, since the state was not invited to any preparatory conference. In the case of the 1972 Cocoa Agreement, accession is extended to the government of any state which is a member of the International Atomic Energy Agency. Since all important states[18] are normally invited to a pre-conference, any other state seeking accession thereafter cannot have its accession producing any legal effect, such as the ability to contribute to the entry into force of the agreement. The accession procedure for non-invited states appears too restrictive, since it is a council that determines their conditions of accession. It will thus appear proper to recommend that all states willing to accede should be granted the right of free accession because any attempt to restrict the accession of as many states as possible will be contrary to the spirit of any agreement which seeks to extend its binding force to as many states as possible. Unlike the EEC, to which accession is subject to the ratification of the nine member states, accession to commodity agreements is subject to the ratification of the acceding states. Consequently, such acceding states should not be allowed to impose conditions[19] for their accession. They should be able to accept the existing legal obligations established in the agreement, since each agreement provides for periodical amendments necessary for combating the fluctuating nature of commodity markets. Finally, all instruments of accession deposited with a depository authority are accordingly thus notified to contracting parties.

(iv) *Withdrawal, suspension, exclusion and amendment procedures of contracting states*: All Commodity Agreements are provided with withdrawal and suspension clauses which could take effect only under certain conditions:

(a) *Withdrawal*: there are two types of withdrawals in commodity agreements – voluntary and compulsory. Any contracting party could at any time withdraw from an agreement after it had entered into force, by giving a notice of withdrawal to its depository authority.[20] It is only natural that such a country will not share from the proceeds of liquidation of the Buffer Stock as well as from the assets of a council, at termination of the agreement. Commodity Agreements specifically provide these conditions (Article XXIII of the 3rd Tin Agreement and Article 73 paragraph 1 of the Cocoa Agreement).

(b) *Conditions for withdrawals*:

1. If a council determines that a country has failed to carry out its obligations under an agreement and that such a failure significantly impairs the operations of the agreement (Article 67 of the Coffee Agreement), it may by a two-thirds distributed majority vote require the withdrawal of such a country and it shall immediately notify the depository authority of such a decision.

2. If a participating country considers that its economic interests have been seriously injured by any action taken by another country, it could withdraw only after the Council has justified its complaints in consonance with a set procedure of withdrawal which we shall examine later.

3. When a participating country is engaged in hostilities, it would withdraw without notifying the Council. The interpretation of this provision conforms to that adopted in war time according to the principles of International Law, as regards the legal effects of war on the application of treaties. This is to say that all treaties between belligerents are considered null and void.

4. If a consumer country considers that its interests are seriously injured by an amendment, it could withdraw after notifying the depository authority. Any member which has not notified its acceptance of an amendment shall also cease to participate, unless its reasons for not doing so are due to consitutional difficulties in ratification.

There is a danger in unilateral withdrawals. This stems from the fact that every country appears to be the only competent authority to determine the gravity of the damage done to its economic interests, although this power is considerably reduced by the procedure of withdrawal. In spite of this, it is gratifying to note that the only known example of a country that has withdrawn from the Tin Council and in fact from any known commodity agreement, was Ecuador (1957–8).

(c) *Procedure of withdrawal*: a participating country that wishes to withdraw from an agreement because its economic interests have been injured could either first complain to a council (Article XIX, paragraph 3 of 4th Tin Agreement) or notify the Secretary-General of the UN in writing that it wishes to withdraw (Article 71 of the 1972 Cocoa Agreement). In the latter case, withdrawal becomes effective 90 days after such a notice. In the former case, if the council decides by a special vote that a country's complaint is justified, it could be allowed to withdraw. The exclusion or withdrawal policy of commodity agreements is dependent on whether the council has decided, by special vote, that a participating country has breached any of its obligations with detriment to collective interests; for instance Articles 67 of the 1968 Coffee and 72 of the Cocoa Agreements respectively. In cases of exclusion or compulsory withdrawals, the council notifies the Secretary-General of the UN and it becomes effective 90 days after the council decision. In the Tin Agreements, this period is 12 months. The period allotted to an effective date of entry into force of a withdrawal is not without a diplomatic purpose. It is supposed to cater for possible negotiations between a complainant country and the council. However, if in spite of negotiations a complainant country still insists on withdrawing, it must settle all its financial obligations contracted on membership. It is at this level that the council finally notifies its decision to the depository authority which in turn notifies all contracting members.

(d) *Suspension and exclusion*: exclusion which is closely linked with compulsory withdrawal appears to have ceded its place to suspension in order to lessen the gravity of breaches of the law; but the procedure of suspension is again closely tied with that of amendment which we shall examine separately below. It suffices here to say that as soon as an amendment enters into force, the council shall determine whether it is of such a nature that consuming countries which do not ratify, approve or accept it, shall be suspended from the agreement. If the council decides that a consuming country's refusal to ratify is of such a nature to warrant suspension, it is automatically suspended unless it provides evidence that its attitude has been due to internal constitutional difficulties in ratification. In such a case, the council could postpone this suspension until these difficulties are alleviated. Suspension has the same legal effects as withdrawal or exclusion for two reasons:

1. a suspended country must fulfil all its financial obligations contracted on signature of the agreement;

2. a suspended state could be reinstated 'on such terms and conditions as it [council] considers equitable'.

However, we still have to find out whether suspension which carries with it a temporary notion, though unlimited in time, could be likened to withdrawal for which the return of a state is less sure. We could then say that as regards the unilateral withdrawal of a country seeking reinstatement into the agreement, it must follow the procedure of accession[21] as if it had never been signatory to the agreement or was never invited to a preparatory conference of the commodity agreement in question. Exclusion is closely linked with compulsory withdrawal because both can be carried out by a special vote[22] of the council as provided by Article 67 of the 1968 Coffee Agreement and Article 73 of the 1972 Cocoa Agreement, if a contracting member has failed to carry out its obligations.

(B) NON-CONTRACTING STATES OF AN AGREEMENT

In order to ascertain that an agreement is applied by as many categories of legal persons as possible, commodity agreements require that their councils make provisions for consultation and co-operation with appropriate organs of the UN institutions. For example the 4th Tin Agreement, like other agreements, requires that the council 'shall make whatever arrangements are appropriate for consultation and co-operation' with the following categories of non-members of the agreement:

1. '. . . members of UNO and its specialised agencies, particularly UNCTAD;
2. members of other organisations within the UN system and appropriate intergovernmental organisations; and
3. non-participating countries which are members of the UN or of its specialised agencies, or which were parties to previous international agreements.'[23]

This is a third-party type of obligation not new in international public law and in commodity agreements. This obligation is flexible to cope with the complexities of applying an agreement. This is to say that the desire to check disloyal and irregular practice in commodity markets is carried out by a simple diplomatic and political action of 'consultation and co-operation'. This practice has proved limitedly successful with the USA, the world's greatest tin-consumer, and Russia, an important producer and consumer because they had on some occasions co-ordinated their policies in co-operation with the Tin Council. For example, the USA has maintained an attitude often qualified as 'benevolent neutrality' for accepting to co-operate with the Tin Council in the liquidation of its surplus strategic stock-piles.[24] As for Russia, she had once accepted to reduce her exports to the Western European market by a simple 'entente', approved at the 17th meeting of the council, between the council and the Russian commercial delegation in the UK in spite of her quondam refusal to grant the USSR an observer status in its 15th meeting in November 1958.[25]

(2) THE APPLICABILITY OF COMMODITY AGREEMENTS ON PERSONS OF CIVIL OR PRIVATE LAW

Not all commodity agreements expressly provide for the application of their provisions on private persons.[26] For example, the Tin and Coffee Agreements do not expressly provide for this type of application while the 1972 Cocoa Agreement does in its Article 13, paragraph 3: 'The council may also make whatever arrangements are appropriate for maintaining effective contact with international organisations of cocoa producers, traders and manufacturers.' Whatever arrangements, here, could be interpreted to mean the conclusion of conventions under any appropriate international organisation with the consent of the Council. These conventions are eventually applicable both to public and private persons. It is the desire for the applicability of legal provisions on these persons that make commodity agreements require that contractual parties ensure fair labour standards in any industry. For instance the Tin Agreements say: 'The participating countries declare that, in order to avoid the depression of living standards and the introduction of unfair competitive conditions in world trade, they will seek to ensure fair labour standards in the industry.' Fair labour standards cannot be achieved in a vacuum, but in a contractual situation where the International Labour Organisation could play a prominent role. The contact therefore required between a commodity council and the ILO is that of encouraging the signing of specific conventions which consider commodity problems. Also the expression, 'whatever arrangements' could be equated with 'consultation and co-operation' which exists in commodity texts. For instance, that commodity agreements provide for the above, with members of UNO and its specialised agencies, also means that the applicability of an agreement on any state which is a member of UNO would depend on the constitutional machineries proper to that state. This is to say that a state could initiate measures to effect the provisions of an agreement. For instance, in Malaysia, when world prices of tin showed considerable increases, with constant reports of black-marketing and stealing of tin, a mobile police force for checking fraudulent practices was set up as an internal arrangement emanating from the co-operation between the Tin Council and the Malaysian government. Consequently, in 1950, a law entitled 'The Emergency (Tin Ore Control) Regulation', later abrogated, was passed to impose restriction on the movements of tin concentrates at night under pain of severe punishments for those in flagrant violation.[27] Commodity agreements therefore use varying indirect techniques to effect the provisions of their texts through links already established with international specialised agencies, which are often invited to preparatory conferences.

SECTION V. STATES AND THE TERRITORIAL APPLICABILITY OF COMMODITY AGREEMENTS

This type of applicability is in respect of a country or territory with 'separate participation',[28] whose participation has been or has not been declared in an instrument of ratification, acceptance or approval of a contracting government. For a territory whose separate participation has not been declared, a contracting government could declare its separate participation by depositing an instrument of accession with a depository authority who in turn notifies all interested governments including the council of the commodity institution. A government notifying a depository authority declares in its instrument that an agreement shall 'extend to any of the territories for whose international relations it is for the time being ultimately responsible . . .'. This is to say that the separate participation of dependent territories ceases immediately on attaining legal independence.

SECTION VI. PROCEDURE OF AMENDMENTS

The application of an agreement depends to a very large extent on the ratification of an amendment, because the contrary could lead to withdrawal or suspension of a participating country. Therefore we shall study this procedure under two sub-headings: (1) Conditions of amendment; (2) Entry into force of an amendment.

(1) CONDITIONS OF AMENDMENT

Commodity agreements largely require a special vote of contracting parties counted separately for the recommendation of an amendment at a council meeting. In this recommendation, the council has to fix a date limit at which all contracting governments must notify the depository authority of their ratifications, acceptance or approvals of an amendment or even its refusal. This date limit could be extended by the authority of the council, if the cause of delay on the part of a contracting party was due to constitutional difficulties in ratification. The conditions under which an amendment could be made are not often precisely stated but they would fall within three conditions. First, that certain difficult situations have arisen capable of obstructing the proper functioning of an agreement. Secondly, that the method of operating an agreement by a contracting member has jeopardised the interest of another member (for example, if an important member expresses its desire to withdraw from an agreement, because its interests have been jeopardised, there could be a proposal for amendment). Thirdly, an amendment could also occur or be proposed because there is a moment of opportunity for adapting an agreement to new politico-economic realities. For example, it was in this vein that the Tin Council proposed an amendment, 'Resolution No. 21 of 18 October 1956: Amendment of the International Tin Agreement regarding Exemption from Taxation'. This was to enable the government of the country in which the headquarters of the council is situated to grant, among other things, exemption from taxation on remuneration paid by the council to its employees other than those employees who are nationals of the country in which the headquarters of the council is situated.

(2) ENTRY INTO FORCE OF AN AMENDMENT

The entry into force of an amendment is automatic for contracting members of an agreement who have ratified it, as soon as the last instrument of ratification, acceptance or approval reaches the depository authority; with the proviso, however, that certain conditions are fulfilled. Such conditions are found for instance in the 1968 Coffee Agreement which reads as follows: .

> The amendment shall become effective 100 days after the Secretary General of the UN has received notifications of acceptance from contracting parties representing at least 75 per cent of the exporting countries, holding at least 85 per cent of the votes of the exporting members, and from contracting parties representing at least 75 per cent of the importing countries holding at least 80 per cent of the votes of the importing members.

Similar conditions for entry into force are established in the Cocoa, Coffee and Tin Agreements. In the Cocoa and Coffee Agreements, 80 per cent and 85 per cent of the total votes, respectively are required from importing members as against 67 per cent or two-thirds of the total votes of all consuming countries in the Tin Agreement. In the Tin Agreement, the number of days required for an amendment to have an effect of law is 90 days; that is three calendar months next following the receipt by depository government of the last ratification, approval or acceptance necessary to comprise all of the votes of producing countries and two-thirds of the total votes of all consuming countries (Article 51, paragraph (i)). In commodity agreements, if an amendment has not entered into effect at the end of the stipulated period, it shall be considered withdrawn (Article 75 of the 1972 Cocoa Agreement); but if a member country has not ratified an amendment within the date limit provided, such a member shall not be bound by the amendment and in fact is expected to withdraw, unless there is proof that its attitude was due to constitutional difficulties in ratification. However we cannot but note the importance attached to the vote of the producing countries in the Tin Agreement, where the refusal of one producer country to ratify, approve or accept an amendment corresponds to a type of veto power since it cannot enter into force, while the consumer procedure is linked with its right to withdraw from the agreement and in fact could give a notice to this effect, if it considers that its interests will be adversely affected by an amendment.

6 Legal Techniques: Conflict Resolution and Headquarters Agreement

SECTION I. THE TECHNIQUES OF CONFLICT RESOLUTION IN COMMODITY INSTITUTIONS

(1) A CASE AGAINST TRADITIONAL INTERNATIONAL LAW IN ECONOMIC CONFLICT RESOLUTION

In general UN parlance conflicts are resolved by different methods; for instance, by negotiation, consultation, arbitration and adjudication. Article 33, paragraph 1 of the UN Charter states this succinctly:

> The Parties to any dispute the continuance of which is likely to endanger the maintenance of international peace and security, shall first of all seek a solution by negotiation, enquiry, judicial settlement . . . .

This is to say that the settlement of conflicts by any of the above methods is a continuous process which must involve the art of negotiations since interests are never similar and permanent. This is why negotiation has been defined as a 'process in which explicit proposals are put forward ostensibly for the purpose of reaching agreement on an exchange or on the realisation of a common interest when conflicting interests are present'.[1]

Consultation, which also is a highly recommended method in commodity agreements, occurs when governments are in communication without being conscious of the existence of a difference between them. This is why commodity agreements recommend 'consultation and co-operation' with various institutions, governments and non-governmental bodies.

Experience of experimental years of arbitration and adjudication since the end of the Second World War, in the settlement of conflicts, has so discouraged the new states that they have grown to have very little or no faith in political and legal institutions of adjudication. We refer here to the International Court of Justice in the adjudication of the South West Africa (Namibia) case between Ethiopia and Liberia on the one hand and South Africa on the other. The ICJ's verdict was that these two African countries, although members of the defunct League of Nations, were not competent to challenge South African administration of this territory.[2] This was a sure case of the failure of international traditional law in solving contemporary political and legal problems involving sovereign states. Another argument against the International Court of Justice and traditional international law is that the proceedings of the court are often unnecessarily long because states are often lukewarm to subject themselves to the verdict of guilt from which emerges the notion of 'a victor and a vanquished'. Before a case goes before the ICJ the two parties to the dispute must agree on the ingredients of the case; that is to say that they would supply the tools with which they would be judged. If in the right to institute legal proceedings, states do preserve the right of rendering justice to themselves in municipal law, they appeal for international justice if they have a contention with another state. In internal justice, which is quite different from the international one, there is maintenance of order because criminals are easily punishable; but penal justice does not exist between states or nationals except that which emanated from the trials of war criminals in Nuremberg and Tokyo after the Second World War.

Administrative justice is still being gradually developed in international institutions so that the only litigious problems that could be decided upon by international jurisdiction are those between states. International justice has another feature. It is voluntary and, as has been said above, states have to agree on the specificity of a case before it could be sent to the international court. This was the case of arbitrage as known in the Middle Ages. In the classical conception of arbitrage, the parties to a dispute had to agree mutually by compromise on the nature and limitations of the issue at stake. They had to choose their judge or court, and had the option of choosing by compromise the type of rules of law that will be applicable in finding a solution to the problem. In this way, states tended to limit the risks of judiciary decisions. The advent of the Permanent Court of Arbitrage (1899), the Permanent Court of Justice (1920) and the International Court of Justice since 1945 have not in any way affected or modified their working mechanism. However, the rigidity of the principle has been softened by the optional clause provision of the ICJ which now permits a state to declare in advance whether it would accept the decision of the ICJ. Thus, unfortunately, the court can only pronounce a judgment based on a pre-established compromise between states in litigation, so that the right to institute legal proceedings by a state is again limited by the right of another state not to accept the decisions of the ICJ.

Another defect of this system is that the ICJ, or the international society for that matter, has no competent machinery for law enforcement. It was in this vein that the government of Thailand refused to carry out the decision of the ICJ in July 1962 asking her to restitute the Temple of Prear Vihear to Cambodia. In a case like this the UN Charter requires the intervention of the Security Council (Article 94 of the UN Charter), but we know how difficult it has also been for the Security Council to enforce decisions because of state sovereignty and great power interests. Successes are assured only in cases where there are favourable forces at work. We can therefore say that when two states agree to go before an international jurisdiction, it is because the problem at stake does not touch their vital interests. We have also examined the case of the UN resolutions passed against France for her atomic explosion in the Sahara, to which the French government was insensitive because the UN could not carry out any sanction against her.[3]

Messrs Northedge and Donelan, so dismayed by the incompetence of political and legal institutions to find solutions to some international problems, have established that out of 50 case-studies of international disputes studied by them since 1945, none appeared to have revealed any encouraging results. They hold that in more than three-quarters of these disputes arbitration or adjudication does not appear even to have been proposed by either side or by third parties as means of settlement. . . .[4]

Before we study the techniques used in commodity institutions as distinct from political legal institutions, two further examples of disrespect for international classical law may be made.

(a) *The USA*: as established by Northedge and Donelan, the USA adopted the notorious Conally Amendment on 2 August 1946 reserving to the USA the right of interpretation of domestic jurisdiction, thus excluding the USA from her previous adherence to the optional clause of the ICJ. In spite of both internal and external criticism, this has not been rectified.

(b) *Great Britain*: in 1957, Great Britain temporarily amended the declaration of adherence to the optional clause of the ICJ statute so as to exclude matters which to her constituted her national security in order to forestall any attempt to re-establish the legality of British nuclear tests in the Pacific. This situation has since been rectified.

The above exercise is simply to show how inadequate international traditional law is to contemporary problems of international economic order which require basic solidarity to accomplish.

In so doing, economic institutions have tried to evolve their own methods of conflict settlements so that a breakdown in machineries of economic co-operation will not disrupt the final principles as set in Article 55 of the UN Charter. From UN experience, over 4,000 sittings of multilateral conferences occur each year, and this is why it offers the greatest source of study in conflict resolution. The UN experiences from the Brookings studies are five:[5]

(i) conflict resolution through conciliation and mediation;
(ii) 'freezing' of conflict through truce supervision;
(iii) reduction of tension through disarmament supervision;
(iv) sublimation of conflict through economic and social activities;
(v) controlling conflict through public opinion.

Because what mainly interests us in our study is that pertaining to economic activities, we shall then proceed to examine techniques used in this area of intense solidarity and activity among nations of the world.

The first and the fourth classifications therefore will aid us in our study.

(II) TECHNIQUES OF CONFLICT RESOLUTION OUTSIDE THE UNITED NATIONS SYSTEM

The GATT

The Gatt, otherwise known as the General Agreement on Tariffs and Trade, which contains 36 Articles, 9 Annexes and other supplementary instruments is made up of a set of rules governing international trade practices and policies.[6] These are highly restrictive rules, although there are some exceptions. For instance, it is provided that any advantages, favours, privileges or immunity granted to third parties by contracting members must be immediately granted unconditionally to the like product originating from or destined for all other contracting parties.

Any of these provisions could be waived[7] by a contracting party to the GATT under 'exceptional circumstances' by a two-thirds vote (Article 25, paragraph 5) acting 'jointly' as contracting party. Although the GATT is not provided with a policing organ, it resolves its problems through a system of techniques of co-operation and accommodation. The GATT does not forbid any contracting party from taking part in any intergovernmental commodity agreement provided it satisfies certain criteria. These take the form of reservations (Article XX(h)) and the proviso required here is that the measures of implementing a commodity agreement should not be 'applied in a manner which could constitute a means of arbitrary or unjustifiable discrimination between countries where the same conditions prevail, or a disguised restriction on international trade'. What this means precisely is that if any commodity agreement falls within the scope of this reservation without infringing the GATT texts, it is regarded as perfectly legal. But in a case where discrimination arises, conflicts therefore arise.

The provisions for conflict settlement are contained in Articles I, II, XI, XIII, XVI, XVII, XXII, XXIII. Article XIII, which appears more vital to our study, stipulates that if any contracting party finds that any benefit accruing to it directly or indirectly is impaired, or that it could not carry out the objective of the agreement because the application by a contracting party of any measure runs counter to it, the following situation is open to it as a redress:

1. Any aggrieved party could petition for a relief in the first place to the offender and if this fails, to the Contracting Parties who are empowered to investigate promptly and pronounce rulings and make recommendations on the issue under dispute.
2. In an extreme case, the aggrieved party is authorised to retaliate by way of righting the wrong or imbalance.

The Havana Charter

It is important to describe this charter briefly, not because it has evolved a distinct machinery for conflict settlement, but because it is a precursor to UN intervention in commodity politics. The Havana Charter, as its name indicates, was consummated in Havana in March 1948 as an International Trade Organisation by the UN Conference on Trade and Employment. It was thus known as the International Trade Organisation Charter or simply the Havana Charter. It was a document of 106 Articles plus Annexes with chapters on Employment and Economic Activity, Economic Development and Reconstruction, Commercial Policy, Restrictive Business Practices and International Commodity Agreements in addition to its organisational and procedural provisions. It was when the final text was in the process of preparation that ECOSOC (Economic and Social Council of the United Nations Organisation) passed a resolution in the form of a recommendation which provided that, while awaiting the outcome of the Charter,[8] UN members should adopt as general guideline the principles contained in Chapter VII pertaining to intergovernmental arrangements, while giving recognition to the possibility of being able to make modifications.

Unfortunately for the authors of the Havana Charter, like the GATT, it never entered into force.[9] However this Chapter VII later became Chapter VI which has received international legal approbation while the charter itself has failed to acquire this approbation. The said Chapter VI addresses to 'Principles' in Articles 60 and 63 entitled 'General Principles Governing Commodity Agreements' and 'Additional Principles Governing Commodity Control Agreements'.

(3) TECHNIQUES OF CONFLICT RESOLUTION WITHIN THE UNITED NATIONS AND QUASI-UNITED NATIONS SYSTEM

We shall study two types of institutions here, the one under the UN system (UNCTAD), and the other which can be considered quasi-UN institution simply because of the enormous organisational capacity of UN and UNCTAD Secretariats in recent times, involved during preparatory conferences. The latter is the case of international commodity agreements under specialised institutions which, although inspired by UNCTAD principles since 1964, are not connected directly with the UN through any agency agreements.

(A) Commodity agreements under a quasi-UN system

Commodity agreements have a highly developed system of resolving their internal conflicts within the areas of their activities. This is because they have found other methods utilised so far in political and legal world organisations inadequate and unrealistic to the requirements of economic and social reality and solidarity.

(a) The panel advisory system

This system has become known as the panel advisory system entrenched in commodity texts. They employ the system of continuous consultation and co-operation as initial approaches to resolving their internal conflicts arising from the application or non-application of agreements. In this panel system, the complainant and the accused must consent to be arraigned before an independent panel established by an executive director. If a member brings up a matter relating to an agreement, consultation is first recommended among the parties. If this fails, the panel advisory system is resorted to; but if it succeeds the executive director simply distributes the report to all contracting parties. Article 59 of the 1968 International Coffee Agreement stipulates that any dispute concerning the interpretation and application of the agreement which could not be settled by negotiation will be referred to the council for decision at the request of a member party to the dispute. Where a dispute has been lodged with the council a majority of members holding not less than one-third of the total votes could require the council, after discussion, to seek the opinion of the advisory panel before it gives its final decision. This procedure is common to all commodity agreements, and the cost of this panel system is often met by the commodity organisation.

As a general rule any complaint that a contracting party has failed to fulfil its obligation will be decided by the commodity council. If it is found that a member has committed a breach of an agreement, the nature and the extent of the breach must first be specified. A breach is established only after a distributed simple majority vote of the council. In a case of an established breach a council could take either of the following measures:

(i) the council could, by a distributed two-third majority vote, suspend that member's voting rights in the council or board until it fulfils its obligation;
(ii) the council could ask the member country to withdraw compulsorily under Article 67 of the International Coffee Agreement (1968).

(b) Composition of the advisory panel

Where a dispute has been referred to a council, unless the council unanimously agrees otherwise, the panel shall consist of:

(i) two persons, one having wide experience in matters under dispute and the other having legal standing and experience nominated by the exporting members;
(ii) two such persons as above are nominated by the importing members;
(iii) a chairman is selected unanimously by the four persons nominated above failing which the executive chairman of the council makes the nomination.

As a general rule, persons appointed to the advisory panel are expected to act in their personal capacity without accepting instructions from any government. Such persons are not expected to be drawn from countries whose governments are contracting parties of an agreement. This is the requirement of the 1972 International Cocoa Agreement (Article 61, paragraph 36) while the 1968 Coffee Agreement does not object to persons from countries whose governments are contracting parties being eligible to serve on the advisory panel (Article 59, paragraph 3(b)). Although the Tin Agreement is explicitly silent, it does require that the persons could be nominated by both the producing and consuming countries. However, the proper practice would be to nominate complete outsiders, as suggested by the cocoa texts, to inspire confidence of the parties in dispute. All the texts however require that in the event of the four members not being able to choose an acceptable chairman, the executive chairman or director is empowered to make the choice himself among the four members already chosen. The expenses of the advisory panel are paid by the organisation and their reasoning and opinion are submitted to the council which makes the final decision after considering all the relevant information and opinion submitted to it.

(B) Conciliation procedures under the UN system: UNCTAD

The concept of conciliation as an institutional mechanism for conflict resolution within the three organs of UNCTAD (assembly, conference and board) was first adopted at its first conference in 1964. This technique was contained in the final act as a recommendation in the Annexe A.V.I. The responsibility for evolving these conciliation procedures was attributed to a Special Committee on Procedures which was appointed by the Secretary-General of the UN. Its terms of reference were contained in the now famous paragraph 25 of Annexe A.V.I. of the final act of the first conference as quoted by R. Krishnamaturi and D.

Cordovez, who are officials of the UN Secretariat.[10] They are as follows:

> (A) The task of the committee shall be to prepare proposals within the continuing machinery designed to establish a process of conciliation to take place before voting and to provide an adequate basis for the adoption of recommendations with regard to proposals of a specific nature for substantially affecting the economic or financial interests of particular countries.
>
> (B) Such conciliation may be carried out through a system of conciliation committees, the good offices of the Secretary-General of the conference or any other means within the framework of the United Nations.

The committee's task in accomplishing the above procedures must be considered in the light of the wish of the interested states to place on record and to publicise their views, and the need to issue reports at appropriate times which would state the areas of accord and disaccord. This is why an explanation of the various positions, and the changes that might occur as regards the implementation of any proposed recommendation, are vital to the interests of the Committee.

> Any Government participating in this Conference may submit to the Special Committee such proposals and recommendations as it considers relevant to (A) above provided they do not imply any amendment to the Charter of the UN or any departure from the principle that each country has one vote. The Special Committee shall include a study of such proposals and recommendations in its report to the General Assembly.

The Special Committee on Procedures met at the UN headquarters from 28 September to 23 October 1964, during which it submitted a unanimous report to the Secretary General in document A/5749. Its recommendations[11] proposed to the General Assembly of the UN as paragraph 25 of the resolution establishing UNCTAD, was contained in Chapter 6 of this report. Two factors made these recommendations necessary: (a) the recognition of the importance of consultation, negotiation and conciliation in the UN system; (b) the need to initiate formal conciliation only in respect of certain categories of proposals; for instance, those which affect the economic and financial interests of particular countries.

How significant is paragraph 25 of the General Assembly Resolution 1995 (XIX) to the general concept of conciliation in economic and financial matters within UNCTAD deliberations?

The significance of the above paragraph 25 cannot be under-rated in any way because it sets forth the rules of the game: procedure, levels of conciliation, methods and by whom conciliation procedures must be taken, areas in which they can be considered appropriate, etc. For any effective negotiation to occur within the machinery of UNCTAD it must never be seen by the various interest groups that conciliation is being used as an instrument of defeat and humiliation. To illustrate what the final goal of conciliation is intended to achieve, in the humble opinion of the author, it may be necessary to recall a political crisis situation between Premier Nikita Khruschev and President J. F. Kennedy over the Cuban missile crisis when the two most powerful Presidents of the world, in 1963, made highly desirable and laudable reciprocal concessions on the future of Soviet missile installations on Cuban soil and the undesirability of American invasion of Cuba under any guise. This will indeed be one of the most recorded acts of statesmanship in contemporary political history, that saved the world from a war conflagration. Therefore it seems to the author that the conciliation procedures of UNCTAD intend to produce the like acts of statesmanship among competing interests of the world in the areas of conflicting world economic interests in commodity trade and the transfer of technology etc., so as to avoid conflagration between the rich and the poor nations of the world by eventually guaranteeing peace through equitable distribution of scarce resources, payment of fair and remunerative prices for both raw and manufactured goods. The main function of UNO has essentially been both mediatory in nature and pacific in settlement procedure while refusing to employ any use of force. The UN has also used public opinion techniques, all those in purely political matters. To avoid the uncertainties into which these put the anxious world, conciliation measures have been evolved for UNCTAD without, however, ignoring the techniques of negotiation. This was why paragraph 25 of Resolution 1995 (XIX) of the General Assembly of the UN can be examined under various levels of techniques.

(a) Levels of conciliation and request for conciliation

Within the meaning of paragraph 25, conciliation could be initiated by any of the specified committees, by preparing proposals, before voting is undertaken so as to provide adequate basis for adopting recommendations, as has been said above. Surely these proposals are those which come before the three organs of UNCTAD: conference, the board and the committees of the board. When it concerns the board, the process of conciliation applies only to those matters, 'with respect to which a committee has been authorised to submit without further approval, recommendations for action'. However the 'Special Committee did agree that while special conciliation could be conducted at the plenary level of the conference, it should normally be conducted at the level of sessional committee concerned' (paragraph 16). This is why it is being stated that in the case of proposals before the committees of the board a formal request or initiative must be made by at least three members of the committee. The purpose of this approach cannot be underestimated, because not only does it guarantee a thorough study of the problem posed, but it also guarantees the inadmissibility of interminable discussions characteristic of a larger committee. In other words this procedure permits the categorisation of problems after deliberations, and if insoluble could be proposed to the board after all unnecessary areas of friction have been removed.

This is why a further request for conciliation within the meaning of paragraph 25 was considered important. A request for conciliation within the meaning of the said paragraph could be made in the following manner: When there are proposals for conciliation before the conference, a request could be made by at least ten members of the conference; before the board by at least five members of the conference whether or not they are members of the board and before the committees of the board, by at least three members of the committee. This means that proposals before the conference and the board are determined by a restricted number of the conference participants and the power of the conference here can be felt since it determines whether conciliation procedures should be undertaken by the board without necessarily including any of its members. However, and this is significant, when proposals for conciliation are made before the committee of the board, this request must be made by at least three members. No doubt, as we had said above, the autonomy of the committee of the board stems from the importance attached to it in terms of ability to achieve more concrete studies and results. It is also significant that although the initiatives for proposals emanate from the various bodies, they must in the first instance be transmitted as appropriate to the president of the conference or to the chairman of the board, and in the case of a request for a proposal before a committee of the board, the chairman of the committee concerned, shall submit it to the chairman of the board. The purpose of this procedure is clear. It is to permit a thorough re-examination of the proposals in consultation with their various bodies before a general discussion takes place, particularly among the various heads of the bodies who are likely to be aided by the technicians or specialists within UNCTAD itself. This well-conceived procedure helps to initiate, from the beginning, behind-the-scenes conciliation before substantive discussions take place.

(b) The presiding chairman and time for request for conciliation

Conciliation process is considered as a last resort of conflict resolution and it does replace the other techniques of negotiation and consultation. Either the president or chairman could initiate conciliation only after an appreciable debate had been undertaken and his technique actually consists of 'feeling' or 'sensing' the pulse of the delegates and he consequently has to be satisfied that the required number of delegates favour the process. If this process is initiated at the committee level, its chairman shall refer the matter to the board after nomination of a conciliation committee. Members of the committee are nominated by the president or chairman of the conference or board after consultation, with the organ in question subjected to the approval of the conference or board.

Among those to be consulted, is the secretary general of the conference and the chairman of the committee who has referred the matter to the chairman of the board.

This committee is selected according to certain guidelines, although the chairman or president appoints the members submitted to the conference or board for adoption without a vote. Where a procedural question arises, a simple majority of the representatives present and voting is required.

Before voting, which takes place only after a debate is concluded, an appropriate interval of about 48 hours for submission of requests for conciliation is allowed. The purpose of the said interval is not only to allow the presiding chairman or president to decide whether to institute conciliation, but also it corresponds to a period of reflection as to which other UN processes of conflict resolution could be used.

The size and composition of the conciliation committee should be small as a rule. It must be made up not only of countries directly connected with the dispute but must be constituted on the basis of equitable geographical representation. This does not mean that countries not especially interested cannot be invited.

(c) Procedure within the conciliation committee and submission of its reports

(i) The committee must endeavour to reach agreement during the same session of the conference or of the board, failing which it could report to the next session of the conference[12] or board, whichever is earlier.

(ii) There is no voting in the committee because it 'would defeat the very purpose of special conciliation', although it could if no solution appears on the horizon.

(iii) The view of the special committee is that the time allotted for conciliation should not be so short as to prevent thorough discussion or so long as to delay adoption of a recommendation (paragraph 32 of the Report).

The mandate of the conciliation committee could be extended beyond the agreed session when it is expected to submit a report, by a simple majority decision of the conference or board as the case may be. The report of the conciliation committee which is made available to the conference is expected to contain two important positions: (1) whether it reached an agreement or not; (2) whether it needs a further extension of time.

In the case of the former, it would contain the agreed draft text of its recommendation. In the case of the latter, the report must indicate areas of agreement and disagreement and their reasons for recommending an extension of time or rejecting it.

The report of the committee shall have priority on the agenda of the organ to which it is submitted. The resolution adopted must show explicit relevance to the report of the committee and to the conclusion, thus:

> . . . Noting the report of the Conciliation Committee appointed on (date) in (document number). Noting also that the Conciliation Committee (was able to reach agreement) (recommends a further period of conciliation) (was unable to reach agreement).

(I) Reports of the board and the conference

The reports of the board to the conference and to the general assembly and the report of the conference to the general assembly shall include, *inter alia*:

(i) the texts of all recommendations, resolutions and declarations adopted by the board or the conference during the period covered by the report.

(ii) in respect of recommendations and resolutions which are adopted after a process of conciliation, these shall also be included in a record of the voting on such recommendation or resolution together with the texts of the reports of the conciliation committees concerned. In the report, the record of voting and the texts of the report shall normally follow the resolutions to which they pertain.[13]

(II) Pro forma of the report of the final act of the first UNCTAD

Resolution 1: Measures for action for the promotion of trade in manufactures and semi-manufactures in developing countries.
(text of the resolution).

Resolution 2: Guidelines for international financial co-operation.
(text of the resolution).

Resolution 3: Preferences
(text of resolution).
This resolution was adopted after a process of conciliation instituted by the board.
(a) The board adopted this resolution without dissent.
(b) The following is the text of the report of the conciliation committee (originally reproduced in document . . . .);
(text of report of conciliation committee).

Resolution 4: Common measure of understanding on shipping questions.
(text of the resolution).

Resolution 5: Terms of financing.
(text of resolution).
This resolution was adopted after a process of conciliation instituted by the (board).
(a) The (board) adopted this resolution by . . . . votes to . . . . , with . . . . abstentions.
(b) The following is the text of the report of the conciliation committee (originally reproduced in document . . . .);
(text of resolution).

Resolution 6: Conditions of economic and technical co-operation. (text of resolution).
This resolution was adopted after a process of conciliation committee (originally reproduced in document . . . . .). (text of Report of Conciliation Committee).

(d) Good offices of the secretary-general of the conference

'The good offices of the secretary general of the conference shall be utilised as fully as practicable in connection with the process of conciliation.' No specific duties are assigned to him but it is expected that he would use his good offices at every stage of the conciliation process. The object of conciliation is to reach an agreed recommendation. But if UNCTAD decides to adopt a resolution by majority vote instead of without a vote which should be the case of an agreed recommendation, it is only proper that such a resolution must make reference to the conclusion reached.

(e) Subjects in regard to which conciliation is appropriate or excluded

We have already described the conditions for automatic institution of conciliation. Here paragraph 25(e) establishes as follows:

(i) Those proposals considered appropriate for conciliation must be of a specific nature affecting the financial or economic interests of particular countries. For example:

- economic plans or programmes or economic or social re-adjustment;
- trade, monetary or tariff policies or balance of payments;
- policies of economic assistance or transfer resources;
- levels of employment, income, revenue or investment;
- rights or obligations under international agreements or treaties.

(ii) Proposals in the following areas do not require conciliation:

- matters of procedure;
- proposals for study or investigation and those related to the preparation of legal instruments in the field of trade;
- establishment of subsidiary bodies of the board within the scope of its competence;
- recommendations and declarations of a general nature which need no specific action;

– proposals which involve action proposed in confirmity with recommendations unanimously adopted by the conference.

The appropriateness or non-appropriateness of the use of conciliation is important, because in highly technical matters there is need for selection to avoid excessive loss of time. For instance that matters of procedure need not be decided through the long process of conciliation is understood when one realises that matters of procedure can be settled with a simple majority vote which is the practice of the UN. In the same vein we could expect the use of conciliation in matters pertaining to specific policies, monetary or trade, because the resolution of a conflict in any of these areas could affect decisions already made on national levels. However a question does arise as to whether points of order could be raised within the organ concerned if conciliation has been proposed for any other item not enumerated among those for which conclusion is necessary or not. R. Krishnamaturi and D. Cordovez, officials of the UN Secretariat, provide an adequate answer: 'In the absence of any specific rule, and in accordance with the normal principles of parliamentary procedure, the appropriate rule of procedure of the conference or the board would seem applicable in such a case.'[14]

(III) CONCLUSION

We have seen from the study of conflict resolution in economic insitutions that there are specific techniques peculiar to them, although those of political institutions are intermingled, e.g. negotiation. We have seen the need for a different system of approach in economic matters as distinct from political ones. In political and legal institutions, resolutions of the General Assembly of the UN and decisions of the ICJ are optionally carried out by states without any sanctionable enforcement, while in commodity institutions the fear of penalty and the need for solidarity lend respect to decisions taken by states. In the ICJ, most of the jurists are too legally conscious with often political motivations. In commodity institutions (agreements) the panel system has come to stop the lacuna whereby flexibility is determined by sovereignty considerations and not concessions or the need to attain higher living standards as provided by Article 55 of the UN Charter or by contractual interests. Since members of the panel are not only lawyers, certain other factors or considerations, which create *quid pro quo* treatments, make decisions obeyed and solutions workable.

SECTION II. HEADQUARTERS AGREEMENT: DIPLOMATIC PRIVILEGES AND IMMUNITIES

The privileges and immunities which accrue to functionaries of commodity institutions, like those of other international organisations, are inspired from the provisions of Article 104 of the UN Charter which grant the organisation legal capacity and from its Article 105, paragraph 2, which runs thus: 'Representatives of the members of the United Nations and officials of the organisation shall similarly enjoy such privileges and immunities as are necessary for the independent exercise of their functions in connection with the Organisation.' Consequently, we could then say, that the granting of immunities and privileges is based on the notion of the necessity for international organisations to function.[15] This is why the legal capacity of commodity councils is considered enormous and important; they could not only conclude a headquarters agreement but also be granted privileges and immunities in respect of their institutions and their functionaries.

All commodity agreements have provision for privileges and immunities, the purpose of which is to insulate their functionaries from the probable arbitrariness of national laws, depending, however, on the nature of government that is operative.

This notwithstanding, non-nationals of a host government are not exempted from liability in respect of damage caused by their motor vehicles and from traffic offences within the host country.[16] As provided by the 1946 UN Convention on Privileges and Immunities, all international institutions are granted legal status. Consequently, commodity institutions are granted the 'capacity to contract, to acquire and dispose movable and immovable property and to institute legal proceedings'.[17] The government of a host country is then referred to as the 'host government' or 'host member'. With this host government, the organisation is empowered to conclude a separate agreement on what is known as a 'seat agreement' or 'headquarters agreement' whose scope is very far-reaching.

(I) HEADQUARTERS AGREEMENT

A headquarters agreement concluded between a host government and an international institution, and which must be approved by its council, could enter into force on signature.[18] It relates to the status, privileges and immunities of the institution, its executive director, its staff and experts including member representatives whilst in the territory of the host government, for the purpose of exercising their functions. This agreement is concluded only after the main commodity agreement has entered into force. Independent of the main agreement, it terminates under any of the following conditions:

(a) by agreement between the host government and the institution; or
(b) in the event of the headquarters of the institution being removed from the territory of the host government; or
(c) if the institution ceases to exist.

(II) THE SCOPE OF THE AGREEMENT

The agreement covers very vital areas of the administration of the institution, such as currency exchange facilities, tax exemption on assets, income and taxation of staff salaries, property of its council, including such legal capacity necessary for the execution of its functions to 'the extent consistent'[19] with the law of each state. The council of the commodity institution is thus exempted from the taxation of its assets, income and other property. The use of the expression '. . . to the extent consistent with its law' does signify that the council shall accept the jurisdiction of the host country within the limits of its national laws consistent with the requirements of international law. This is because the international society has not yet reached the stage at which international organisations could enjoy the status of absolute supranationality. For instance, in respect of tax exemptions, the host government shall grant exemption from taxation on remuneration by the council to its employees other than those of its nationals.

This was the case of the 3rd Tin Agreement to whose council in August 1956, the UK government granted tax exemptions on its operations. To achieve this, a law had to be passed in 1957 entitled 'Legal Status and Tax Exemptions of the Tin Council: Amendment'. It became applicable as soon as this amendment entered into force on 19 July 1958.

During the first council meeting, 2–6 July 1956, the UK delegation made it clear that by virtue of Article IV, paragraph 2 of the 1st Tin Agreement (1956) and the UK internal legislation, her government was not in a position to grant immediate tax relief to the employees of the council who were not of British nationality. This was why the Tin Council, during its second meeting, 15–19 October 1956, recommended to member governments the ratification of an amendment that would make the British government fulfil her obligations. This amendment was open for signature from 18 October 1956 to 17 July 1958.

By virtue of a headquarters agreement which could also be concluded with one or other members of the agreement,[20] the functionaries of the institution, such as the secretary, manager, buffer stock manager and other staff members, are granted tax exemptions on their salaries. These tax exemptions, which exclude the nationals of the host country, pose definite problems of inequality of advantages in status among the staff of the institution. With regard to UNO,[21] this no longer poses a problem because, when the USA refused to grant tax exemptions on salaries of its nationals working therein, the UN Secretariat decided to reimburse the totality of their taxes, so that they could be at par with their counterparts.[22] This was after a UN Administrative Tribunal had ruled to this effect. This highly desirable practice would be recommended to other international institutions; much more so because nationals of a host country do not usually enjoy diplomatic advantages which accrue to their counterparts.

(III) SOURCES OF DIPLOMATIC PRIVILEGES

The sources of diplomatic privileges are the following:

(i) Constitutional texts of international organisations, e.g. UN Charter Articles 104 and 105, paragraph 2; Treaty of Economic Community of West African States and its Protocols, Article 60, paragraphs 1–4 and 37, paragraph 2 respectively.

(ii) General conventions on privileges and immunities, e.g. UN Convention on Privileges and Immunities of February 1946 or those on specialised institutions of 21 November 1947[23] or 1961 Vienna Convention.

(iii) Texts of commodity agreements and their headquarters agreements.

The scope of applicability of these conventions depends on the number of ratifications received from contractual member states. This practice has been aggravated by the fact that certain states refuse to ratify them. For instance: (i) the USA refused to ratify the UN general convention on privileges and immunities; (ii) France acted likewise in respect of UNESCO.[24]

Because of this unfortunate practice, if there had not existed other arrangements or agreements of a bilateral nature, the status of international organisations in host countries would never have been defined. This is to say that a headquarters agreement issue from a commodity agreement is a bilateral arrangement between a host government and an international commodity institution, defining the status of this institution and the privileges and immunities of its functionaries. This agreement is more precise than the general convention on privileges and immunities, and tends to solve problems that are specific to each country. Besides headquarters agreements, the texts of commodity agreements tend to extend the scope of such agreements to other countries where the functionaries of such institutions are likely to perform their official functions. The purpose is to guarantee protection to representatives and functionaries as they could be called to sit outside the headquarters of the institution.[25] In commodity institutions like in general international organisations, the host country does not have to formally agree to accept a state representative before accreditation as in normal diplomatic practice between states, where a state has to agree to the nomination of an ambassador before his credentials are accepted.

In other words, states are free to nominate any representative they wish, to commodity institutions without formal agreement or consent from either the institution or the receiving state. However, the names of representatives and their alternates must be communicated in advance.

By virtue of the double role of state delegations as diplomats or delegates and functionaries, there has grown a need for representation without constraints in the proper performance of their duties. For this reason, we shall examine certain aspects of their diplomatic status namely: (a) inviolability; (b) immunity from jurisdiction; (c) tax or fiscal privileges.

(A) Inviolability

(i) The scope

The chairman, representatives of member-countries and observers attending meetings and secretarial staff enjoy immunity from personal arrest, detention, seizure of luggage, inviolability of documents and papers. The draft headquarters agreement as negotiated between the Cocoa Producers Alliance and the government of the Federal Republic of Nigeria and other similar agreements include immunity from legal process even after termination of their mission, in respect of acts done by them or words spoken or written in the exercise of their functions; the right to use codes and receive documents or correspondences; exemption for themselves and their spouses from all measures restricting entries, from charges for visas and from aliens' registration formalities. This is also true of the OCAM Agreement in its Article 23, paragraph 3. This includes, however, currency and exchange control facilities accorded to other delegates attending international conferences in the host country and custom facilities as regards personal luggage accorded to representatives and delegates.

Without these privileges and immunities it would be difficult for these categories of persons to function adequately. The protection needed by an ambassador and his staff is comparable to that of an international organisation whose functions also border on diplomatic activities. It is interesting to note that these areas of inviolability as contained in the Cocoa Headquarters Agreement are applicable irrespective of the state of diplomatic relations existing between the governments concerned and the Nigerian government, although these immunities are not extended to Nigerian citizens.[26] This means that even in a period of war or international crisis-situation between Nigeria and the country of a national in the secretariat of the Cocoa Council, this national is diplomatically covered or protected. This is because a secretariat staff may not necessarily be a state representative but one recruited in his own right filling his country's quota representation.

However, in case of war or crisis as described above, it is in the interest of the person concerned, or his government, if he represents the interests of that government to initiate a withdrawal or recall to avoid expulsion or being regarded as persona non grata. Another question is that arising from a proof that a member of staff of the institution has abused the privileges accorded him by a host government. According to set provisions[27] in headquarters agreements, no staff member of the institution would be forced out of the host country through an expulsion order, by its authorities, without having abused the privileges accorded him for the proper execution of his duties. Before an expulsion order takes effect, it must receive the prior approval of the Ministry of External Affairs of the host country who, in turn, is expected to have consulted with any of the following undermentioned legal persons:

(a) the government of a member state if it concerns a representative of the state or his family;
(b) the chairman of the council of the organisation if it concerns a member of its executive council or his family;

(c) the secretary general of the organisation if it concerns any other member of its staff.

In any of the two examples mentioned above, we could expect that the person concerned would be given, according to normal diplomatic practice, a reasonable period of time to leave the country and, until he left, would continue to be beneficiary of the privileges and immunities to which he and his family are entitled.[28] Inviolability also covers archival materials such as all records, correspondence, documents, manuscripts, photographs, films and recordings. This is similar to the requirements of Article 24 of the 1961 Vienna Convention in respect of archival materials of a diplomatic mission. It states that the archives and documents of a diplomatic mission are inviolable at any given moment wherever it is located. Article 5 of the Harvard Law School Draft states: 'A receiving state shall protect the archives of a mission from any violation and shall safeguard their confidential characters, wherever such archives may be located within the country of the receiving state . . .'. Since in normal diplomatic practice a mission is inviolable, it is more so for its archival materials which may not be located at the embassy quarters. This is why, in the case of commodity institutions, their agreements specify in respect of their archives that '. . . wherever located, shall be inviolable'. This inviolability is absolute and must remain so even if the institution ceases to exist and until the materials are transferred to a continuator organisation or to its next headquarters. This is also the case with the archives of diplomatic missions. For instance, in 1944 during the Second World War, the Swiss government did not ransack the German embassy and its archives. Rather, they were sealed off and the embassy kept under political surveillance. This does not exclude the right of the belligerent to destroy its own archives, as this is usually their practice before their officials quit.

(ii) Properties

Article 22, paragraph 3 of the 1961 Vienna Convention states: 'Les Locaux de la Mission, leur ameublement et les autres objects qui s'y trouvent ainsi que les moyens de transport de la Mission, ne peuvent faire l'objet d'aucune perquisition, requisition, saisie ou mesure d'exécution.' Article 8, paragraph 2 of the Cocoa Draft Headquarters Agreement re-echoes this provision by immunising the properties of the alliance from 'any form of requisition, confiscation, search, expropriation or sequestration'. This, however, does not exclude the right of search if a luggage or a car belonging to the alliance or its functionary is suspected to be carrying goods whose importations have been banned, as allowed by Article 36, paragraph 2 of the Vienna Convention.

(iii) Communication

The host government permits and protects unrestricted communication consistent with the legitimate functions of the organisation. As in normal diplomatic practice, the receiving state permits the use of facilities to communicate with external agents and home governments. It does also respect the secrecy of the organisation, and for this reason it is allowed the use of code or cypher. However, if wireless transmitters are to be installed, there would be need for prior consent of the appropriate authorities. As in normal diplomatic practice, the mail bag of the institution, which must not be opened or withheld, must not contain anything outside official materials.

(iv) Special protection for premises

The premises of a commodity institution are inviolable like those of a diplomatic mission. A host government must take all appropriate steps to protect them against any intrusion or damage and against any disturbances of the peace or impairment of their dignity. No officer or official of the government or any person exercising any public authority shall enter the premises of the alliance except with the consent of the secretary-general and under conditions approved by the secretary-general . . .[29] (Article 5, paragraph 3).

This provision recalls to one's mind the cases of political demonstrations and refugee attacks on foreign legations. These acts occur more frequently against political institutions than against economic ones. The limit of protection expected of a receiving state is well explained in the incident which took place in the Rumanian embassy in Berne (Switzerland) in 1955.[30] A group of Rumanian refugees from Germany forcefully entered into the Chancellery and residence of the Rumanian Head of Mission in Berne during a night raid, 14/15

February 1955. In this encounter, the embassy driver was severely wounded and later died in hospital. While the chargé d'affaires escaped, other members of staff were caught in. The Swiss police then encircled the premises having been authorised by the chargé d'affaires to penetrate into the embassy and capture the intruders. But the police refused to penetrate on the grounds that the embassy staff were in the premises. In spite of the fact that the aggressors later liberated the staff, the Swiss authority still felt it was improper to attack the embassy because the neighbouring houses would need prior evacuation. They thought it was better to negotiate. However, 38 hours after the seizure, the aggressors decided to surrender in the afternoon of 16 February 1955. They were then arrested and documents in their possession recovered and returned to the chargé d'affaires.

The aggressors were then taken before the Swiss Federal Tribunal, which found them guilty and were consequently imprisoned on 22 June 1955.[31]

Tied to the protection expected of a host country is the question whether such protection should also be extended to peaceful demonstrations. This is a recent question which even the Vienna Convention did not examine, for example, in October 1961 when the USSR exploded her nuclear devices, its permanent mission in New York was subjected to a series of peaceful demonstrations. This was also the case of the British High Commission in Lagos subjected to peaceful demonstrations by the University of Ibadan students who frowned at possible British military bases in Nigeria at independence. Demonstrations are not normally frowned at, provided they are peaceful. But it is generally the case that embassies often get destroyed by demonstrators. Because of the high costs involved, an embassy or institution cannot be protected with all the might of the host government until there is proof of a possible demonstration.

However, in the case of destruction, compensations are normally paid, although this rule of law is not often adhered to. For instance, when angry crowds demonstrated against the British High Commission in Lagos for the alleged involvement of Britain in the attempted abortive coup of 13 February 1976 led by Lt Col B. S. Dimka, the British High Commissioner, H.E. Mr Le Quesne, demanded compensation shortly afterwards.

The Federal Government of Nigeria acted promptly by requesting his immediate recall because the demand was made when the nation was still mourning the assassination of its head of state, General Murtala Muhammed.

(B) Immunity from jurisdiction

The Cocoa Producers Alliance as an institution like the ECOWAS Organisation or the OCAM institution, is immune from jurisdiction and execution unless they are waived in a particular case or in respect of an enforcement of an arbitration award. Since privileges and immunities are granted to the officials and experts in the interest of the institution and not for the personal benefit of the staff, it is stipulated in the headquarters agreement of the Cocoa Producers Alliance that the secretary-general shall always have the right and duty to waive the immunity of any official or expert, where it is judged to impede the course of justice.[32] In the case of the secretary-general, the waiver is the commodity council. The institution also enjoys immunity for acts accomplished by its staff in their capacity as officials with respect to their speeches and writings.[33] Sometimes, this provision is not respected by host governments. For instance, in April 1955, during a meeting of the 5th Committee on Industry and Petroleum of the ILO in Venezuela, the Venezuelan government expelled a labour representative of the ILO for attacking her at its opening session.[34]

This action was, by the status and standards of international organisations, illegal because this representative made the speech in the interest of his function.

In the case of the OCAM Agreement, immunities can be waived according to Article 26a – c, in respect of the administrative secretary-general; directors of divisions, and other functionaries by the conference of heads of state acting jointly with the government of the country of the secretary-general; by the chairman of OCAM acting jointly with the government of the country of the particular director and secretary-general after consultation with the governments of the countries of other staff and experts respectively.[35]

With the ECOWAS Treaty, the immunities and privileges stipulated for its entire staff are similar to those accorded by the host government Nigeria, to other diplomatic missions and to international organisations in Lagos and in member states. However, other privileges to be granted by member states in connection with the community shall be determined by the Council of Ministers.[36]

(C) Tax or fiscal privileges

In the course of performing its function, a commodity institution gets to import certain items of necessity. For this reason, it is normally exempt from imposition of taxes and rates relating to the non-beneficial portions and from exchange control. All goods and equipment directly imported for official use, including any publications, are exempt from taxes with the proviso, however, that it complies with the regulations which protect public health and those for the prevention of diseases in plants and animals. However, with regard to goods whose importation and exportation is prohibited or restricted its functionaries enjoy the same privileges and facilities granted to international organisations in the host country. It also benefits from custom duties exemption in respect of the import and export of its publications, moving pictures, films and sound recordings.

Conclusion

We have seen from the study above that the provisions of headquarters agreements are still largely inspired from classical sources or conventional documents, and adopted to soothe particular politico-economic situations. This is to say that the techniques of classical international law and diplomacy are still being largely employed in modern economic international law and diplomacy, because of the absolute non-supranational nature of commodity institutions. They have therefore not developed their specific peculiarities sufficiently enough to make them very distinct from conventional political documents, but share to a very large extent common drafting techniques and terminology proper to economic documents desirable of rapid entry into effect and of encouraging the socio-economic development of signatory states, in order to improve the living standards of their peoples. However, they enjoy some supranational concessions.

7 Tin in International Metallic Diplomacy: Case Study One[1]

INTRODUCTION: NOTES ON THE IMPORTANCE OF TIN

Since the bronze age, tin has been known as one of the best non-ferrous metals. It is unique in the sense that when it coats a piece of steel electrolytically, it is resistant to rust and acids. New uses for tin have been discovered in some fields of application such as cast-iron and steel, electroplated coatings, plastics, paints, industrial fungicides, disinfectants and agriculture.[2] From time immemorial, the Royal Duchy of Cornwall in the United Kingdom is considered to be the Mecca of those who were interested in the tin industry. Prospecting started there probably 2,000 years before the occupation of Great Britain by the Romans in 55 BC. Much had also been said about it after 1066 in various official documents and towards 1198 black tin was said to have been refined. Cornwall was therefore the principal source of supply at the middle of the thirteenth and fourteenth centuries.

The commercial route for tin from Cornwall was through the Column of Hercules to the Mediterranean countries of Greece, Alexandria, Egypt and Rome which were the principal consumers of tin. Today, this current of trade has been completely reversed because tin now comes principally from developing countries (Malaysia, Bolivia, Indonesia, Thailand, Nigeria and Zaïre) and it is exported principally to Europe and the USA. This new current of trade poses some problems in the world market. As developing countries are producers and developed ones are consumers and suppliers of capital, the profits which accrue to producers also come from taxes at exports and other mineral rights paid by the foreign capitalist owners. This is to say that these sources of revenue are very important to their national economies. For instance, in Bolivia, tin represents 74 per cent of her mineral exports. Thus any adverse fluctuation on world prices is bound to have repercussions on their budgetary provisions. In those circumstances, it was difficult for the developing countries to attain the annual rate of growth in revenue as established by the UN Development Programme. But these countries depend enormously on importations of capital equipment and other manufactured products for the implementation of their programme of development. There is also the problem of foreign exchange which is posed, because one actually notices that there is a continuous tendency towards an imbalance in foreign trade, because their importations of foreign goods increase at a faster rate than the profits which accrue to them from the sales of their raw materials to developed countries.[3] As has been pointed out above, raw material industries are chiefly owned by private foreign capitalist interests from the advanced countries, for example tin in Malaysia and Nigeria. Thus if the Tin Agreement has to be properly executed, support from governments and private-interest groups is necessary because any imperfection in the programme of stabilisation of world prices could render a number of individuals jobless and miserable in a given country. It is therefore necessary to co-ordinate policies and objectives. 'If the objectives of groups within a community are contradictory, then there is conflict and the community ceases to exist. A political community is defined by the way in which partly contradictory and partly compatible purposes come to terms.'[4] It is therefore the desire to find equitable compromises to divergent interests in a newly found community established by International Agreements on Commodities that the Tin Agreement is here studied. This agreement, renewable every five years, is entered into by two contracting parties: consumers and producers.

If tin poses some difficult problems on the world market, it is because of its scarcity, geographical localisation, production and consumption. As a result of these its market displays triple characteristics:

1. From the view point of supply and demand, production takes place in developing zones such as Asia, Africa and Latin America (Bolivia), although some developed countries are small producers (6, 322 tons in 1962).
2. From the viewpoint of market structure, it is very sensitive to fluctuations of economic activity. It is for this reason that producers and consumers whose interests are often divergent, have agreed to put their efforts together to find an adequate solution to the market problems of tin. This market has passed through a period of complete economic liberation to that of private 'en-

tentes'. These private 'understandings' were later transformed into international agreements meant to regulate tin movements as regards production, price, stocks, policies, etc. We could therefore say that, after 'ententes', came a period of the Havana Charter and then later that of the International Committee on Tin which gave place to the Tin Council under the aegis of the UN.

3. The demand for tin is more sensitive to variations in revenue than to variations in prices because it is used in the manufacture of finished products such as automobiles, radio sets, engines of all sorts, tinplates, etc. This is to say that its overall demand could change following a drastic change in the demand of its uses. This change could happen either because consumption habits have changed or because distribution of revenue has varied.

SECTION I. DIPLOMATIC NATURE OF TIN CONFERENCES

INTRODUCTION:

At the moment, profound research studies are being carried out under the aegis of the Tin Research Institute in London because tin is a much-needed metal in all growing industries. Because of its rational importance, producers and consumers are concerting all efforts to establish methods of controlling its prices in the interplay of supply and demand. Of all metals, tin happens to be more adaptable to control systems for the following reasons:

1. it is non-perishable;
2. its supply could be controlled particularly, because it cannot be obtained by synthetic methods, although we cannot exclude the possibility of a risk of substitution in certain other uses;
3. it is not easily affected by climatic conditions like agricultural products are;
4. it is an essential compound when used as an industrial alloy;
5. producers are relatively few.

After the First World War (1914–18), trade in tin went through a very difficult period because of a contraction in demand, lack of transport facilities and overproduction in the principal producer countries. There was consequently a fall in prices as for example in 1918, when prices which were at £331 sterling fell to £165 in 1931 with maximal fluctuation of more than 26 per cent on average. Such was the position when many private enterprises asked for state intervention. For example, in 1919 the Federal Government of Malaysia took over the buying of tin and was thus able to increase its prices in 1920 although a little later it became evident that the pursuit of such a policy was not practicable in view of the continuous fall in prices.

(A) Past attempts at stabilisation through 'ententes'

(1) The Bandung Conference and the Association of Tin Producers

Because of the aforementioned difficulties, the governments of the Federation of Malaysia and the Dutch West Indies convened a Bandung Conference in 1921, where a 'Bandung Pool' was constituted. Their action consisted in transferring tin from the world market and stocking it. This was the practice until 1923 when prices rose to £213 per ton and to £227 in 1928, although there was a fall in 1924 (£98). According to the terms of this agreement, each contracting party was forbidden to stock more than 5 per cent of his total monthly stock. If another attempt at stabilising the tin market was made, it was because of the economic depression in European countries whose industries' demand for tin dropped, at a time when producer countries, encouraged by the rising prices of 1926 (£291) and 1927 (£289) were producing more tin. Such was the position when 'The Association of Tin Producers' was formed in June 1929 by Nigeria, Burma, Malaysia and Siam (Thailand) in order to control production. Bolivia and the Dutch West Indies later joined, when they discovered that prices were falling continuously.

(2) The International Committee on Tin

This came into being on 27 February 1931 when the principal producers of tin met in London to draw up an agreement. The first agreement, signed on 1 March 1931 and lasting for three years, was meant to establish an equilibrium between production and consumption with the purpose of preventing fluctuations in prices. The signatories were Nigeria, Burma and Malaysia but when Thailand joined in 1931, 95 per cent of production was already under control. This committee created a 'tin pool' on 24 August 1931. A second agreement, which lasted from 1934 to 1936, was made up of five new members: France, Indo-China, Belgian Congo, Ruanda-Urundi, Cornwall and Portugal. Its purpose was not only to prevent a fall in prices but principally to absorb excess stocks.

(3) The International Tin Study Group (1947)

The post-war period witnessed a scarcity of tin because of the destruction of mines and equipment by the Japanese military invasion of South-East Asia, so that, in spite of an increased production in Nigeria and the Belgian Congo, production was still insufficient for world demand. Thus a Joint Committee was set up from 1942 to 1946 to apportion export quotas until 1947 when the International Tin Study Group was formed to study and find solutions to problems of supply and demand. This was a small group composed for the first time both of consumers and producers. They were, in 1956: Western Germany, Australia, Belgium (Belgian Congo and Ruanda-Urundi), Bolivia, Canada, British dependencies (including Malaysia and Nigeria), USA, France, India, Indonesia, Italy, Japan, Netherlands, UK, Thailand. In 1950, after a working group had drawn up a draft agreement, it recommended that the Secretary General of the UN should convene a conference, which met in October/November 1950. As this group was unable to accept the agreement it adjourned in 1953. This was the group that presented another draft but was later retired with a titular secretary and had all its papers transferred to the International Tin Council in April 1957.

(4) The United Nations Conference

This conference met in two sessions in October 1950 and November 1953 in Geneva. Among governments represented were those of the International Tin Study Group, including the USA who made valuable contributions, while the USSR was an observer. Unfortunately by October/November 1950, while other producer and consumer countries were favourable to a Tin Agreement, the USA expressed the view that the moment had not yet come to establish an agreement. This was because there was a sudden fall in prices in 1953 (£639 and £649 in November and December respectively) during the negotiations. If, by this date, the prices were as high as they were in October–November–

December 1950 (£882, £1,083 and £1,164 respectively) the USA could probably have subscribed more to the cause of establishing an agreement. It was the above-mentioned fall in prices that favoured the approval of the text of the International Agreement on Tin on 9 December 1953 by a plenary session of the conference in Geneva. The USA did not sign this document, although she adopted an attitude which has come to be known as 'benevolent neutrality'.

(5) Interim committee

This was set up during the Geneva Conference in 1953. In 1954–56 it held two sessions during which work preparatory to the formation of the International Tin Council was carried out. On 29 June 1956, it was replaced with a conference of all signatories who decided that the date of the entry into force of the Tin Agreement should be 1 July 1956.

(B) Preparatory conferences under the UN system

Introduction: The preparatory conferences of 1961 and 1966 agreements have a semi-institutional and diplomatic character

Among the techniques used by the UN for the eventual stabilisation of the market of basic commodity products,[5] a place must be reserved for the preparatory conferences and administrative institutions. Most of the private international institutions which intend to undertake such stabilisations appeal to the UN to convene such preparatory conferences because of its enormous diplomatic and technical capacity. Thus the UN has come to have a big role to play in organising institutions with intent to stabilise commodity prices. This has become more formalised since the creation of the UN Conference on Trade and Development in 1964 from whose principles international commodity agreements are now inspired, thus usurping the role formally played by the GATT. This is why we shall examine the diplomatic and quasi-institutional characters of the preceding agreements before analysing, in Section IV, the permanent and administrative institutions of the Tin Council in which binding laws are formulated.

All the agreements on tin since 1956 have applied institutional techniques through preparatory conferences. These are provisional organs adopting an institutional form in which much diplomatic activity is carried out. For instance, the preparatory conferences to the 1961 and 1966 Agreements on Tin were provided with a secretariat and subsidiary organs which were the frameworks within which negotiations were carried out. The necessity for a conciliation between the respective requirements in a negotiation, if they must conserve an intergovernmental feature, must take into account the fears and mistrust of negotiators because the international society itself has not reached a stage of intense solidarity. This explains why provisional institutions conserve a diplomatic character. However, these preparatory conferences, which are quasi-institutions, also carry out profound research on problems posed by virtue of their high degree of technical expertise. The diplomatic atmosphere thus created means that there must be a conciliation between divergent interests if the agreement would have to be eventually signed. This is why it would be worthwhile discovering these characteristics within the two agreements of 1961 and 1966.

(I) The 1961 Tin Agreement

On 12 of March 1959, the Tin Council took the initiative of inviting the Secretary-General of the UN to call an international conference that would study the conditions under which the Tin Agreement of 1956 could be renewed. This initiative *per se* is very diplomatic and justified by virtue of the quasi-universal nature of the UN. Consequently, this request of the Tin Council was transmitted to the Provisional Commission for the Co-ordination of International Agreements on Basic Commodity Products, pursuant to Resolutions 296(XI), 373(XIII) and 557 F(XVIII) of the Economic and Social Council. This commission, in a report dated 8 May 1959 to the Secretary-General of the UN, regretting the absence of certain major consumers of tin in the 1956 agreement, concluded that a conference organised under the aegis of UNO could contribute towards increasing the membership of the Tin Council.

The UN conference of 1960

This conference was held at UNO headquarters in New York from 23 April to 24 June 1960; that is, for 62 days. The above-mentioned commission was responsible for drawing up the timetable and rules of procedure of the conference. The participating countries were 35 in number, out of which 23 were delegations and 12 observers. Their credentials were examined by the Credentials Committee presided over by Mr J. M. Kisch (UK). As it is customary with the UNO whenever she is the organiser of an international conference, the Secretary-General or his representative often declares the conference open. Thus Mr Philippe Seynes, an Under-Secretary of the Economic and Social Affairs Division of the UN, declared the conference open and welcomed all the participants to New York.

This conference set up an *ad hoc* secretariat in which top administrators of both the UN and the Tin Council rendered very useful services. For instance, Mr R. Judd, head of the Commercial Section of the UNO, was Secretary of the conference while Mr William Fox, Secretary of the Tin Council, carried out the functions of a Secretary to the Administrative Committee. The two principal organs of this conference were the Executive and Credentials Committee. What is interesting about these committees is that even observers are given the opportunity to contribute their knowledge, not only because they could later decide to accede to the agreement but because those who are representatives of specialised agencies could lend the weight of their knowledge and experience to these deliberations. These committees often create sub-committees to examine more detailed aspects of problems posed. For instance, the sub-committee of the Executive Committee which sat eleven times received reports from other committees and undertook the drafting of the agreement which was finally adopted on 24 June 1960. Nigeria figured prominently in the Administrative, Economic and Credential Committees.

Countries participating in the conference

There are two principal categories of participating countries: (1) those who are producers and consumers of tin or those whose intention it is to accede later, but temporarily partake in the process of treaty drafting so as to get fully aware of the problems posed; (2) those who express their reservations by remaining as observers and who, like the active participants, could sit in specialised committees.

(A) Representatives

Of the 23 intergovernmental delegations representing the interested states, 6 were those of producers while 17 represented the consumers. The producer states were: the Belgian Congo (Zaire) and Ruanda Urundi, Bolivia, Federation of Malaysia, Federation of Nigeria, Indonesia and Thailand while the consumers were Australia, Belgium, Canada, Denmark, Federal Republic of Germany, France, Guinea, India, Italy, Japan, Mexico, Netherlands, Republic of Korea, Spain, Turkey, United Arab Republic and United Kingdom.

(B) Observers

Austria, Brazil, Cuba, Dominican Republic, Norway, Peru, Rumania, Sweden, USSR, USA, Venezuela and Vietnam.

The delegation[6] of participating countries

The nature of the composition of each delegation reflects to a great extent its importance as a producer or consumer. A delegation could be high-powered because it is a great producer such as Malaysia, or could be scanty because its interests are not great, such as Guinea. A close examination shows that most of the producer representatives are plenipotentiary and extraordinary ambassadors except Nigeria and Belgian Congo (Zaire). The consumer representatives having the rank of ambassadors are Belgium, Federal Republic of Germany and the United Arab Republic. These ambassadorial representations, which contribute very little in a technical negotiation, show the importance which these countries attach to politics rather than to technical expertise. Since these representations are mostly diplomatic it would be necessary to examine some of them.

(A) Represented countries

The countries represented were 23 in number out of which we shall examine only four or five of them.

(I) Producing countries The *Bolivian delegation* was made up of an extraordinary ambassador and two alternates who were themselves of the same rank. The presence of His Excellency, Dr Manuel Barrau, who was later the first Vice-Chairman of the Tin Council for 1962–63, is noteworthy. He was also Chairman from 21 July to 27 October 1962

when Mr George Peter, a quondam Chairman for 1956–62, left for an appointment in the UN. In this delegation there were two technicians, an embassy councillor and a first secretary of their permanent mission in New York.

The *Malaysian delegation* was high-powered by virtue of her being the first world producer of tin. Her representation was made up of an ambassador with full powers, and an alternate, Sir Vincent del Tufo, who died in November 1961. Sir Vincent del Tufo was a personality highly esteemed in the Council of Tin when he became a Malaysian delegate as from 1956. He was a chairman of the Working Group on statistics from 1956–60, first Vice-Chairman from 1959 to 60 and 1961 to 62. In this delegation were also five representatives, three advisers and two other advisers who were joint secretaries.

Nigeria was represented by her delegate to the Tin Council, Mr L. H. Goble, CMG. He was Vice-Chairman of the Tin Council from 1960 to 1961. There were also three alternates: an administrator of the Ministry of Mines and Power, a Chief Deputy Inspector of Mines and Power, and a diplomat of the Nigerian Embassy in New York, Mr P. C. Asiodu. The representation is very important by virtue of its technical expertise and Nigeria's premier position as an African producer. The Nigerian delegation was composed of advisers from the private sector of the tin industry: Mr A. M. Koskinas from the Nigerian Chamber of Mines, Mr J. Ivans Spans from the Nigerian Chamber of Mines in London and Mr J. L. Farrington, the Chairman of the Nigerian Chamber of Mines.

The *Indonesian delegation* was represented by His Excellency Mr Sukardjo Wirjopranoto, an ambassador with full powers and their permanent delegate to New York. He was Vice-Chairman of the third plenary session to this conference. On this delegation was an adviser minister of the Economic Division of the Indonesian Embassy in London, including six ordinary members who were highly qualified experts.

(II) Consuming countries The *Australian delegation* was made up of a diplomat of the Australian High Commission in London, an alternate, an Under-Secretary of the Department of Trade and an adviser from their permanent mission. Although the Australian delegation was not as large as that of Belgium, for instance, she is a greater tin consumer than

the latter. Australian consumption was 3,800 tons (1960), 4,482 tons (1962) and 4,660 tons in 1963 while for the same period Belgium's consumption was 2,800, 3,125 tons and 3,435 tons respectively. Note must be taken of the presence of an important personality, Mr Y. Coppieters Wallant, Head of Belgium's Foreign Trade and Foreign Affairs Ministries. He was Vice-Chairman of the Tin Council from 1963 to 1964.

The *French delegation* was relatively large by virtue of her being the third consumer-member of the agreement (11,050 tons in 1963) after the UK (20,636 tons in 1963) and Japan (15,896 tons in 1963). Her delegation was made up of Mr Pierre Legoux, an honorary Inspector General of Mines who was himself a Vice-Chairman of the Tin Council in 1960–61, two alternate representatives, an Engineer-in-Chief of Mines and a civil servant of the Ministry of Economy and Finance; two advisers, one of whom was a plenipotentiary minister and a second secretary of her permanent mission in New York. To this delegation, political representation seems secondary since it was principally made up of experts.

The *Guinean and Turkish delegations* That of Guinea was composed of two representatives one of whom was a First Secretary and the other an embassy attaché of her permanent mission. The Turkish delegation was far less important than that of Guinea, in spite of her position as a small consumer (750 tons in 1963). Guinea is not even a consumer. Turkey was represented by a commercial adviser to her embassy.

The *Japanese delegation* was very large by virtue of her position as a second member consumer of the agreement (15,896 tons) after the UK (20,636 tons) in 1963. This delegation was entirely made up of experts (technicians) without any political representation, except for the three advisers representing the private sector.

The *UK delegation* was very important because of her position as a first consumer member of the agreement (20,636 tons in 1963). It was technical in composition for it was drawn from various offices like the Commonwealth Office, Board of Trade and diplomatic missions, so that on the whole it was political, economic and social by virtue of the representations of the Commonwealth Relations Office and the Colonial Office.

(B) Observers

These were twelve in number with fifteen delegations, among whom was a lady delegate from Vietnam who was a permanent observer. Most of the delegations were drawn from their permanent missions, in other words, they were experts. The only political representations were Cuba, Venezuela and Vietnam. Among them were also the USSR and the USA who, by their delegations, showed how interested they were in the tin market.

We cannot also underestimate the importance of specialised agencies as regards the application of the agreement because of their financial assistance since the 'Council shall make whatever arrangements are appropriate for consultation and co-operation' with them, pursuant to Article IV, paragraph 20, of the 3rd Agreement. Those specialised agencies who were present as observers were: ILO, FAO, IBRD and IMF.

(C) Chairmanship

The French delegate, Mr George Peter, who was the Chairman of the Tin Council from 1956, was unanimously elected as Chairman of the Conference on 24 May 1960. Two other very important personalities were elected Vice-Chairmen. They were the delegates of Canada and Indonesia, Messrs Harvey and Wirjopranoto who by their great diplomatic experience and their knowledgeability of the problems posed in the tin market, were elected second and first Vice-Chairman respectively. There were two things worthy of note in these elections: (1) Mr Wirjopranoto was elected *in absentia*; (2) the candidates were proposed by non-member representatives of the Tin Council, Germany and Japan, who nominated the Chairman and the Vice-Chairman respectively.

After these elections, the Chairman proposed the setting up of a Credentials Committee composed of Spain, Nigeria, the Netherlands, Federal Republic of Germany and the UK. The proposal was favourably accepted.

At the last plenary session, 24 June 1960, the Chairman of the Conference presented the text of the agreement presented by the Administrative and Economic Committees and approved by Executive Committee for adoption. Mr Legoux (France), in the name of all the delegations of consumer countries, proposed the adoption of the draft agreement. This was supported by Sir Vincent del Tufo (Federation of Malaysia) in the name of all producer members. However, the representatives of Japan and Germany expressed their reservations in the name of their governments, relative to the effect that they would not be bound by this adoption, which they said would be tantamount to 'acceptance'.

During this conference, Mr MacMahon (UK) speaking as a Vice-Chairman of the Tin Council, read out a communiqué approved by the Council on 23 June and which was meant to be published at the end of the conference. Its last paragraph ran thus:

> The Council has recommended to member states to conclude, at the termination of the present International Agreement on Tin, on the 30th June, 1961, a new agreement which would have been examined and approved in May and June 1960 by the United Nations Conference on Tin.

The Chairman, before declaring the conference closed, remarked that the new text of the agreement could serve as a model for future agreements. He thanked the Secretary-General of UNO for having placed the services and the building of UNO at the disposal of the Conference. He officially extended his appreciation to all the representatives of governments and to the personnel of the secretariat of UNO for their welcome co-operation.

(II) The 1966 Agreement

Introduction

On the initiative of the Tin Council on 23 March 1964, the Secretary General of the UN convened a Conference at the New York headquarters from 22 March to 1 July 1965 with the view to renewing the existing agreement on 1 July 1966. As in the case of the previous agreement, the Tin Council request was transmitted to the provisional commission for the Co-ordination of International Agreements on Basic Commodity Products, pursuant to Resolutions 296 (XI), 373 (XIII) and 557F (XVIII) of the Economic and Social Council. In its reply to the Secretary General on 19 November 1964, the chairman of the commission recommended that a UN Conference on Tin be convened in 1965 and that all should be done to prepare the necessary basic documents in conjunction with the Tin Council Secretariat. Thus, the Tin Council had to submit a working paper on a draft agreement.

Contrary to the procedure followed in the previous agreement, this conference was convened under the auspices of the UN Conference on Trade and Development. This procedure was in accordance with Resolution 1955 (XIX) of the General Assembly of UNO, taken at its 19th Session, which created UNCTAD as one of its organs. Pursuant to this resolution, UNCTAD was empowered to take any necessary measures with the competent organs of the UN with the view to negotiating and adopting any multilateral legal instruments within the fields of trade.

The opening conference

At the first plenary session Mr Perce R. Judd, Director of the Commodities Division of the UN, welcomed all the delegates to the conference in the name of Mr Paul Prebisch, Secretary General of UNCTAD, who could not attend. Mr Harold W. Allen, Chairman of the Tin Council, was unanimously elected as Chairman of the Conference while Messrs Eduardo Mendez Pereyra (Bolivia) and Theodore Idzumbuir (Democratic Republic of the Congo) were elected first and second Vice-Chairmen respectively.

As in the previous agreement, an Executive Committee, composed of the representatives and observers, was created. This committee held ten meetings, during which it set up the Credentials Committee composed of Canada, Spain, Nigeria, Netherlands and the Federal Republic of Germany. Mr S. O. Soyode (Nigeria) was elected chairman.

Countries participating at the conference The increase in the number of participants to this conference compared to that of 1960, is a clear indication that countries are becoming more interested in the tin market. Out of the 48 participants, 28 were delegates and 20 observers. All their credentials were examined under the Chairmanship of Mr S. O. Adebo (Nigeria).

The representatives were the following: Australia, Belgium, Bolivia, Canada, Republic of Congo (Zaire), Denmark, Federal Republic of Germany, France, India, Israel, Italy, Japan, Lebanon, Liberia, Malaysia, Mexico, Netherlands, Nigeria, Panama, Republic of Korea, Ruanda, Southern Rhodesia, Spain, Thailand, Turkey, UK, USA, Yugoslavia (total 28).

Two facts retain our attention during this conference: (1) the absence of the United Arab Republic, Guinea and Indonesia who were present at the 1960 Conference; (2) the participation of eight new countries: Israel, Lebanon, Liberia, Panama, Ruanda, Southern Rhodesia, USA and Yugoslavia. The USA was an observer in the 1960 conference.

It is worth noting that the Nigerian delegation was made up of His Excellency Chief S. O. Adebo, Extraordinary and Plenipotentiary Ambassador to the Permanent Mission; two alternates, Messrs S. O. Soyode, Commercial Attaché of the Nigerian High Commission in London, E. A. Ifaturoti, Chief Inspector of Mines, and Mr M. E. Whitefield, Chairman of the Nigerian Chamber of Mines.

The US representation was largest by virtue of her being the first world consumer of tin. Her delegation was made up of Mr George R. Jacobs, Deputy Director of the State Department, 16 alternates, 11 of whom were representing private commercial interests and 5 the state administration. This importance in private representation shows the enormous influence which private American commercial companies have over her national tin policy.

Observers. The observers were: Austria, Brazil, Bulgaria, Cameroun, Colombia, Cuba, Czechoslovakia, Ecuador, Finland, Ghana, Hungary, Iraq, Kuwait, Norway, Philippines, Poland, Portugal, Sweden, Switzerland, USSR (total 20).

Among these were some who participated as observers in 1960 but who were absent in 1965, except the USA who had become an active participant. They are Vietnam, USA, Rumania, Peru, Dominican Republic and Venezuela, that is six in number. The 14 others who attended for the first time in 1965 were: Bulgaria, Camerouns, Colombia, Czechoslovakia, Ecuador, Finland, Ghana, Hungary, Iraq, Kuwait, Philippines, Poland, Portugal and Switzerland. It is interesting to note the increasing interest shown in the stabilisation of the tin market by the presence of the People's Democracies such as Bulgaria, Czechoslovakia, Hungary and Poland. While Yugoslavia actively participated in the negotiations only Czechoslovakia signed the 3rd International Agreement on Tin.

We must also note the presence of Ghana, Cuba, and a few others who, although non-producers of tin, took part in the 'travaux préparatoires'.

Finally among the delegations were the following specialised agencies: ILO, IBRD; IMF and GATT. The FAO which was represented in the 1960 Conference evacuated its seat for GATT in that of 1965. This is, however, understandable because the FAO is a purely agricultural organisation. But the most interesting event there was the presence of a new representation, that of the EEC, by virtue of their increasing interest in the tin market. However, their representation was of a consultative capacity.

Conclusion

What strikes the student of this type of economic diplomacy most, is the difference in method in the procedure of adopting the draft agreement of 1965 compared to that of 1960. In the final agreement it was the chairman of the conference who proposed the adoption of the draft agreement already examined by the Executive Committee including the legal and drafting commitees; while in the 2nd Agreement of 1960, it was the French delegate, M Legoux, who proposed the adoption in the name of consumers. It was supported by Sir Vincent del Tufo (Malaysia) on behalf of the producers. What the chairman did at the beginning of the conference, was simply to draw the attention of all the participants to the draft agreement. This innovation in method was simply due to the desire for rapidity of action and the avoidance of certain implicatory formalities. Besides, what contributed to facilitating the adoption of the draft was the unquestionable dexterity with which the Chairman conducted the meeting and this was true of the 1965 agreement.

SECTION II. VOTING PROCEDURES IN THE THIRD AGREEMENT

Although the voting procedures are inspired from the UNCTAD Conference of 1964, they conform to the additional principles on control measures, established by Article 63b of the Havana Charter of 24 March 1948.[7]

(A) NORMAL PROCEDURES IN THE DISTRIBUTION OF VOTES ACCORDING TO ARTICLE IV, PARAGRAPH, C, 13–18

According to this Article, the total number of votes held by members of the Tin Council is 2,000; 1,000 each for the producers and consumers taken separately. The contributions made to the Administrative Account are based on the number of votes held (Article V, paragraph 3).

(i) Producing countries

Producer votes are re-determined (a) yearly during the re-distribution of one-twentieth of the percentage of each producer country and (b) on accession or withdrawal of any participating producer country.

According to this procedure, 1,000 votes are divided among producers in such a way that each country gets an initial vote of 5. Thereafter, the remaining votes are calculated in the following way: the percentage of world production of each country in direct proportion to the total percentages is multiplied by the difference between the total of the initial number of votes (35) and the total number of votes held by the producer countries (1,000) pursuant to Annex A or to the provisions of Article VII, paragraph 10.[8] Consequently, the number of votes for each country will be the initial number of votes plus the supplementary votes. For example, the votes for Nigeria:

$$\frac{6.55}{100} \times \frac{(1000-35)}{1} = 63.2075$$

i.e. approximately 68 votes after adding the five initial votes.

(ii) Consuming countries

The agreement stipulates that a total of 1,000 votes held by the consumers shall be distributed amongst them:

(a) annually on the basis of the consumption of each country during the last three years;
(b) on accession of a new consumer member; and
(c) on withdrawal of a consumer member.

Consequently, the number of votes held by a consuming country is equal to its five initial votes plus supplementary votes based on tonnage. These supplementary votes are calculated thus: the proportion in tonnage of each consuming country in direct proportion to the total number of tons consumed by consumer countries, as they appear in Annex B, is multiplied by the difference between the total number of votes and the total of the initial number of votes. For example, for Germany in Annex

B her total number of votes =

$$\frac{11{,}726}{147{,}451} \times \frac{1000-105}{1} = 71+5 = 76$$

that is 76 votes without fractional votes.

The voting method among consumers invites four observations:

1. If there are more than 30 consuming countries the total number of initial votes must not exceed 150, with each consumer country having as initial votes 'the highest whole number consistent' with the above requirement of 150 votes.

2. The council must determine and publish the tonnage of a country in any of the four categories of legal persons stated below:

(i) a country that does not figure in Annex B, but has ratified, approved or accepted the agreement;
(ii) a country that expresses its intention to ratify, accept or approve the agreement;
(iii) a country that accedes to the agreement as a consumer country;
(iv) a country that changes its category from a producing country to a consuming country pursuant to Article III, paragraph 3.

In any of the above cases, it is the council that is competent to fix the date of entry into force of these tonnages pursuant to Article IV, as if it was a tonnage established in Annex B of the agreement. Here, it is worthy of note that a simple intention to ratify, accept or approve the agreement produces a legal effect which gives right to determining and publishing the tonnage of a country in the above categories in the same capacity as that possessed by countries who had already ratified, accepted or approved the agreement.

3. The council may amend Annex B during its first meeting and must publish the revised Annex which shall enter into force *in situ* for the purpose of Article IV.

4. At the meetings of the council which shall take place during the second quarter of each year, the council must re-examine the tin consumption figures of each consuming country during each of the past three calendar years. It shall publish an average consumption, and the revised tonnages applicable as from 1 of July which follows, as if they were the tonnages established in Annex B.

The above procedures in distributing votes make room for four other remarks:

1. no participating country shall have more than 450 votes;

2. fractional votes are not admissible;
3. decisions of the council are taken by a simple distributed majority unless otherwise stated, and any abstentions are not regarded an affirmative or a negative vote; a delegate cannot divide his votes, on voting;
4. if one or more of the countries listed in Annex A or B fails to ratify or notify intention to ratify, accept or approve the agreement and the total number of votes becomes less than 1,000, the difference will be divided among the other participating countries (consumers and producers) as the case may be, as nearly in proportion to the votes they already hold, less in each case the initial votes, as is consistent with there being no fractional votes (Article IV, paragraph 17). This also applies to Articles V, X, XIX, XX, XXI, XXII or XXIV.

(B) EXCEPTIONAL PROCEDURES IN THE RE-DETERMINATION OF VOTES DURING THE APPLICATION OF THE AGREEMENT

(I) Annual procedures for re-determining the percentages of producing countries according to Annex G

The agreement provides for a new re-determination of votes at the first meeting of the council after the agreement enters into force. This procedure shall be divided into several stages of re-determination.

First re-determination

This takes place during the first meeting of the council by attributing new percentages of votes to producing countries according to their production during the last four quarters. However these four quarters must not have been declared a 'control period', thus the percentages and votes of producing countries were re-determined during the first meeting of the Council in London on 1 July 1966 within the scope of the 3rd Agreement, as shown in Tables 7.1 and 7.2.

TABLE 7.1 Percentage and votes of producer countries

Country	*Percentage*	*Votes*
Bolivia	16·92	172
Republic of Congo Kinshasa	4·56	50
Indonesia	10·79	111
Malaysia	46·74	450
Republic of Nigeria	7·01	74
Thailand	13·98	143
TOTAL	100·00	1,000

Source: Press Communiqué of the Council of 7 July 1966.

TABLE 7.2. Votes of consumer countries as at 1 July 1966

Country	*Votes*	*Country*	*Votes*
Australia	57	Italy	70
Austria	12	Japan	197
Belgium/Luxemburg	40	Korea	8
Canada	60	Mexico	19
Czechoslovakia	33	Netherlands	45
Denmark	12	Spain	23
France	127	Turkey	14
India	55	United Kingdom	228
	TOTAL = 1,000 votes		

Source: Press Communiqué of the Council of 7 July 1966.

Second and third re-determinations

These are made at yearly intervals following the first re-determination on condition, however, that no period subsequent to the four quarters preceding the first re-determination has been declared to be a 'control period'.

The method of re-determination is as follows: the percentages are calculated according to the production of each country during the last period of production (for which figures are available) after the renewal of the agreement by 24 months for the second re-determination and 36 months for the third. This procedure is valid for future re-determinations except after a period declared 'control period'.

(II) Future re-determinations after a period has been declared a 'control period' according to Rule 3 of Annex G of the agreement

When a period has been declared a 'control period', there will be no re-determination of percentages until after a further four consecutive quarters for which production figures are available. This is the condition under which Rule 7 of Annex G established the following procedure:

1. for the first re-determination after this control period, percentages shall be in direct proportion to the total tin production of each producer country in the latest 12 consecutive calendar months for which figures are available and in the four quarters immediately preceding the control period;
2. for future re-determinations the procedure as above will be followed for a period of 24 and 36 consecutive months for which figures are available as long as a period has not been declared a 'control period'.

(III) Voting procedures during council meetings

According to the voting rules established in the Rules of Procedure No. 17, voting is carried out by roll call except on a contrary decision of the council when a delegate manifests a refusal. Although this procedure, meant to promote rapidity in decision-making, conforms with the purposes and objectives of the agreement, since it could produce a contrary decision at the request of a delegate, it would be most desirable to resort to a secret voting system so that delegates could be more frank in the expression of their votes. According to the Rules of Procedure, the roll call could begin with any group of delegates from the following countries: UK, France and Spain.

Finally it is the duty of the Chairman of the Council to release the results, whether negative or positive, including abstentions. These results must be entered into the minutes. It is also understood that in voting, each delegate must put in all the votes held by him for or against a motion, or abstain. The votes of a delegate are indivisible. Most important is that all council decisions are taken with a simple distributed majority[9] except on contrary decision of the council according to Article IV, paragraph 18.

(C) LEGAL CONSEQUENCES OF A REFUSAL TO APPLY THESE PROCEDURES BY PRODUCING COUNTRIES, WHO ARE MEMBERS OF THE AGREEMENT

This is where the coercive powers of the council appear. They are stipulated in Annex G of the agreement.

1. Any producer country which fails to communicate its production figures for any period of 12 months to the council, one month after a minimum of four countries have done so, would have its production, for that period of 12 months, calculated by multiplying by 12 its average monthly rate of production for any period for which figures are available and from this 5 per cent would be deducted.

2. For the purposes of re-determination of percentages, production figures before 42 months preceding the date of re-determination will not be recognised as valid.

3. The council is empowered to reduce the percentage of any producer country if it fails to export the total authorised by the provisions of paragraph 4 of Article VII, with the view to sharing it among other producers 'in proportion to their percentages in any revised table of percentages which may be published'. This measure also applies to any increased total of exports which this country must have accepted in accordance with paragraph 7 of Article VII and in this case, the council could increase the total authorised exports for the control period in question by a fraction which, in its opinion, 'will ensure that the total permissible export amount required will in fact be exported' (Article VII, paragraph 8b). However, this reduction shall not take place under four conditions:

(i) If the producer country in question renounces, in conformity with the 'consent' required by Article VII, paragraph 7, a part of the total permissible exports. In such a case, the council could be more lenient during its moment of decision-making.

(ii) That this renunciation be brought to the knowledge of the council in a declaration 'not later than one calendar month after the date upon which such permissible export amount has become effective' (Article VII, paragraph 8a).

(iii) With the exception of the first re-determination carried at the council's first meeting, the percentage of a producing country cannot be more than 10 per cent during any period of 12 months (Article VII, paragraph 8a).

(iv) In accordance with Article VII, paragraph 6b, certain circumstances are considered exceptional, particularly if they impede the application of the agreement as regards exports. Although any country could determine what its exceptional circumstances are, it is still the duty of the council to 'waive or modify the full application of the rules' by a distributed two-thirds majority. These exceptional circumstances are set out in Rule 13 of Annex G, thus:
   - (a) during a national disaster;
   - (b) when big labour crises paralyse the tin industry for a considerable length of time;
   - (c) when there is a serious interruption in energy supply or (in the case of Bolivia) transports on any of the principal communication systems linking the coastal areas. This calls for two remarks:
      - (i) Bolivia has been specifically mentioned here not only because of her importance as a second world producer, but also due to the frequent military operations which take place there between her rebels and government forces;
      - (ii) this provision is also applicable to any country with the same political unrests as Bolivia. Thus, it is flexible and conforms to a socio-political reality.

(D) ADMINISTRATIVE AND FINANCIAL COMPETENCE OF THE TIN COUNCIL AND THE VOTING PROBLEM ARISING THEREFROM

(I) Administrative and financial competencies and voting problems

Pursuant to Article V, the council keeps two important accounts for the execution and administration of the agreement. In the administrative account are kept all office expenses of the council including the salaries of the chairman, the secretary, the manager and the staff. The council also keeps the accounts of the buffer stock in which all expenses on its operations or transactions are entered as well as expenses in respect of storage, commission, insurance, telephone and telegraph facilities.

As a result of these competencies, the council at its first meeting after the entry into force of this agreement shall 'determine what its financial year shall be and approve estimates of contributions and expenditure on the administrative account for the period between the date of entry into force of the agreement and the end of the financial year' (Article V, paragraph 2a – b).[10] Here appears a discretionary power of the council because it also possesses the power to approve a supplementary estimate for the rest of the year, if it appears that the amount already approved is insufficient (paragraph 2b). After this exercise, the council could now fix the contribution of each member country, to the administrative account, in sterling. This contribution shall subsequently be paid in full to the secretary of the council by each country upon notice of assessment after it has been calculated on the basis of votes held. Thus for every vote held,[11] a participating country shall pay one two-thousandth of the required total, provided that no country shall pay less than £100 sterling for any financial year. This payment could be effected either in sterling or in any money freely convertible into sterling, on the London foreign exchange market.

This provision of the agreement calls for a comment because this method of payment conforms to the principles adopted in a weighted voting system. It is perfectly conceivable that a country holding more votes in the council, and consequently wielding more political influence because it could direct the course of decision-making, should contribute more financially to the administrative coffers of the council, and vice-versa. Nevertheless, this system presents a very important disadvantage, in the sense that the proper functioning of the agreement shall be dependent upon the possibility or the impossibility of obtaining, on any given question, the favourable votes of a country with the highest quota. Such a country could paralyse the proper functioning of the agreement, as we shall see later, at a time when international economic conjuncture dictates a favourable voting. A refusal to cast its votes in conjunction with another member in the same community of interest would produce the same effect as when they cast their total votes, depending on their options on specific issues. For instance a recommendation of an amendment which requires a distributed two-third majority[12] could easily be thwarted by the refusal of the most important producer and consumer with a little sympathy from another member. This is also true of a simple distributed majority based on the weighted system principle. This problem will become more acute on membership of the USA, to whom 344 votes are allotted in Annex B of the agreement for being the largest world consumer. She shall find herself in a position of force and at this moment, the council shall no doubt be urged to seek another method of approach in working the mechanism of the agreement. This is why it would be desirable to have contributions to the adminstrative account shared equally amongst producing and consuming members of the agreement. The adoption of such a highly desirable system, if we must establish an equilibrium of forces between participating countries, will not, however, entirely eliminate all the difficulties on the path of developing countries. For example, the difficulties arising from the desire of developing countries for membership of all important organisations of economic and social nature. A question arises at this point as to whether they could continue to make the usual heavy financial contributions to all these organisations in spite of fluctuating advantages, particularly when their interests as producers or consumers are very minimal? Thus, in order to solve this contradiction, which arises from a desire to make all the institutional mechanism function adequately with the purpose of attaining the set objective, we shall propose two possible recommendations for commodity products generally:

1. Certain markets could be declared 'selective markets' consisting of important basic products which suffer very frequent fluctuations. Any agreement concluded in this category should incorporate the practice of the principle of equal votes and equal financial contributions from all participating countries. Other markets would be declared 'non-selective'.
2. All financial requirements either for 'non-selective' or 'selective' markets, or both, should be supplied from the administrative budget of the UN with increased quota contributions from member states. This will enable contracting parties to any form of agreement, to practise the principle of equal votes. Some countries could then group themselves together in order to exercise the same votes.

In this way, all powers on voting will be equal and thus conform *stricto senso*, to the majority rule, the nature of which is such that no conflict arises as members, having entered into the organisation voluntarily, become equally bound and equally exposed to the risk of being beaten by the majority during any voting exercise.[13] This voting system will provoke a return to normal classical method of negotiations which will replace power politics and consequently favour a true expression of will in terms of equality in number of votes. In order to support this principle, we shall draw from the speech of the Indonesian delegate made at the third plenary session of the United Nations Preparatory Conference in May 1960. This delegate[14] mentioned that according to the 1956 Agreement on Tin, export percentages were fixed by a decision taken at simple majority of the members and this enabled certain powerful groups to determine the policy adopted to the disadvantage of his country (Indonesia). He then urged the conference to examine whether this non-equitable procedure could be maintained. It is the desirability for a weighted system that is being seriously questioned here. At this juncture another striking example is necessary: during the first meeting of the council in July 1961, the floor and ceiling prices in the 2nd Agreement were the subjects of intense discussion. The producers, establishing a common front, proposed an increase in floor prices from £730 to £880 and in ceiling prices from £880 to £1000 per ton. This proposal, when put to vote, was defeated because consumers could not obtain the simple majority required of them. Nevertheless, the members of the council generally agreed that the margin of prices existing at that time did not conform to the objectives of the agreement. Consequently in January 1962, when this proposal was re-examined, the council thought it proper to increase the floor price from £730 to £790 and the ceiling price from £880 to £965 sterling. At this point, we are compelled to ask ourselves two questions:

1. Would the consumers have voted favourably for a price level inferior to that originally asked for by the producers? This seems probable because the consumers had to re-examine the producer's proposal later, and in this case, the producers could have studied the possibility of a negotiable compromise before voting in 1961.
2. Was the voting pattern of the consumer countries an expression of a simple demonstration of force or a test of the producers' wit? This is again probable, because they seemed quite awake to the importance of their votes as a counter-weight.

Whatever the case might be, it is crystal clear from the above analysis that a simple majority calculated on the basis of a weight system is a double-edged weapon capable of paralysing the proper functioning of the agreement for two reasons:

1. Before 1961 producing countries made great and justifiable sacrifices in reducing their productive capacity through export restrictions.
2. After 1961, when the need for tin started to grow, one could have expected a consequent reflexion of this need in terms of sufficiently high prices. But contrarily, by August 1967 prices were fluctuating

just at the floor price until they fell below this level where the stock manager had to be compelled to support the prices through buying in the open market.

From the above, we could conclude that the problem of inadequate functioning of the agreement is not principally that of non-appurtenance of the USA to the Council of Tin but that of a defect in the system of contributions to the administrative accounts and in the voting system which give greater importance to power politics rather than to economic realism. This observation does not, however, cloud the necessity for America's immediate membership of the council if an effective world control of the tin trade has to be accomplished. In this respect, we must not forget the necessity for the control of her liquidation policy, under the aegis of a multilateral community of interests. This observation rather recognises the importance of not throwing the responsibility for the weakness of the agreement exclusively on a third party because we must always aspire to make it workable even in the non-membership of this third party, which for the purposes of this analysis is the USA. Finally, it would be highly desirable if the council ceases to borrow for the purposes of the adminstrative account either from national or international banks, as this does not solve the problem of unilateral contribution of producer countries to the said account. The only laudable source of financing therefore remains the administrative account of the UN, to which both consumers and producers would be accountable.

(II) Sanctions arising from contributions to the administrative accounts

An important problem which arises from these contributions is that of *sanctions*. The sanctions which follow a refusal to contribute into the coffers of the account have conferred a true coercive power in the hands of the council so that the agreement could be honoured. Thus, the council is empowered to deprive any participating country of its voting rights at meetings if it had not made its contributions to the administrative account 'within six months of the date of notice of assessment' (Article V, paragraph 5). This power goes further to deprive the said country of any other rights held in the agreement, 'including such proportion of its rights to participation', on liquidation of the buffer stock in accordance with Article XIII, if within a period of 12 months it has not made his contribution. This power is an expression of a sense of justice and proportionality by the council because 'this proportion of the rights of participation' deprived of the said country must be 'equivalent to the unpaid contribution' (paragraph 5). It is however understood that the said country shall be re-established in its proper rights after honouring its financial obligations.

If the duty of the council is to publish 'as soon as possible' audited administrative and buffer stock accounts at the end of each financial year, the buffer stock accounts have a special treatment. They must not be published earlier than three months after the end of the appropriate financial year to which they relate. The expression 'as soon as possible' guarantees to the council a wide field of action and reveals an inherent flexibility, because for the two above cases, their publications could take place any time after the three months indicated. It will therefore be correct to say that these flexibilities take into account certain technical difficulties likely to arise at the end of the financial year. Finally, all expenses incurred by delegates and their alternates, including advisers, are not the responsibilities of the council but those of their respective governments. Such expenses include travel and lodging of delegates when they are attending council or committee meetings.

SECTION III. FUNCTIONING MECHANISM OF THE TIN AGREEMENTS: SOURCE OF LEGAL OBLIGATIONS

All the agreements on tin signed under the aegis of the UN, to the present day, are provided with two mechanisms for stablising prices: a buffer stock and an export control mechanism. But before analysing them it would be necessary to examine the functioning principles of these agreements.

(1) THE FUNCTIONING PRINCIPLES OF THE 1956, 1961 AND 1966 AGREEMENTS

In order to appreciate better the working principles of these agreements, we shall first of all examine briefly the evolution of price margins as they emanate from the working of these agreements.

(a) Evolution of price margins

The 1953 Agreement was ratified on 1 July 1956 and up to 30 June 1961 the price margins of this agreement were only modified once. This was in 1957 when the Tin Council increased the floor price from £640 to £730, leaving the ceiling price at its original level of £880. During the period of the 2nd Agreement, 1 July 1961–30 June 1966, the price margins in the

TABLE 7.3 Price margins: 1st revision of the 1956 Agreement

	Up to 22 March 1957 in £sterling per ton	*After 22 March 1957 in £sterling per ton*	*Intervention of the buffer stock*
Ceiling price	–880	880–	Could sell if it has tin.
Upper third	800–880	830–880?	May sell.
Middle third	720–800	780–830	No action unless council decides otherwise.
Lower third	640–720	730–780	May buy.
Floor price	–640	730–	Buys if it has funds.

TABLE 7.4 Subsequent revisions (figures in £ sterling per ton)

2nd Revision (12 Jan. 1962)	*3rd revision (4 Feb. 1962)*	*4th revision Nov. 1964*	*5th revision (1 July 1966)*	*Powers and duties of stock manager*
Ceiling price 965	1000	1200	1400	Must sell if he has cash.
Upper sector 910–965	950–1000	–	1300–1400	May sell.
Middle sector 850–910	900–950	–	1200–1300	No action unless the council decides otherwise.
Lower sector 790–850	850–900	–	1100–1200	May buy.
Floor price 790	850	1000	1100	Must buy if he has cash.

Sources: *Tin Council Report 1963–64*, p. 11.
Press Communiqué of the Tin Council of 7 July 1966.

agreement were revised three times. The 3rd Agreement of 1 July 1966 did not come into effect until its price margins were revised and this was the fifth time since the 1956 Agreement (See Tables 7.3 and 7.4).

(b) The buffer stocks

Before examining how the agreements function in practice, we shall now examine their functioning principles.

(i) The functioning principles

The 3rd International Agreement, like the two preceding ones, is provided with two mechanisms: the buffer stock and an export control system. The total contributions of producer countries to the buffer stock is established at 20,000 tons in the 3rd Agreement as it was in the 2nd. The 1st Agreement provided for 25,000 tons. The total amount of contributions (20,000 tons) in the 2nd Agreement is made up thus: 12,500 tons in tin metal and the equivalent of 7,500 tons in cash established at floor price, unless the Council of Tin decides otherwise in its first meeting. In the 3rd Agreement, the total of 20,000 tons is made up thus: one-half is due on entry into force of the agreement while the other half would be due on a date decided upon by the Council.[15] The contribution of the portion in tin metal must be made not later than three months from the date of such a decision. The 3rd Agreement, like the 2nd, grants producer countries the possibility of transferring tin metal from the buffer stock of the 2nd Agreement on condition, however, that the country in question gives its consent. These contributions, made on the basis of percentages established in Annex A of the agreement, are re-examined during the first meeting of the Tin Council according to the provisions of Article VII, paragraph 6 and Annex G.

The operations of the buffer stock fall within a margin of prices between a ceiling and floor price divided into three sectors. The manager of the buffer stock must sell tin at his disposal, at a recognised market price or at London market price as soon as the world price is equal to or above the ceiling price, until prices fall below this level or his stocks are exhausted. He could also sell when the prices fall within the upper third. He could buy tin when the price is equal to or below the floor and also within the lower third structure. But immediately the price falls within the middle third, the buffer stock manager could neither buy nor sell until he has been authorised by the council. In the 2nd Agreement of 1961, the majority required for this authorisation was stricter than in the 1st Agreement because it needed a distributed majority of two-thirds. The 3rd Agreement does not qualify this majority and in this case, it must be a simple distributed majority as stated in Article IV, paragraph 18. According to Article VI, paragraph 2 of the 3rd Agreement, the ceiling and floor prices are those in force at the expiration of the 2nd Agreement, but in practice this was not so because its margins were revised.

(ii) Functioning of the agreements in practice

To determine whether these agreements are functioning properly or not, we shall have to examine the price behaviour in respect of the buffer stock.

(A) Prices and the buffer stock

The role which the buffer stock plays depends on the movement of prices in the world market. It sells tin metal to the world market when prices become too high and buys when they fall very low, in accordance with the levels of intervention which we have already examined above. This is why we shall only have to study how world prices react on the functioning of the buffer stock and vice-versa.

(i) Period characterised by export control (1956 –60)

The buffer stock did not intervene by buying tin during the first nine months of this period because the world price was between the upper third and the middle third margins, but its action became very necessary at the end of March 1957 when the floor price was revised from £640 to £730. This revision brought the price between the middle third and the lower third structures where the buffer stock manager is expected to buy tin in order to raise prices by creating scarcity, thus preventing a continuous fall in prices and making him the stockholder of a greater quantity of tin needed to combat excessive rise in prices at the ceiling. For the first time since the 1956 Agreement the world price fell to the floor price (£730) at the end of 1957 due to Russian exports into

Western European markets and to a reduction in the USA consumption.

According to Article IX, paragraph 2e of the 1956 Agreement, the buffer stock manager must buy tin at floor price,[16] whenever the London market price falls below this level or it is at this level, until the market price rises above it. The council could not impose its control on exports until 15 December 1957 when the stock held a minimum of 10,000 tons of tin metal required to enable it to act. Thereafter, although exports were reduced, the European market was still flooded. This obliged the buffer stock manager to buy at a rate of 1,000 tons per week until he exhausted all his available funds. Because of the financial difficulties[17] thus provoked, following the provisions of the agreement, producers had to contribute the equivalent of 5,000 tons in monetary value (£3,650,000). This enabled the stock manager to accumulate a total of 15,000 tons by the end of December 1957. However, because of the financial difficulties of the manager, producers were authorised by their governments to establish a special fund. This enabled the manager to accumulate a total of 22,440 tons when prices were between £730 and £740 so that by 30 June 1958 the stock held 23,300 tons. However, after a heavy buying period between January and June 1958 by the manager, he refused to continue this policy on 18 September 1958. The consequences were disastrous, following degradation in prices. The London market was closed in the afternoon of that day with a fall by £90 and the New York market price fell from 0·94 to 0·86 dollars per lb. The Tin Council had no alternative other than to negotiate with the Russians on a possible reduction of their export quota into the Western European market. This quota was established with their consent at 13,500 tons. Thus as from January–February 1959 prices began to soar until the special fund got exhausted. It was only at this point that stocks of tin held by the buffer stock were sold into the market to control excessive rises in prices and to maintain an equilibrium between prices and the fund. In spite of the labour strikes in the USA, prices were maintained between £720 and £795 because of the demand from other countries. It is noteworthy that the 2,500 tons of tin from the non-commercial stocks of the UK sold towards the end of the third quarter of 1959, were subjected to the same sales conditions as those from the buffer stock, thus stabilising the London market price at £795 at the end of the fourth quarter.

As from 1960, irregularities in demand about fluctuations in prices particularly as from 30 June 1960 when the council decided not to allow any further interventions at the middle sector of the price margins. Straits tin fluctuated between £784 and £800 with a sudden rise on 30

June 1960, to £807. Two reasons explain this rise, increase in consumer demand and a reduction in production and in stocks as foreseen by statistics. In spite of the rumours as to a possible increase in the ceiling and floor prices and in the sales of stocks, prices remained high in such a way that by 7 June 1961, the price was already threatening the ceiling at which point the buffer stock manager is expected to intervene with sales of tin. On 21 June 1961, when the buffer stock exhausted its stocks of tin, the price shot above the ceiling.

In conclusion, a close observation of the evolution of prices at this period (1956–61) shows that the working mechanism of the buffer stock is a very delicate one because the moment its funds are exhausted, the buffer manager finds it impossible to control prices. This is the problematic aspect of its functioning. The solution to this problem depends therefore on the eventual contributions of producers and consumers. It is also noteworthy that statistics play a big part in determining the behaviour of the International Tin Market and that non-member countries of the agreement affect the proper functioning of the buffer stock with their sales at a time when these could be detrimental to producer interests.

(ii) Period characterised by fluctuations in prices

Because tin in the buffer stock of the 1st Agreement was exhausted before it expired, nothing was transferred to the 2nd Agreement. Thus it became necessary to make contributions in money equivalent of 20,000 tons of tin metal because tin was scarce in the international market. With scarcity came rises in prices, but as the buffer stock had no tin metal to combat this tendency, it became a great problem. If prices systematically fell later, it was because the USA had announced their intention to dispose of a surplus of 164,000 tons of tin metal from their strategic stockpile. Consequently the London market price fell from £960 to £910 while in the USA the price fell to £845 when the American Congress authorised the sales of 50,000 tons. This brought the price to the lower sector (£790–£850) where the buffer stock manager may buy if he has money in his coffers. The price rose slightly, oscillating between £858 and £874, when he decided to act. But prices continued to fall with the sales of the General Services Administration at a rate of 200 tons a week until about the end of October 1962 when the Cuban crisis effected a price increase. At the end of December the buffer stock manager had bought about 3,270 tons from the £15½ million put at his disposal, but prices were still low until demand from Socialist countries brought the level to between £910 and £965. For the year 1962–63 the buffer stock bought 3,275 tons and sold 1,940 tons with an insufficient quantity of 1,335 tons left behind. A continuous increase in price for 1963–64 towards the ceiling (£1,000) exhausted the buffer stock of its tin on 28 October 1963. This provoked an increase in the ceiling and floor prices, from £790–£965 in 1962 to £850–£1,000, when the Tin Council met on 4 December 1963. But this measure did not seem to have stopped the continuous increase in prices which readily reached £1,225 in the London market.

(B) The weakness of the buffer stock

The weakness of the buffer stock stems not only from the impotence of the agreement when its stocks of tin and money are exhausted, but also from the very fact that the method of contributions to its coffers is faulty and does not conform to a reality. Contributions are only made to the buffer stock by producer countries while the advantages derived from its functioning accrue to both producers and consumers. This is to say that such one-sided contributions are illogical; much more so that they are so high. It was for this reason that the contributions which were the equivalent of 25,000 tons in the 1st Agreement of 1956 were reduced to 20,000 tons in the 2nd Agreement of 1961. If we consider the fact that, in spite of producer contributions world prices were still unfavourable, we cannot help asking ourselves what advantages accrue to producers from their contributions. This was why the Malaysian delegate Mr Ramani remarked during the fifth session of the preparatory conference in New York in 1965, that only the producer suffers from the difficulties of the buffer stock. He went on to ascertain that the principles from which the negotiators were inspired were those which gave more to those who had, and took more from those who gave. The producer, condemned to the old floor price, is again forced to grant subsidy to consumers by extracting the cost of maintaining prices between the ceiling and floor levels, from his meagre resources. Surely, Mr Ramani did not give the impression that producer countries do not draw benefits from their contributions, but maintained that in the final analysis, consumer countries have proved themselves better negotiators following the classical definition of a diplomatic success which consists in taking from the other all that one desires without ever letting loose what he has firmly in his grasp. This was also the view expressed by the delegate of

Thailand, Mr Sethaput, during the second plenary session of the preparatory conference in New York in 1960. Even though he expressed the view that the 1956 Agreement had functioned with some measure of success, he generally criticised the contribution equivalent of 25,000 tons[18] of tin metal because it was a heavy responsibility for producer countries to bear all alone.

For the above reasons, we cannot help recommending that either the financial resources of the buffer stock should come from the coffers of the UN or that producer and consumer countries should make equal contributions to it. While the consumers make their contributions in money, the producers should do the same in tin metal. In this way, the buffer stock will be better equipped in money and tin to deal with market fluctuations, because in actual fact the true problem of the buffer stock is that of insufficient resources which producer countries, by virtue of their poverty, are not able to remedy all alone.

(C) Export controls

The powers bestowed upon the Tin Council by this agreement as regards export controls are to be found in Article VII, paragraph 2 of the 3rd Agreement as follows:

(I) Export control

(a) Pursuant to Article VII, paragraph 2, the council could declare any period 'a control period' and fix the total authorised exports for this period. Thus the limitation of exports depends on the 'positive decision of the council' (paragraph 2c) on condition however that the buffer stock holds at least 10,000 tons. There are two other factors which make an exception to this rule:

- (i) an export control period could be declared when the buffer stock holds 5,000 tons if a control period is declared for the first time after an interval when no limitation had been in force;
- (ii) by a two-thirds distributed majority the council could reduce the tonnage to 10,000 or 5,000 for any control period.

(b) The council could invite any consuming country, which is also a producing country, to limit its exports during a control period. The extent of such a limitation shall be determined by a common agreement between the council and the consuming country.

(c) The council could, with a distributed two-thirds majority, amend the provisions of Annexes C and G concerning the conditions under which tin could be regarded as exported for the purposes of export control and the rules of re-determining the percentages attributed to producing countries.

(d) If the net exports of a producer country during a control period exceed his authorised exports for that period by more than 5 per cent, the council could require the said country to make an additional contribution to the buffer stock, proportional to his excess exports, either in cash or in metal. Such proportions[19] and the dates of the contributions shall be decided by the council (paragraph 7b). On the other hand, if during four successive periods of control, including the period under examination in paragraph 9b, a producing country exceeds its permissible exports by 1 per cent, the council could decide to reduce its total exports during each of the four subsequent control periods by one-quarter (1/4) of the total exported in excess or by a fraction not exceeding one-half. But if, after these four periods, the said country exceeds its permissible exports during any four successive control periods, the council could, apart from the reduction already imposed in paragraph 9c, do the following:

(i) deprive the country in question of a part of its right to participation on liquidation of the buffer stock, which part 'shall on the first occasion not exceed one-half of its rights to participation' (paragraph 9b);
(ii) restore to the country in question the portion of its rights so forfeited on such terms and conditions as it (council) may determine.

(e) The council could decide that exports from producer countries shall include the tin content of any mineral production of the country in question.

(II) On special exports (Article VIII)

(a) The council could, with a distributed two-thirds majority, authorise a participating country to carry out 'special exports'. In conformity with Article VII, paragraph 4, this could include its permissible export quota when the conditions[20] in Annex D are fulfilled or at such terms which the council deems necessary. That the council could also modify these conditions (paragraph 4) is a discretionary power conferred upon it by the agreement. Finally, we would ask ourselves what could have been the fate of the tin market during over-production periods in the absence of such control measures.

(2) COMPARATIVE STUDY OF THE 1956, 1961 AND 1966 AGREEMENTS

A comparative study of these agreements can best be made by examining the differences which exist between the two previous agreements and the third one of 1966. This is to say that we shall have to find them out within specific domains of the agreements themselves.

(1) Within the buffer stock

The 3rd Agreement, like the two previous ones, provides for two means of action: the buffer stock and an export control mechanism, the only difference in them being in the quantity of tin metal held in the buffer stock. While the 1st Agreement held 25,000 tons equivalent, the 2nd and 3rd held 20,000 tons in the form of contributions. According to the provisions of the 2nd and 3rd Agreements, the council could borrow money to satisfy the needs of the buffer stock 'upon the security of tin warrants held by the Buffer Stock' (Article X, paragraph 6a). Compared to the 1st Agreement this provision is an important change because the 1st Agreement of 1956 refused the council any right of borrowing. The total amount of money to be borrowed by the council must have been approved of, by a majority of votes cast by the consuming countries and all the votes cast by the producers. Thus the chairman of the Tin Council was able to borrow the sum of £10 million for the purposes of the buffer stock, under the authority of the council, for the 3rd Agreement of 1966. This sum was borrowed from a consortium of banks in London, with Hambros Bank at the head. If the agreement requires a unanimity vote of the producers, it is because the sum is meant for the buffer stock, to which they are the only contributors. Moreover, the consumers are not under any obligations[21] but when, in the future, it becomes necessary for both contracting parties to make equal contributions, the consumers would no doubt be equally obliged.

The 2nd and the 3rd Agreements bestow upon the council the right to suspend the buffer stock manager's operations of buying and selling, whenever it finds that they go against the objective of the agreement. The rigidity of the 1st Agreement did not permit this right.

In respect of the functioning principles of the agreement, the previous agreements required a distributed two-thirds majority of the council to enable the buffer stock manager to intervene in the middle sector of the price margins. But on the other hand, the 3rd Agreement of 1966 seems satisfied with a 'special authorisation' (Article XI, paragraph 3a) whose voting procedure could be determined by the council.

(2) In respect of exports

In the three agreements, the control periods are spaced out in quarters and the council must evaluate supply and demand every quarter. Unlike the 1956 Agreement, which permitted barter arrangements only after an amendment was carried out in its annex, the agreements of 1961 and 1966 authorise special exports on a distributed two-thirds majority basis. Exports which are meant to be part of government strategic stocks are not considered as exports, under export control measures. There is a new provision in the 1966 Agreement which was absent in that of 1961: during export control periods, the council could ask consumer members of the agreement who are also producers to accept a certain reduction in their exports. This provision is very realistic because the production of the consumer members of the agreement was gradually making progress: 5,098 tons in 1960; 6,119 tons in 1961 and 6,322 tons in 1962.

(3) Within the domain of disposals from non-commercial stockpiles

While 'disposals from non-commercial stockpiles' constitute an Article in the 3rd Agreement of 1966, that of 1961 provided for it under 'Ancillary provisions', thus laying emphasis on the role which they could play on the world market during a period of scarcity. Unlike the 2nd Agreement, the 3rd does not fix any date-limit to those countries wishing to dispose of tin from non-commercial stocks. While the 2nd Agreement requires that such intention to dispose of stocks must be publicly notified six months in advance, the 3rd stipulates that the council must simply be duly and publicly informed of the plan so that it could enter into discussions with the countries in question with the view to making recommendations. This is undoubtedly a concession made to the USA in order to coax her into joining the agreement.

(4) In respect of voting procedure

While the 1956 Agreement required a simple majority vote of all participating countries counted together for all decisions of the council (except when there is an expressed contrary decision of the council) the provisions of the 2nd and the 3rd Agreements require a simple distributed majority except when the council decides otherwise. For a great number of important matters, a distributed two-thirds majority is required.

The percentage of exports for a producing country for the purpose of control in the 2nd and 3rd Agreements cannot be reduced by more than 10 per cent (except for the first re-determination for the purpose of control) during any period of 12 months (Article VII, paragraph 6a). On the other hand, the 1st Agreement of 1956 provides for a re-determination of percentages of exports once a year and for a given country the percentage cannot be reduced by more than 5 per cent.

According to the 2nd and 3rd Agreements, the number of votes of consumer countries is not determined by their average imports and consumptions as it was in the 1st Agreement of 1956, but by their average consumptions only.

(5) Within the domain of the entry into force of the agreement

In the 1st Agreement of 1956, the number of votes required for its final entry into force was 900 for the producers and 330 for the consumers, out of a total of 1,000 each. There seems to have been an improvement on these numbers as a new agreement comes into effect.Thus the 2nd Agreement of 1961 required 950 for the six producers and 500 for the fifteen consumers. In the 3rd Agreement of 1966, while the number of votes for the six producers remain unchanged (950), those of the sixteen consumers were reduced to 400. These changes had to come in as a result of the various difficulties encountered in ratification in the past, by participating countries.

In respect of purposes and objectives of the agreements

While the purposes and objectives of the two previous agreements were inspired from the principles of the Havana Charter of 1948, those of the 3rd Agreement of 1966 reflect the principles which recognise the state of poverty of the Third World. The principles referred to are those of the UN Conference on Trade and Development held from 23 March 1964 in Geneva.[22]

CONCLUSION

The various amendments carried out in all the agreements go to portray that the secretariat of the Tin Council not only studies the experiences of the past from closed quarters, but also draws from the suggestions made during preparatory conferences.

SECTION IV. PERMANENT AND ADMINISTRATIVE INSTITUTIONS OF THE AGREEMENT

In order that the agreement might function properly, permanent institutions become necessary to carry out an evolutionary study in conjunction with the community of the signatory states. Such institutions are in two main organs: (1) intergovernmental organs such as the council and its various committees; (2) organs that are independent of participating governments such as the secretary, secretariat and the manager of the buffer stock. We shall for the purpose of this study examine the second type of these organs.

(1) THE SECRETARY

According to Article IV, paragraph 7, the secretary is appointed by the council who determine his terms and conditions of service. The secretary is expected to be a personality with considerable administrative and diplomatic qualities. He is responsible, like the buffer stock manager, to the chairman of the council, in all that concerns the application of the agreement. Like the chairman and the buffer stock manager, he is held by all sorts of obligations. For example, he is not expected to have had financial or commercial interests in the tin industry. The duties of the secretary cover a wide field; including meetings and reports on accounts and budgets. Pursuant to Rule 6 of the Rules of Procedure of the council, the secretary must send to each representative a written notification and a draft agenda for a future meeting, at least eight days and at most 21 days before the day scheduled for the meeting.[23] Rule 16 stipulates that the secretary shall make adequate arrangements for all simultaneous interpretations at council and committee meetings. The secretary ensures that all council reports are sent to the participants in the three official languages. Rule 18 requires that a draft of the council minutes in the working language must be sent to all participants immediately after the meeting for possible amendments which must be notified to the council within 21 days of the date of despatch. It is only when this document has been approved by the council that a report established in the three main official languages is despatched to the designated representatives of participating governments (Rule 3).

On 31 March latest, of each year, the chairman of the council must submit to the Finance and Establishment Committee, a draft budget of the income and expenditure relating to the administrative account for the next financial year and a statement setting out estimates of the contributions to be made by each participating country. This is where the secretary plays an important role: it is his duty to transmit this draft, on which he makes his remarks and amendments, to the Finance Committee, representatives of participating governments according to Rule 3, 30 days at least before the date of the meeting at which the draft budget will be the object of discussion. Pursuant to Rule 25 of the Rules of Procedure, it is the secretary's duty to keep an administrative account. He also establishes, after the end of each financial year, all accounts relative to the previous year including a report on incomes and expenses. All these accounts, including a certificate from the auditor after auditing them, are sent to the Finance Committee which makes its remarks and passes the accounts on to the council for its approval. The secretary, 21 days[24] before the end of each quarter, must furnish the Finance Committee with a statement of incomes and expenditures of the previous quarter; this shall in turn be transmitted to all council members.

A thorough examination of the attributions of the secretary shows that he must be in close liaison with the council and its committees to whom he must give his material aids coming from the service of the secretariat.

(2) THE SECRETARIAT

The secretariat, which is the administrative organ of the council, is placed under the authority of a secretary. In order that it might function properly its personnel, and that of the buffer stock, are internationally recruited, with preferences given to the nationals of participating countries. These recruitments are made by the chairman of the council after consultation with the secretary and the buffer stock manager. Their conditions of service and employment must be approved by the council. These functionaries are expected to keep professional secrecy. They must not reveal any 'information concerning the operation or administration of this Agreement' except those which may be authorised by the council (Article IV, paragraph 9) or which may be necessary for the execution of their duties.

(3) THE BUFFER STOCK MANAGER

The manager of the buffer stock, like the secretary of the council, is appointed by the council (Article IV, paragraph 7a). The council determines the terms and conditions of service. In order that he might carry out his functions properly, he, like the chairman and the secretary of the council, must not have held any interests in the tin industry. According to Article XI, paragraph 1, he is responsible for the proper functioning of the buffer stock, particularly in respect of the operations of buying, selling and maintenance of tin stocks. These responsibilities will come to an end as soon as the agreement is terminated. Following this termination, the manager shall prepare an estimate of all expenditure necessary for liquidating the buffer stock in accordance with Article XIII. He shall deduct from his buffer stock account a sum which, in his opinion, will be sufficient to cover the expenses of liquidation. On the other hand, if this total proves insufficient he could 'sell a sufficient quantity of tin metal to provide the additional sum required' (Article XIII, paragraph 5).

Pursuant to Rule 28 of the Rules of Procedure we could classify the manager's attributions into four:

1. The manager opens buffer stock accounts in the name of 'The International Tin Council' in banks approved by the Finance Committee. These banks are often in London because the seat of

the council is there. In these accounts he credits all contributions and incomes of the buffer stock.

2. The manager keeps account books in which figure all the incomes and expenditures of the buffer stock. These accounts, audited in conformity with Article V, paragraph 6, must comprise a report on incomes and expenditure. They must be published three months after the end of the financial year to which they relate.
3. The manager keeps a register of all contributions made in metal to the buffer stock, including all stocks held, specifying the country where they are held and of all operations of buying and selling. The chairman and the auditor have easy access to these registers.
4. The manager could, with the approval of the chairman, invest the surplus funds of the buffer stock in order to cover its immediate needs, either in treasury bills or in banks approved by the council.

(4) THE LEGAL STATUS OF THE SEAT OF THE COUNCIL: IMMUNITIES AND PRIVILEGES

The privileges and immunities of the council functionaries emanate from the provisions of Article 105, paragraph 2 of the UN Charter: 'Representatives of the members of the United Nations and officials of the Organisation shall similarly enjoy such privileges and immunities as are necessary for the independent exercise of their functions in connection with the Organisation.' Consequently, we could certify that privileges and immunities are based on the notion of the necessity[25] for international organisations to function. Thus we could conclude that the legal capacity of the Tin Council is very great because it could even conclude 'a seat agreement' or be granted privileges and immunities on the territory of each member state.

(1) In each member state

The council is granted all exchange facilities, including such legal capacity necessary for the execution of its functions 'to the extent consistent' with the law of each state (Article IV, paragraph 28). It is also exempted from the taxation of its assets, income and other property. '. . . to the extent consistent with its law', means that the council shall accept the jurisdiction of the host country within the limits of its powers because the international society has not yet reached the stage at which international organisations could enjoy the status of absolute supranationality. For example on 3 August 1956, the UK Government granted the Tin Council tax exemptions on its operations. The result of this was the passing of a law in 1957 (Legal Status and Tax Exemptions of the Tin Council: Amendment). This became applicable as soon as this amendment entered into force on 19 July 1958. During the first council meeting from 2 to 6 July 1956, the UK delegation mentioned that by virtue of Article IV, paragraph 22 of the Agreement[26] and their internal legislation, her government was not in a position to grant immediate tax relief to the employees of the council who were not of British nationality. This was why during the second meeting, from 15 to 19 October 1956, the Council recommended to member governments the ratification of an amendment that would make the British government fulfil her obligation. This amendment was open for signature from 18 October 1956 to 17 July 1958. The following is the text of the Amendment:

Resolution No. 21 of 18 October 1956: Amendment of the International Tin Agreement regarding exemption from taxation.

The International Tin Council.

Desiring to make an amendment to the International Tin Agreement, opened for signature at London on the 1st March, 1954, recommends, pursuant to paragraph 1 of Article XVIII of the Agreement,

(a) the following amendment to the contracting governments for their ratification or acceptance.[27] paragraph 22 of Article IV shall be deleted and the following paragraphs shall be inserted in the place thereof:[28]

'22. The Council shall have in each participating country to the extent consistent with its laws, such exemption from taxation on assets, income and other property of the Council as may be necessary for the discharge of its functions under this agreement.

'23. The government of the country in which the Seat of the Council is situated shall grant exemption from taxation on remuneration paid by the Council to its employees other than those employees who are nationals of the country in which the seat of the Council is.'

(b) that twenty months from the date of this Resolution be fixed as time within which Contracting Parties shall notify the Government of the United Kingdom of Great Britain and Northern Ireland of their ratification or acceptance of the amendments which have been deposited by the number of consumers and producers required in conformity Article XXI paragraph 3.[29]

(2) A seat agreement

Many international agreements recognise the importance of a 'seat agreement' which grants immunities to their civil servants. Consequently, the International Tin Council is empowered to conclude such agreement with the government which seats the council. By virtue of this agreement the salaries of its functionaries,[30] such as the secretary, manager of the buffer stock and other members of staff are granted tax exemptions (Article IV, paragraph 30). This tax privilege poses a real problem. For instance, in UNO (where the USA refuses to grant its nationals who are civil servants tax exemptions) UNO reimburses them the total of their taxes, so that they could be on the same footing as their counterparts.[31]

Finally, the legal personality of the seat equally extends to international organisations such as 'the UN, its appropriate organs, particularly UNCTAD, and its specialised agencies' (Article IV, paragraph 2) because the council would enter into 'consultation and co-operation with them'. For example the Council could draw up conventions on labour or health with the ILO and WHO for the protection of tin-mine workers, because, in conformity with Article XVI, participating countries have promised 'to ensure fair labour standards in the tin industry' in order to avoid depression in living standards and the practice of unfair competitive conditions in world trade.

SECTION V. AN EXAMINATION OF THE 4TH INTERNATIONAL TIN AGREEMENT AS AN INSTRUMENT OF COMMODITY STABILISATION

(A) TECHNICAL SITUATION

1. The general weakness of the mechanism of stabilisation in the tin agreements stems from the fact of the compulsory and unilateral contributions made into the buffer stocks arrangements only by producer countries. But the advantages derived from a successful functioning of the agreements accrue to both consumer and producer. The voluntary contributions which are meant to be palliatives in both Article X, paragraph 7 of the 3rd Agreement and Article 22[a] of the 4th

Agreement do not solve the problem. While the 3rd Agreement limits voluntary contributions to participating countries, the adopted 4th Agreement includes the invitees to the 1970 UN Conference on Tin. This is to acknowledge the fact that the scope of voluntary contributions has been increased in the 4th. The purpose of this is far more a desire to facilitate the future accession of those countries which participated in the adoption and signature of the agreement but which might fail to ratify it, than a desire to increase the coffers of the buffer stock. These provisions are meant to leave voluntary contributions open to both contracting parties willing so to do, on consent of the council because they could at any time ask for a refund. Here again, the refund is made subject to the conditions which the council will deem necessary. This is to laud the efforts of the 4th Agreement for having moved a step further since the notion of invitees covers the following categories:

(i) contracting parties of the 4th Agreement;
(ii) those whose intention to ratify the agreement would be notified accordingly. This category could ask for a refund if eventually they fail to ratify the agreement;
(iii) those who participated in the negotiation, adoption and signature of the agreement, but fail to ratify it.

It however excludes those members of the previous agreement and the members of UNO and its specialised agencies which are normally qualified for accession. At this level of accession in the 4th Agreement, the notion of equity has been introduced 'in respect of voting rights and financial obligations, as between the countries seeking to accede and other countries already participating' (Article 48[c] of the 4th International Agreement on Tin).

The above postulations are not to say that we have now arrived at the ideal goal of the buffer stock. The fact is that we do not see the logic in asking the consumers to vote at all when the need to borrow for the buffer stock arises (Article 24[a] of the 4th Agreement), as such borrowing would depend 'upon the security of tin warrants held by the buffer stock',[32] to which only the producers contribute. The only set of consumers that could contribute to such decision-making must be those who would make voluntary contributions and in such a case it is a simple consent of the few contributors that would be needed. This is to establish that all consumers should not be called upon to exercise the weight of their influence in laws which all of them would not have helped to create, since they are not subject to compulsory contributions. In the final analysis, then, 'No obligation shall be laid upon any participating country under this article without consent of that country' (Article 24 [c] of the 4th Agreement) is contradictory in purposes and intent because it neither satisfies the need for a compulsory contribution of the consumers nor justifies the consent of a group of consumers who have not made any contributions. It therefore boils down to the fact that the previous provision of the 3rd Agreement has not in fact been modified, as the 4th Agreement would want to make us believe. Furthermore, the liquidation procedures of the 3rd and the 4th Agreements at termination of the agreement, do not provide for voluntary contributions, and even the 3rd Agreement deliberately excludes them (Article XIII, paragraph 6 [bi]). This is undoubtedly because the council is already competent to determine the conditions of refund, so that this same procedure could be retained at liquidation on termination of the agreement. Article 31(b) of the liquidation procedure of the draft 4th Agreement stipulates: '. . . the share of each contributing country in the buffer stock shall be refunded to that country'.

The purpose of the above exercise is twofold. First, by comparing the adopted 4th International Agreement on Tin with the 3rd Agreement, it becomes easy to see how the minds of the negotiators work. Secondly, in the light of our above analysis, a genuine solution to the problems of the buffer stock would depend on compulsory contributions of all contracting parties to its coffers – the producers in metal and the consumers in acceptable currencies. This will help the producer countries within the concept of equity in international co-operation, in conserving for immediate purposes of development a part of their hard-earned foreign currencies which is otherwise being kept in the form of securities or metals producing uncertain results. Furthermore, the coffers of the buffer stock would become more replenished in the overall increasing power of contributions needed to fight against scarcity of funds when prices of tin soar above the ceiling price and when there is no more tin in the buffer. This has been the major problem within the stabilisation mechanism of the Tin Agreement. On the other hand, a continuous price degradation in the world market would almost automatically lead to a reduction of exports from producer countries, with all its attendant consequences on the economy of these countries.

2. Among all existing metals, tin has been the only one provided with an agreement; but there could be need in the future to control other metals like iron ore, antimony, tungsten, lead and zinc, to which particular attention has to be paid.[33] These are the fields with increasing

production and exports in both industialised and developing countries. North America is blessed with large desposits of most minerals from which she taps for her domestic consumption. Canada exports all major metals except tin and even undertakes imports of bauxite for re-exportation in metal form. Japan relies mostly on Australasia for imports because of proximity, which lessens transport costs. With tin and manganese as exceptions, the USA and Canada chiefly buy from Latin American countries. Within a total of 3·0 US billion dollar exports for developing countries in 1960, copper earned 1·2 US billion dollars, iron ore (517 million US dollars), tin (248 million dollars) and it is estimated that their share in the trade is bound to increase because of the decrease in the production of developed countries, and their exports will grow at an annual rate of 5 per cent to reach 6·2 US billion dollars at constant prices by 1975.[34] Nevertheless the increasing world production of the following selected metals shown in Table 7.5, excluding those of mainland China and North Korea, are pointers to a future need for the stabilisation of certain categories of metals. The table shows an increasing production of iron ore and fluctuating variations for antimony, tungsten and bauxite. The supply of these metals depends on the extent of industrial demand, particularly of non-ferrous alloys and steel. These facts also pose the problem of the need for the iron and

TABLE 7.5 World production of selected metals, 1953–1966*
(in metric tons)

Year	*Iron ore*	*Bauxite*	*Antimony ore (Sb content)*	*Tungsten (concentrates, WO_3 content)*
1953	159,000	42,000	22,500	27,970
1958	182,100	19,400	24,400	14,850
1959	193,300	20,500	32,600	13,060
1960	232,100	25,100	32,900	17,020
1961	233,000	25,870	31,600	19,620
1962	242,500	27,600	32,900	17,710
1963	252,500	26,950	35,000	12,530
1964	158,000	29,880	41,300	14,240
1965	308,700	34,120	40,200	13,110
1966	319,300	37,140	39,900	14,370

* *Statistical Year Book 1967*. The figures are expressed in metric tons and exclude Mainland China and North Korea for which production figures for iron ore were 1958 (30,000 tons) 1960 (55,000); 1966 (40,000 tons) and 1958 (1552); 1960 (3108) and 1966 (6,000) respectively.

steel industries in certain producer-countries as a measure against possible over-production in the future and a gradual preparation towards stabilisation.

(B) LEGAL POSITION

Certain innovations and modifications have arisen in the 4th International Agreement on Tin in respect of entry into force (Article 46), collective voting rights (Article 50) and the authentication of texts through working languages (Article 56). First, Article 46 stipulates that for the entry into force of the adopted 4th Agreement the votes of at least six producing countries holding at least 950 votes, and at least nine consuming countries holding at least 300 votes, of the 1,000 stipulated for each side of the contracting parties, would be the requirements for the definite entry into force of the agreement. The reduction of the required votes for consumers from 400 votes in the 3rd Agreement to 300 in the 4th points to difficulties in ratification by consuming countries and therefore intends to facilitate the entry into force. While producer requirements have remained stable, increasing only once from 900 votes in the 1st Agreement (1956) to 950 votes since the 2nd, consumer votes have been reduced constantly after the 1956 Agreement (330 votes), after the 2nd Agreement (500 votes), 400 for the 3rd and now 300 for the 4th Agreement, without any noticeable structural change within the consumer group.

Secondly, Article 50 provides for the participation of any intergovernmental organisation with responsibility to negotiate. This organisation would not have the right to vote, but could exercise the voting rights of its members collectively on matters within its competence. This is an innovation which no doubt prepares an honorary seat for the EEC.

Thirdly, Article 56: 'Authentic texts of the agreement' has added the Russian language to English, French and Spanish languages in which the text of the agreement could be regarded as being equally authentic. The absence of the Russian language in the 3rd Agreement (Article XXVII) and its inclusion in the 4th augurs well for the admission of a new member from the Socialist world.

8 Coffee in International Agricultural Diplomacy: Case Study Two

INTRODUCTION

The international coffee agreement is a five-year agreement, unlike other agricultural products provided with agreements.[1] The 1st International Coffee Agreement entered into force provisionally on 1 July 1963, and into force definitively on 27 December 1963, as soon as all forms of constitutional ratifications were accomplished and notified accordingly. Its purpose, like other similar agreements, is to stabilise coffee prices and assure an equilibrium between production and consumption. The contractual members are consumers and producers of coffee who by this agreement have set up a comprehensive set of quota mechanisms limiting the exports of producer members of the agreement. The 1968 Agreement provides for certificates of origin and re-export (Article 43) which requires that all coffee exported by contractual members of the agreement be accompanied by 'a valid certificate of origin in accordance with rules established by the council and issued by a qualified agency chosen by that member and approved by the organisation' (Article 43, paragraph 1 of the 1968 Agreement). This is to say that all importer countries who are members of the agreement should refuse importation from non-member countries and reject coffees not accompanied by these valid certificates.

Coffee is an important commodity for study for four reasons:

1. Membership of the alliance embraces about 67 contractual members (43 exporting and 24 importing) and coffee affects the lives and economy of Latin American and African countries.
2. In terms of scholarship it presents a vast area of study like other recent agreements, e.g. wheat, sugar, tin, olive oil and cocoa.[2]
3. Coffee agreements, like the others, demonstrate a growing pattern in commodity agreements because they all contain mechanisms of

control, procedures in negotiation, drafting, territorial application and final provisions.

4. It is an area, like others, presenting co-operative and conflicting situations involving techniques in contemporary international economic diplomacy.
5. Thc jurists of dcvcloping countrics from my own practical experiences appear to neglect the study of commodity agreements from an interdisciplinary point of view, and even from the point of view of their study, as techniques of international legislation towards the achievements of the provisions of Article 55 of the UN Charter. Yet it is important because of the need for concessions made on the sovereignty of states. For instance there is need for consent by states to the application of the weighted voting system reflecting national financial strength in terms of contributions, and in the control techniques used by international administration thus set up by a commodity agreement on national policies.

For the above reasons the study of coffee requires a comprehensive knowledge of its attendant problems in the areas of exports, planting, political factors, etc.

SECTION I. THE COFFEE PROBLEM

Coffee is a bean-like seed ground into powder before consumption. There are three major types grown in tropical areas of the world: Brazils, grown in Brazil; Milds, in other Latin American countries; and Robustas, from Central Africa. The duration of the agreement appears to conform to its cyclical period of fruit-bearing which is from three to five years, and it could continue to bear fruit for the next 25 – 40 years. Its importance in world trade comes next after petroleum, with exports valued in excess of $1\frac{3}{4}$ US billion dollars a year.[3] In the coffee year 1962 (October 1961–September 1962) production amounted to about 71 million bags, each bag weighing 60 kilograms, i.e. 132 pounds. The producers are Latin America (18 countries) and Africa. In 1962 total world exports were 45·3 million bags and the largest consumer was the USA which imported more than half of the world's imports (see Table 8·1). Germany, France and Italy excel in European imports which account for about two-fifths of world imports. There is also some coffee consumption in parts of Eastern Europe, Africa, the Near East and Asia.

TABLE 8.1. Total world coffee exports and production (1961–2)

	*World**	*Brazil*	*Colombia*
Total production	71	35 % (49 %)	7·8 % (11 %)
Exportable production	58	28 % (48 %)	6·8 % (12 %)
Exports	45·3	16·1 % (36 %)	6·5 % (14 %)

Source: *Law and Contemporary Problems*, 28 (1962), p. 332.

* Expressed in millions of bags, each of 60 kilograms.

The 1962 Agreement, in its Article 72, provides for review within the last six months of the 1964–65 coffee year. This agreement was scheduled to terminate on 30 September 1968 after an initial life of five years. The council thus authorised the board to undertake its review and extension beyond its 30 September 1968 deadline or renegotiate or amend it if necessary. This was why the council decided at its August–September 1966 session to set up a high level working group for 1966–67 to co-ordinate and obtain maximum reliable information on the coffee market economy. It was also empowered to appoint fact-finding missions to certain countries. Certain fundamental factors affect the coffee trade. They are trade barriers, quotas and internal taxes. While the USA imposed almost no restrictions on coffee,[4] the EEC imposes barriers like import duties, quantitative restrictions and internal taxes. Total import duties and internal taxes amounted to 200 per cent of import value. Coffee imports into France are subject to quantitative restrictions in favour of her African associates of the EEC, for they received higher prices.[5] Coffee like most commodities is produced in developing countries and it is a mono-crop in these areas.[6]

There were 54 original signatories to the 1962 Agreement, 32 exporting and 22 importing countries. Today according to the 1968 Agreement, there are 43 exporting and 24 importing countries. Out of the original signatories, 4 failed to ratify within the first three years (i.e. 2 exporting and 2 importing); 8 (5 exporting and 3 importing) other countries not signatories at the New York Conference decided later to accede. The coffee market presents a number of problems. For instance:

1. Like tin it suffers from over-production which can be exemplified from the Korean War period when prices were always on the upward trend and demand could not determine its supply because coffee as a cyclical plant takes about 3–5 years to bear fruit. This is

also the problem with cocoa, where producers cannot quickly reduce production.

2. Like cocoa it suffers from the problem of storage facilities because it is expensive to hold stocks for a long period.

These are reasons for low prices when they overflow the world market. For instance in the past the Second World War period, frosts and demand factors in Brazil from 1948 to 1953 led to increased prices which in turn encouraged increased planting in Central Africa. By 1955, production had surpassed demand and the result was degradation of prices. Between 1954 and 1962 the average wholesale price of coffee fell from 79 cents to less than 35 cents. That is, by more than 50 per cent because world stocks had increased to 66 million bags which was the equivalent of the world's supply for 18 months. To worsen these problems the African countries had entered the world market with their Robusta coffee sold at relatively lower prices while the Latin American countries' economy was suffering because of consequent imbalance in their foreign trade transactions. These circumstances, like in those of tin, made it necessary to seek ways of stabilising the coffee market, although political necessities on the side of the USA had made these attempts faster because at this time the commodity trade was gradually becoming an instrument of her foreign and aid policies as we shall see later.

SECTION II. DIPLOMATIC NATURE OF COFFEE CONFERENCES

(A) PAST ATTEMPTS AT STABILISATION

Attempts at stabilising the coffee market were for a long time the individual concern of Brazil, the chief world producer before the Second World War. But before then several discussions had ensued for about 60 years.[7] Brazil's approach consisted in limiting her own exports and stockpiling and buying stocks. Between 1931 and 1944 she had to destroy some 78 million bags of coffee to stabilise prices.

First attempt

This was in 1940 when 14 Latin American countries and the USA concluded an Inter-American Coffee Agreement.[8] The agreement not only divided the US market among Latin American countries but also required the USA to limit her imports from non-member countries. This agreement, which ended after the war, did help considerably to increase prices and most important was the improvement in the relationship between the Latin American countries and the USA.

Second attempt

In 1954, after an initial boom, the coffee market was again suffering some decline in prices and an international action was thought necessary. There was consequently a meeting of American Ministers of Finance and Economy acting as the Inter-American Economic and Social Council of the Organisation of American States which commissioned the council's special Committee on Coffee to carry out studies on the world coffee situation with the purpose of finding adequate solutions to the problem. The result of this feasibility study were not acceptable to the USA because it failed to include European consumers and African producers.

Third attempt

By 1955–56 pressures were mounting for an international agreement because the huge coffee crop in 1957–58 had produced over-production and consequent degradation of prices. Consequently, seven Latin American producers: Brazil, Colombia, Costa Rica, El Salvador, Guatemala, Mexico and Nicaragua got together in Mexico City in October 1957 and concluded an emergency Mexico City Agreement. This agreement was based on quarterly allocation of export quota to each contracting party to the agreement. This attempt did not achieve the desired results.

Fourth attempt

As the USA became gradually immersed in the problems of the developing world generally and with her traditional interest in the coffee market in particular, she convened in 1958, at her own initiative, a Coffee Study Group, made up of 20 producers and consumers, whose headquarters was in Washington, DC. This group paid particular attention to two major problems: (1) that of declining prices; and (2) that of establishing a long-term equilibrium. Consequently in 1958, the Latin American Coffee Agreement was negotiated and signed by 15 Latin American producing countries. The agreement, which took effect in October 1958, provided for a system of export quotas based upon a certain percentage for each country of its total exportable production.

Fifth attempt

The above led to another short-term international coffee agreement which entered into force in October 1959 for a period of one year. This agreement again specified quotas for each contracting party under the following alternatives: (1) 90 per cent of its exports in its best year between 1949 and 1958; (2) for any contracting party with less than two million bags of exportable production, 80 per cent of its current estimate of exportable production. However the quota exercise did not include exports to certain non-traditional markets of Eastern Europe, Africa and Asia. The importance or significance of this agreement was that it included non-Latin-American producers, for in addition to the traditional 15 of the Latin American Coffee Agreement, France and Portugal signed the new short-term agreement on behalf of their respective African territories. Nevertheless, consumer countries were still excluded or not represented. But in September 1960, this agreement was extended for another year with membership increased to 28 producing countries which accounted for about 90 per cent of the world export of coffee.[9] These short-term agreements were unsuccessful for the following reasons: (1) the quota allocations were determined at levels unrealistic in terms of world prediction; (2) certain member signatory countries violated quota allocations which were difficult to police or control because of the non-membership of consumer countries; (3) these agreements were more like temporary arrangements which did not grasp the main issue of over-production which plagued the international coffee market.

The turning point

Because of the evasion of the root causes of the problems, the Coffee Study Group had to produce ten volumes of reports on coffee problems which explained the need for a more general agreement which must include the USA, a world major consumer. This was still at a time when the Eisenhower administration was hostile to international commodity agreements, although she was a signatory member to the sugar and wheat agreements (being a wheat producer). The attitude of the USA was therefore seen as important to an international agreement. The myth of her hostility to international agreements was uncovered in March 1961 when President Kennedy made his now famous speech at Punta del Este (Uruguay) on the 'Alliance for Progress'. In this, President Kennedy declared the intention of the USA 'to co-operate in a serious case-by-case examination of commodity market problems'.[10] Consequently at a special meeting of the Organisation of American States, Inter-American Economic and Social Council in Punta del Este, the head of the United States delegation, the Secretary of the Treasury, Dillon, formally declared that the USA was 'prepared to join a workable coffee agreement, to use its good offices to urge the quotas through the use of import controls'.[11] This was therefore a breakthrough in the series of attempts to organise the international coffee market by means of an international agreement.

(B) PREPARATORY CONFERENCES UNDER THE UN SYSTEM

With the above-mentioned formal pronouncements, it became evident that the USA was prepared to negotiate and prepare a long-term agreement. At the Punta del Este Conference[12] three resolutions were adopted unanimously, which set forth principles for the examination and implementation of the Coffee Study Group (Resolution C.1). Resolution C.2 dealt with regulatory measures and seasonal financing while Resolution C.3 set up a committee to negotiate the elimination of restrictive practices on coffee consumption. The third resolution was directed chiefly at common market practices.

By September 1961, the Coffee Study Group had increased its membership to 34 countries, and in order to prepare for a long-term draft agreement, this group appointed a ten-nation Co-ordinating and Drafting Committee whose chairman was Mr W. Michael Blumenthal of the USA, Deputy Assistant Secretary of State for Economic Affairs. This committee subsequently chose three representatives in their personal and expert capacity to prepare this draft in conjunction with the secretariat of the Coffee Study Group. When the group met, it was generally agreed that this draft should not only include a system of export quotas determined on the bases of world consumption but also the consumers of coffee who would play a vital role in the policing of the quota system. The promotion of increased consumption and the control of production and stocks were also some of the objectives of the draft. The encouraging outcome of these preliminaries led to a decision that the Secretary-General of the UN be asked to convene a conference for June or July 1962 to negotiate an international agreement. Consequently a twelve-nation pre-conference co-ordinating committee was created to continue discussions with the view to ironing out areas of agreement and to sending delegations to countries likely to be interested in the agreement. The said request was then transmitted by the Secretary-General of the UN to the Interim Co-ordinating Committee for the International Commodity Arrangements (ICCICA) of the Economic and Social Council (ECOSOC) which recommended that the conference be convened. Subsequently, in conformity with ECOSOC Resolution 296(XI), the Secretary-General convened a UN conference on coffee on 9 July 1962 at the UN headquarters in New York.[13] Those invited were all the 104 members of the UN, several non-members with an interest for coffee, members of the Coffee Study Group, members of the UN Interim Commission of the International Trade Organisation (ICTITO); the FAO; Ruanda-Burundi. There were also observers from UN specialised agencies including the World Bank and IMF. One may ask why the Coffee Study Group had to request the UN to sponsor the conference as in the case of most commodity conferences of our times. Some of the reasons may be the following:

1. it conformed to the recognised practice and rules established by ECOSOC, e.g. participation of all countries must be on equal bases;
2. such role of the UN will give the conference a universal character and the opportunity for contributions from its highly technical staff with a vast knowledge of drafting and other techniques;
3. a pre-conference co-ordinating committee was detailed to pay several visits to participating countries in order to explain not only the importance of the agreement but also divergent viewpoints and conflicting positions which needed solutions in advance of the conference.

For this purpose, the committee fixed the date of the conference and its rules of procedure, and settled the thorny question of selecting a conference chairman.[14] The chairman of this conference was the

Canadian Deputy Minister of Trade, Mr Mitchell W. Sharp, who resigned in 1958 to enter private industry and politics. He had played significant roles in a number of commodity and trade conferences.

(C) THE NEGOTIATION AND ADOPTION OF THE AGREEMENT

(I) Conference negotiations

The conference, which opened on 2 July 1962 at the UN headquarters, was attended by 58 nations representing various delegations, observers from 13 other countries and 3 specialised agencies.[15] Since it finally adjourned on 28 September 1962, the negotiation period covered about 86 days. This conference, which had a number of issues[16] to settle in order to achieve its objective of establishing an agreement, was saddled with what we might call 'politics of group interest' normally characteristic of commodity negotiations since they concern the world of producers and consumers. While the importers were not too keen to accept sharp price increases, the exporters were highly desirable of achieving an international agreement not only capable of stabilising prices but also of increasing them. Although the small producers and consumers feared that their interests were insignificant and would not be cared for, they appeared consoled by the established voting principle of 'one country one vote' which they could employ to the fullest in their contributions to decision-making at the conference. There were other regional group interests: the Latin American and African producers. The Latin Americans were most willing to have an agreement because they were aware of the African penetration into EEC preferences which they were also willing to enjoy in an international agreement. The most dependent of the Latin American group on coffee were Brazil and Colombia who are main producers, while 13 other producers, together with Puerto Rico had formed a Federation of Coffee Producers of America (Federation Cafetera de America or FEDECAME). The African group, which had formed themselves into Inter-African Coffee Organisation (IACO) because of their preferential position with the EEC, were very lukewarm, particularly the franc-zone area, in reducing their trade with the EEC and losing the technical assistance from their former colonial masters. The African group could be divided into three further group interests:

1. countries under French jurisdiction enjoying the EEC preferential treatments;
2. countries of East Africa: Tanzania, formerly Tanganyika, Kenya and Uganda still under British trade systems and influence;
3. Ethiopia, Nigeria, etc.

The attachment of the EEC to the African group appeared to make them unwilling to assume any far-reaching obligations, for instance in tax reduction.

(II) The problem of procedure and working languages

In accord with ECOSOC rules, the question of procedure is very important in a large conference of this nature as this could determine its success or failure;[17] for instance the choice of a chairman follows certain set patterns, as we have already seen at the pre-conference. The procedure is common to all commodity negotiations with slight modifications according to the nature of the problems posed by the particular commodity. As in the tin conferences, the delegates assemble either in a plenary or a committee seated alphabetically in parallel positions[18] facing a central podium on which the chairman sits. Those seated with the chairman on the podium are the important secretariat officials, the executive secretary of the conference and its legal adviser who are all normally members of staff of the UN Secretariat. In the case of the Cocoa Conference of 1968, the staff was drawn from the UNCTAD Secretariat in Geneva where it took place. During these conferences, although the working languages are those of the UN, practical experiences show that there is a tendency to use English. This creates conflict, up to the point of some delegates from other language groups refusing to participate unless papers are produced in their languages. Such difficulties could sometimes arise from the nature of the composition of the secretariat staff or from the time limitations, or from simple diplomatic discourtesy because of rivalry on the importance or precedence given to one language over the other. The most visible difficulty, however, arises from technical difficulties of interpretation and translations. During these meetings the secretariat provides facilities for simultaneous interpretations into the working languages which are often English, French, Spanish, Russian and Portuguese.[19] Sometimes the use of these languages leads to errors in translation and interpretation. For example at the 1968 UN Conference on Cocoa in

Geneva, during which the Cocoa Draft Agreement was being negotiated, the Ivory Coast delegate, referring to the US delegates previous intervention, said that he took the African delegates for a 'petit-negre'[20] which was simultaneously interpreted as a 'small Negro', when in actual French expression or usage, it means a black toy often given to French children for familiarisation purposes. The US delegate, taking offence at what he thought was a reference to American internal black race problems in a cocoa conference, expressed indignation and the whole talks almost went to blazes but for the quick explanation of the Ivory Coast delegate after the explanatory intervention of the author who is bilingual. The US delegate, not satisfied with his explanations made in an African sense of humour, did not hesitate to make further enquiries from the author and other bilingual delegates during the short recess that followed in order to confirm the validity of his explanations.

The conference is convened by a pro-tem chairman who is generally on the staff of UNO, while the Interim Co-ordinating Committee for International Commodity Arrangements prepares the provisional draft agenda and rules of procedure[21] before the start of plenary conference to which they are submitted for proposal and adoption. Then the conference elects a chairman by unanimous vote and he is supposed to be independent.[22] Several vice-chairmen, often heads of delegations, are chosen geographically or according to interest groups. There are also committees set up to reflect specialisation of functions, e.g. Credentials Committee and Executive Committee; this is usually of the whole house, with the chairman being that of the plenary. Finally a steering committee of the conference chairman and vice-chairmen, and the chairmen of main committees,[23] is set up. As soon as the plenary adjourns into the Executive Committee of the plenary, the conference then becomes closed to outsiders. The plenary only meets again for formal decisions. But it is noteworthy that it is in the Executive Committee that policy statements which may include the expression of diplomatic niceties are made. It is also the Executive Committee that submits the Draft Proposal of the Agreement to the specialised committees. For instance a Legal and Drafting Committee, made up of five or six jurists from the delegations chosen in their personal and expert capacity, provides legal and drafting services to the conference. All the specialised committees are expected to submit their reports to the Legal and Drafting Committee which further examines them before they are included as revised articles in the Agreement after a decision to this effect is taken by the Executive Committee of the whole house.[24] After the revised articles have been adopted, one after the other, the Executive

Committee then adopts the entire provisions of the Agreement in a pro-forma draft. It is at this point that the Legal and Drafting Committee is called up to re-examine the entire text, in order to ascertain the proper use of terminology, clarity of thought and style of presentation, and make any necessary changes. Hereafter the conference meets no more in its Executive Capacity but in a plenary to formally adopt[25] the Draft Agreement and any formal act or resolutions that may arise. It is however to be noted that, although the 1962 Coffee Conference did not create or appoint a legal and drafting committee, a small Legal and Drafting Group came into a *de facto* existence.[26] When the conference reconvened on 28 September 1962, and after all the usual encomiums expressed by delegations, the draft text as submitted was approved and opened for signature. Only 23 states signed on this day but by the 30 November 1962 deadline, the Agreement had been signed by 54 governments,[27] 32 from the coffee-exporting countries having 95·1 per cent of total world exports, and 22 from coffee-importing countries having 94·7 per cent of total world imports. The agreement entered into force provisionally on 1 July 1963 and the first session of the Council started on 27 December 1963 when the requisite number of signatory governments had deposited their instruments of ratification or acceptance. The International Coffee Organisation was to function through the International Coffee Council, its Executive Board, Executive Director and Staff.

Finally it is important to note that most negotiations take very informal postures. For instance they take place in the corridors, hotel rooms, dining halls or under invitation conditions at dinners and mid-day meals. These techniques appear common to all commodity negotiations for they were largely employed at the 1968 Cocoa Conference in Geneva and at other Cocoa Producers Alliances Conferences attended by the author.

SECTION III. THE COFFEE AGREEMENTS

For the purpose of this study, two important and latest international agreements on coffee could be examined – the 1962 and 1968 in which the '1972 Geneva Document' would be mentioned.

(A) THE 1962 AGREEMENT

This agreement, which was opened for signature from 28 September to

30 November 1962 inclusive, in English, French, Russian, Spanish and Portuguese was signed by the USA and twenty-three others on 30 November 1962. Those who were entitled to sign were those governments represented by invitation to the 1962 United Nations Coffee Conference and by the government of any state represented before independence as a dependent territory at that Conference. This Conference, held in New York in July, August and September 1962, was attended by representatives of 71 coffee-exporting and coffee-importing countries, some specialised international organisations and observers. Delegations drawn from 58 countries participated actively in the negotiations while others had observer status. This agreement, among other objectives, was meant 'to achieve a reasonable balance between supply and demand on a basis which will assure adequate supplies of coffee to consumers and markets for coffee to producers at equitable prices, and which will bring about long-term equilibrium between production and consumption' (Article 1, para. 1). The importance of this objective cannot be underrated because it concerned the stability in foreign-exchange earnings of coffee-producers in 35 countries of Africa, Asia and Latin America since a decline of 1 cent per pound in coffee prices would reduce their foreign exchange earnings by 70 million dollars a year.[28] It was therefore a very important agreement to the poor countries of the world, particularly to the Latin Americans for whom coffee accounts for 23 per cent of the total export earnings of the region and which provided employment for 12 million persons. It was therefore a major accomplishment for the Alliance for Progress, as it replaced a short-term agreement started about three years before by 28 coffee-producing countries, which represented about 93 per cent of world exports in 1962.

General provisions of the agreement

This agreement, made up of a preamble (which recognises the importance of coffee to the economies of many countries and their dependence on this commodity for their export earnings and consequently for their development programmes) contains 74 Articles in 19 Chapters as follows: I – Objectives; II – Definitions; III – Membership; IV – Organisation and Administration; V – Privileges and Immunities; VI – Finance; VII – Regulation of Exports; VIII – Certificates of Origin and Re-export; IX – Regulation of Imports; X – Increase of Consumption; XI – Production Controls; XII – Regulation of Stocks;

XIII – Miscellaneous Obligations of Members; XIV – Seasonal Financing; XV – International Coffee Fund; XVI – Information and Studies; XVII – Waiver; XVIII – Disputes and Complaints; XIX – Financial Provisions. The International Coffee Organisation administers these provisions and supervises the operation of the agreement. The governing council of the Organisation is the International Coffee Council, made up of all the members of the Organisation represented by a representative each, and one or more alternates. A member could designate one or more advisers to accompany its representative or alternates. The basic votes for each contracting category (exporting or importing) are 150. Each member country is entitled to 5 basic votes unless the total membership of each contracting group exceeds 30, and in which case, the total number of basic votes for each category must be adjusted in such a way that the total does not exceed 150. Within the exporting group the remaining votes of 850 shall be allotted to each country in proportion to its basic export quota. For the importer group the remaining votes will be divided in proportion to the average volume of their respective coffee imports in the preceding three-year period. This is to say that each contracting group hold together 1000 votes. While no fractional votes are allowed, no member must hold more than 400 votes. Voting is carried out by a distributed simple majority unless otherwise stated in the agreement. This is to say that for more important decisions a two-thirds distributed majority vote is called for.

For the organisation and administration of the agreement, there is the International Coffee Council, its Executive Board, its Executive Director and its staff. The Executive Board, to which its members could be re-elected, consists of 7 exporting members and 7 importing members elected for each coffee year. Its Chairman is appointed by the Council for each coffee year and may be re-appointed. He has no right of vote although his alternate could in his place.

In order to enforce the application of the provisions of the agreement, the agreement provides for a system of 'Certificates of Origin and Re-Export' in Chapter VIII, Article 44. These certificates are required to accompany every export of coffee from any member in whose territory that coffee has been grown, and must have been issued by a competent and qualified agency chosen by that member. While the original copy of such certificates accompanies the exported coffee, its duplicate is sent to the coffee organisation by that member. In the final analysis it is an internationally recognised world-wide organisation that would verify these certificates of origin in order to ascertain the quantity of coffee exported by each member. These rules also apply to re-exports of coffee and these notwithstanding, the Council could, for reasons best known to itself, declare certification by a particular agency unacceptable to it. While the provisions on export should enter into effect not more than three months after the entry into force of the agreement, that on re-export shall be at a time when the Council so decides. This is to say that after the time-lag provided above, all importing members agree to disallow the entry of coffee from outside the signatories of the agreement and in fact any importation not accompanied by a Certificate of Origin. This agreement, unlike all previous short-term arrangements, covers all types of coffee, the definition for coffee according to Article 2 being: 'the beans and berries of the coffee tree, whether parchment, green or roasted, and includes ground, decaffeinated, liquid and soluble coffee'. The agreement provides that signatory members should find all possible ways of progressively reducing and eventually eliminating obstacles to increased trade and consumption and to communicate their findings to the Council within 18 months after the agreement goes into effect. On regulation of imports, Article 45 provides that in order to prevent non-member exporting countries from increasing their exports at the expense of members, each member shall, subject to certain conditions[29] 'limit its total annual imports from non-member countries as a group to a quantity not in excess of its average annual imports from those countries as a group during the last three years prior to the entry into force of the Agreement for which statistics are available' (paragraph 2). However the application of such limitations could be deferred by the Council.

There are no price levels established in the agreement as it was meant to maintain a price level not lower than the general level prevailing in 1962 by equating exports to world demand. However provision is made for the adjustment of quotas to prevent excessive rise and fall in prices occurring within brief periods. The agreement does not contain any specific production or stock control mechanisms, but the Council would, after the first year, recommend production goals and stock policies in order to equate supply with demand during the application of the agreement. Any attempt to refuse the recommendations of the Council by any member would lead to sanctions.

Final provisions of the agreement

The agreement was open for signature at the UN headquarters until and including 30 November 1962 to two categories of legal persons: (1) all governments invited to the 1962 United Nations Coffee Conference; (2) the government of any state represented before independence as a dependent territory at that Conference (Article 62). There is a right of accession to the government of any state member of the UN or of its specialised agencies upon conditions which the Council was alone competent to establish (Article 65). Instruments of Ratification were deposited in accordance with the respective constitutional procedures of contracting members with the Secretary-General of UNO not later than 31 December 1963 (Article 63). The agreement expressly provides that no reservations be made with respect to any of its provisions (Article 66). It would come into effect definitively after governments representing at least 20 exporting countries having at least 80 per cent of world exports of coffee, and governments representing at least 10 importing countries with at least 80 per cent of world imports based on 1961 figures, deposit their respective instruments of ratification or acceptance (Article 64). Article 63 provides that no contracting party may withdraw voluntarily before 30 September 1963. Thereafter, it could, by giving a written withdrawal notice any time to the Secretary-General of UNO which is the depository of the Instruments of Ratification. Such voluntary withdrawals shall become effective 90 days after the notice is received. Article 69 provides for a compulsory withdrawal on condition that the Council by a two-thirds distributed majority vote has determined that any member has failed to carry out its obligations to the extent that they have impaired, significantly, the operations of the agreement. Article 70 provides that any withdrawing member shall have its settlement of accounts determined by the Council and in fact it is duty bound to pay amounts due from it to the Organisation at the time its withdrawal becomes effective, except with the proviso that its withdrawal is connected with its inability to accept an amendment. In this case the council will determine its accounts in an equitable way. Article 71 determines the life of the agreement as five full coffee years unless extended or terminated before its expiring date, to be determined by the Council. Article 72 provides that a review of the agreement shall hold at a special session during the last six months of the coffee year ending 30 September 1965. Article 73 provides for a possible amendment of the agreement with a distributed two-thirds majority under certain conditions. Article 74 stipulates that the right of notification is the responsibility of the Secretary-General of UNO and that the texts of the Agreement are authentic in the English, French, Russian, Spanish and Portuguese languages.

(B) THE 1968 COFFEE AGREEMENT COMPARED

There are great similarities in the overall objectives of both the 1962 and 1968 Coffee Agreements except for certain structural and provisional changes in the 1968 text. For instance, in Article 15 of both agreements dealing with the 'Composition of the Board', the Executive Board now consists of eight exporting members and eight importing members instead of seven on each contracting side as in the 1962 Agreement. We shall therefore examine these changes from specific provisions of the 1968 Agreement: Privileges and Immunities (Article 22); Export Quotas (Articles 31 and 37); Processed Coffee (Article 44); Removal of Obstacles to Consumption (Article 47); Production Policy and Stocks (Articles 48 and 49); Diversification Fund (Article 54); Waiver (Article 57); Consultation, Disputes and Complaints (Article 58 and 59).

(I) Privileges and Immunities (Article 22)

The legal personality of the International Coffee Organisation has been spelt out succinctly. While the 1962 Agreement, in its Article 22 paragraph 2, simply establishes the legal personality of the ICO in member countries as would be consistent with their laws, the 1968 Agreement appears less vague in the sense that it spells out the areas of this capacity or personality, namely: 'Capacity to contract, acquire and dispose of movable and immovable property and to institute legal proceedings.' Another area of this legal capacity is in the area of a headquarters agreement. The ICO now has the legal personality of concluding an independent agreement with 'the host Government . . . relating to the status, privileges and immunities of the organisation, of its Executive Director and its staff and of representatives of Members while in the territory of the host Government for the purpose of exercising their functions' (Article 22, paragraph 2). For the purpose of this agreement, the host government is the United Kingdom, since the seat of the ICO is in London.

Both agreements, however, provide that the host government should grant exemption from taxation on the remuneration paid to the ICO employees although this may not apply to nationals of the host country in the employ of the ICO. The host government is also expected to grant exemption from taxation on the assets, income and other property of the Organisation.

(II) Export Quotas: Articles 31 and 37

Article 31, paragraphs 1–2 now requires that basic quotas shall no longer be allotted to any exporting member whose average annual authorised exports for three preceding years are less than 100,000 bags until its average annual exports reach 100,000 bags. However, any exporting member for which no basic quota had been allotted would have in the coffee year 1968–69, its quota fixed.[30] In the subsequent years the quota shall be increased by 10 per cent of that initial quota until the maximum of 100,000 bags is attained, subject to certain conditions.[31]

Article 37 paragraphs 1–3: These are additional provisions for adjusting export quotas. In addition to the old Article 41 of the 1962 Agreement, which stipulates that the Council shall 'ensure that supplies of all types of coffee that consumers require are available', the Council shall also now ensure that prices for the different types are equitable and that sharp price fluctuations do not occur within brief periods. The Council is also empowered to adopt price differentials and price brackets by a distributed two-thirds majority for various types of coffee. It is also empowered to adjust quotas in relation to the movement of the prices of the principal types provided that the limit set by the Council to the amount by which annual quotas may be reduced shall not exceed 5 per cent.

(III) Processed coffee (Article 44)

One of the obstacles to the 1968 Agreement during its negotiation was the vehement objection of certain manufacturers of processed coffee in importing countries to the discriminatory practices which existed in respect of processed coffee and green coffee. In the forefront of this opposition was the USA, who were opposed to Brazil's attitude for instituting an export tax on green coffee but not on processed coffee, thus making processed coffee cheaper in the USA market than their manufacturers could achieve. For this reason, it was agreed to provide for Article 44, a new provision in respect to processed coffee. It provides that no member should apply discriminatory practices against another member as regards processed coffee as compared with green coffee. This provision does not, however, apply to certain special situation of markets.[32] If there is complaint to the effect that discrimination exists, an arbitration panel of three persons shall be set up to determine the validity of the complaint. The panel shall consist of:

(i) one person designated by the complaining member;
(ii) one person designated by the member against which the complaint has been made; and
(iii) a chairman mutually agreed upon by the members involved or, failing such agreement, by two persons designated under i and ii (paragraph 2b).

If a discriminatory treatment has been proved the defaulting member is given a period of 30 days after it had been duly notified of the panel's conclusions, to rectify the situation in accordance with the panel's conclusions. Otherwise the member whose interests have been jeopardised could 'take counter measures which shall not go beyond what is necessary to counteract the discriminatory treatment determined by the arbitration panel and shall last no longer than the discriminatory treatment exists' (paragraph 3b).

(IV) Removal of obstacles to consumption (Article 47)

Article 47 has been drafted in stronger terms and appears less cumbersome in content than the previous one. The Council now recognising the need for the increase of coffee consumption, has adequately called for the removal of all administrative and legal obstacles hindering this objective. For instance, all import arrangements applicable to coffee: tariffs, quotas, operations of government import monopolies, official purchasing agencies, which hinder the objective of increased consumption are expected to be removed. Finally, while members are expected to inform the Council of all measures adopted by them, for the implementation of these provisions, the Council is empowered to make recommendations to members as to the best ways of achieving the above objectives.

(V) Production policy and controls (Article 48)

The production of each producer member must be adjusted to a goal which does not exceed the amount required for domestic consumption, permitted exports and stocks. In relation to this, the Council could by a distributed two-thirds majority establish a stocks policy in producing member countries (Article 49). Consequently each exporting member could submit its production goals to the Executive Board. This shall be considered as approved if the Executive Board does not reject it by a distributed simple majority vote. But if rejected, the Board shall recommend production goals for that exporting member. In the light of the Board's recommendations, the Council could by a two-thirds distributed majority vote establish individual production goals for exporting members. Although these individual production goals do not confer entitlements to specific levels of exports, nor are they binding, producer members are expected to comply with these provisions. If any member fails to comply, it shall not enjoy any subsequent increase in its annual export entitlement and may have its voting rights suspended until the Council is satisfied that the member has fulfilled its obligations, or may be required to withdraw from the Organisation. To ensure production goals of producing countries, a special obligation is imposed on any international body to which importing members belong, not to offer technical or financial assistance or support proposals which are against the objectives of the agreement (paragraph 10). Reference made to the international organisation is no doubt that of the EEC.

(VI) Diversification Fund (Article 54)

The Diversification Fund was established to further the objectives of limiting the production of coffee so that demand could equate supply. Contributions to this Fund are only compulsory to exporting members whose export entitlement is over 100,000 bags. There are also provisions for voluntary contributors who are in any other category of contracting parties and other sources, with the proviso that the condition of such contributions shall be agreed between the Fund and the parties concerned (paragraph 2). The compulsory contributions of an exporting member is made in quarterly instalments of an amount equivalent to US $0·60 per bag, times the number of bags it actually exports in excess of 100,000 bags each coffee year to quota markets. These contributions are made for five consecutive years and this started with the 1968–69 coffee year. The rate of contributions may be increased to a level not exceeding US $1·00 per bag by a distributed two-thirds majority vote of the Fund. These contributions will facilitate the funding and execution of approved programmes and projects in the territories of the exporting participant. However 20 per cent of the contribution payable in freely convertible currency shall fund other programmes approved by the Fund, and an additional percentage payable in freely convertible currency, shall aid the administration of the Fund. Failure to meet with the above obligations could lead to the suspension of the voting rights of the defiant exporting member in the Council, whose export entitlement will not also be increased. Any further defiance for a continuous period of one year could lead to the compulsory withdrawal of such a member from the Organisation 90 days thereafter, unless the Council by a distributed two-thirds majority vote decides otherwise.

(VII) Waiver (Article 57)

The Council may grant waivers by a two-thirds distributed majority vote to relieve a contracting member of an obligation because of exceptional circumstances, force majeur, constitutional obligations or even international obligations under the UN Charter for territories administered under the trusteeship system. The former condition, that there was imposed a serious hardship or inequitable burden or an unfair advantage on another, is no more required. However in granting a waiver the terms and conditions must be explicitly stated. Furthermore it is now specifically mentioned that no waiver will be granted in respect of an excess of permitted exports or failure to comply with production or stock policies.

(VIII) Consultations (Article 58)

This article on consultations did not exist in the previous agreement. It is therefore a new provision. It recommends the use of consultations as a method of conflict resolution. On request by either party during such consultation, an independent panel could be set by the Executive Director with the consent of the other party. This panel shall employ its good offices in conciliating the parties. On the other hand if a party refuses to accept the setting-up of a panel, or if the consultations yield no fruitful results in terms of a solution, the matter could be referred to the Council in accordance with Article 59 which deals with Disputes and Complaints. There is also a new provision in this Article 59 on Disputes and Complaints. Before a matter is referred to the Council, a majority of members holding not less than one-third of the total votes may require the Council after discussion, to seek the opinion of an advisory panel.

This panel normally consists of five persons, two of whom are nominated by the exporting members and the other two by the importing member. The fifth is a chairman selected unanimously by the other four persons already nominated.

(C) FUNCTIONING OF THE COFFEE AGREEMENT IN PRACTICE

The high prices of the 1950s when demand exceeded supply encouraged plantings in Africa, Asia and Latin America with the result that the emergent surpluses caused decrease in prices in the later 1960s. Between 1957 and 1961, a number of short-term international agreements were signed on quota and crop-retention schemes. With the 1962 Agreement now provisionally in force, the period 1 July 1963–30 September 1966 was significant because it witnessed how the agreement functioned under an institutional framework of the ICO which served as the instrument for the administration and supervision of the agreement. During the said period, the Council met nine times and the Executive Board 19 times.[33] Let us then examine its administration under specific provisions of the agreement.

Export quotas and prices

During this period (1 July 1963–30 September 1966), the ICO achieved its main objectives of establishing a fair balance between demand and supply through quota adjustments. In 1963–64 the quota provisions had to be negotiated in order to halt rising prices created by reports of crop shortage in Brazil, by increasing quotas although they were later reduced to uplift the downward price movements. This was the first sign of co-operation between the signatory members of the agreement. To start with, a system of adjusting quotas was introduced under Resolution No. 67 of March 1965. This resolution provided for a daily price of coffee based on the simple arithmetic average of the prices (ex dock New York) of the three main groups of coffee, namely mild arabicas, unwashed arabicas and robustas. A system of price ranges was established, between 38·00 and 44·00 US cents per lb, within which the Board could adjust quotas upwards and downwards within defined limits if prices soared either beyond or below the ceiling and floor prices. Within this period, this resolution remained in operation and it helped to stabilise prices despite the growing gap between production and consumption. Because of over-production, stockpiles in developing countries reached a record level of about 70 million bags by the end of 1965–66. Consequently some eight countries were in 1963–64 granted waivers to the tune of 1,148,000 bags in accordance with Article 60 of the agreement, while for 1964–65, another four countries were granted 857,000 bags under Article 28, paragraph 2, as an increase in quotas. In 1965–66 special waivers were again granted to 15 members to the tune of 1,357,000 bags as a relief pending a decision on the review of basic quotas. All these waivers were granted with the proviso that prices did not fall beyond a certain level. However the constant fall in prices led to a suspension of waivers. For instance, half the waivers of members producing mild arabicas were suspended, that is a loss of 335,000 bags. Ethiopia, who is the only producer of unwashed arabias, had its waiver suspended, in the last quarter; that is a loss of 12,000 bags. During the period 1965–66, market reports revealed that there were large-scale evasions of the provisions of the agreement because of the uncertainty over basic quota revision rendered necessary by stockpile. For example, over 2½ million bags reached traditional quota markets from exporting members, without being debited to quotas. They were transhipped through non-member countries or had been diverted from, or while en route to, the non-quota markets.[34]

Control measures

A system of Certificates of Origin and Re-export established to check all coffee shipments from member countries became fully operational in late 1964–65. This was because of the delay in America's legislative process of ratification. This delay is important to note because America is the largest importer of coffee. Because of the 'tourist' coffee illegally moving outside, quota members pressed for control measures which resulted into *two* important resolutions initiated at the Council Session held from 22 August to 6 September 1966. They were to be applied only in the 1966–67 coffee year. The Resolutions were:

(i) Resolution No. 117

This called for the application of Article 45, paragraph 3 of the agreement to regulate imports of coffee by members from non-member countries. Under this resolution a concerted action was undertaken by contracting members to limit individually its total annual imports from non-member countries to a quantity not in excess of its average annual imports from those countries as a group during the last three years prior to the entry into force of the agreement. This dealt a blow on non-members trafficking on 'tourist' coffee.

(II) Resolution No. 118

This called for the introduction of a system of export stamps to be used in conjunction with Certificates of Origin. Each exporting member was provided with a quantity of these stamps each quarter in accordance with their authorised exports for that quarter. Other types of measures for a selective adjustment of coffee supply were also introduced to ensure that the types of coffee required by consumers would be at their disposal in accordance with Article 41. But because the expectations of several members were quite different from the provisions of the agreement, the matter was referred to the Advisory Panel in accordance with Article 61 paragraph 3. The case at issue was that while most members preferred a selective quota adjustment system several provisions of the agreement favoured a pro-rata system. The Advisory Panel's report indicated that departures from the pro-rata principle would only be possible in very special circumstances under the agreement as it stood. Therefore a compromise solution had to be sought. Consequently when the selective system was introduced in Resolution 115 of 6 September 1966,[35] it was merely for a trial period of one year, 1966–67. It applied only to special export authorisations totalling 1,083,500 bags and waivers granted to 16 countries totalling 1,732,000 bags. The annual export quotas for 1966–67 of 43·7 million bags therefore were only to be adjusted on a pro-rata basis if the Council considered a change necessary.

Goals and remedial action

The price and quota drive for stabilisation during the period up to 1966 were seen as short-term measures. This was because stockpiling and quota barriers could not go on for long. Therefore a long-term objective was to establish an equilibrium between production and consumption. Three alternatives were then open to the organisation: (1) increase consumption at all cost; (2) establish realistic production goals; (3) help members diversify and develop their economies so that they can be less dependent on coffee. Therefore, to achieve these goals, certain remedial actions were taken.

1. In August 1964, the Council established a world coffee production committee and created a Fund for compulsory contributions from exporting members to finance promotional and public relations programmes. For 1964–65 contributions were assessed at the rate of 15·00 US cents per bag of three-quarters of each member's total authorised exports under quotas for the previous coffee year. Five million US dollars were thus collected and allocated for campaigns in 11 countries in 1965–66. A sum of 7 million US dollars was raised in 13 countries in 1966–67. Most of these campaigns took place in the USA – the greatest consumer – with declining consumption figures and in the UK and Japan, known traditionally as tea-drinking nations, in order to make room for coffee-drinking.
2. The ICO tried to encourage members to eliminate or reduce tariffs and taxes capable of increasing prices to consumers.
3. The ICO campaigned against the sale of adulterated coffee and substitutes.
4. The ICO evoked Article 55 of the agreement which requires that if coffee products contain less than the equivalent of 90 per cent green coffee as basic raw material, the sale and advertisement under the name of coffee should be prohibited. It called on members to bring their legislation in line with this Article.
5. The ICO, in its August–September 1966 session, established a Coffee Diversification and Development Fund and set up a Working Group to review a draft proposal submitted by the Executive Director for this purpose. Waivers became dependent on the contribution which a recipient member makes to the schemes of Diversification and Development in its own country.

The 1972 'Geneva Group'

The USA had renewed the 1968 Agreement only in March 1972, although it was still valid until 1973. This US renewal came in after twelve months' delay because the approval of the US Senate for the renewal of the 1968 Agreement was obtained only after assurances that coffee prices would not be raised to compensate producers for the dollar devaluation which had reduced commodity prices generally among producers. In order to compensate for this loss, the producers had asked for structural price changes within the ICO. They asked for an increase, in dollars, by 4 cents from the beginning of 1972 but the ICO would not reach an agreement. Thus emerged the 'Geneva Group'[36] which decided to limit their exports so that they could not exceed the quota agreed upon on 15 February 1972. This group[37] made up of Brazil, Colombia, the Ivory Coast and Portugal (acting for Angola), met in Bogota and drew the draft of what has come to be known as the Geneva Document. This document, whose aim was to control supplies of coffee and increase prices, was to them more justified after a compromise increase of 2 cents were rejected by the USA and Canada. According to the document, there would be a meeting of a Co-ordinating Committee of two representatives of each signatory state every three months to review the market situation. This document contains several provisions; namely, the establishment of a buffer stock with a 'commercial body' meant to buy surplus coffee fetching too low a price. Such coffee would be released when the market indicator price is rising. The purpose of the buffer stock is to prevent individual producer members from undertaking separate deals with consumers such as that which Brazil had entered into with the USA. The Committee was to have had its first meeting in Paris in May 1972.

However, in spite of the disagreement within the ICO, as we have already mentioned, quotas were later increased despite an increase in world exports during the later months of 1971–72 season ending in September.[38] This increase was due to a strong upward surge in price movements because of the frost situation in Brazil. Because they could still not agree on the indicator price ranges for the next season, at their August/September meeting, the ICO however fixed a substantial increase in quotas for October–December. As prices continued to soar, all the operations of the ICO were in principle suspended until September 1973. Nevertheless, the 'Geneva Group' of producers decided to maintain some limitations on their exports.

The International Coffee Agreement officially expired on 30 September 1973 although its machinery had earlier broken down as we have just explained, because the ICO lifted all export restrictions on coffee on 12 December 1972.[39] Instead of negotiating a new agreement under the ICO, the African members of the UNCTAD Board insisted that there should be coffee 'consultations' under UNCTAD between October 1973 and March 1974. This was during the Board's 13th Session in September 1973. When the Latin American group proposed a return to the International Coffee Agreement, the Afro-Asian majority, backed by the Communist bloc, overruled. In this way, the resolution was taken without a vote, after a very strong opposition from the Latin American bloc which accounted for 70–80 per cent of world coffee production in spite of their refusal to participate in any 'consultations' under UNCTAD auspices. The result was that the western developed market countries had to oppose the Afro-Asian proposal. Another reaction then surfaced by early 1974 from the small producers of Central America who were willing to join the London-based sales company established by Brazil, Colombia, Ivory Coast and Angola which already control about 60 per cent of world coffee production. With this new position it became clear that no 'consultaions' could hold effectively without these two groups of producers and consumers. This would have created a virtual monopoly except for the USA, the greatest world consumer, who might reduce her imports from Brazil rather than pay increased prices. Consequently, the African coffee-growing countries might also open up new markets by underselling the cartel.

SECTION IV. VOTING PROCEDURES

We have already seen in the preceding section how votes are generally distributed among each contracting group of the agreement. We are therefore concerned here with how those votes are manipulated in the functioning of the agreement in terms of its decision-making processes. However it is noteworthy that in these parts of the provisions of the 1962 and 1968 Agreements, there are no structural changes.

(A) VOTING IN THE COUNCIL (ARTICLES 13–14)

According to Article 13, paragraph 1, each representative may cast its votes fully but any contracting member could authorise any member within its contracting group to represent its interests and to exercise its voting rights at any meeting of the Council. In respect to decisions of the Council, they are made by a distributed simple majority vote unless otherwise stated in the provisions of the agreement (Article 14, paragraphs 1–3). For all other actions which require a two-thirds majority vote, the procedure is established in a graded system moving downwards. For instance: (1) if due to a negative vote of any three or less members of any of the contracting groups, a distributed two-thirds vote is not obtained, the proposal shall again be put to vote within 48 hours provided a decision to this effect is reached by a distributed simple majority vote and by a majority of members present in Council; (2) if again a two-thirds vote is not obtained because of two or less negative votes of any contracting group, it will again be put to vote within 24 hours; (3) if the matter is again put to vote by the same process without achieving the desired results, that is, a two-thirds majority, because of the negative vote of any one member of a contracting group, the proposal is considered adopted. The above consideration shows that the Council takes important decisions with a two-thirds distributed majority and simple procedural ones with a simple distributed majority. Finally it is important to note that the Council members have all undertaken to accept the Council decisions as binding.

(B) VOTING OF THE EXECUTIVE BOARD (ARTICLES 17–18)

Article 17 stipulates that while major decisions remain the prerogative of the Council, it would delegate certain functions (which it could also revoke at any time by a simple distributed majority) to the Executive Board by a simple distributed majority. This is to say that there are some important functions which the Council cannot delegate to the Board according to Article 17 (paragraphs 2a – k). These exceptions are the following:

(a) approval of the administrative budget and assessment of contributions to it according to Article 24;
(b) suspension of voting rights under Article 45, which deals with Regulation of Imports, or Article 59 on Disputes and Complaints;
(c) determination of quotas with the exception of the adjustment of quarterly export quotas;
(d) establishment or revision of individual country and world production goals under Article 48, which deals with Production Policy and Controls;
(e) establishment of a policy relative to stocks under Article 49;
(f) waiver of obligations of a member under Article 57;
(g) decision of disputes under Article 59;
(h) a decision to require compulsory withdrawal (Article 67);
(i) extension or termination of the agreement under Article 69; and
(j) recommendation of amendments to members under Article 70.

The voting procedure in the Board is established in Article 18. It stipulates that voting by proxy is not allowed and that each member is expected to cast the number of votes allotted to it under the provisions of paragraphs 6 and 7 of Article 16. No fractional votes are allowed.

(C) ELECTION OF THE BOARD (ARTICLE 16)

The Board is elected by both contracting groups of the Council and voting takes place in the following way. Each member-country may cast all the votes at its disposal for a single candidate of its choice in accordance with Article 12 which we have already examined in Section III(A): General Provisions of the Agreement. It could also cast any other votes exercised by it under Article 13, paragraph 2, which states that any contracting group may authorise the representation of its interests by any of its group interests in respect to the exercise of its voting rights at any Council Meetings (Article 16, paragraph 2). According to Article 15, the Executive Board consists of eight members on each side of the contracting group elected for each coffee year. On electing these candidates, eight candidates which receive the largest number of votes shall be elected with the understanding that no candidate shall be elected on the first ballot unless it receives at least 75 votes (paragraph 3). During this voting if less than eight candidates are elected on the first ballot, the rest will be elected by those members who did not vote for any of the already elected candidates. For each further ballot after the first one, the minimum number of votes required for election shall be successively diminished by *five* until eight candidates are elected. That is, for example, if six candidates were elected in the first instance, the minimum number of votes required will be 70 for the 7th and 65 for the 8th candidate.

If a member is elected it is considered that it had received the number of votes originally cast for it, that is 75 votes in addition to the number of votes assigned to it provided that its total number of votes do not exceed 499 (paragraph 6). If the votes received by an elected member exceeds 499, those members which voted or assigned their votes to such a member shall arrange among themselves for one or more of them to withdraw their votes from that member and assign or reassign them to another elected member so that the votes received by each elected member shall not exceed the limit of 499 (paragraph 7).

(D) VOTING RIGHTS AND ASSESSMENT OF CONTRIBUTIONS FOR THE ADMINISTRATION OF THE AGREEMENT

Voting rights as determined by the financial contributions of contracting members of the 1968 Coffee Agreement is considered in Chaper VI – Finance (Articles 23–25). These articles also consider the sanctions attendant on failure to contribute within a given period and the contributions of those who wish to accede after entry into force of the agreement. As for the delegations to the Council, Article 23 stipulates that the expenses to attend meetings in the Board, Council or Committees of the Council are borne by the individual governments. We shall therefore examine the above under two headings.

(a) Administrative budget and assessment of contributions

Article 24, paragraphs 1–3 considers this vital area of decision-making. It is important as a study for the following reasons: (1) it reveals, like in other commodity agreements, the importance of a weighted voting system as distinct from equality of votes as practised in political institutions; (2) it explains the law-making processes and the application of law in terms of sanctions; (3) it highlights the importance of contractual obligations in international economic institutions; (4) it opens up channels for the verification of sanctions as to whether they are applied. The assessment of financial contributions to the administrative budget of the agreement is an exercise determined in the second half of each financial year of the agreement. This assessment, carried out on the basis of each contracting member, is in proportion to the number of votes held by a member at the time of the approval of the budget, and which bears to the total votes of all the members put together. However, if there is a change in the distribution of votes at the beginning of the financial year (Article 12, paragraph 5) for already assessed contributions, such shall be adjusted accordingly.[40] For the purpose of Article 24 in determining contributions, the vote of each member is calculated without considering whether a member's voting rights have been suspended or whether this had once given rise to the distribution of votes. It also deals with what happens to a member joining the Organisation for the first time after the entry into force of the agreement, that is when acceding (Article 24, paragraph 3). The initial contribution of such a member is assessed by the Council on the basis of the number of votes to be held by it in accordance with Article 12, paragraphs 1–2[41] and the period remaining in the financial year in question. However, the assessment upon other members for that year shall remain unaltered.

(b) Sanctions and mode of contributions (Article 25)

According to Article 25, paragraph 1, the contributions to the Administrative Budget must be paid on the first day of the financial year, in freely convertible currency. But if any member fails to pay within six months of that date, its voting rights will be suspended both in the Board and in the Council unless the Council decides otherwise by a two-thirds distributed majority and in which case, such a member will not be relieved of its obligations or denied of its voting rights. But if its voting rights have been suspended in accordance with Article 25, paragraph 2 or under Articles 38, 45, 48, 54 or 59 of the 1968 Agreement,[42] the member remains responsible for the payment of its obligations (see Table 8.2).

SECTION V. PERMANENT AND ADMINISTRATIVE INSTITUTIONS OF THE AGREEMENT

The ICO, which was first established in 1962, administers the provisions of the agreement under a Chief Administrator who supervises this administration. This organisation functions through the ICC, its Executive Board, its Executive Director and staff (Article 7, paragraphs 1–3).

THE EXECUTIVE DIRECTOR AND ITS STAFF (ARTICLE 20).

The Executive Board of sixteen members recommends the Executive Director whose terms of appointment are spelt out by the Council. Those terms are comparable to those applicable to corresponding officials of similar inter-governmental organisations (paragraph 1). The Executive Director is the Chief Administrative Officer who is responsible for the administration of the agreement. For instance, since the ICO is also an institution of co-operation and consultation,

TABLE 8.2 Distribution of votes (Annex C)

Country	*Exporting*	*Importing*
Argentina	–	16
Australia	–	9
Austria	–	11
Belgium*	–	28
Bolivia	4	–
Brazil	332	–
Burundi	8	–
Canada	–	32
Colombia	114	–
Congo (Democratic Republic of)	20	–
Costa Rica	21	–
Cuba	4	–
Cyprus	–	5
Czechoslovakia	–	9
Denmark	–	23
Dominican Republic	12	–
Ecuador	16	–
El Salvador	34	–
Ethiopia	27	–
Federal Republic of Germany	–	101
Finland	–	21
France	–	84
Ghana	4	–
Guatemala	32	–
Guinea	4	–
Haiti	12	–
Honduras	11	–
India	11	–
Indonesia	25	–
Israel	–	7
Italy	–	47
Jamaica	4	–
Japan	–	18
Kenya	17	–
Liberia	4	–
Mexico	32	–
Netherlands	–	35
New Zealand	–	6
Nicaragua	13	–
Nigeria	4	–
Norway	–	16
OAMCAF	(88)	–
OAMCAF	(4)†	–
Cameroon	15	–
Central African Republic	3	–

Country	*Exporting*	*Importing*
Congo (Brazzaville)	1	–
Dahomey	1	–
Gabon	1	–
Ivory Coast	47	–
Malagasy Republic	13	–
Togo	3	–
Panama	4	–
Peru	16	–
Portugal	48	–
Rwanda	6	–
Sierra Leone	4	–
Spain	–	21
Sweden	–	38
Switzerland	–	19
Tanzania	15	–
Trinidad & Tobago	4	–
Tunisia	–	6
Uganda	41	–
USSR	–	16
UK	–	32
USA	–	400
Venezuala	9	–
TOTAL	996	1,000

* Includes Luxembourg.
† Basic votes not attributable to individual contracting parties under Article 5(4)(b).
Source: International Coffee Agreement, 1968.

information and studies, the Chief Administrator co-ordinates the activities of non-governmental organisations concerned with international commerce in coffee and with experts in coffee matters (paragraph 1). Consequently the ICO through its Executive Director acts as a centre for data collection of statistical nature on world production, prices, exports and imports distribution and consumption of coffee. These include technical information on the cultivation, processing and utilisation of coffee. The co-ordinating responsibilities of the Chief Administrative Officer can therefore not be underrated. In fact when the Council authorises studies on the impact of governmental measures in producing and consuming countries on production and consumption, it could be understood that the impact of the Secretariat is not simply that of collection but also that of recommendation to governments. In this way secretariats of international organisations are able to influence State decisions. This is to say that the calibre of the

Secretariat Staff will determine the confidence reposed on it. This is why the Director and his staff are not expected to have any financial interests in the coffee industry, coffee trade or coffee production. However the agreement appears silent as to whether the Executive Director could renounce any of these interests before he takes up the appointment, as is the case with the tin agreements. He is expected to receive no instructions from any other authority external to the Organisation nor is he expected to receive instructions from any member and by implication, his home country. All these prerequisites are meant to guarantee the independence of the Secretariat vis-à-vis member-governments. The members of staff are therefore expected to keep professional secrecy although preference is given to the nations of participating countries in their recruitment.

Part Two

Conflict and Co-operation in Commodity Diplomacy

9 General Economic Scope of the Problem

SECTION I. ECONOMIC SITUATION

In the process of finding adequate solutions to the problem of commodity stabilisation, developing nations have searched incessantly over the years for the establishment of contractual arrangements because, as principally primary producers, fluctuations in world prices of their commodities do affect the development growth of their nations. In this process, they had in the past ignored political issues arising therefrom and the appropriate approach towards tackling them. This could be inferred from the fluid nature of the negotiation tactics of the 'Group of 77' during the 2nd UNCTAD Conference in New Delhi in 1968, for their lack of preparedness and consequently cohesiveness. However today this situation has been reversed because of their greater awareness of their relationship with the consumers of raw materials and manufacturers of finished goods. This awareness expressed itself during the 3rd UNCTAD Conference in Santiago, Chile, in 1972 and during the 1974 Raw Material Conference in New York for the establishment of a new international economic order. The role which the exploitation and commercialisation of raw materials play in the world scene can only be appreciated by the importance attached to them in these negotiations, by both producers and consumers who concert efforts to regularise the forces of supply, demand and prices. A product like tin, for instance, has been a great source of power politics because of its strategic use in the manufacture of military equipment and luxury goods like automobiles, radios, etc. So also oil politics have engendered power politics because of oil's strategic importance. The bulk of agricultural products form the basis of anxiety for the developing world who possess little or no technological prowess for the transformation of these perishable products, often torn asunder by the vicissitudes of price fluctuations. The producer nations have fought shy of this problem in the past by their inability to establish institutional or juridical arrangements for controlling these free market forces. The result has been that developing countries have often been hard-hit by their terms of trade. The 'Group of 77' established under the banner of UNCTAD in 1964, was one of the approaches adopted by them. On the other hand, the developed nations themselves have found answers to these tactics by quickly co-ordinating their policies within institutional arrangements like the EEC, OECD, GATT, etc.

The relative positions of the developing world of producers vis-à-vis consumers in world trade and development calls for great concern because more than 80 per cent of the export earnings of the developing countries come from their sales of primary products. Added to this, is the fact that while the GNP of the developed economies had an annual growth rate increased from 3·2 per cent in the second half of the 1950s to about 5 per cent in 1960–66, the developing poor nations in terms of total real product was 4·6 per cent in the period 1955–60 and 4·5 per cent in 1960–65. During the first five years of the development decade, the poor nations passed the target growth only once, that is in 1964, and their economic growth has since persistently fallen. For instance between 1960 and 1969 the share of the poor nations in world trade fell from 21·3 per cent to 17·8 per cent, and more particularly with primary commodities which fell from 54 per cent to 42 per cent between 1953 and 1967. But when we compare the volume of trade among developed market economies and between socialist countries with intra-African trade, the disillusionment of the poor nations can easily be understood. About 52 per cent of world trade in 1966 belonged to the developed market economies and the socialist countries have grown at an average fast rate of 11·6 per cent between 1960 and 1966. While the developed market economies had their share of world trade increased from 61 per cent in 1950 to 70 per cent in 1966, and the socialist countries of Eastern Europe from 8 per cent in 1950 to 10·2 per cent in 1960, the developing countries had their share embarrassingly and steadily declining from under 31·2 per cent in 1950 to 19·1 per cent in 1966. If oil exports were excluded the decline over the same period would be from 24·4 per cent to 14 per cent. Unfortunately exchanges within the developing countries had also diminished to 3 per cent in 1966, particularly the share of primary commodities in total world trade which has persistently contracted compared to manufactured products which had risen considerably. On the African scene itself, intra-African trade has not made any appreciable progress since independence. For 44 African developing countries the GDP has been calculated to be less than that of the Benelux countries (Belgium, Netherlands and Luxembourg) while the total GDP of 14 West African states is less than the GDP of Turkey.[1]

SECTION II. PROBLEMS OF COMMODITY MARKETING: THE EXAMPLES OF CITRUS FRUITS (ORANGE, LIME, CITRON, GRAPEFRUIT), BANANAS AND TEA

(i) CITRUS FRUITS

The main exporting countries are the USA, Israel and the developing countries of southern Europe. World exports have risen at 4 per cent per annum so that the rate of the share of citrus fruits by exporting countries was 18 per cent in 1969 for Cyprus, 6 per cent for Lebanon and 5 per cent for Jordan.[2] Other exporting countries are: Algeria, Morocco, Tunisia, Egypt, Brazil, Argentina, British Honduras and Cuba. While total exports from developing countries rose in 1960 at 6 per cent per annum, prices have declined with marketing difficulties because according to FAO projection for 1980 there may be surplus oranges and grapefruits. Protectionist tendencies have increased in later years, for instance in Japan, EEC and the USA,[3] and this is bound to be so with the continuous enlargement of the EEC. Although the new entrants to the EEC do not grow citrus fruits, the consequences will be affected in the rise in their duties to 15 per cent or 20 per cent ad valorem[4] for sweet oranges and tangerines.

(ii) BANANAS

The main exporters are Ecuador, for which banana exports account for 50 per cent of its export earnings; Honduras, 62 per cent; Costa Rica, 28 per cent; Panama, 54 per cent; and Somalia, 27 per cent. There are two main problems facing producers generally: (1) there is no identification of interests among producers; (2) the existence of preferential trading arrangements designed to encourage or protect banana cultivation in certain countries having traditional links with consumer countries. This protectionism exists in various forms, e.g. important restrictions from non-preferred suppliers and preferential rates of import duty or internal tax.

(iii) TEA

Tea shows a downward trend in price of about 3·5 per cent average per annum because there is a tendency towards over-production. Exports of tea in the 1960s rose at 1·8 per cent per annum. In the 1970s the annual value in terms of exports fell from 580 million US dollars in 1959–61 to 504 million US dollars in 1968–70. However the tea market appears profitable to small holders. Although there are no major barriers to tea trade in developed countries, the EEC applies a 5 per cent duty on package of tea while the Federal Republic of Germany imposes an excise tax of DM 4–15 per kg (80 per cent ad valorem) in addition to a turnover tax of 5·5 per cent. These taxes therefore discourage consumption. Some forms of action have been taken since 1969 by the FAO Inter-governmental Group of Tea in co-operation with UNCTAD. For instance, producing countries agreed on specific export quotas for 1970 pending an international agreement. This was later extended in 1971 through 1972–75. In 1971, a working party on long-term measures recommended the appointment of conciliators to promote agreement on export quotas among exporting countries. Consequently, two officials from the FAO and the UNCTAD, each of whom were appointed as conciliators, visited many countries. From the three examples of products just examined, it is clear that there is need for long-term stabilising agreements to regulate forces of supply and demand.

SECTION III. WORLD COMMODITY SITUATION

(a) UNDERLYING FACTORS

Since the 1970s the international commodity trade had drastically been influenced by many factors. Firstly, there was the recession in industrial market economy countries which brought a change in the Brettonwood system of fixed exchange. Secondly, a shortlived 'boom' in prices of primary foodstuffs and raw materials occurred in the later part of 1972–74. Thirdly, OPEC countries quadrupled the prices of petroleum between September 1973 and January 1974 in spite of the substantial rise in 1971. Fourthly, the international society experienced an unprecedented acceleration of inflation between 1970 and 1975. The declining exchange value of the US dollar vis-à-vis other currencies was closely associated with the eventual change in the fixed exchange rate in 1970–73 during the international monetary upheavals. This had two major effects on commodity trade and prices. Firstly, the exchange-rate uncertainties brought about intensive speculation in commodity markets and no doubt led to fluctuations in prices and even higher prices in 1972–74 because of accelerated economic activity in the western world, particularly Western Europe; the USA and Japan. Secondly, the depreciation of the US dollar led to increase in world prices except where the USA was principal buyer of a commodity.

(b) VALUE OF COMMODITY EXPORT OF DEVELOPING COUNTRIES

Between 1967–9 and 1972–74 the nominal value of exports of developing countries in terms of food and raw materials increased on average at a rate of 14 per cent, while their fuel export also increased by 37 per cent. Because of the world inflationary situation, their purchasing power over manufactured goods was by no means lower. The aggregate value in 1975 of exports of developing countries other than the main exporters of petroleum and manufactured goods was about 2 per cent lower in nominal terms, and about 13 per cent lower in real terms, than in 1974. This adversely affected the external payment deficit on current account of the non-oil-exporting countries, which rose from $33·5 billion in 1974 to an estimated $45 billion in 1975.[5] Although high petroleum prices characterised the year 1974–75, the volume of exports declined because of recession and the efforts of consumer importing countries to economise fuel usage. This was responsible for the decline in the export value of petroleum in 1975 by about 10 per cent in nominal terms.

In 1970–73 about 75 per cent of food and raw material exports went to developed market economy countries, while about 17 per cent was accounted for as trade among developing countries and 9 per cent as trade with socialist countries of Eastern Europe and Asia. While the real value of exports in 1967–69 and 1972–74 increased in some few cases like sugar, beef, oil cake and meals, timber, phosphate rock, zinc, for others like rice, wine, tea, bananas, jute, wool, hides and skins and manganese ore, the rate of increase was about 2 per cent. The rate of export earnings from increased production was limited by several factors: (1) low income and price elasticities of demand for tropical beverages and tin; (2) competition from substitutes like natural fibres, rubber and copper; (3) persistent tendencies of over-supply of bananas, oranges, iron ore and manganese ore (see Table 9.1).

TABLE 9.1 Export trends of selected commodities from developing countries: 1967–69 to 1972–74

Commodity	*Value (percentage change per annum)* Nominal[a]	Real[b]	*Average value 1972–74 (in million $)*
(A) *Food beverages*			
Raw sugar	24·5	13·4	3718
Rice	4·2	−4·0	714
Wheat	12·0	3·7	287
Cóffee	9·8	1·8	3805
Cocoa	9·2	1·1	1061
Bananas	6·3	−1·3	573
(B) *Raw materials*			
Cotton	10·2	2·1	2·396
Rubber	11·4	2·6	1667
(C) *Minerals of metals*			
Copper	9·8	1·2	3702
Iron ore	9·9	1·6	1302
Tin	9·5	1·0	882

[a] In current dollars.
[b] Dollar value divided by the UN index of unit values of manufactured goods exported by developing countries.

Source: FAO, *Trade Year-Book* and national trade statistics. Also selected from UNCTAD IV, Doc. TD/184/Supp. 1, *The World Community Situation and Outlook*, item 8, supporting paper, p. 17.

(c) VALUE OF COMMODITY IMPORTS OF DEVELOPING COUNTRIES

The main imports of developing countries are foodstuffs which in 1971 and 1974 nearly trebled, while that of fuel more than quadrupled. This was due to a general rise in prices including that of petroleum, which rose fourfold between September 1973 and January 1974. In countries with scarce fuel resources, a rising volume of fuel imports is justified by their economic development exigencies. However, a rise in the imports of foodstuffs does indicate inadequate progress made in the agricultural sector and a desire for exotic tastes over local ones. Since their increase in food production depends upon expansion of fertiliser and pesticides imports, it is noteworthy that the cost of these imports has also risen steeply since 1967–69. This was so for large increases in 1972 and 1973 in the cost of manufactured pesticides and fertilisers coming from developed-market economy countries. These increases were due mainly to rises in prices following shortages of supplies, increase in the prices of raw materials and fuels and the cost of inflation in manufacturing industries concerned (see Tables 9.2 and 9.3).

TABLE 9.2 Value of commodity imports of developing countries
(US billion dollars fob)

Imports	*1971*	*1972*	*1973*	*1974*
Food	9·1	10·1	15·1	24·0
Raw materials	4·2	4·8	7·2	–
TOTAL	13·3	14·9	22·5	–
Fuels (chiefly petroleum)	5·6	6·7	8·7	24·5

Source: See UNCTAD IV, Doc. TD/184/Supp. 1, *The World Commodity Situation and Outlook*, item 8, supporting paper, p.27.

TABLE 9.3. Value of fertilisers and pesticides – import of developing countries

Fertilisers	*Rate of change 1967–69 to 1972–74*	*Value*			
		1972	*1973*	*1974*	*1974 (million dollars)*
Crude fertilisers	15·6[a]	10	−7	–	111[a]
Manufactured fertilisers	7·5[a]	30	46	–	112[a]
Pesticides	10·6[a]	14	32	–	412[a]

[a] 1973.
Source: FAO Trade Year-Book.
See also UNCTAD Doc. TD/184/Supp. 1, p. 29 (see Table 9.1).

SECTION IV. EXPERIENCE OF INTERNATIONAL COMMODITY AGREEMENTS

Let us examine in brief some of the experiences of commodity agreements concluded to the date of writing, in order to see to what extent they have fulfilled their text provisions.

(a) COCOA

Since the 3rd UNCTAD Conference in Santiago (Chile) only the International Cocoa Agreement has been concluded. The price and quota provisions of this agreement, concluded in 1972 under UNCTAD auspices and re-negotiated in October 1975, have never been operative because the market price of cocoa has been rocketing above the ceiling price range established in the agreement.

(b) THE 5TH TIN AGREEMENT

This was negotiated in June 1975 under UNCTAD auspices and replaced the 4th Agreement, which expired on 1 July 1976. Like other tin agreements, this one establishes two operating functioning mechanisms: buffer stock and export control mechanisms. The new agreement provides that producing countries shall make contributions to the buffer stock amounting to the equivalent of 20,000 tons of tin metal. Unlike earlier agreements, this includes an implied target of the equivalent of 20,000 tons of tin metal for additional contributions by consuming countries.[6] It was agreed that 30 calendar months after its entry into force, the Council must review the results obtained from consumer contributions and in function of that may decide to convene a negotiating conference to amend the agreement. The Tin Agreement is the only international commodity agreement incorporating provisions for market regulations which are actually in operation.

(c) THE WHEAT TRADE CONVENTION

This has no economic provisions and the Food Aid Convention of the International Wheat Agreement 1971 expired on 30 June 1974. The provisions have since been periodically extended by protocol to 30 June 1976, while awaiting the report of the preparatory group appointed in February 1976 by the International Wheat Council to examine the possible bases for a new international agreement to replace the International Wheat Agreement.

(d) INTERNATIONAL COFFEE AGREEMENT

The price and quota provisions of the 1968 Agreement ceased to operate in 1973 due to lack of agreement between the exporting and importing member countries of the agreement. They could not reach a consensus on the issues of prices and export quotas. Consequently when the agreement expired in 1973 it was extended by protocol without economic provisions, first to 30 August 1975 and next to 30 September 1976. However, it is worth noting that it was at a special meeting of 61 exporting and importing countries in London in 1975 that the 1976 International Coffee Agreement, which is to last for six years, was adopted. Like in previous agreements, a system of exporting quotas constitutes its mechanism for stabilising the market system. However, it has a new feature which consists of a division of the global export quota decided upon annually by the ICC into a fixed part, amounting to 70 per cent of the global quota and a variable part, amounting to 30 per cent. The fixed part is allocated to exporting countries in direct proportion to their basic tonnages, while the variable part is allocated in proportion to the size of stocks held by them with a proviso, however, that no country should be given allocation from the global variable quota in any amount exceeding 40 per cent of the volume of the quota. The functioning of price mechanism remains the same as in previous agreements. For example, quotas will be introduced or suspended if specific indicator prices fall below the floor, or exceed the ceiling, of a predetermined price range. There are also provisions for distribution of export shortfalls to other exporting member countries.

(e) OLIVE AND SUGAR AGREEMENTS

The Olive Agreement, which does not contain economic provisions, has been extended until 1978. For the 1968 International Sugar Agreement, the free market prices rose above the maximum specified in the agreement and the commitments of producers and exporter countries to supply a minimum quantity of sugar to importing members at a price not higher than a maximum 'supply price' came into force in December 1971. Although the 'supply price' was raised, the market price remained above it until the agreement expired at the end of 1973. During the negotiations of 1973 under the auspices of UNCTAD, no agreement was reached on prices and on the demand of exporting countries for purchase commitments by importing countries. There was, however, a new agreement which did not contain economic provisions but which simply maintained in operation the International Sugar Organisation authorised to study the possibility of negotiating a fuller agreement.

SECTION V. CO-OPERATION ATTEMPTS BY PRODUCERS OF AGRICULTURAL COMMODITIES

(a) BANANAS

In March 1974, a Union of Banana Exporting Countries (UPEB) was formed by five Central American banana-producing countries[7] in order to co-ordinate banana marketing policies and to increase returns to producer countries. Member countries had to impose export taxes on bananas in order to improve their real returns from banana exports which had shown unsatisfactory rate of growth over several decades.

(b) COFFEE

Following a failure to have an International Coffee Agreement in 1973, four major coffee producers (Angola, Brazil, Colombia and Ivory Coast) in association with the Café Mondial, concerted efforts to maintain prices of coffee by restricting export supplies or buying in the market.

(c) SUGAR

In 1974, 22 Latin American and Caribbean countries, accounting for 61 per cent of world sugar exports, agreed to co-ordinate their efforts in sugar exporting by forming the Group of Latin American and Caribbean Sugar Exporting Countries (GEPLACEA).

(d) RUBBER

The Association of Natural Rubber Producing Countries (ANRPC) since its inception in 1970 has been exploring the possibility of using buffer stock as an instrument for stabilising the price of rubber. Consequently, an UNCTAD Preparatory Conference, under an Integrated Programme for Commodities convened in Geneva from 17 to 21 January 1977, tried to explore the possibilities of an international agreement between producers and consumers. However, earlier efforts had been made by the producers of natural rubber of the ANRPC (Indonesia, Malaysia, Singapore, Sri Lanka and Thailand) to draw up an International Natural Rubber Agreement on price stabilisation in Jakarta, on 30 November 1976, at the 5th Assembly of the ANRPC. The objective, like in most commodity agreements, is to achieve a balanced growth of supply in relation to demand, to assure remunerative and equitable prices to producers and to assure supply to consumers. The scheme will be governed by an International Rubber Council with Headquarters in Kuala Lumpur. It does provide for both international and national buffer stocks which will be financed from external and international sources.[8]

The principal producers of natural rubber which are concentrated in Malaysia, Indonesia, Thailand and Sri Lanka produce about 85 per cent of the world's natural rubber.[9] Small producers are India, Liberia, Nigeria, the Philippines and Papua–New Guinea. Singapore is known to be the largest single re-exporter. The exports of natural rubber by the principal natural rubber producers between 1970 and 1975 accounted for about 25–35 per cent of the total export earnings of Malaysia, 5 to 19 per cent in the case of Indonesia, 8 to 15 per cent in the case of Thailand and 13 to 23 per cent in the case of Sri Lanka.[10] Consumption of natural rubber by rubber-products manufacturing industries in producer countries is less than 5 per cent of the total production of natural rubber. The natural rubber international market suffers severely from great price fluctuations because natural rubber producers are not as organised as the producers of synthetic rubber who are principal consumers from the developed countries. Synthetic rubber accounts for more than 70 per cent of the bulk supply of rubber. For instance in 1948 natural rubber supplied 74 per cent of the international rubber market, but drastically fell to 33 per cent in 1974 because of synthetic rubber production. We can also estimate the gross value of exports of Natural Rubber for the ANRPC member countries, as indicated in Table 9.4.

TABLE 9.4 Gross value of exports of natural rubber for ANRPC member countries

Year	*Indonesia*	*Malaysia*	*Singapore*	*Sri Lanka*	*Thailand*	*Total (US $000)*
1973	391,372	1,023,347	635,365	87,415.9	203,622.4	2,341,122
1974	479,189	1,249,654	863,777	110,389.0	237,092.9	2,940,102
1975	358,240	780,502	523,176	84,754.5	171,657.5	1,918,330

Source: Proposed International Arrangement for Natural Rubber.

SECTION VI. CO-OPERATION ATTEMPTS BY PRODUCERS OF MINERALS AND METALS

(a) BAUXITE

Eleven countries,[11] which account for 70 per cent of world output of bauxite, formed in 1975 the International Bauxite Association (IBA) whose objectives were to achieve for participating members fair and reasonable advantages from the exploitation, processing and marketing of bauxite and its products, including the rational development of its industry.

(b) COPPER

In November 1975, the membership of the Intergovernmental Council of Copper Exporting Countries (CIPEC) was enlarged. The original members (Chile, Peru, Zaire and Zambia) were later joined by Indonesia as a full member and by Australia and Papua–New Guinea as associate members. Because of the falling prices of copper the members of CIPEC had to reduce production and exports of copper as from December 1974. In 1975 they declared support for multilateral negotiations between the consumers and producers. Consequently, on 23–26 March 1976, an *ad hoc* intergovernmental consultation on copper was held under UNCTAD auspices where consensus was reached in favour of establishing a permanent intergovernmental consultative body on copper.

(c) MERCURY

In 1974 a group of mercury-producing companies from Algeria, Italy, Mexico, Spain, Turkey and Yugoslavia held a conference in Algiers where they decided to harmonise producers' action to defend a floor price for mercury.

(d) TUNGSTEN

In April 1975 a Primary Tungsten Association was formed by representatives of producer-companies from Australia, Bolivia, France, Peru, Portugal and Thailand who met in La Paz. Those who attended the meeting as observers indicated their support for the new organisation. They were Brazil, Canada, China, Mexico and the Republic of Korea. The objective of this association is to promote tungsten consumption and price stability. UNCTAD is also considering, within its committee on tungsten, whether to establish an international stabilisation arrangement for this commodity.

(e) IRON-ORE

The Association of Iron-ore Exporting Countries (AIEC) was formed in 1975 by Algeria, Australia, Chile, India, Mauritania, Peru and Venezuela, who were later joined by Sierra Leone, Sweden and Tunisia.

SECTION VII. THE PROBLEM OF CONFLICT AND CO-OPERATION

Against this background knowledge the anxiety of the developing world to catch up with the developed world in their attempts to find adequate and compensatory markets for their raw materials can be understood. These attempts have met with limited successes resulting in the establishment of international agreements on tin, coffee, wheat, sugar and cocoa, after difficult years of patient and some times conflictual periods of negotiations. For instance, failures persistently characterised the negotiations on a cocoa agreement for many years, so that the Secretary-General of the UNCTAD, Señor Manuel Perez Guerrero, rightly described the cocoa phenomenon as the 'most erratic and speculative commodity'. This is also to say that the established agreements have met with some measure of co-operation between the world of consumers and producers. This restrictive co-operation does not exclude further co-operation and conflict during their application. The politics of co-operation and conflict which emanate from any institutional framework within which the nations of the world discuss commodity problems are dictated by the nature of their respective national policies. There is co-ordination of national policies as soon as an institutional framework is established for those who belong to it, as against those who are 'outsiders'; for instance the Tin Agreement vis-à-vis the USA and her disposal policy. Within UNCTAD, the 'Group of 77'[12] has constituted itself into a force for achieving its objectives. The signatories of the Final Act of the 1st UNCTAD Meeting in Geneva in 1964, which was adopted at the end of the conference, expressed the determination to 'seek a better and more effective system of International Economic Co-operation, whereby the division of the world into areas of poverty and plenty may be banished and prosperity achieved by all . . .'.[13] The co-ordination of their policies, and the continuous search for more practical approach to the problems of an international economic order, have made this group a bargaining force, though a little fragile.[14] For this reason, the study of international public policy issues cannot be made without considering a co-ordinated system.

With a product like cocoa, for instance, for which an agreement has been reached only recently, co-operation is expressed in terms of co-ordination of national policies within the Cocoa Agreement and also within the Cocoa Producers Alliance that carries out collective bargaining with the consumers. Within UNCTAD sessions in Geneva (1964), in New Delhi (1968) and in Santiago (Chile) in 1972, there were instances of areas of agreement which resulted in the formulation of general principles of trade and there were also areas of conflict which formed the basis of further negotiations. This was the case also in the 1974 Raw Material Conference in New York. In international negotiations on commodities, conflicts and co-operation arise from the confrontation of various national postures, and this is dependent on whether a product is regulated by an agreement or not. When there is an agreement, there is co-operation among the members who have formed or identified themselves within a contractual community of interests. This functional co-operation is also extended to UNO, its specialised agencies, other organisations within the UN system and appropriate intergovernmental organisations, and even to non-participating countries which are members of UNO, and to contracting parties of a previous international agreement.[15] With an organisation like the Çocoa Producers Alliance, conflict arises between its members and the consumers during negotiations, while there is co-operation within its fold, in order to achieve greater bargaining power.

Another consideration in the study of conflicts and co-operation in commodity diplomacy is the appreciation that the separation of the world into 'haves' and 'have-nots' has produced a new set of crisis situations which make it practically impossible to solve such fundamental problems as hunger, inflation and resource shortages in spite of the increasing apparent co-operation and world interdependence. One of these crisis situations has so far been expressed in terms of confrontation between the OPEC countries and the western world who have refused to share the benefits of modern technology with developing countries. In a situation like this, conflicts are bound to characterise their relationships. Furthermore international economic financial institutions have not helped the situation either, and some great powers themselves have refused to be part of schemes to regulate commodities. All these points demonstrate the need for a new type of bargaining relationship which should replace the imposition of decisions on the weak by the strong. It has therefore become recognised that the traditional approach must be abolished because, in as much as the inadequate purchasing-power of the developing countries emanates from the inflation and recession in developed countries, so long will there be confrontation on oil prices. The integrated programme for commodities suggested by the developing countries during the 4th UNCTAD Conference in Nairobi was one of the methods designed to meet a new approach. The commodity-by-commodity approach preferred by the western countries was not preferred, since it limits the number of agreements to a few and gives too much prominence to narrow commercial and short-term national interests at the expense of the longer-term interests of world commodity economy. This integrated commodity programme covers a wide range of commodities in the external trade relationship of the developing world. There are seventeen commodities in this programme which include ten 'core' ones accounting for 75 per cent of the export value of developing countries. This programme also consists in the establishment and operation of international stocks and the provision of a fund which would provide an opportunity to create decision-making machinery for both developing and developed countries alike. The fund would then be expected to lend to individual commodity organisations operating international stocks who need finance to buy stocks, while repayment would be effected as the organisations acquire funds from stock disposals. It is proposed that the subscriptions to this fund be made by exporter–importer countries of the commodities covered by the programme and by certain petroleum exporters in balance of payments surplus who would extend long-term loans to the fund. The programme itself also aims at negotiating maximum and minimum prices reviewed at regular intervals for a wide range of products of interest to developing countries. If the UNCTAD secretariat endorsed this proposal, initiated in the Manila Declaration and programme of action by the Group of 77,[16] it was crystal clear that it wanted to make the integrated programme a general framework for governmental negotiations. However it must be acknowledged that this programme cannot succeed unless under certain conditions namely:

1. That this programme must go beyond mere price objectives and embrace the participation of developing countries in the marketing, distribution and processing of primary products; and in fact it must be recognised that the price structures must periodically take account of fluctuations and inflationary tendencies in the developed market economy countries.
2. That access to markets for primary products into developed market economy countries must be facilitated because, as we have seen in the first part of this book, demands for primary products in developed markets which necessitated increased production by farmers in the developing countries did not bring in the corresponding increase in prices because of over-production.
3. That there must be adequate machinery for compensatory financing for the stabilisation of export earnings in order also to minimise resort to nationalisations of foreign capital investments in developing countries.

Another area of conflict has been the relationship between transnationals and developing economies. In some countries, transnationals or their affiliates have also become producers of primary commodities. This means that they are capable of transferring commodities to parent bodies or companies at internal book-keeping prices which maximise the global profit of the multinationals. Where this obtains, the return to the individual producer has been very inadequate and the shares of the developing countries in the final price has been established at 10–15 per cent.[17] One of the responses of the developed western economy countries, to the anxieties of the developing countries, was the initiation of multilateral trade negotiations within the framework of the GATT.

According to the Tokyo Declaration, the objectives of these negotiations were to liberalise world trade and to secure additional benefits for the trade of the developing countries. But the outcome of the 4th UNCTAD Conference seems to have negated these objectives, as we shall see later in this book. However it is sufficient to note that negotiations began seriously at the beginning of 1975 after the USA had passed her Trade Act of 1974. In February 1975, the Trade Negotiations Committee within the framework of the GATT principles and philosophy, established six groups to organise and conduct negotiations on tariffs, non-tariff measures, the sectoral approach, safeguards, agriculture and tropical products. These negotiations have not produced any appreciable results, since the GATT and its Articles are still not reformed, nor has priority treatment been accorded to tropical products. In fact a number of obnoxious import duties which take the form of tariffs and non-tariff obstacles had been imposed in developed countries mainly from the fear of their local pressure-groups and other business interests wishing to protect their local industries from the import competition of the developing world in spite of the provisions of the Lomé Convention.[18] Such obstacles as have been imposed relate to quantitative restrictions, export subsidies and even in some special cases with the GATT, trade liberalisation negotiations were limited to products of special export interest to developed countries as compared to the trade export interests of the developing countries. Within this same GATT, it is true that the developed countries had agreed to grant tariff reduction on a non-reciprocal basis to export products of interest to developing countries including a standstill on tariff and non-tariff barriers on similar products. These types of concessions also conducted under the UNCTAD auspices did not receive any disapproval in establishing a Generalised System of Preferences (GSP) whereby the developed countries would accord, on a preferential basis, duty-free and reduced tariff concessions to imports from developing countries. However the test to these agreements proved disappointing when the negotiations in the Kennedy Round paid greater attention to products which did not form the main exporting items of the developing world and above all tariff cuts were drastic on such items.[19] Thus the Kennedy Round offered no advantages to the poor nations and even the standstill on the imposition of new trade barriers was not respected by developed countries. Assuming that there were some relative advantages which accrued to the developing countries in the GSP, the narrow coverage of products of the developing countries in this respect made a mockery of these concessions because the majority of imports from developing countries were outside the GSP concessions. In order to overcome these conflict situations between the poor and rich nations, Fabio R. Fiallo suggests a shift in method from what he calls a 'debate-type' as distinct from a 'game-type' of strategy. A debate-type consists in persuading the opponent or counterpart, in order to obtain a general consensus, while a 'game-type' would recommend a *quid pro quo* type of concession from both sides. 'Negotiations relating to trade liberalisation, however, have reached a stage where general good-will declarations will inevitably have to be superseded by action arrived at securing concrete results. Such action is to entail a complex and sophisticated negotiation strategy.'[20] These proposals are no doubt interesting to appreciate in the light of the past experiences of the developing world in spite of the provisions of Article 55 of the UN Charter on international co-operation. No doubt these charter provisions here have failed to help the poor nations. The question therefore arises as to what type of *quid pro quo* concessions could be made. In the past, before the creation of the OPEC institution the developing world was not thought of as having any concessions to make, as against the aids and development programmes introduced into the developing world by the rich world, which represent only about one-third of the world's population. Yet it escaped the minds of the poor nations that the provision of raw materials to the developed world, at prices dictated by them for a long time was undoubtedly a type of unpleasant aid to the rich. With this aid the rich nations had come to claim superiority over the poor in terms of advancement in the development of technology and the attainment of higher living standards which Article 55 of the UN Charter had promised to all UN members. However, it has now become clearer to OPEC countries that they possess a very important weapon with which to negotiate the complexities of third-world exigencies as negotiated within UNCTAD conferences. These debates, however, cannot exclude the fact that, in the relationship between the rich and poor nations, a certain amount of international moral rectitude is expected of the rich nations to compensate for the years of exploitation and colonialisation into which the third world had been placed. There was also a need to raise the standards of living of the entire world, as required by Article 55 of the UN Charter. Nevertheless, the developing world must not forget that they are depleting their resources which are being stockpiled by some developed countries. All these require an eventual reassessment, which we shall discuss in our final remarks in this book.

Furthermore, those who believe absolutely in the GATT must realise that she does not embrace the entire international community. This is why UNCTAD, in spite of the failures of its various conferences, still represents the best forum for negotiating and initiating international commodity agreements. After all, the membership of the GATT is only about 83 countries, while UNCTAD has about 146, including countries of the Eastern bloc which do not belong to the GATT. The UN therefore recognises that liberalisation of trade is but one aspect of the problems of the developing countries; these also extend to problems of the need for the transfer of technology, problems of transnationals etc., as will be evidenced when we discuss negotiation positions at the 4th UNCTAD in Chapter X, Section 1, paragraph 3. The difficulties of the developing world in the field of trade has therefore led to series of diplomatic activities within international institutions, for example at the 6th and 7th Special Sessions of the UN, the UN Industrial Development Organisation conferences and at UNCTAD conferences.

Our purpose, therefore in the subsequent chapters, is to examine negotiation positions as they relate to conflict and co-operation within the UN system and in quasi-UN systems before discussing the Treaty of the Economic Community of West African States as a response, in a regional setting, to a world economic situation as at present, and as already discussed in previous chapters.

10 Commodity Diplomacy Within the United Nations System

SECTION 1. UNDER UNCTAD CONFERENCES

Commodity diplomacy has for more than half a century preoccupied the minds of the international society. The first commodity to have preoccupied the minds of governments was tin. Series of conferences were held to regulate its market after the first Bandung Conference was created, until 1956 when it became provided with a proper agreement under the aegis of UNO. But since the formation of UNCTAD, all commodities have since been negotiated under its aegis except the Raw Material Conferences which took place in 1974 directly under the General Assembly of UNO. Since the economic boom of the Korean War, the share of the developing countries in world trade has persistently fallen, and since the bulk of raw material trade is vital to the economy of the developing world, a more global approach to finding solutions to trade problems became necessary. Thus the first conference of the UN on Trade and Development was convened in Geneva in conformity with Resolution 1785 (xvii) of 8 December 1962 of the General Assembly of the UNO from the 23 March to 16 June 1964.[1] The Final Act adopted expressed the determination of the members to seek a 'better and more effective system of international economic operation . . .' while its recommendations called for a solution by means of new guidelines for trade and international co-operation, with particular regard to problems affecting developing countries and irrespective of differences in economic and social systems.[2] The purpose of this conference was twofold: firstly, it sought to enlarge the role of the UN in the fields of international trade, and secondly, it added to the broad concepts of negotiation and co-operation in conformity with Article 55 of the UN Charter. Consequently, the adoption of the General Assembly Resolution 1995 XIX of 30 December 1964, creating

UNCTAD as a permanent organ of the assembly, established the growing conviction that the economic aims of the Charter would best be furthered by a bold new programme of international economic co-operation. In the very words of the Secretary-General of UNO, the first Conference has 'ushered in a new chapter in the history of the United Nations' endeavours to accelerate the economic development of the developing countries. The Conference has shown the way towards a more just and rational international economic order.' In the first few years of UNCTAD, it was thought of by some cynics as a forum for uncompromising confrontation. Yet 'consensus' and flexibility have become methods that characterise the crystallisation of group interests within UNCTAD for three reasons: Firstly, the developing countries seemed to have abandoned the expression of their views in irrevocable terms so as not to incur the absolute displeasure of the developed countries. Secondly, the developing countries did not realise that they had economic concessions to offer in conformity with the *quid pro quo* method characteristic of classical commercial negotiation, except recently in the areas of oil, and so their demand was solely based on the concepts of international co-operation formulated in Article 55 of the UN Charter and those of the new international economic order. Thirdly, the developed countries have grown to learn that a negative attitude towards negotiation with the poor nations might throw them into embarrassingly extreme ideological positions. However, UNCTAD could not within its first four years be 'credited with significant concrete results for it appeared to be playing a role in the realm of ideas and to be influencing the evolution of decision-making in the realm of international trade'.[3]

It was in the 2nd and 3rd UNCTAD Conferences in New Delhi (1 February–29 March 1968) and Santiago respectively that the commodity problem became a real item for discussion and negotiation. These UNCTAD conferences posed the problem under item 10 for the 2nd Conference and items 12 and 13 of its agenda for the 3rd Conference. These items were considered by their First Committees, set up during the 37th and 82nd plenary meetings on 1 February 1968 and 13 April 1972 respectively. One of the agreed aims of the 1968 meeting was to achieve 'through appropriate forms of negotiation, specific results that ensure real progress in international co-operation for development' in spite of the fact that the developed countries had earlier on reiterated their intention not to 'negotiate' with a view to arriving at binding decisions.[4] The items pertinent to commodity problems in the agenda of both conferences were:

I. *Item 10 of the agenda of the New Delhi Conference*
Commodity problems and policies:

(a) Review of recent developments and long-term trends in commodity trade, including activities of commodity groups and other commodity bodies in the light of recommendations and other provisions of the Final Act of the 1st Conference.
(b) Main elements of commodity policy including international commodity arrangement and other techniques of commodity market stabilisation:
    (i) operation and financing of buffer stocks,
    (ii) role of and financing of diversification programmes,
    (iii) basic principles and guidelines for pricing policy designed to achieve the highest possible receipts from export of primary commodities.
(c) Programme for the liberalisation and expansion of trade in commodities of interest to developing countries.
(d) Problems arising from the development of synthetics and substitutes.[5]

II. *Items 12 and 13 of the agenda of the Santiago Conference*
Item 12: export promotion of (a) commodities, (b) manufactures.
Item 13: Commodity problems and policies: (a) access to markets and pricing policy including international price-stabilisation measures and mechanics; marketing and distribution system of primary commodities;
(b) competitiveness of natural products; (c) diversification.

The commodity problem, as enumerated above, forms the basis of our search for areas of conflict and co-operation. Attention must then be drawn to the problems of disposal of surplus stocks, synthetics and substitutes, a pricing policy, the financing of diversification programmes and export promotion. During both conferences under consideration, the developed countries saw, in these proposals for an international commodity policy, the opportunity for declaring their stand on a 'commodity-by-commodity' approach because of the enormous difficulties involved in drafting a general agreement on commodity arrangements. The committee, in its general debate on a commodity policy, finally agreed to the commodity-by-commodity approach during the 1968 New Delhi Conference. The basic principles and guidelines reached for a pricing were that there was need to improve the trend of export earnings from the sale of primary products, and that prices should be stabilised at levels remunerative both to the producers and consumers whose interests must come into play.

The various positions of conflict and co-operation will now be examined under three broad types of proposals:

(I) Proposals of the New Delhi Conference.
(II) Proposals of the Santiago (Chile) Conference.
(III) Proposals of the Nairobi Conference.

(I) PROPOSALS OF THE NEW DELHI CONFERENCE

(A) Proposals not agreed upon entirely

(a) Problem of buffer stocks

For any agreement on commodity to be concluded the question of buffer stock, if required for a particular agreement, must be settled adequately because it is the mechanism of regulation which as a result of its functioning produces legal obligations. The unfortunate situation in the buffer stock arrangement in an already concluded agreement[6] is that contributions to its coffers have not been made on the basis of equity. While the advantages which arise from the stabilisation of any commodity accrue both to consumers and producers alike, the compulsory contributions have tended to be titled only towards the producer side with recent slight modifications as to the possible voluntary contributions of the consumers. This is true of many commodities like tin[7] (Article VIII, paragraph 22 of the 4th Agreement) and coffee (Article 54, paragraph 2). But the basis of agreement of the committee was that buffer stocks should be provided with regular income determined on the basis of equity both for the developing and developed countries, such that it does not impose an unnecessary burden on the developing countries. The interpretation of this in recent agreements is that pre-financing of the buffer stock be made on behalf of the producers through borrowing from banks and international financial institutions, and such borrowing would depend upon the security of tin warrants held by the buffer stocks (Article 24, paragraph 9 of the 4th International Tin Agreement) to which only producers contribute.[8] Yet consumers can be called upon to exercise the weight of their influence in laws which all of them would not have helped to create since they are not subject to compulsory contributions. This is why it will be interesting to examine the points of disagreement between the developing and the developed countries in the light of the buffer stock contribution in order to understand its functioning. Two points formed the basis of their disagreement: firstly, the source of pre-financing; and secondly, the principle of market intervention by a buffer stock. *For the first*, on the source of pre-financing, the developing and socialist countries of Eastern Europe proposed that an international financing institution should be able to advance sufficient resources[9] in addition to voluntary contributions expected of developed countries, whenever there was need. But the developed countries shared a different view. They proposed that all possibilities should be considered, including private sources of capital from an international financing organisation, or voluntary contributions by governments in the form of loans or in any other form. The proposal by the developing countries, that financing should be carried out by the producing developing countries and the consuming developed countries, was unacceptable both to the developed-market economy countries and the socialist countries. The developed countries felt that, as this problem had been negotiated and decided in the 3rd International Tin Agreement[10] it should not be the subject of a further discussion during the conference. *For the second*, on the principle of market intervention by a buffer stock, both the developing and the socialist countries shared the same viewpoint. They proposed that buffer stock should function with the 'largest flexibility' so that it can intervene to defend the maximum and minimum prices whenever they were threatened, at every sector of the market so as to create an impact on the market (be it 'spot' or 'features' market). The developed countries decided to choose the expression 'appropriate flexibility'; but, taking into consideration other techniques of stabilisation, they proposed that the intervention of the buffer stock be in accordance 'with the conditions set out in the particular agreement and under the control of the International Council in question'.

(b) Synthetics and substitutes

One of the growing threats to commodity trade is the increasing production of synthetic products and substitutes which compete favourably with natural products. These therefore tend to reduce the demand for natural products on which the developing countries depend for their foreign-exchange earnings. Among the products for which synthetic substitutes exist are: cocoa, rubber, cotton, silk, sugar, vegetable oil, jute and nitrates. In addition to this synthetic production, the fact that the developed consumer countries make use of the availability of stocks to pressurise the producers makes the problem a more pathetic one. The growing but unfortunate practice in developed countries is that they spend colossal sums of money on research into these materials, sums of money which could better have been invested in the manufacture of cheaper machinery and equipment needed for the development of the poor countries. In this connection, however, the developed countries share the view that development in the field of synthetics and substitutes is an integral part of technological progress basic to the economic growth and welfare of all countries, and an important factor in promoting demand for primary commodities. But this policy is very injurious to the economy of the developing countries because of the discriminatory practices of big international monopolies of the developed-market economy countries. Yet when restriction is proposed by the developing countries, their refusal is total because the production of synthetics in the developed-market economy occurs largely in the private sector which is normally difficult to control. Some even go further and suggest the complementarity of natural and synthetic products, thus recommending that both producers and consumers should exchange statistical information, and discuss production plans and the possibility of joint promotion of consumption. For these reasons it would be interesting to further examine areas of conflict and co-operation during this conference.

(a) Areas of further conflict

That the expansion and promotion of synthetics have narrowed the markets of natural products, and consequently led to price degradation, does not seem to have been the subject for controversy between the producers and consumers although the latter stress the importance of the effect of synthetics in developing countries. The need to discourage the production of synthetics and substitutes was proposed by the developing countries because of their competitiveness with natural products.

This policy, they maintained, should be carried out particularly when market needs are capable of being met by the natural products. While some socialist countries were prepared to accept this proposal with some slight modifications, the developed-market economy countries simply called on 'governments and producers of synthetics to bear in mind the desirability of taking due account of the balance between supply and demand'. It called upon the conference to accept that where natural products are found to be able to satisfy national demands it is 'desirable, in principle and in the context of national policies, that no special encouragement should be given to the production of directly competing synthetics'. When the need for accessibility to markets was discussed, the developing countries proposed the progressive removal of tariff and non-tariff barriers on natural products, particularly those on semi-processed and processed forms. The developed-market economy countries, in their turn, preferred 'to consider measures for a gradual reduction of these tariffs in primary or processed form which face excessive competition'. The problem of elimination of tariff and non-tariff barriers on agricultural products entering developed countries is crucial to the poor nations because all developed countries at present protect their domestic agriculture. For instance, in the EEC, this is practised because of the large agricultural labour force therein. It will therefore be difficult to dismantle protectionism without comparable consideration for other countries like the USA, Canada and Australia, who are also agricultural. So far, however, in respect of non-tariff barriers, progress has been very slow. Only the EEC, Japan and Norway have tried to comply with the strategy provision of the development strategy which recommends implementation 'as early as possible in 1971'.[11]

(b) Areas of co-operation

It was generally agreed at the conference that in the technical-assistance programmes of the developed countries, provisions should be made to render assistance to the developing countries producing natural products 'which suffer competition from synthetics and substitutes in order to help them to diversify into other areas of production, including processing of primary products'. It also recommended that UNCTAD should, in co-operation with competent specialised agencies, study methods of market promotion of natural products particularly with respect to: (a) areas of complementarity between natural products and synthetics; and (b) tariff and non-tariff barriers including internal charges affecting trade in natural products in the raw, semi-processed and processed form.

(II) Proposals of entire disagreement

(a) Pricing policy

The need for an adequate pricing policy is vital to the eventual economic growth of the developing countries. This was why the conference agreed on a set of general principles that would form guidelines but were unable to agree on the specific principles involved. The purpose of a pricing policy should be to secure remunerative and equitable price levels that would spur on the developing countries not only to greater developmental goals but also to increase their productivity and maintain fair labour standards. It is therefore necessary that developed countries share the burdens of supporting minimum price levels. For these reasons already fixed prices in international agreements must remain for an appreciably long period, so as to ensure a reasonable predictability in the export earnings of developing countries and constitute an element of an action-orientated programme designed to correct structural and cyclical disequilibriums. These formed the very basis of the position of the developing countries, while the developed market economy countries felt that the objectives of a pricing policy should be 'to secure stable price levels remunerative for the producer and equitable for the consumer in order to contribute to the achievement of the overall targets of economic development of the developing countries as set by the General Assembly of the United Nations and by the UNCTAD'.

Against this background must be examined recent price trends in commodity trade towards the end of the last decade. There was a general increase in world prices, enjoyed both by the manufactures and primary commodities. On the average, prices increased by about 4 per cent above the 1968 levels so that there was a modicum of improvement of 2 per cent in the terms of trade of developing countries. But the snag arises that, for developing countries persistently in deficit in their balance of trade, such price increases could do more harm to the economy (see Table 10.1).

(b) Disposal of surpluses and strategic reserves

Stockpiling and disposal of surpluses are issues of great concern in world commodity politics. They have produced great conflicts between the poor and the rich nations who undertake such a policy for national political-interest purposes. The policy to stockpile and dispose of surpluses is often dictated by the internal political and pressure-group

TABLE 10.1 Terms of trade of developing countries (1963 = 100)

1955	*1960*	*1961*	*1962*	*1963*	*1964*	*1965*	*1966*	*1967*	*1968*	*1969*	*1970 (1st quarter)*
Developing countries trade with the world											
Export unit	103	100	97		103	103	104	103	103	107	108
Import unit (cif)	99	99	100		101	102	102	102	101	103	104
Terms of trade[a]	104	100	98		102	100	102	101	101	103	104

[a] Unit value index of exports divided by unit value index of imports. (The export index is on an fob basis whereas the import index is on a cif basis; – this is in line with the fact that the bulk of the insurance and freight costs for developing countries accrue to developed countries.)

Source: UNCTAD DOC.NO. TD/B/309 of 7 August 1970. *Review of International Trade and Development*, 1969/70, part I.

situations prevalent in the stockpiling countries. Nearly all developed countries have indulged enormously in this practice, in order to control the world price situation of commodity products. This situation puts the poor nations of the world under perpetual subjugation of the rich. For instance, the national policies of consumer countries like the USA, Great Britain and Canada, who stock tin for military purposes, are sometimes determined by the positions of their internal commercial forces such as in the USA and the Federal Republic of Germany. They are also a reflection of a spirit of co-ordination and co-operation depending on whether a country is a member of a regulating council or not. This was why the importance of controlling disposals of stocks preoccupied the minds of the conference delegates to the 2nd UNCTAD Conference in 1968. Here the developing countries proposed that strategic reserves and production surpluses should be disposed of in such a way that they do not 'adversely affect the exports of the developing countries, the investment of capital in the exploration and development of new supplies', while the developed countries put their emphasis on the need to avoid 'serious adverse effects on the normal commercial markets and trade of these products'. The developing countries' proposal that the disposal of strategic reserves should rather supplement than compete with natural products did not meet with the approval of developed market economy countries, who suggested that it should take into account the investment of capital in the exploration and development of new supplies. Both sides did agree that, as an integral feature of a disposal policy, there should be consultations between the governments making the disposal and the government of the producing countries and the international organisation concerned with stabilisation. In the face of prevailing difficult conditions of low prices, the developing countries proposed that they should be allowed to 'consult and co-operate among themselves in order to co-ordinate effectively their policies in the commodity field'. Although this naturally met with a stiff opposition from the developed market economy countries, developing countries as of today have become wiser for it, with the formation of a Cocoa Producers Alliance responsible for co-ordinating their national policies with a view to establishing a strong front against the consumers in cocoa negotiations.

(II) PROPOSALS OF THE SANTIAGO CONFERENCE

The 3rd UNCTAD Conference met in Santiago (Chile) from 13 April to

16 May 1972, to further the discussions of the problems left unsolved during the 2nd Conference in New Delhi in 1968. During the 82nd plenary meeting, on 13 April 1972, UNCTAD established its First Committee[12] and at its 83rd plenary it adopted 22 items in which items 12 and 13, already stated above, relate to commodity. This Committee held 22 meetings during which it considered items 12a and 13a-c.

(a) Area of co-operation

Export Promotion (item 12a). The first committee considered this area during its 18th meeting on 6 May 1972. The developed countries of both the Western and Eastern hemisphere expressed the need for co-operation with the developing countries in the field of export promotion measures, training of experts in marketing and foreign trade because these could be highly profitable both for primary products and manufactures faced with synthetic products. The member states of the developing countries reminded the committee of the recommendations of the 'Group of 77' at Lima[13] relating to export promotion. The resolution, adopted without dissent, urged the following:

(a) studies and research, including an exchange of commercial information on a continuous basis on the export prospects for products from developing countries;
(b) standardisation, packaging, design and quality control of products from developing countries;
(c) organising international trade fairs for the purpose of increasing export opportunities for developing countries.

(b) Area of Disagreement: Access to Markets and Pricing Policy Including International Price Stabilisation Measures and Mechanisms

While the 2nd UNCTAD Conference laid the foundation for the basis of a generalised system of preferences, the 3rd UNCTAD did not reach agreement on many practical issues, for example the suggestion by some developing countries that study and consideration be given to broad multi-commodity measures such as multi-commodity buffer stock, compensatory financial arrangements and schemes to provide guaranteed prices for specific quantities, did not meet the approval of the developed economy countries who preferred the commodity-by-commodity approach. While the 'Group of 77' called for intergovernmental consultation within UNCTAD because GATT cannot provide satisfaction, the developed countries felt that GATT negotiations would provide advantages in the areas of agriculture and industrial trade. While the developing countries felt that access to markets and pricing policy were most important for discussion, developed countries considered them as separable aspects of an overall international commodity policy. The positions of the developed countries were as contained in the draft resolution submitted by them. The signatories were 18: Australia, Austria, Belgium, Canada, Denmark, Federal Republic of Germany, Finland, France, Ireland, Italy, Japan, Luxembourg, Netherlands, New Zealand, Norway, Sweden, Switzerland and the United Kingdom. They also recognised Resolution 73(x) of the Trade and Development Board as adopted on a pricing policy and liberalisation of trade. The resolution of the developing countries presented by the 'Group of 77' established its basis as emanating from the International Development Strategy for the Second Development Decade. This resolution decided on the following:[14]

(i) an access to market and pricing policy for primary commodities of special interest to developing countries;
(ii) a stand-still policy by developed countries, that is, that no new barriers be placed on primary commodities;
(iii) that tariffs by developed countries on processed or semi-processed primary commodities from developing countries be removed;
(iv) that there be a reduction and ultimate elimination of taxes, fiscal charges and levies on all commodities from developing countries;
(v) a reduction of tariffs on a preferential non-discriminatory and non-reciprocal basis in favour of developing countries prior to any multilateral negotiation.

(c) Agreed decisions of the Trade and Development Board

As the UNCTAD Conference could not reach a substantive agreement on the draft resolutions on access to markets and pricing policy submitted to it by the First Committee, workable decisions had to be reached by the Trade and Development Board on a number of items.

Areas of agreed conclusions

1. The Board agreed that the Committee on Commodities should organise intensive intergovernmental consultations on agreed commodities or groups of commodities. It should also set up appropriate consultative groups that could reach concrete and significant results on trade liberalisation and pricing policy early in the 1970s. The scope and procedures to be followed to achieve these objectives should be established by the Committee.

2. The Board established the following criteria for determining the commodities subject to intensive consultations.

(i) The magnitude of the role played by the commodity in the export trade of the developing country.
(ii) The incidence of problems of access to markets and/or pricing policy and the need for balanced attention between the two.
(iii) A representative list of commodities with special consideration for the interests of the least developed among the developing countries. The list must be small enough to be dealt with within a reasonable period of time.

3. The Board also tabled the draft resolution submitted by a group of developing countries.[15] This draft specified 27 commodities, 18 on the basis of Conference Resolution 83(ii) of 26 March 1968 and others added to, which should be the subject of intensive consultations. The draft was also made up of proposals concerning objectives, procedures and timing of the consultations. Because of lack of time the Board could not consider the draft fully. However, the Secretary-General of UNCTAD was mandated to continue to intensify his consultations in accordance with paragraph 3 of the Conference Resolution 83(iii) with due consideration for the list of commodities submitted by a number of African countries and statements made by the developed market economy countries.

(III) PROPOSALS OF THE NAIROBI CONFERENCE

(A) Diplomatic nature of the Conference

(i) Preparatory conferences

In conformity with General Assembly Resolution 1995(xix) of 30 December 1964 and pursuant to Resolution 3216(xxix) of 6 November 1974, the 4th Session of the UNCTAD was held in Nairobi (Kenya) from 5 to 31 May 1976.

Before this conference, the Trade and Development Board had served as a 'preparatory committee' for this session of the conference, when it began preparations at its 14th session, during which it recommended in its decision 113(xiv) of 13 September 1974 that the General Assembly should accept the invitation of the Government of Kenya to hold the 4th session of the conference in Nairobi. The General Assembly in its Resolution 3216(xxix) accepted this with appreciation. Consequently, the Board at the first part of its 15th session in August 1975, adopted a consensus on a list of selected broad policy areas, indicating the specific issues to be taken up in each policy area at the 4th session of the Conference.[16] The General Assembly later endorsed the consensus of the Board as well as the arrangements for the organisation of the work of the session, by its Resolution 3459(xxx) of 11 December 1975 and then urged all member states to adequately prepare at the national, regional and inter-regional levels in order to ensure that such negotiations were action-orientated so that decisions could be promptly and efficiently implemented. As part of the preparations, a number of regional intergovernmental meetings were held at ministerial levels both in African and Third World countries as well as in Western and Eastern Europe.

In the third world countries were held the following meetings:

(i) The 4th Conference of Trade Ministers of the OAU member-countries in Algiers in November 1975.
(ii) First Extraordinary Meeting of the Latin American Council of the Latin American Economic System (SELA) in Caracas in January 1976.
(iii) Third Ministerial Meeting of the Asian Group in Jakarta in January 1976.

The results of these meetings were considered at the 3rd Ministerial

Meeting of the 'Group of 77' held at Manila, from 26 January to 7 February 1976, where the Manila Declaration and Programme of Action[17] were adopted and presented to the Conference, by His Excellency Mr Ferdinand E. Marcos, President of the Republic of the Philippines on behalf of the 'Group of 77'.

In Europe: representatives of the OECD countries met several times in Paris in the months preceding the 4th session, to consider their government's preparations. The UNCTAD Secretary-General addressed the Conference of the OECD Council on 13 April 1976.

In the USSR: Ministers of Foreign Trade of the member countries of the Permanent Commission for Foreign Trade of the Council for Mutual Economic Assistance met in Moscow in March 1976 to exchange views among themselves. They were addressed by the Secretary-General of UNCTAD on 26 March 1976.

In the Commonwealth: In February–March 1976, a Commonwealth Experts Group established by the heads of government at Kingston in 1975, met in London. This group was invited to propose for their consideration: 'in the context of the current international dialogue, a comprehensive and interrelated programme of practical measures, directed at closing the gap between the rich and poor countries'.[18]

The purpose of this meeting was to consider some issues for discussion at the 4th UNCTAD Conference in Nairobi. The report was prepared and signed by the Experts Group in their personal capacities and not as representatives of governments or countries. It was at a subsequent meeting in Hongkong in September 1976 that the Commonwealth Finance Ministers considered a further report.

(ii) Opening of the Conference and its method of work

In order to consider substantive proposals for action and to advance negotiations, the Trade and Development Board held its 7th Special Session in March 1976 during which the Board endorsed a number of arrangements pertaining to the organisation of the 4th Session. On its recommendation, the 4th Session was preceded by a meeting, held on 4 May 1976, of senior officials representing the states participating in the conference. The report of this pre-conference was presented by its chairman Mr K. K. S. Dadzie (Ghana), President of the Trade and Development Board. The 4th UNCTAD Conference was then opened in Nairobi, Kenya from 5 to 31 May 1976 under the temporary presidency of Mr Albelardo Silva Davidson (Chile) before its President Mr E. T. Nwamunga, Minister for Commerce and Industry of Kenya, was elected. During this session, a method of work which determined the ultimate method of negotiation was established.

After the report of the Pre-Conference Meeting was submitted by the President of the Trade and Development Board, who was its Chairman, and the recommendations therein accepted, the Conference elected a Rapporteur and 32 Vice-Presidents. The agenda was then adopted and the resolution approving the report of the Credentials Committee was also adopted without dissent. A General Committee, to which items 8–16 of the agenda[19] were referred, established five negotiating groups provided each with a Chairman, Vice-Chairman and a Rapporteur. Reports of the groups in which agreements were reached were transmitted to the plenary with recommendations that they be adopted, while those which were the object of disagreement were transmitted through the Chairman to the President's Contact Group. For instance, on 25 May 1976, item 8 on commodities; item 11 on money and finance and transfer of real resources for development; and item 10 on recent trends in international trade and development (review of developments in the international monetary field) were referred to this group, whose membership consisted of the President, 15 members from the 'Group of 77'; 10 from Group B (countries of western democracies); 5 from Group D (countries of Eastern Europe); China, and 6 co-ordinators of regional groups.

The Bureau of the Conference consisted of 35 members; the President and 32 Vice-Presidents of the Conference, the Chairman of the General Committee and Rapporteur of the Conference. It later co-opted the Chairman of the five negotiating groups,[20] the regional co-ordinators and the Rapporteur of the General Committee. The Conference was also assisted by a group of 11 'Friends of the Rapporteur' composed of 2 members each from Africa, Asia and Latin America; and two members each from Groups B and D; and one from China. In attendance at this Conference were 132 states who were members of UNCTAD, several specialised institutions of the United Nations, 28 intergovernmental bodies and 14 non-governmental organisations.

(B) Co-operation and conflict from positions held by delegations at the 4th UNCTAD Conference

The opening of the conference with a general debate, from heads of delegations drawn from persons of ministerial ranks or equivalent, was meant to provide an opportunity for general policy statements representative of group interests. As in previous UNCTAD Conferences, the technique of consensus approval of resolutions helps to develop international development policies which are intended to set in motion a process of restructuring world economy within the UNCTAD institution that has become the most advanced trade and commodity institution, universally representative and specialised, within the United Nations system. It is meant to concretise our global objectives of trade, development and international economic co-operation. The 4th UNCTAD Conference had therefore two main objectives to accomplish; namely, to launch programmes and policies with long-term impact on development problems and to take decisions that are fundamental to short-term needs of the developing world. It is within this context that the consensus technique of decision-making has come to stay. Consensus technique has no legal effect but its evolvement has been dictated by the fear of international moral sanction and public opinion both accentuated by the provisions of Article 55 of the United Nations Charter, the plight of the poor world and the futurity of a global peaceful society. The technique of consensus adoption without dissent which characterised the process of decision-making at the 4th UNCTAD Conference did not, however, mean obligation to apply text resolutions since they were qualified with reservations. They have unleashed a process of continuous negotiations which form the very basis of UNCTAD decision-making processes at such meetings since it is hoped that one day some of these decisions might meet with general application. These conferences *per se* are of vital importance as a political event; for if successful they could improve relations between states and between group interests, but if a failure, they could aggravate and foster crisis and tensions. It is in this perspective that we shall discuss positions of conflict and co-operation in the light of the agenda items, a few of which will be the object of our discussions. They are:

(a) Integrated Programme on Commodities (item 8);
(b) Manufactures and Semi-manufactures (item 9),
Transfer of Technology (item 12), and
Institutional Issues (item 16).

(a) Integrated Programme on Commodities (Resolution 93 (iv) on agenda item 8): Nature of the Resolution and Positions held by Delegations

(i) Nature of the resolution

The integrated programme which arose from two basic papers is closely related to the issues raised in the Programme of Action on the New International Economic Order adopted at the 1974 Raw Material Conference during the 6th special session of the United Nations Assembly. The two papers were proposals submitted to the Nairobi Conference by the Group of 77[21] and the Group B[22] countries representing the Western world. There were also supporting papers prepared by the UNCTAD Secretariat.[23] In them the Secretary-General had proposed an Integrated Programme for commodities envisaging separate arrangements for individual commodities, taking account of their distinctive peculiarities like financing facility, buffer stocks arrangements, etc. This is to say that the ideas presented by the Group of 77 were not entirely the same as those of the Secretariat, for the Group of 77 had wanted consideration of products in a package. However, the main features of the Secretary-General's proposals were:

(i) the establishment of international buffer-stocks for selected commodities;
(ii) creation of a Common Fund to finance these stocks;
(iii) establishment of compensatory financing arrangements for residual fluctuations in prices and earnings not provided for by buffer-stocks in commodity arrangements;
(iv) establishment of multilateral supply and purchase commitments by governments of producing and importing countries;
(v) acceptance of ways of encouraging processing of producing countries and diversification of their production including method of its implementation.

However, at the 4th UNCTAD Conference, an integrated programme for commodities was adopted without dissent, which is not to say that there were no reservations or observations. The adopted resolution covered the following areas:[24]

I. *General objectives*, which were, among others, not only to improve the terms of trade of developing countries, eliminate the economic imbalance between developed and developing countries, but also to expand and diversify the trade of developing countries.

II. *Commodity coverage*, is a list of 18 products of export interest to developing countries; namely bananas; bauxite; cocoa; coffee; copper; cotton and cotton yarns; hard fibres and products; iron ore; jute and products; manganese; meat; phosphate; rubber; sugar; tea; tropical timber; tin; and vegetable oils, including olive oil and oilseeds. Other products could be added on further negotiations.

III. *International measures and timetable.*[25] It was agreed that a Common Fund should be negotiated not later than March 1977 and that a series of preparatory meetings on individual products should be held in order to produce draft proposals for consideration by February 1978. The Common Fund was meant to involve contributions from both developed and developing countries irrespective of whether a particular country is a party to an individual commodity agreement or not. The UNCTAD Secretariat had estimated the capital requirements of the Fund at 6 billion dollars out of which only 3 billion dollars were the initial requirement.

(ii) Positions held by delegations

(a) Group of 77

This group saw the resolution adopted as not fully representative of its views although it marked a turning point in international economic relations. They held the view that the merits of the Common Fund had been established since what remained was the negotiation of its modality and details in a future conference.

(b) USA

She appreciated the common desire of the Conference to reach agreement which led to a consensus. Nevertheless she had a number of reservations and observations, namely:

(i) She interpreted Section IV of Resolution 93 (iv), on the need to convene meetings for negotiations on individual products, to mean that each meeting would determine the nature of the problems affecting particular commodities and the measures appropriate to each. To her, therefore, those preparatory meetings proposed were mere consultations prior to decision on whether to embark on negotiations.

(ii) It was also her understanding that the Secretary-General of UNCTAD would utilise existing commodity bodies but where there was none, *ad hoc* groups could be convened. In this way the USA could be seen as still adhering to her commodity-by-commodity approach.

(iii) Since there might be advantages in linking the financial resources of individual buffer stocks, the USA would participate without any commitment in preparatory meetings in order to examine whether further agreements for financing of buffer stocks including common funding were desirable.

(iv) She had accepted Resolution 93(iv) on the understanding that its various provisions, including those on commodity arrangements and compensatory financing, did not alter reservations on the concept of indexation.[26] Therefore, support for the Resolution did not imply any change in the views of the USA on the new international economic order and the Charter of Economic Rights and Duties of States.

(c) Federal Republic of Germany

The Republic of Germany was of the opinion that although she had joined the consensus, this was not to say that she had agreed to the concept of the new international economic order. Rather, she had simply agreed to a number of practical steps designed to improve the structure of world economy and consequently was prepared to play a role in the preparatory meetings and negotiations, the outcome of which would determine which commodity agreement would be acceptable and whether a common fund would be the best form of financing buffer-stocks. She also held the view that it would not be in the interest of developing countries to create a dirigiste mechanism for centralised management and therefore rejected the idea of indexation.

(d) Colombia

Although she joined in the consensus on Resolution 93(iv), she maintained that any integrated programme for commodities should specifically and unambiguously exclude commodities that were already governed by an existing agreement or one that was in the process of being ratified. Her delegation was not entirely convinced of the appropriateness of the Common Fund for financing commodities, historically characterised by structural overproduction with consequent price degradation. She therefore wished that coffee should be excluded from the list of commodities enlisted in the programme.

(e) Canada

She was ready to participate in the implementation of the integrated programme and recalled her previous promise at the 7th Special Session of the United Nations, to examine sympathetically, along with other donors, the concept of a Common Fund meant to finance buffer-stocks in the light of the results of the proposed consultations and negotiations. However, this would again depend on the number of commodities for which agreements based on the buffer-stock were negotiated. In spite of her support for stabilisation and liberalisation measures, she thought that it would be difficult to harmonise them although, through such efforts as stabilisation for natural products, competitiveness with production of synthetics and substitutes could be better achieved.

(f) New Zealand and others

New Zealand had no fundamental objection to the Fund since she had, during the 3rd Ministerial Meeting of the Group of 77 in Manila, promised to contribute $50 million to the proposed Fund. Out of 19 countries that expressed willingness to contribute, 5 indicated specific estimates as follows: India ($25 million); Indonesia ($25 million); Norway ($25 million); Yugoslavia ($30 million); Kenya ($1 million). Finland, Malaysia, the Netherlands, Nigeria and Sweden had announced their willingness to contribute although Finland and Sweden would wish to subject their participation to the broad participation of other countries. The other 14 countries were: Algeria, Ghana, Iran, Iraq, Kuwait, Mexico, Pakistan, Peru, Romania, Saudi Arabia, Sri Lanka, United Arab Emirates, Venezuela and Zambia.

(iii) Progress made on the Common Fund Negotiations

In conformity with Resolution 93(iv) paras 1–3 of the 4th UNCTAD Conference a negotiating conference on the Common Fund, convened by the Secretary-General of UNCTAD Gamani Corea adjourned its sitting on 3rd April, 1977. These negotiations represented a test case for the true intentions of the negotiators although their previous positions were already known. This meeting failed to achieve any concrete decisions except to reconvene not later than November 1977. 'We cannot fail to express in the most unequivocal terms that the conference is ending in complete failure', said Georges Alvares Maciel, the distinguished representative of Brazil at the closing session, while speaking on behalf of the Group of 77. He put the causes of the failure both on the developed market economy countries and all the socialist states with the obvious exception of China. This is why we shall at this juncture examine the positions of some selected delegations, as they will enable us to arrive at some useful opinions when examining Section II, paragraph 3 of this chapter.

(a) Group of 77

While the developed economy countries believed that the Common Fund was but a part of the integrated programme, the Group of 77 regarded it as the essential part of the programme convened to function independently as an international financial institution. They wanted the developed economy countries to accept from the start the principle of the Fund whose modalities would later be negotiated, but the developed economy countries preferred to examine its various implications before commital.

(b) USA

Her position is summarised by the final declaration of her spokesman, Mr Stephen Bosworth, after the meeting had adjourned: 'it would be premature for us to agree to setting up the proposed Fund at this time. . . . We are not prepared to commit ourselves to something until we know what that something is', and further went on to add that the Carter Administration had not formulated its policy on the subject[27] since the previous US Administration was hostile to the concept of the

Fund. No doubt this was a clear indication that the US officials were more in favour of utilising the World Bank facilities than creating an independent financial institution for the Common Fund.

(c) Group B countries

Mr Gordon Barass (UK), on behalf of this group, did not think the conference was a failure because some progress had been made in 'broadening the areas of consensus concerning some of the elements of the Common Fund' and added that this group remained 'politically committed to continue negotiations towards the establishment of the Common Fund'. As Ursula Wasserman puts it: 'these statements were of course meant for public consumption, for behind the scenes we witnessed not only the irreconcilable positions of the developing countries on the one hand and the industrialised countries on the other, but also vast differences of opinion among the Western developed countries (Group B) themselves'.[28]

(d) Some European nations

Scandinavian countries, Belgium, the Netherlands and Ireland found favour with the concept of the Fund as espoused by the developing countries and the UNCTAD Secretariat. In March 1977 the EEC Summit Meeting in Rome had also accepted this concept and reached an agreement on a Common Fund but not as conceived by the developing countries. It is therefore significant to note what a Dutch delegate to this conference, Suzanne Bischoff Van Heemskerck, said to Ursula Wasserman in order to appreciate the dimension of the problems involved:

> As representative of a country which more than a year ago publicly supported the establishment of a Common Fund, one is certain to be frustrated when after 16 months of discussion in the Committee on Commodities, at UNCTAD IV, at three preparatory meetings and a negotiating conference which turned out to be a fourth preparatory meeting, the international community is able to agree only on a further round of negotiations being required. What, for example, happened to the sixteen countries who in Nairobi, following the statement of the Dutch Minister of Development Pronk, promised to

> work actively towards the implementation of the integrated programme? As a member of Group B, we are used to the lack of political will – as the Group of 77 call it – the search for economic arguments against the establishment of a Common Fund, arguments which may well be disputed – and one is not surprised at the lack of results. After almost two years of heated discussions within the E.E.C., the Summit meeting on 25/3/77 agreed that there should be a Common Fund which, in effect, simply means exclusion of the option of 'no common fund' as advocated by the Federal Republic of Germany. This is a small step forward. However, small steps forward, now and again, convince me of the usefulness of continuing the struggle.[29]

(e) China

The Chinese delegate did not hesitate to throw the responsibility of the failure of the Meeting on the Super Powers, particularly one Super Power, who professes its willingness to take an active part in negotiations, and tries to substitute its own schemes for the concept of the Common Fund in absolute reference to the USA whose desire is to shift the responsibility of financing buffer stocks to the World Bank. He continued,

> the other Super Power has openly declared that the stability of the market is not of its concern, as if this Super Power did not even exist in this world. . . . It has played dumb and slurred its words . . . styling itself the natural ally of the developing countries . . . it has given sham support to the Common Fund while opposing it in reality.

This was in reference to the USSR and East European countries.

(b) Transfer of technology, manufacture and semi-manufactures and institutional issues

General adoptions without dissent characterised most of the positions held in the above areas by the negotiators without however underplaying the importance which the Big Powers give to reservations.

(*i*) *Technology*

The need for strengthening the technological capacity of developing countries is referred to in four basic documents: (1) The Declaration and Programme of Action on the International Economic Order adopted by the General Assembly at its 6th special session.[30] (2) Charter of Economic Rights and Duties of States.[31] (3) The objectives of the International Development Strategy for the Second UN Development Decade, in particular paragraph 64 and the General Assembly Resolution 3517 (xxx) of 15 December 1975 on the review and appraisal of progress in the implementation of the International Development Strategy. (4) Manila Declaration and Programme of Action adopted by the 3rd Ministerial Meeting of the Group of 77.[32] On this question of transfer of technology, substantive agreement could not be reached on a code of conduct because the Group B countries preferred a non-legal code which would be voluntary in nature, universally applicable and directed to source and recipient enterprises and their governments. For Group D countries it was the question of eliminating restrictive practices and political discrimination while the Group of 77 preferred a multilaterally binding instrument as the only effective method of regulating the transfer of technology to developing countries. This was also the African viewpoint.

(*ii*) *Manufactures and semi-manufactures*

Resolution 96(iv) of item 9 was adopted without dissent to cover the following areas: improving access to markets in developing countries for manufacture and semi-manufactures; industrial development co-operation and restrictive business practices. The resolution stipulated that semi-manufactures of developing countries to markets of developed countries should be improved by:

(i) general system of preferences which are non-reciprocal, non-discriminatory and which shall cover many products of exports to developing countries;
(ii) a duty-free entry to manufactures and semi-manufactures;
(iii) simplification, harmonisation and improvement of rules of origin of the GSP to facilitate better utilisation of the scheme;
(iv) allowing the GSP to apply beyond a ten-year period envisaged. This GSP should not be used as an instrument or political and

economic weapon of retaliation against developing countries adopting policies intended to safeguard their national resources;

(v) developing countries should make new policies on encouraging domestic factors of production;

(vi) on restrictive business practices: (a) negotiation should be carried out to establish a set of multilaterally agreed equitable principles and rules for the control of restrictive business practices having adverse effect on multilateral trade; (b) elaboration of a model law or laws that would help the developing countries devise appropriate legislation.

While they were generally agreed on the GSP, Australia accepted the stand-still provisions but qualified her position in respect of GATT, holding the view that any safeguard measures therein must not be subjected to consultations, multilateral surveillance and compensation because she felt that the most effective method of control was by national laws and regulations. Although the USA supported the GSP over the envisaged ten-year period because her scheme expires in 1985, she held the view that she could have abstained from some sections if the resolution were put to vote. However, she favoured policies facilitating the normal evolution of industrial production in response to market forces without government intervention. New Zealand reserved her position in respect of multilateral surveillance while supporting the resolution.

(*iii*) *Institutional issues*

Group B and the USA would not want the independence of GATT or the IMF affected by the reform of UNCTAD and were therefore opposed to the setting up of a new institutional machinery. They reiterated their non-support for the Declaration and the Programme of Action on the New International Economic Order and the Charter of Economic Rights and Duties of States. Group D considered that any reform of UNCTAD must be responsive to the General Assembly Resolution 1995 (XIX), particularly that on trade, and must therefore co-operate with ECOSOC and other UN organs. Consequently, any institutional changes within UNCTAD must be such that reinforced the elimination of colonialism and neo-colonialism from trade and suppressed any attempt to encroach upon the sovereignty of states over their natural resources. Group D, while preferring the transformation of

UNCTAD into an international trade organisation without any immutability of the UN Charter, felt that such a reform must conform to the resolutions adopted at the 6th and 7th special sessions of the General Assembly and the Charter of Economic Rights and Duties of States. However, it is significant to note that in a recent Working Party on Trade Expansion and Regional Economic Integration among Developing Countries[33] under the auspices of the UNCTAD Secretariat the idea of reform did not follow the above lines. Rather it suggested the creation of an intergovernmental consultative body within the UNCTAD Secretariat whose duties would be consultative and coordinative.

On rescheduling of debts, considered by the Negotiating Group III under Money and Finance and transfer of real resources, as no formal agreement was reached, it was referred to the plenary where Group D expressed the view that they would have abstained because its provisions were not applicable to them since their credit relations with developing countries were different from those between developing countries and developed capitalist countries. Group B however welcomed the adoption by consensus although the USA added that her policy remained that of engaging in debt rescheduling within the framework of the GATT creditor clubs.

On the problems of developing island countries and the least developed of developing countries including landlocked countries (Resolution 98(IV)), Group B were pleased to concur with the consensus but made reservations and interpretations in respect of the idea of the Special Fund for the least developed countries since they preferred to support it through existing funds or programmes geared to their needs whether bilateral or multilateral.

SECTION II. UNDER THE GENERAL ASSEMBLY OF THE UNITED NATIONS

(I) THE 6TH SPECIAL SESSION OF THE GENERAL ASSEMBLY ON THE PROBLEMS OF RAW MATERIALS AND DEVELOPMENT

For the first time in the annals of UNO, the conflict and co-operation diplomacy between the third world and rich nations of the international society shifted from the specialised organs of the UN system to the General Assembly itself. This was at the 6th Special Session of the General Assembly, convened at the initiative of President Houari Boumedienne of Algeria to study the problems of raw materials and development. The conference opened up from 9 April to 2 May 1974 when it completed its work after adopting, on 1 May 1974, without a vote, a declaration of basic principles on a new international economic order. This Special Session, in the words of the Chinese UN Permanent Representative, reflected the attitudes of the 'awakened and united third world' because this was the first time the General Assembly had devoted itself to the consideration of economic measures. The discussions, which formed the basis of co-operation and conflict, were centred on already adopted documents prepared by the Group of 77 of the non-aligned nations of the world. The two resolutions passed by the General Assembly on the basic principles mentioned above were largely based on two documents made up of a Draft Declaration and a Programme of Action on Principles of a New International Economic Order. They were discussed for about three weeks by an *ad hoc* committee of the General Assembly which set up a working party to outline a programme of emergency measures later added to the programme of action.

Addressing the General Assembly during this session were seven heads of states from Algeria, Gabon, Gambia, Liberia, Mauritania, Mauritius and Sierra Leone and two Deputy Prime Ministers from the Republics of China and Yugoslavia. It was also attended by seventy-three Foreign Ministers and thirty-seven other Ministers amongst whom was His Excellency Dr Okoi Arikpo, Commissioner for External Affairs of Nigeria, who addressed the General Assembly in very strong terms, on 15 April 1974. Dr Arikpo said, *inter alia*, ' . . . the tragedy of our times is that, in spite of the political advances of the past generations, the world economic order has remained firmly rooted in its 19th century foundations, where military and technological power regulate world market prices'. Also discussed during this session were seven draft resolutions which dealt with various aspects of emergency measures to help developing countries 'most affected by economic crises'. These resolutions were referred to the 56th Session of the Economic and Social Council for examination.[34] The basic documents which formed the basis for the New International Economic Order contain very interesting provisions which will be examined below.

(II) BASIS FOR A NEW INTERNATIONAL ECONOMIC ORDER

(a) Provisions of the declaration and action programme

On 1 May 1974, the General Assembly of the UN approved, without a vote, a Declaration establishing the principles on which an International Economic Order should be built. It also includes a Programme of Action which takes into consideration special measures aimed at alleviating the sufferings of those countries most affected by the international economic crisis.

(i) The declaration[35]

The Declaration on the Establishment of a New Economic Order, made up of twenty principles, stresses the right of a state to full permanent sovereignty over its natural resources over which it is entitled to exercise effective control and exploitation, 'with means suitable to its own situation, including the right of nationalization or transfer of ownership to its nationals'. The Declaration also establishes the principle that all states, territories and peoples under foreign occupation or apartheid have the right to restitution and full compensation for the exploitation and depletion of, and damages to, the natural and all other resources of those states, territories and peoples. In matters of trade the Declaration calls for a 'just and equitable relationship between the prices of raw materials, primary products, manufactured and semi-manufactured goods exported by developing countries and the prices of raw materials, primary commodities, manufactures, capital goods and equipment imported by them'. Another principle calls for the regulation and supervision of transitional corporations by taking measures in the interest of the national economies of the countries where such corporations operate. After the enumeration of its twenty principles, the Declaration establishes that nations 'must have an even greater role in the establishment of a new international economic order' and finally calls on member states to exert maximum efforts in the implementation of the Declaration, 'which is one of the principal guarantees for the creation of better conditions for all peoples to reach a life worthy of human dignity'.

(ii) The programme of action

This programme as adopted by the General Assembly consists of a set of 'urgent and effective measures' for coming in aid of the developing countries. It contains sections on raw materials and primary commodities, the international monetary system and financing of development, industrialisation, transfer of technology, the Draft Charter of Economic Rights and Duties of States, promotion of co-operation among developing countries and the exercise of permanent sovereignty of states over their natural resources. It also calls for efforts to facilitate the functioning of producers' associations, including their joint marketing arrangements, orderly commodity trading, improvement in export income of producing developing countries and their terms of trade and sustained growth of the world economy. As regards external debt contracted on hard terms, the programme calls for international action to mitigate adverse consequences arising from this situation and urges debt renegotiation on a case-by-case basis with a view to concluding agreements on debt cancellation moratorium, re-scheduling or interest subsidisation. It also called for increase in food production inputs and the purchase of fertilisers from developed countries on favourable terms and efforts to promote exports of food products of developing states through just and equitable arrangements by progressive elimination of protective and other measures that constitute unfair competition.

(iii) Special measures programme

As part of the above programme, the General Assembly created a Special Fund into which voluntary contributions from industrialised nations and others could be made, in order to provide emergency relief and development assistance. The Special Fund was expected to begin operations by 1 January 1975 at the latest.

(b) Reservations and acceptances of some participating countries

After adopting the Declaration and Programme of Action, the General Assembly heard several speakers explaining their respective positions. Only a few, but important, delegations from developed countries expressed reservations on various provisions, while all the developing countries endorsed the documents as a matter of course, the South

African delegation was exposed to several attacks from the developing countries, and in view of certain objections it neither supported the Declaration nor the Programme of Action in spite of the need to support the principles on assistance to developing countries. Let us then examine *four* main reservations from the USA, the Federal Republic of Germany, France and Canada.

(I) United States of America

The US Ambassador to UNO, Mr John Scali, expressed disappointment at the inability of the conference to emerge with unanimous agreement on how international economic problems could best be solved. He questioned the sense in 'voting through' difficult and controversial questions and the idea of 'consensus' which emerged from the conference. 'My delegation believes the word "consensus" cannot be applied in this case', and it 'does not in fact, whatever it is called, represent a consensus in the accepted meaning of the term.' The document, according to him, contained elements supported by member states, but it also contained elements which members 'large and small, and on every continent' did not endorse. For the USA, how to assure immediate and effective relief to the developing countries most hard hit by recent changes in world economy, was their concern. Mr Scali said that the Declaration and the Special Programme contained provisions which his country could not support. *For instance*:

1. The Permanent sovereignty over natural resources. He regretted that the compromise solution on this subject embodied in the Assembly Resolution 1803 (XVII) of 1962 was not reproduced in the Declaration. The Declaration 'does not couple the assertion of the right to nationalize with the duty to pay compensation in accordance with international law'. For this reason, the formulation is incomplete or unacceptable.
2. The USA did not support the provisions that referred to restitution and full compensation for exploitation of and damage to certain resources and peoples.
3. The idea of producer-association was neither a viable means of promoting development nor of fixing a relationship between import and export prices. Artificial attempts to manage markets which ignored economic realities and legitimate interests of consumers as well as producers ran the risk of political con-

frontation on the one hand and economic failure on the other.

4. Regarding the provision dealing with the activities of the multinational corporation, the USA believes that the corporation must act as good corporate citizens of states in which they operated and thus were subject to the regulation and supervision of those countries in which they operated. Such regulation and supervision must be non-discriminatory or otherwise conform to the norms of international law.
5. The Programme of Action contained 'too many objectionable features'. The USA's fears about commodity agreements are well known. She thus was prepared to consider them on a case-by-case basis. The USA cannot allocate a specified share of its market to developing countries. He concluded by pointing out that the Assembly had not yet agreed on the type of co-ordinated action that would provide immediate relief. 'Words could not feed the starving or help the impoverished.'

(II) Federal Republic of Germany

Mr Walter Gehlhoff on behalf of Germany accepted the documents but made reservations on producers' associations. He also questioned the right of nationalisation which does not talk about adequate compensation. As for the convention containing the code of conduct for liner conferences, adopted in Geneva in April 1974, his governments had no intention of influencing insurance costs. As regards the Special Measures Programme, his government would concentrate on those measures which it considered effective. Regarding the multilateral trade negotiations, the EEC subscribed to the Tokyo declaration by which such talks should be conducted on the basis of mutual advantage and commitment.

(III) France

Mr Louis de Guiringaud hailed the outcome of the special session but expressed reservations on nationalisation which should contain a clearer reference to modes of compensation. The renegotiation of debts should not be dealt with in a blanket form but on a case-by-case basis only in crisis situations.

(IV) Canada

While Mr Saul F. Rae accepted the right of a state to permanent sovereignty over its natural resources, his government had reservations concerning nationalisation which was inconsistent with the principles of international law. As regards the Programme of Action, his government could have abstained from voting if it were called for, because of the manner in which a number of economic, trade and monetary issues with long-term implications were approached. Supporting the Special Measures Programme, he mentioned that his government had provided 100 million dollars in aid over and above its normal aid programme to the hardest-hit countries. He suggested the use of the World Bank because his government had agreed to contribute 276 million dollars to the fourth replenishment of International Development Association.

(III) WILL THE ADOPTED DECLARATION ON THE NEW INTERNATIONAL ECONOMIC ORDER AND THE CHARTER OF ECONOMIC RIGHTS AND DUTIES OF STATES ADOPTED AT THE 7TH SPECIAL SESSION OF THE UN ASSEMBLY BE GIVEN ANY LEGAL EFFECT THROUGH IMPLEMENTATION BY MEMBER STATES OF THE UN?

We shall examine these questions from two principal perspectives. Firstly, the question of the right to full and permanent sovereignty over natural resources in which the Draft Declaration and the Programme of Action on the Principles of a New International Economic Order will be discussed. Secondly, the adoption of the Charter of Economic Rights and Duties of States as seen through the attitude of the Big Powers before answering the above questions from the discussions which follow.

(A) Full and permanent sovereignty over natural resources arising from the Declaration and the Programme of Action

This area met with vigorous criticisms from some developed countries such as the Federal Republic of Germany, France and Canada as we have already seen in Chapter X, Section II (11b), because they hold the view that the proposal on nationalisation without adequate compensation was inconsistent with the principles of international law as it did not make provision for the right to adequate compensation in conformity with Resolution 1803 (XVII) of 14 December 1962 which ought to have been reproduced in the draft text.[36] The question that comes readily to mind, is whether the adopted declaration of principles will be implemented by those states that have expressed reservations concerning the right to nationalisation without adequate compensation, although this point seemed to have been cleared in a subsequent Charter of Economic Rights and Duties of States adopted later in the General Assembly session of 12 December 1974 in its Article 2, paragraph C, which states that each state has the right:

> to nationalise, expropriate or transfer ownership of foreign property in which case appropriate compensation should be paid by the state adopting such measures, taking into account its relevant laws and regulations and all circumstances that the state considers pertinent.

This has not deferred in details from the original position of the Declaration of Principles on the New International Economic Order as we shall see later. Since they also objected to the notion of 'consensus' involved in the adoption of the text, can an adoption without signature and possibility of sanctions be taken seriously in terms of application? To answer these questions, we must look into previous practices and origins of the issue before arriving at a conclusion.

(i) UNCTAD Trade and Development Board

The issue of permanent sovereignty over natural resources, the exploitation of the reserves of a country by the nationals of another, the problems of definitions, of nationalisation, principles and standards of compensation, the exhaustion of national remedies have all received critical attention at the General Assembly in 1962 when Resolution 1803 (XVII) on Permanent Sovereignty over Natural Resources was adopted. The adopted text of this resolution recognised the inalienable rights of people and defined certain criteria for their exploitation in the interest of economic development of countries.[37] Ten years later, in October 1972, the UNCTAD Development Board at its 12th Session passed a resolution relative to rights of countries to nationalise companies undertaking extractive activities.[38]

The debate arose from the 'Kennecott Case' in which a French court blocked payment for a shipment of Chilean copper while it examined the question as to whether Kennecott should have received compensation for the nationalisation of its assets in Chile. The Kennecott Copper Company was a United States corporation which endeavoured to obstruct payment on 1250 tons of shipment of the Chilean State Copper Corporation (Codelco) bound for France. Kennecott had claimed property rights over the cargo and consequently petitioned the French court, le Tribunal de Grand Instance, to obtain the proceeds of the transaction totalling about 1·9 million dollars.[39] The whole dispute between Kennecott and the Chilean government arose from a constitutional amendment on natural resources. This amendment, which included Kennecott's 49 per cent equity in Compania Minera el Teniente, provided for the nationalisation of Andean Mining Company and all major copper-mining enterprises, and established a set procedure for calculating compensation, terms of payment and recourse procedure. This dispute, properly speaking, arose from a clause therein which provided that all or part of the 'excess profits' of nationalised companies and their predecessors made between 5 May 1955 and 31 December 1971 should be deducted from payable compensation. So, when it was discovered that the Teniente Copper Mine had made excess profits totalling about $410 million, exceeding by $10 million the value of Kennecott's investments between 1955 and 1971, the company was declared unworthy of any compensation. What displeased the company was not so much the nationalisation, which it accepted, but the method of determining compensation. It therefore appealed to the Special Copper Tribunal[40] which dismissed the case on 16 August 1972. Kennecott had no other recourse and was therefore compelled to initiate legal proceedings in France.

(ii) The argument over permanent sovereignty: the case of Kennecott versus Chile at the UNCTAD Trade and Development Board

At the October 1972 session of the UNCTAD Development Board, the above-mentioned case came under serious diplomatic tussle and debate. Chile, who was aggrieved by the subjection of her municipal law responsibility to a Paris Court, described the French Court's provisional order as flagrant violations of both international law and the principles of non-intervention and self-determination of peoples as set forth in the UN Charter. She therefore accused Kennecott of attempting to strangle her economically in Western Europe where she obtains her foreign exchange earnings. The eight Latin American countries at the Board,

These texts were all co-sponsored by the developing countries because they understood very quickly that it was in their interest to establish a common front in order to seek concessions from the developed countries. It was evident from the reservations expressed during the 1974 UN Raw Materials Conference that the Western Powers were not pleased with the third world majority obtained therein, and so they were not ready to compromise on the subsequent December 1974 Charter of Economic Rights and Duties of States as could be seen from the pattern of Western opposition expressed in terms of votes which were 6 against and 10 abstentions. When the UNIDO also adopted the Lima Declaration[45] on 27 March 1975 in Lima (Peru) the pattern of votes also expressed, indicated their opposition. For instance, there were 82 votes for and one against (USA) and 7 abstentions (Belgium, Canada, Israel, Italy, Japan, Federal Republic of Germany, United Kingdom). This declaration had called for the 'maximum possible increase' in the share of developing countries in world industrial production from 7 per cent to at least 25 per cent by the year 2000, through a process of consultations. It set out the main principles of industrialisation and defined the means by which the international community as a whole could undertake action of a broad nature in the field of industrial development with a view to establishing a New International Economic Order.[46] In all those discussions, if the developing countries had advanced radical views, it was because they argue that the present economic order has engendered a situation of inequality, injustice and inequity. They do not see how an old order that existed during the colonial period should be allowed to perpetuate itself into a post-colonial period. For them, therefore, there was need for both legal and economic equality although they were not ready to concede anything to the developed countries because of the subjugation, exploitation and economic plunder that they had undergone during the colonial era. This was why, for instance, the developing countries had insisted on the drawing-up of a legal document for an international code of conduct for the transfer of technology contrary to the views of the developed western countries. Thus they want concessions from the industrial countries without reciprocity or losing sovereignty.

Measures taken after the Declaration on the International Economic Order

The first measures taken after the above Declaration in favour of the

Special Programme of action was the drawing up of a provisional list of 29 countries[47] considered most seriously affected by the 1972–74 economic crises for which an overall deficit of about 4550 million dollars was projected for 1974 and 1975. Among these countries were 19 African countries. These measures were contained in an adopted report to the General Assembly by a 36-member intergovernmental body on a special programme of emergency relief assistance to developing countries. It contained recommendations on the scope, machinery and modes of operation of the Special Fund set up by the General Assembly at its 6th special session. The Fund was set up to serve as a central monitoring body for bilateral and multilateral assistance and in general as a focal point for emergency relief and development assistance to the countries so affected by the world economic crises. The Fund, which was meant to be replenished from voluntary contributions by governments, non-governmental organisations and other sources, was empowered to make grants and loans on concessionary terms, participate in investments and allocate assistance to the most needy countries. The eligibility to this Fund would be reviewed periodically by a Board of Governors composed of 36 countries whose role would be to formulate policies and which Board would be made up of potential donors and recipients serving for 3 years.[48] During this *ad hoc* committee meeting which concluded its work on 7 October 1974, some Western delegations (France, Federal Republic of Germany, United Kingdom) expressed reservations, while the Soviet Union held the view that it would not be appropriate for the UN organ to monitor or control any aid given bilaterally, since this would amount to interference in the internal affairs of states. However, the UN Secretary-General finally announced the names of 45 States[49] wishing to contribute to replenish the Fund and some of these comprise the members of the EEC, USA and petroleum-producing countries of OPEC.

The second measure included the international code of conduct on the transfer and development of technology to developing countries. The Nairobi Conference in its Resolution 89(iv) at its 4th session, like its predecessor the Santiago Conference in its 3rd session, had recommended that the Secretary-General of UNCTAD study the possibility of a new international legislation regulating the transfer of technology. These led to the setting up of an intergovernmental group of experts comprising member-states who were commissioned to elaborate on the code and formulate draft provisions that were either mandatory or optional without prejudice to the final decision on the legal character of the code. To this end, the General Assembly was asked to convene at its 31st session a UN conference under UNCTAD auspices scheduled for 1978 so as to negotiate on the draft and adopt final document embodying the code of conduct including the decision on its legal character. This group held its first session from 8 to 19 November 1976,[50] during which they decided to establish three working groups covering different chapter-headings; namely, preamble, principles and objectives, definitions and scope of application, special treatment to developing countries and restrictive business practices. They finally came out with a corporate draft text defined 'Definitions and Scope of Application' made without prejudices to possible textual changes and additions to be made by governments in the future. This group had met twice in 1975, during which meetings the Group of 77, Groups B and D shared different view points. For instance, while the Group of 77 expressed the view that all countries have a right to access to technology, and that its attainment can only be achieved through an internationally binding document that could regulate its transfer,[51] Group B stood for a non-legally binding document which would consist of guidelines of a voluntary nature[52] setting out general and equitable principles applicable to governments and to the transfer in which private primary resources would be needed.[53] Another area of UNCTAD's study vital to developing countries was that of the reverse transfer of technology, otherwise known as brain-drain. Its study concluded that in 1970 alone, the income that was transferred from developing countries to the USA was about 3·7 US billion dollars while, for the same period, the development assistance of the USA amounted to 3·1 US billion dollars.[54] Because the drain consists principally in the flow of qualified personnel like doctors, engineers and scientists, to the developed countries, the UNCTAD Secretariat had to propose that compensation be paid to affected countries in financial terms through the development of appropriate taxes. The importance of technology can no more be underrated, because even Robert Solow had attributed the 87·5 per cent of the growth of per capita income in the USA over the period 1909–49 to technological progress and the rest to the use of capital.[55] The development of the USSR was also rapid because it controlled its labour force and established anti-emigration laws, while a country like East Germany had to build a Berlin Wall.

From the positions we have examined so far, it is clear that the developed world would not accept the terms of the Group of 77 but might accept training of manpower requirements in some restricted areas. Two basic proposals emerge from this problem:

Firstly, developing countries must pay greater attention to the establishment of research centres into which transnational corporations should be asked to contribute financially without control. There are some developing countries that have established their patent laws to protect their research findings and manufactures and in spite of this they only own about 1 per cent of world stock of patents and at the same time grant monopoly rights on imports to foreign patent holders. Among the countries that have tried to develop new laws and formulate national policies in the area of transfer and development of technology are Mexico, Argentina, Brazil, the Andean Pact countries, India and Spain. However, when one examines the development approaches of China and India in the 1950s, it is easy to appreciate the effects of capital goods industries on their economies. While India concentrated on capital goods on a big scale, China during this period concentrated on manufacture of machine tools and industrial equipment in order to manufacture iron and steel, cement-making machinery, oil-drilling and transport equipments. Consequently, while in India by the end of her 3rd Plan only about 55 per cent of all machinery requirements was met from domestic sources, China in the first five years had about 5 per cent of capital construction investment – spent on machine building and consequently 85 per cent of the machinery and equipment for the second plan was produced in the country including very sophisticated equipments.[56] Consequently the developing countries must develop indigenous technology for their advancement.

Secondly, developing countries could begin to develop the idea of technological progress within regional economic groupings where the contracting parties could pull their resources together. It is true that clever multinational corporations could still penetrate, but their influence would be minimised by the advantages of economic co-operation and integration that might arise therefrom.

OPEC and the western developed countries within the problems of the New International Economic Order

When the OPEC countries collectively sought for world increase in the prices after the October 1973 crises, it was evident that for the first time there was solidarity within the group, and that raw materials could be effectively used as a weapon of politico–economic survival without however neglecting the negative role it also had on the small non-producer countries of the Group of 77. While the western countries reacted by favouring their affected group within the OECD countries through oil facility of the IMF, the OPEC countries decided to come to the aid of the poor countries,[57] particularly Arab and Muslim countries. The West also reacted through some of their scholars like Professor Edward McWhinney of the Simon Fraser University, who came out with three alternative approaches[58] in tackling the pressures created by the OPEC and the third world in respect of their raw materials. The three options suggested by him were as follows:

Firstly, the West should concentrate their development efforts within the Western triangle created by USA, Japan and Western Europe.

Secondly, in order to separate the third world and the fourth, which are the poorer nations, the West could concentrate on key nations of the third world in order to reach agreement with the OPEC countries and other raw-materials-producing countries.

Thirdly, the most positive option would be to incorporate all the nations within a 'new and more inclusive global economic order' in order to settle not only economic problems but also those problems emanating from environmental deterioration, the world population explosion and food scarcity through special bilateral deals or trade-offs with the more important producers of raw materials among the third world majority.

These options of Professor McWhinney express beyond doubt the thinking of the dominant class of the western world, who believe that the present world problems could still be solved by classical diplomatic means of divide and rule. He does not realise that the present international society has passed that stage and that we are interdependent, and that only this could save the world, where the third world is becoming more and more aware of the present inequality in development and will continue to react to it. He does not appear to have absorbed the requirements of Article 55 of the UN Charter and its logical consequences which the original authors of this article had foreseen. He should therefore not pull the hands of the clock backwards.

(C) Some salient conclusions arising from the questions posed at the beginning

Although we could say that the Raw Material Conferences held so far have awakened the conscience of the world to the economic problems of developing countries, we cannot but be sceptical about the possible application of the entire provisions of the Declaration of Principles on the International Economic Order and the Charter of Economic Rights and Duties of States for the following reasons:

Firstly, it is obvious from the above analysis so far made that political resistance has come from hostile votes or abstentions or reservations expressed by some very important trading partners like the USA, France, Germany and Canada on the provisions concerning nationalisation because it did not consider the possibility of adequate compensation. These countries, which are all highly industrialised with the USA as the leader, voted against not only the Charter of Economic Rights and Duties of States but also the Lima Declaration of 1975 and the Declaration of Principles on the New International Economic Order. The importance of the USA in these negative attitudes cannot be underrated because she is the greatest buyer of most raw materials. Nevertheless, the result of the intransigence of the developing world in respect of compensation, although this had been catered for in the Charter of Economic Rights and Duties, could have been the reluctance on the part of the entrepreneurs of the developed countries to invest capital in developing countries. If the 'Group of 77' had adopted these tactics, it was no doubt in recognition of the amount of exploitation that had taken place in their respective countries, as has been seen from the Kennecott versus Chile case and the refusal of developed countries to pay adequate prices for their commodities while prices of finished products are determined by the developed markets without international consultation. The areas of vexation from the developed countries can still be traced to the creation of producer associations, indexation of prices of raw materials vis-à-vis finished products imported by developing countries, reimbursement of customs duties on importations from developing countries.[59] It becomes therefore obvious that co-operation from the developed countries in terms of paying favourable prices for raw materials might help to keep the balance. However, it could be deduced from the nature of the reservations and acceptances made that some developed countries first had to accept the basic documents so as not to incur the displeasure of the poor nations. Such is the nature of compromises in international diplomacy. But the possibility of the tactics of evasion cannot be overruled since these documents are not basic international agreements. An adoption without signature and possibility of sanctions cannot be taken seriously in terms of application. Therefore, the entire application of the basic documents will undoubtedly run into difficulty unless the conflicting interests are resolved in future negotiations.

Secondly, Dr Kissinger's military threat to oil-producing countries was an unacceptable indication of intent to display the classical notion of diplomacy where the stronger takes everything without granting adequate concessions to the weaker.[60] The recourse to gun-boat diplomacy confirms the fears of the developing world that the UN is incapable of solving world tensions when the interests of Big Powers are involved. In this way Dr Kissinger did not intend to strengthen or 'develop friendly relations among nations' but intended to practise a 'violation of the rights of peoples and nations to sovereignty over their natural wealth and resources'. But since this is contrary to the spirit and principles of the UN Charter, the development of international co-operation and peace would continuously be a far cry. Dr Okoi Arikpo, Nigeria's External Affairs Commissioner at the last UN Conference on Raw Materials in May 1974 in New York, rightly spoke when he said *inter alia:*

> the tragedy of our times is that, in spite of the political advances of the past generations, the world economic order has remained firmly rooted in its nineteenth-century foundations where military and technological power regulate world prices.

However, the developing nations should always be ready to challenge this type of threat because world developments have confirmed beyond doubt that military might is not an absolute determinant of world diplomacy.

Thirdly, the desire of the rich nations to provide for prompt compensation is another deterrent to the application of the Declaration. Paragraph 4 of Resolution 1803 quoted in our previous analysis makes reference to appropriate compensation and not to prompt compensation.

Furthermore, what constitutes adequate or appropriate compensation is even difficult to define because the notion of compensation has been tied to national constitutional requirements, that is, 'in accordance with rules in force in the state taking such measures in the exercise of its sovereignty' (paragraph 4). There is therefore a moral issue involved in what constitutes compensation, which moral issue can approach a solution if the developed countries agree to pay commensurate prices for raw materials, contribute positively to the development of the poor countries and agree to subject the prices of finished products to international consultation as is the case with raw materials. This issue, consequently, will continue for a long time to plague the conscience and morality involved in international investments since exploitation and nationalisation are generally accepted notions which have not yet been precisely defined. Unless these issues are resolved, the expression of independence through the right to natural resources as expressed in Article 55 of the UN Charter, will continue to jeopardise and compromise world peace and co-operation.

SECTION III. CO-OPERATION AMONG THIRD WORLD INTERNATIONAL ECONOMIC INTEGRATION ORGANISATIONS

INTRODUCTION

As a reaction to the experiences of the developing countries in respect of the problems of their commodity marketing vis-à-vis the prices of finished goods from the developed nations, which the developed countries have refused to be put under a system of indexation, the absolute decline in their terms of trade since the two development decades and the tortuous experiences to which their national development processes have been subjected because of their roles as primary producers, regional integration organisations now proliferate in the different continents of the third world. The incessant search over the years for adequate pricing policies within contractual arrangements made up of producers and consumers and in forums for economic discussions in the areas of commodity stabilisation and marketing, has not proved satisfactory because of the politics now identified with certain strategic raw materials stocked by principal consumer countries. Moreover the Common Fund Negotiations, to which the developed countries have not been sensitive enough and which in fact broke down in December 1978,[61] either because they prefer a borrowing system from existing International Financial Institutions or a system of voluntary contributions to Commodity Agreements or because the USSR payments systems are quite different from those of the West, have now convinced the Third World that they must look inwards and be self-reliant. This was indeed one of the conclusions of the Manila and Mexico City Conferences of the non-aligned ministers and the Group of 77. The developing world has therefore responded by encouraging the creation of regional economic groupings and co-operational links within these groupings across continents.

(I) UNDER THE UNCTAD AUSPICES AS RESPONSE TO THE FAILURES OF THE INTERNATIONAL ECONOMIC SYSTEM

(A) Co-operation among interregional economic groupings

As a follow-up to the Mexico City Conference, a working party made up of fifteen subregional and interregional economic groupings with fourteen UN and specialised agencies including five experts of the UNCTAD Secretariat, met under the banner of the UNCTAD in Geneva from 8 to 18 April 1978.[62] This meeting resulted from the resolutions made by the Group of 77 at their 3rd ministerial meeting at Manila, and at the Mexico City Conferences of 13–22 September 1976 during which far-reaching decisions were taken including an expression of a strong political will to establish close co-operation links within themselves and regional economic groupings in order to achieve self-reliance. The Mexico City Programme[63] had suggested the drawing-up of guidelines for measures of support of concomitant action at the interregional level, to be implemented by developing contries as a whole. According to this programme, the multilateral financial institutions in close co-operation with the secretariats of regional and sub-regional groupings, as well as appropriate bodies of the UN system, should undertake identification, preparation, promotion and financing of inter-country projects in all fields of economic co-operation among developing countries. The agenda items of the General Meeting could therefore be classified into two main headings:

(a) institutional and co-ordination arrangements;
(b) substantive issues arising from the agenda items.

(a) Institutional and co-ordination arrangements

These arose from the decisions of the Mexico Conference in September 1976 on economic co-operation among developing countries during which three areas of action were identified.

(i) Measures of support action at the interregional level to be implemented by developing countries as a whole

The working party recommended the establishment of subsidiary intergovernmental bodies which concern: (a) the promoting and implementation of the broad aspects of the Mexico Programme, for example in the areas of trade, production, infrastructure and services; (b) establishment of multinational marketing enterprises for a given commodity; (c) the technical and financial support of the UN should be sought to strengthen co-operation in the areas of education, training, human resources and employment.

(ii) Establishment of links among sub-regional and regional groupings

These links would be in the areas of: exchanging information on matters of common interest, assisting other member countries in the co-ordination and harmonisation of their positions in global negotiations, undertaking joint research and training activities, development of joint marketing and import arrangements, etc. In order to make this workable, it was recommended that interregional visits by the senior officials of their groupings, and consultation between the public and private sectors including associations of manufacturers and traders as well as investors of these countries, should be encouraged. The support of the UN system and the UNDP would be of vital importance if these goals must be attained.

(iii) Participation in co-operation and integratioı. schemes of countries that are at present outside such schemes

This section is highly controversial because it involved complex and difficult problems – complex and difficult because non-members of an existing economic grouping cannot benefit from the achievements of a grouping without being a member. Such preferential treatment is unjustifiable in terms of the provisions of contractual arrangements which provide for possible dismissals and withdrawals. Therefore if a non-member enjoys the fruits of collective endeavour without being a member of the grouping, the agreement will be meaningless. Although the Mano River Union, between the Sierra Leone and Liberia, permits the participation of non-members in its schemes, this is apparently an exception, because after all it is not an international organisation but a bilateral union using multilateral techniques since this might be one of its methods of encouraging further participation of neighbouring countries *ad interim*. It was therefore not surprising that the working party concluded that the participation of countries outside existing schemes should not be treated in a general way, since each regional and sub-regional grouping is itself different from all others in many respects. It was therefore recommended that the UNCTAD Secretariat, in consultation and co-ordination with appropriate organisations of the UN system, should:

(a) make contacts with governments of developing countries eligible to accede to specific economic groupings and seek their views on the matter;
(b) ascertain their technical assistance needs with the view to encouraging necessary co-operation.

Coincidentally, when this meeting was being held in Geneva, the ECOWAS Heads of State Summit Conference in Lagos had thrown more light on this problem by their resolution to help Cape Verde Islands and Guinea-Bissau pay their budgetary contributions for two years in order to facilitate their membership and continuity within the organisation.

(iv) Establishment of a consultative body or mechanism of co-ordination and promotion of activities of integration groupings

In order to be able to centralise and co-ordinate arrangements, an Inter-Secretariat Consultative Group (ISCG) made up of secretariats of sub-regional and regional groupings of the developing world was recommended, on a provisional and informal basis. Its role would not only be advisory to the Group of 77 that suggested its establishment, but would also, in this capacity, assume responsibility with UNCTAD and other organisations for the preparation of substantive studies and for providing servicing facilities to the Group of 77 on economic co-operation among developing countries and also to the various organisations within the UN systems. Its functions are also to make proposals for action required at the interregional level in consonance with the Mexico Conference objectives and to facilitate 'participation in co-operation and integration schemes of countries that are at present outside such schemes', in line with paragraph A. 1–1(c) of the Mexico City programme. The ISCG would be organised and serviced by UNCTAD.

(v) Other recommendations were:

(a) That the UNCTAD Secretariat, in conjunction with other regional commissions and in consultation with regional groupings, submit proposals for the establishment of a financing facility for short- and medium-term financing for trade expansion among developing countries.
(b) That the UNCTAD Secretariat, in consultation with UNIDO, UNDP and other relevant UN bodies, prepare a study on the role of consultancy and engineering services in developing countries.
(c) That in conformity with Resolution 87 (iv) of the 4th UNCTAD Conference in Nairobi and the Mexico City Programme, the Group of 77 should:

    (i) encourage member governments to give financial support to regional centres for the transfer and development of technology;
    (ii) invite the UNCTAD Secretariat to explore ways and means of supporting and assisting these centres and promoting exchange of experience among them.

(b) Substantive issues on co-operation techniques arising from the Agenda items

The items covered were the following: generalised trade preferences (sub-item 4 (c)); investment, production, training, employment and services (sub-item 4(b)); infrastructure, transport and communications (sub-item 4(d)).

(i) Co-operation in trade preferences

The problem of trade preferences had been for a long time the subject of various negotiations between the poor and rich world, either at UNCTAD Conferences, GATT Multilateral Trade Negotiations or even between the ACP countries and the EEC. For the developing world, therefore, this meeting of third world regional groupings was seen as an alternative method of finding solutions to their balance of payments problems in commodity marketing. The GATT, which had been the forum for discussions under its multilateral trade negotiations, had not measured up to the expectations of the developing world since no substantial progress has been made so far. The meeting of the Working Party on Trade Expansion was therefore also seen as a forum for re-stating the intentions of the Group of 77 through their regional groupings so as to work out possible approaches for discussion at the next UNCTAD Conference, in Manila in 1979. Two specific areas drew their attention:

(i) the establishment of a global system of trade preferences among developing countries;
(ii) co-operation in state-trading and the setting up of multinational marketing enterprises.

These two considerations are vital, if thought is given to the fact that the developing world do not all share the same political and consequently trading systems. In so doing they are trying to be self-reliant, as required by the Mexico City Programme. A generalised system of trade preferences could succeed only if closely identified with co-operation in the fields of production, finance and payments. This consideration cannot be taken in isolation of the long-standing positions of the Group of 77 as regards coverage of a wide range of commodities which the 4th UNCTAD Conference established at about 18. For these reasons the working party recommended that preferential treatment should extend to manufactures and not to agriculture alone. This idea is new in so much as it is not connected with the demand of the Group of 77 for indexation of both raw and finished manufactured goods as regards pricing policies. Therefore a global system of preferences must not be limited to tariff preferences alone, but must include other preferential measures, such as non-tariff barriers, long-term contracts and concomitant action in the area of finance and marketing. Although the latter has not been given a global dimension it is limited to certain concessionary measures granted by the EEC to the ACP countries under the Lomé Convention, yet certain fears are now being nurtured in some quarters that oil seeds may soon come under thick barrier walls in the EEC countries in order to protect their internal market.[64] In order to achieve the objectives of the developing world, therefore, there arises an incumbent need to study the implications of disparities in import regimes of developing countries in order to be able to evaluate the equivalence of concessions among them. Although these studies are being presently conducted in the ECOWAS research schemes, the working party felt the absolute need to provide mechanisms linking preferences with joint ventures in the areas of export and import policies and in respect of the least-developed countries, and agreed that within a global system of trade preferences, special and non-reciprocal measures should be granted in their favour. Two measures became imperative:

1. preferential links should be established on the regional level between groupings, while for interregional level, information seminars and workshops could be organised;
2. in sub-regional groupings, those that developed common foreign trade policies should negotiate global schemes as a single unit. This is not new because it is already been practised by the EEC (Article 228, paragraph 7 of the Treaty).

(ii) Co-operation in joint investment; training, employment and services (sub-item 4(b))

Some of these objectives are not dissimilar to the conclusions reached later at the Niamey/MULPOC/ECA Meeting of Intergovernmental Organisations in the West African sub-region as we shall see later in section II (B) (iv): ECOWAS in relation to international organisations.

Agriculture, which is the mainstay of the developing world and which is their principal foreign-exchange earner, is still limited to regional or sub-regional co-operation. Their problems also extend to the non-complementary nature of their economies since they produce identical products; physical infrastructure, especially irrigation schemes in arid areas; feeder roads, particularly with the landlocked countries and drought-ridden regions. Two suggestions then emerged from the working party: (1) the importance of co-operation in consultancy services as a means of developing the technical capacity of developing countries, and expansion of the scope of their markets in order to save foreign exchange; (2) correlation of investment and production planning of countries concerned, in order to avoid duplication of efforts.

(iii) Monetary and financial co-operation, (sub-item 4(c))

This sector is of great importance to the developing world since their transactions with the developed economy countries in respect of payments for imported manufactured goods are made in the currency of the exporting country. In this respect, the importance of a clearing and payments arrangement cannot be underrated in order to facilitate trade among the developing world. For these reasons the working party supported the creation of a Co-ordination Committee on Multilateral Payments and Monetary Co-operation as a means of studying and discussing problems arising therefrom in respect of trade expansion. It then recommended to the Group of 77 that there was need to undertake studies relating to the creation of a developing countries Payments Union, a Liquidity Unit and a Commercial and Merchant Bank for developing countries.

(iv) Development of infrastructure, transport and communications facilities (sub-item 4 (d))

Exports from developing countries undergo very exorbitant transport charges because they lack this very important item of trade distribution. It was therefore recommended that in order to solve this problem it would be necessary to harmonise transport policies that would eventually lead to: (a) the establishment within secretariats of economic groupings, of units responsible for the analysis of freights, volume of traffic and earnings derived from shipping; (b) the convening of periodic meetings of shipowners and council of shipowners at regional and interregional levels; (c) the exchange of information on the result of negotiations with liner conferences. In order to achieve this, the working party entrusted this responsibility to the UNCTAD Secretariat, which should collaborate with secretariats of groupings and other relevant organisations.

(B) Some salient remarks

There is no doubting the fact the working party has reacted to the many failures in negotiations between the rich and the poor nations, particularly the Common Fund and Preferences negotiations. However it is significant to note that because they are incapable of setting up an independent secretariat for the study of their problems the UNCTAD Secretariat is still resorted to for conducting their studies and establishing co-operation links *ad interim*. This points to UNCTAD as the only competent institution, to which the Group of 77 belongs, capable of preparing groundwork papers for the group in preparation for the 5th UNCTAD Conference in May 1979 in Manila. This is to confirm that their responses to the problems of the third world cannot be interpreted as an intention to establish a type of north/south dialogue based on confrontation or an opposing force against the rich nations. Rather, as it did emerge at the working party, it was a desire to find self-reliant solutions to the problems of the third world. What strikes an observer at these international meetings attended by experts of the third world is that many youthful functionaries representing their various governments and organisations had cultivated from past experiences a phobia or suspicion that the UN organs are mere tools of the Great Powers who have now evolved a new method of having a collective grip on subregions and national economies. Paradoxically they do not deny the importance of UN institutions or refuse their limited technical roles for instance in the areas of research. In fact the original authors of the UN Charter meant to encourage greater roles for multilateral aids emanating from its agencies, rather than encourage bilateral aids based on bipolar ideological camps or emanating from sovereignty considerations. The negotiations on the rescheduling of debts going on within the UNCTAD institution, and all its conferences so far and the fluctuating nature of national currencies on the international market, are probably pointers that the founding fathers of the Charter may in the future have their way in spite of the growing fears of the growing generations of the developing countries about the neo-colonial use of these United Nations institutions.

(II) REGIONAL ECONOMIC CO-OPERATION INSTITUTIONS WHICH CO-OPERATE WITH THE UN SYSTEM

We have seen that from the economic groupings that attended the meeting of the working party on trade expansion, over fifteen organisations from the third world participated actively. Within the African continent alone there are about 124 intergovernmental co-operation organisations fairly distributed among all the problem areas facing the world today.[65] Significant, however, is the number of economic communities, common markets, customs unions and other multilateral organisations in Africa alone, which number about twenty-three.[66] This proliferation of economic institutions is symptomatic of a region in a dilemma of how to get out of her socioeconomic problems, since in essence they have common objectives. Prominent among them are the economic groupings in East, West, North and Central Africa.[67] On the West African sub-region, two main economic communities will be the subject of our study for the purpose of identifying their differences, similarities, structures, problems and prospects. These institutions are the CEAO (Economic Community of West Africa) and the ECOWAS (Economic Community of West African States).

(A) The CEAO

The solidarity among the francophone West African States is of long historical significance. For more than twenty years, they had developed a community of economic interests within economic co-operation organisations. For instance, the Union Africaine et Malgache (UAM), that is, the African and Malagasy Union; the Economic Co-operation of African and Malagasy Union (UAMCE) which later became OCAM (the African and Mauritian Common Organisation) on 26 June 1966. From about 1959 to 1966, the failure of the Customs Union of West Africa to satisfy the needs of the sub-region led to the creation of the CEAO (Communauté Economique de l'Afrique de l'Ouest) on 17 April 1973, the date of the signature of its Treaty in Abidjan. It is made up of six francophone states of the West African sub-region, namely, Ivory Coast, Upper Volta, Mali, Mauritania, Niger and Senegal who are all members of a larger ECOWAS community. The six countries of the CEAO live in a contiguous zone, speak the same official language, share about the same political philosophy (ideology) in spite of some differences in political regimes, share the same monetary system (CFA francs) except Mali whose francs are Malian, and Mauritania whose monetary system is Uguiya. In spite of these slight monetary differences, they all share a common administrative system which was a legacy of the French colonial era, and they all have close ties with France. All these point to the fact that there is greater homogeneity within the CEAO countries whose population is about thirty million, than within the ECOWAS countries made up of three colonial systems (francophone, lusophone and anglophone) and whose population is about 125 million. Most of the CEAO countries are in the Sahelian zone, except Ivory

Coast and Senegal, while Upper Volta, Mali and Niger are far removed from the coastal area.

The six member-countries have similar economic structure because they are essentially agricultural. For instance, in this sector alone the Ivory Coast has about 83 per cent of her population; Upper Volta (83 per cent); Mali (90·5 per cent); Mauritania (85 per cent); Niger (92 per cent) and Senegal (75 per cent).[68] The three Sahelian countries depend on their neighbours for access to the sea, and the Niger Republic appears more economically viable because of her uranium extraction and exports. Within the CEAO, the Ivory Coast and Senegal contribute the lion's share to the tune of about 80 per cent of the Community Development Fund because they are the two more economically advanced countries and have consequently in the last five years refused to take advantage of the Fund so as to help the poorer ones.

Objectives: The fundamental objectives of the Community as established in Articles 3–4 of Title I of its Treaty, are to achieve eventual integration of the economies of the contractual member-countries, particularly in the areas of agriculture, animal husbandry, fishing, industry, transport and communications, tourism, intraregional exchanges in the areas of agriculture and industry. In order to achieve these lofty objectives, in terms of execution, there are three main instruments:

(i) *The Community Fund for Development*, whose role is not only that of compensation arising from fiscal losses due to the application of regional preferences in the industrial sector but also to contribute to industrial development projects.

(ii) *Regional Co-operation Tax*, is substituted for all the duties and taxes on importation in each member-state with the exception of internal taxes on products of national origin.

(iii) *The Fund for Solidarity and Intervention for the Economic Development of the Community (FOSIDEC)*, guarantees loans made by contractual member-states and has an annual budget of five milliards of Francs (CFA) into which they contribute. It grants loans or gives guarantees to national financial institutions of development in order to finance specific projects. Priority is normally given to the least industrialised states. The Fund does not participate in the administration of a company or enterprise so formed, but however, reserves the right of representation in its Board of Directors.

With the birth in May 1975 of the ECOWAS, whose objectives are similar, questions have been asked as to whether the CEAO should not or would not eventually disappear. Some look at both institutions as potential rivals although both have been declared complementary institutions by the ECOWAS Council of Ministers, in a Resolution[69] on the establishment of co-operation between the ECOWAS and the CEAO, in which the council held the view that it 'is the best strategy for raising the standard of living of the people' in the sub-region, among other declarations. Although this resolution appears to be a temporary strategy for the recognition of the reality, it must be emphasised however that African states pay such great attention to political and sovereignty considerations in most of their transactions that this is likely to pose untold problems to the ECOWAS which is an amalgam of 16 states of three different linguistic affinities, political systems and administrative procedures.

(B) The Economic Community of West African States

This community, made up of sixteen member-states[70] came into force provisionally on 28 May 1975 when fifteen heads of state and governments signed the treaty in Lagos.

(i) Objectives

The objectives of this community are the eventual integration of the sub-region by the gradual elimination of customs duties, abolition of quantitative and administrative restrictions on trade, harmonisation of agricultural policies, abolition as between member-states of the obstacles to free movement of persons, services and capital, among others. All these, according to Article 12 of the Treaty, shall take a period of fifteen years to accomplish.

(ii) Structure

There are two major administrative institutions within the community: the Secretariat whose headquarters is in Lagos and is headed by an Executive Secretary who is the overall administrative head of all the institutions of the community and the Fund for Co-operation,

Compensation and Development headed by a Managing Director who is second in hierarchy within the community with its headquarters in Lomé (Togo). To this Treaty, five protocols are attached. Nevertheless, the institutions of the community as listed in Article 4, paragraph 1 of the Treaty are as follows:

(a) the Authority of Heads of State and Government;
(b) the Council of Ministers;
(c) the Executive Secretariat;
(d) the Tribunal of the Community; and
(e) the following technical and specialised commissions:
- the Trade, Customs, Immigration, Monetary and Payments Commission;
- the Industry, Agriculture and National Resources Commission;
- the Transport, Telecommunication and Energy Commission;
- the Social and Cultural Affairs Commission.

Under the Executive Secretary are two Deputies and a Financial Controller whose appointments are statutory and political in nature and whose responsibilities are those of executing policies enunciated by the Council of Ministers and the Authority. While Article 8, paragraph 2 stipulates that the Executive Secretary 'shall be appointed by the Authority to serve in such office for a term of four (4) years and be eligible for re-appointment for another term of four (4) years only', the Treaty is silent on the length of period that his Deputies and the Financial controller appointed by the Council of Ministers, would serve. This silence could be interpreted in three ways:

Firstly, it could mean that these statutory officers could stay as long as the Executive Secretary and, in this case, their maximum duration would be eight years at most. This interpretation if carried out would be detrimental to the superior interests of the Community since a new Executive Secretary would have no one of statutory rank to understudy, all of them having been appointed in 1977.

Secondly, it could also mean that all statutory officers are permanent staff. In essence, this would be contradictory in terms with the political nature of their appointments, although to a great extent it will help to create continuity in the administration, particularly if a new Executive Secretary becomes appointed. In practice, since the appointments of the Deputies and the Financial Controller are made by the Council of

Ministers, who have not fixed their length of service, this interpretation appears more valid but contradictory. However the ideal recommendation would be for the statutory officers to stay in office for a maximum period of nine years (four in the first instance and five on renewal), thus giving them one extra year to be understudied by a new Executive Secretary and two new Deputies and a Financial Controller.

Thirdly, since the statutory officers are political officers designated by their countries and appointed by the Council of Ministers, it could be interpreted that each country reserves the right of recall or withdrawal of its representative after informing the Council of Ministers. This is unlike the case of the Fund for Co-operation where Article 28, paragraph 5 stipulates that 'the Managing Director shall vacate his office if the council after consultation with the Board of Directors so decides'. This is also true of his Deputy who can be appointed and dismissed in the same manner (Article 28, paragraph 10), their holding offices for a term of four years for the first instance with a maximum of eight years, notwithstanding (paragraph 4).

(iii) The Authority of Heads of State and Governments and the Council of Ministers

These two institutions of the community make decisions on matters of policy in the form of directives and decisions.

(a) The Authority

As the governing institution of the community the Authority has responsibility for the general direction and control of the performance of the executive functions of the community (Article 5, paragraph 1–2 of the Treaty), It makes decisions and directives[71] which are binding on the institutions of the community (paragraph 3). The Authority, which meets once a year, rotates the office of Chairman yearly[72] among members of the Authority. According to Article 7 of the Treaty, it is the responsibility of the Authority to determine the procedure for the dissemination of its decisions and directives including those of the Council of Ministers in matters relating to their coming into effect. According to this procedure,[73] all its decisions and directives, including those of the Council of Ministers, shall be published by the Executive

Secretary in the *ECOWAS Official Journal* within fifteen days of their adoption. It is thereafter incumbent on the Executive Secretary to notify all institutions and parties affected by the decisions and directives of the Authority and the Council of Ministers within the same period of fifteen days. Unless otherwise specified by the Authority its decisions and directives shall take immediate effect (paragraph 3), while those of the Council of Ministers shall take effect on the 30th day following their publication in the *ECOWAS Official Journal* or on the date so specified in them. The adopted text of the procedure which was duly signed by Lt General Olusegun Obasanjo, the Nigerian Head of State and the President (Chairman) of the Authority in Lagos, on 22 April 1978 on behalf of the Authority, is to be kept in the archives of the ECOWAS Secretariat.

When one examines, critically, the provisions of the ECOWAS Treaty and the Procedure for Dissemination already adopted and signed, there exists some lacuna. For example, neither of these documents have specified in greater details the category of legal persons to whom the decisions and directives are applicable, whether corporate or private persons, except in reference to states and community institutions which are definitely not the only subject of community law, nor have they established the instruments of enactments of the laws emanating from these decisions and directives. Therefore the importance of an enactment procedure is vindicated by Article XIII of the Protocol relating to infringement and sanctions which requires that member-states must introduce legislation for penalties against persons who furnish or cause to furnish an untrue document in support of claims in another state. It further states in paragraph 4 that continued infringement may be referred to the Council of Ministers through the Commission without prejudice to the ECOWAS Tribunal (Article 11, paragraph 1 of the Treaty) whose decision is final in respect of settlement of disputes referred to it (Article 56 of the Treaty). Article 39, paragraph 3c of the Treaty on Movement of Capital refers to nationals in the acquisition of stocks and shares etc. Article 35 (stage II) of the Treaty on the Evolution of a Common Agricultural Policy refers among other things to the need for such a policy in the areas of processing and marketing of agricultural products, animal husbandary (although it does not state, like in Article 39, paragraph 1b of the Treaty of Rome with precision that the objective of an agricultural policy shall be to ensure fair standards of living for their agricultural community with particular reference to the individual earnings of persons engaged in agriculture), stabilisation of markets, availability of supplies and the need for such supplies to reach consumers at reasonable prices. These are reasons why the adopted and signed Procedure for Dissemination could have been more explicit and precise in terms of details of means and methods. After all most of the ECOWAS states do practise both private and public enterprise systems in which corporate bodies and persons are involved. Within the agricultural area, the farmer whose products are subject to price fluctuations and whose products will be the ultimate object of decision-making in terms of uniformity in prices within the ECOWAS region, will be the direct subject of community law.

Unlike the treaty establishing the European Coal and Steel Community which includes an enforcement procedure of the decisions and recommendations of its High Authority in Article 15 and the EEC treaty which provides for this in its Article 192, the ECOWAS treaty decided deliberately to leave the onus of determining the procedure for dissemination to its Authority (Article 7). In this procedure already signed, there are very important omissions, in the light of our analysis above, on enactment and enforcement procedures under national legislation in spite of the binding nature of the Authority's directives and decisions on all the institutions of the community. This was why the High Authority of the Coal and Steel Community further required in Article 15 that the 'High Authority shall determine the manner in which this Article is to be implemented'.

The author is therefore of the opinion that a separate protocol would have been preferable, since it is supposed to contain particulars of negotiations or additives of an incomplete treaty instead of a simple procedure. On the other hand if the idea of a procedure is maintained because it goes into force on signature, we must not however ignore the consequences of its provisions on possible changes in national constitutions. If we argue that the decisions and directives of the Authority are binding on all community institutions and therefore consider the heads of state as subject of the law, since they represent a people within a given boundary called state, then we are mainly referring to executive agreements which are normally political. A treaty cannot be binding on a people unless its national constitution makes such a provision allowing for the supremacy of international treaties over its national laws. On the other hand, if this constitution does not provide for this supremacy, then there would be need for a modification of the constitution before the treaty can be applicable. This is why most treaties are subjected to different constitutional methods of ratification while seeking the least time-wasting approach, depending on whether a country has a parliamentary system of government or a military or one-party system. A protocol of the nature which is ultimately recommended here, on the basis of the above reasoning, is such that provides for means and methods of enactment which are bound to modify existing institutions or suggest the creation of new ones because states are not the only subject of community law, since private persons of civil law, corporate and other legal persons are bound to apply laws so created. This is vindicated by Article XIII of the protocol relating to infringement, since it requires a legislation as already discussed above. The above reasoning would have been unnecessary if the ECOWAS treaty already ratified contained all the salient ingredients, as did the Rome treaty to which much reference has already been made. Consequently, the contents of the protocol should follow the following structure from which a prototype is provided.

Part I: *The basis and definitions of the protocol* in which the areas in the treaty and its annexed protocols, containing the scope and nature of the directives, decisions, recommendations, regulations, etc., should be established and defined.

II: *Procedure for enactment*, which should have covered the decisions and directives of the Authority and the Council of Ministers as they are applicable to legal or natural persons (corporate or persons of civil law) and to member states.

III: *Publication and entrance into force* should have contained the legal consequences of the publications of the decisions of the Authority and Council of Ministers in the *ECOWAS Official Journal*, as shall be seen in the prototype below.

IV: FINAL PROVISIONS.

PROTOCOL RELATING TO THE PROCEDURE FOR THE PROMULGATION OF DECISIONS AND DIRECTIVES MADE BY THE AUTHORITY AND THE COUNCIL OF MINISTERS OF THE ECOWAS

A PROTOTYPE

In conformity with Article 7 of the ECOWAS treaty which stipulates that the Authority shall determine the procedure for the dissemination of its decisions and directives and those of the Council of Ministers and for matters relating to their coming into effect, the following procedure is hereby established:

PART I BASIS AND DEFINITIONS FOR THIS PROCEDURE

Article 1 The Authority shall make decisions and directives which shall be binding on all institutions of the Community (Article 5 paragraph 3 of the Treaty).

DIRECTIVES shall be made on policy issues and shall be binding as to the results to be achieved upon each member state to which they are addressed but shall leave the choice of method and means to the discretion of national authorities.

DECISIONS shall be binding in all their entirety upon those to whom they are addressed. The addressee can be a member state or legal or natural persons,,that is, either to a government, to an enterprise, or private individual. They shall be administrative in nature in implementing community law thus evolved. For instance, granting of exceptions, authorisations, imposition of fines and penalties, etc. They shall be enforceable by rules of civil procedure in each member state. These decisions shall generally be made on persons other than states and by the tribunal of the community.

Article 2 The Council of Ministers shall make regulations (Article 10, paragraph 2 of the treaty), recommendations to the Authority on policy matters (Article 6, paragraph 2b), decisions and directives (Article 6, paragraph 3) which shall be binding on all subordinate institutions of the Community.

RECOMMENDATIONS AND DIRECTIVES of the Council of Ministers shall relate essentially to matters of policy while its Regulations shall relate not only to the terms and conditions of Service (Article 8, paragraph 6), financial regulations (Article 55), powers of the External Auditor (Article 10, paragraph 2), the operation of the FUND but also to proof and verification of proof of goods originating from member states (Article XII of the protocol relating to the definition of the concept of products originating from member states of the ECOWAS).

Article 3 Recommendations, directives and decisions of the Council of Ministers shall state the reasons which have motivated them, while also referring to any proposals or opinions that shall have been made by the technical or experts commissions.

PART II PROCEDURE FOR ENACTMENT

Article 4 The procedure for the enactment shall be in two categories as follows:

(a) *Decisions made by the Authority having an effect of law on legal or natural persons*

Each member-state shall designate a 'National Authority' which shall set forth the procedure of ordering enforcement of the decisions of the Authority and the tribunal of the community. Enforcement shall then be governed by the rules of civil procedure that is in force in the given member-state where the decision is expected to be carried out. For instance,

(i) the beneficiary of a decision of the Authority or judgement of the tribunal shall in the first place obtain a certified copy from the Secretariat of the ECOWAS or from the tribunal of the community. The beneficiary or party concerned shall then present this copy to his 'National Authority' with his application for enforcement. The duty of the National Authority shall only be to verify the authenticity of the decision by checking whether or not the signatures appearing on the decision document are authentic. To facilitate this process, the Secretariat of the ECOWAS would have sent specimen signatures of the heads of state and government and those of the judges of the community tribunal to all 'National Authorities'.

(ii) Once this authenticity is established, an ORDER for its enforcement shall be appended to the decision by the said National Authority and it shall then acquire the same legal force as a national court or administrative order. The party can then proceed to enforcement in accordance with national law by bringing the matter directly before the competent national institution or authority. From this moment onwards, the national rules of civil procedure shall apply with the exception that suspension of the enforcement may only be decided by the tribunal of the community. However, the courts of the country concerned shall have jurisdiction over complaints that enforcement is being carried on in an irregular manner.

(b) *Directives made by the Authority having an effect of law on member-states*
The Authority shall give directives binding as to the intended result to be achieved, upon each member-state to which they shall be addressed. However, they shall leave to the national authorities the choice of form and methods of enactment which shall constitute the appropriate measure when existing national legislation needs modification or the enactment of new provisions. Consequently, member-states shall be free to decide whether these provisions will be legislative or administrative in nature. The directives shall be able to create or have direct effect of law, that is, create rights for the citizens which the national courts must uphold.

(c) *Recommendations, decisions, directives and regulations of the Council of Ministers*
Recommendations shall be made to the Authority on matters of policy (Article 6, paragraph 2b of the treaty) by the Council of Ministers.
Decisions, directives and regulations binding to all subordinate institutions shall be administrative in nature with immediate applicability, unless the Authority decides otherwise (Article 6, paragraph 3).

(d) *Regulations* of the Council of Ministers, other than those mentioned in Article 2 above, shall be binding in their entirety and directly applicable in all member-states. For instance, fixing of import levies or compensatory amounts on commodities or the making of customs immigration regulations. Furthermore a regulation of the nature provided in Article XII of the protocol 'concerning proof and verification of proof of goods originating from member-states' of the protocol relating to the definition of the concept of products, shall be of general application and shall be binding in its entirety and directly applicable in all member-states. This will also apply to all other regulations mentioned in the annexed protocols, for example Article III relating to re-exportation of goods from third-world countries.

PART III PUBLICATION AND ENTRANCE INTO FORCE

Article 5 Directives and decisions of the Authority shall be published in the *ECOWAS Official Journal* of the community within fifteen days and shall have immediate force of law upon such publication. While decisions shall enter into force after the procedure established in Article 4(a), directives shall be notified to those to whom they are addressed and shall enter into force upon such notification. However, directives which have not been enforced within 120 days in a member-state shall lapse and shall then be referred to the tribunal of the community unless there is ample reason to believe that the cause of the non-application has been due to constitutional or internal problems.

Article 6 Directives and decisions of the Council shall be notified to whom they are addressed within fifteen days of their adoption and shall take effect upon such notification after publication in the *ECOWAS Official Journal*, on the 30th day following their publication or on the date specified in them. Therefore, these acts need not be published in the official *Journal* unless they affect the rights and interests of the citizens of several member-states.

Article 7 Regulations of the Council of Ministers, other than those mentioned in Article 2 above, shall be of general application and shall be binding in its entirety and directly applicable in all member-states. Regulations shall enter into force on the date specified in them or on the 30th day following their publication in the *Official Journal* of the Community.

PART IV FINAL PROVISIONS

Article 8 *Deposit and Entry into Force*

1. This protocol shall enter into force provisionally upon signature by heads of state and government of member-states and definitively upon ratification by at least seven signatory states in accordance with the constitutional procedures applicable for each signatory state.
2. This protocol and all the instruments of ratification shall be deposited with the Executive Secretary of the ECOWAS which shall transmit certified true copies of this protocol to all member-states and notify them of the dates of deposits of the instruments of ratification and shall register this protocol with the OAU, the UN and such organisations as the Authority shall determine.
3. This protocol shall be annexed to and shall form an integral part of the treaty.

IN WITNESS WHERE OF, WE THE HEADS OF STATE AND GOVERNMENT IN WEST AFRICA, HAVE SIGNED THIS PROTOCOL.

Done at Lagos on the . . . . in single original in English and French languages, both texts equally authentic.

Signed Heads of state

(b) The Council of Ministers

This Council which consists of two representatives of each member-state (Article 6, paragraph 1) has as responsibility to review the functioning and development of the Community (2a), make recommendations to the Authority on policy matters, give binding directives and decisions to all subordinate institutions of the community, unless it is otherwise stated by the Authority. The Council meets twice yearly under a Chairman[74] and one of such meetings immediately precedes the annual meeting of the Authority. It could meet on an extraordinary session only 'after consultation between the Chairman and other members of the Council and after at least one-third of the Members of the Council has signified their consent' (Rule 12 of the Rules of Procedure of the Council). The quorum of any Council meeting is two-thirds of the total membership of the Community, and the decision-making procedure is that of unanimity which in practice has been consensus. Nowhere in the treaty is reference made to this.

(iv) The Fund for Co-operation, Compensation and Development

This fund, whose headquarters is in Lomé (Togo), was first headed by a Managing Director (Dr R. Horton of Liberia) who has, since August 1979, been replaced by another Liberian, Robert Tubman. This followed the decision of the Authority at their Dakar meeting of 28–29 May 1979 as a measure to resolve the personality conflict within ECOWAS. The Fund is made up of a Board of Directors and other officers and staff as the Board of Directors may consider necessary (Article 24 of the protocol). This Board consists of Ministers who are members of the Council of Ministers appointed one by each member state (Article 25, paragraph 2), for a period of one year (Article 25, paragraph 3), with an alternate who 'shall be a person possessing high competence and wide experience in economic, financial and banking affairs' (Article 25, paragraph 6). The Board is presided over by a

Chairman for a period of one year on rotational basis. Each state reserves the right to revoke the appointment of its representatives (paragraph 5). This means that an appointed representative of the Board whose term of office is revoked in the Board will also have his term revoked at the Council of Ministers level although the treaty is silent on this, in spite of the fact that both institutions are represented by the same minister. Although the Council of Ministers reserves the right to ask the Managing Director to vacate his office, as we have already seen, this does not apply to the Executive Secretary of the ECOWAS whose appointment is made by the Authority but who paradoxically can only attend the meetings of the Board of Directors of the Fund without a right to participate, while its Managing Director could. That both have no voting rights is conceivable as servants of the community, but that the Executive Secretary can make no observations but sit there as a spectator is abnormal as the 'principal executive officer of the Community' (Article 8, paragraph 4), who reports on the functioning of the Community to the Council of Ministers. This becomes even more absurd after the Council of Ministers and the Authority had decided on the question of hierarchy between the Managing Director and the Executive Secretary in favour of the latter.[75]

Objectives of the Fund

It is intended to finance national and community projects; guarantee foreign investments made in member-states (Article 2(e) of the protocol); provide means to facilitate the sustained mobilisation of internal and external financial resources for contractual member-states and the Community (Article 2(f)); and among others to provide compensation to countries that have suffered losses due to the application of the treaty. To this end a total of 500 million US dollars was earmarked as operating capital with 50 million dollars to be paid up in each of the first two years of its operation, 1977 and 1978.

(v) Co-operation between ECOWAS and other international organisations

(a) Within the first operative year of the community (1977 and 1978), its Secretariat under Dr Aboubakar Diaby Ouattara (Ivory Coast), his two Deputies Dr J. Nti (Ghana) in charge of Administrative matters, Dr

D. M. Traore (Guinea) in charge of Economic Affairs, Alhaji F. O. Lawal (Nigeria), Financial Controller, and a group of task force members[76] who are technicians in their various disciplines, were loaned to the Secretariat for the initial establishment of all infrastructural requirements of the Secretariat by some member-states.

Within the period 1977–78, the Secretariat had established working relationship with other international organisations in the areas of technical assistance and had meetings with all the sub-regional organisations in West Africa. For instance, the following institutions are collaborating closely with the secretariat: UNCTAD, ECA, IBRD, IMF, BOAD, Mano River Union, West African Clearing House, ADB, FAO, UNDP and the Nigerian Institute of Social and Economic Research, Ibadan. Unfortunately, due to very complex reasons bordering on personality problems the Committee of West African Central Banks provided for by Article 38, paragraph 3 of the treaty as consisting of governors of central banks of the sub-region, has not been properly co-operating with the Secretariat until lately. Their functions are to make recommendations to the Council of Ministers on the operation of the clearing system of payments and other monetary issues (Article 38, paragraph 2). We cannot doubt the importance of this committee to the West African Clearing House, and the help it could render to the Council of Ministers in monetary policy formulations, towards integration objectives.

(b) Furthermore, in pursuance of its policy of co-operation, the first meeting of experts of intergovernmental organisations in West Africa, convened by the Secretariat, was held in Lagos on 6 and 7 February 1978 to discuss how best to integrate policies, utilise scarce resources, identify regional projects, draw up joint participation programmes and co-ordinate international financial and technical assistance, because it was discovered that very many similarities exist in their objectives and forms of intervention. Consequently, for short-term purposes, they identified four main areas of regional integration and promotion of development programmes; namely:

(i) developement of food crops and improvement of distribution and marketing systems for agricultural products;
(ii) communications in the areas of transport and telecommunications;
(iii) training of personnel within the regional setting in an institutional framework;

(iv) co-ordination of agronomical research and the dissemination of results to the states of the sub-region.

They also identified other scientific areas; namely: (i) epizootic disease joint control programme; (ii) co-ordination of health programmes for the eradication of endemic diseases; (iii) energy, industry and mines. Consequently, a small Committee made up of ECOWAS as co-ordinator, ECA, WADB, CEAO, Mano River Union and OMVS (Organisation for the exploitation of the Senegal River Basin), was set up to look into further details, and examine areas similar to those studied by integration institutions.

(c) *The Cotonou Meeting.* The Cotonou Meeting of Experts of West African Intergovernmental Organisations (27–29 June 1978) was the second after the Lagos one. It was meant to adopt the recommendations of its select committee relating to methods of co-operation among intergovernmental organisations. The recommendations of these experts, unfortunately, neither put into consideration the decisions reached by their Council of Ministers at the Niamey ECA/MULPOC Conferences of 12–17 June 1978, nor were their recommendations reflexive in practice of the treaty provisions of the communities in the West African sub-region in relation to their power structures. While the meeting of intergovernmental organisations held on 15 June 1978, during the Niamey/MULPOC conferences, decided among other things that the intergovernmental organisation scheduled to meet in Cotonou should identify common areas in which MULPOC could be of assistance to them, the Cotonou Meeting did not include this item on their Agenda. Even the recommendation of the MULPOC Council of Ministers that matters relating to the Ife-Centre for Aerial Surveys should be examined more beneficially, did not also figure in their agenda. It was, however, most disappointing at the MULPOC meeting that the ministers paid very little attention to this very vital technical training need of the sub-region, in spite of the foresight of the Nigerian Commissioner, Dr Omoniyi Adewoye, who persistently pressed for higher recognition. In the first instance, it was a height of irresponsibility and dishonesty on the part of the experts or the Conference Rapporteur to have changed a paper presented by the Director of the Ife-Centre as a Resolution, to a mere Motion of Information because they were afraid to carry out the financial responsibilities incumbent on such recognition.

If therefore the decisions reached at the Cotonou Meeting appear unrealistic and full of contradictions, it was for the following reasons:

Firstly, the Cotonou Meeting of Experts recommended that the chief executives of intergovernmental organisations in the sub-region should co-operate among themselves within a structural framework built on the following:

(i) that the meeting of heads of intergovernmental organisations be charged with defining and directing the general policy of co-operation and economic integration in the sub-region;
(ii) that the Experts Committees of intergovernmental organisations be responsible for examining and proposing to the meetings of their chief executives measures aimed at promoting and strengthening co-operation;
(iii) that the Permanent Select Committee for Co-operation be made responsible for establishing co-operation, following it up and submitting proposals to the Experts Committee;
(iv) that the Permanent Select Committee be made up of seven members to be appointed for two years. The following organisations were selected: ECOWAS (Chairman, and co-ordinator); CEAO; WADB; OCAM; Mano River Union; WARDA; West African Clearing House.

Secondly, a Draft Declaration of General Agreement[77] on co-operation was drawn up and recommended to the Monrovia Meeting of Chief Executives scheduled for the last week of October/November 1978:[78]

(a) The heads of intergovernmental organisations cannot be charged with defining and directing matters of policy since these are the direct responsibilities of the Council of Ministers of these organisations as provided by their constitutional texts or treaties. The chief executives of these organisations are principal executive officers responsible for the execution of policies of the Council of Ministers and the Authority, and for administrative matters only. For instance the ECOWAS Treaty, Article 8, paragraphs 4 and 9; and the CEAO Treaty, Article 35 of Chapter V.
(b) a draft declaration on co-operation cannot be signed by chief executives without the express permission of the Council of Ministers. The example of the Project Agreement between the ECA and the ECOWAS signed in Lagos in September 1977, without the formal approval of the Council of Ministers, was queried because it carried financial implications for the community. Furthermore, this declaration does not contain any terms of reference.

(c) That these Chief Executives may take decisions on some programme of action involving financial expenditure is very certain. What this means therefore, in the light of the recommendations of the Cotonou Meeting, is that each executive would have to carry such decisions first to his decision-making body for approval. Here, the chief executives in their respective organisations may meet with disapproval because of the scope of financial implications, and may decide to modify them because they share divergent views with their decision-making bodies. As this, indeed, is a long and fruitless procedure, the recommendations reached at the Niamey/MULPOC Council of Ministers Meeting would have been a better solution. In other words, the highest instance should be a Council of Ministers responsible for community affairs or for international organisations in each member-state, represented in the intergovernmental organisations. This would constitute a general policy organ of competent decision-makers without making the ECOWAS Council of Ministers the policy organ if we must take the fears expressed at the MULPOC Conference by the CEAO representatives[79] into consideration.

(vi) Juridico-diplomatic and power structure problems within the ECOWAS institutions

(I) Decision-making processes

Although the ECOWAS treaty is silent on the voting procedure of the Authority and the Council of Ministers, this may be inferred from Article 6, paragraph 6 which suggests the unanimity rule because where an objection is recorded to a proposal submitted for the decision of the Council of Ministers without this objection being withdrawn, the proposal is referred to the Authority for decision. On the other hand, the Fund prescribes a simple majority for its decisions with each member-state having the right to cast only one vote at the Board of Directors Meeting (Article 27, paragraphs 1–2), which is the responsibility of its Managing Director to convene with a two-thirds majority of Board Members. In practice, the meaning given to the unanimity rule is that of consensus in both the deliberations of the Authority and the Council of Ministers. The voting method used in practice consists in considering thorny issues in camera by heads of delegations, while the non-problematic ones are considered in the plenary. This has become an acceptable method of decision-making since the first meeting of the

Council of Ministers. For instance, in their meeting of 18–19 November 1977, questions discussed in plenary were nine in number while those in camera were four.[80] Problems posed by this procedure are numerous:

Firstly, once a member-state refuses to accept a proposal either at the level of the Council or the Authority, it is considered a veto. This was why consensus and conciliation methods of resolving problems were decided by the dèliberate omission of any voting procedure in the treaty. These methods were put to test when the question of hierarchy between the Liberian Managing Director of the Fund, Dr A. R. Horton, and the Ivorian Executive Secretary of the ECOWAS Secretariat, Dr A. D. Ouattara, was to be settled at the Council of Ministers Meeting of 18–27 July 1977. Because of the ambiguities in the treaty and in its annexed protocols, and the resultant conflicts between the executive secretariat and the Fund, the Council of Ministers, after extensive discussions, established a committee comprising The Gambia (Chairman), Sierra Leone, Republics of Benin and Mali, to investigate and report back within thirty days. The Council of Ministers' decisions[81] which among others were to recognise ECOWAS as 'one corporate body subsuming all its institutions including the Fund' with the Executive Secretary as head, did not meet with the approval of the Liberian delegation whose leader expressed reservations that any references that tended to imply that the treaty or its protocol is modified in any of its provisions was not agreeable to his delegation. In spite of further declarations by the Authority at their meeting of 21–22 April 1978, confirming the decision of the Council of Ministers, these declarations were only considered as an 'authoritative interpretation of the provisions of the Treaty and the Protocols as well as an amplification of the intentions of the FOUNDING FATHERS'. The Authority made, among others, the following declarations:[82]

(i) ECOWAS is a single, indivisible entity, with some measures of autonomy to the Fund (and other constituent institutions of the Community) particularly in matters of banking and financial nature:

(ii) Administratively, ECOWAS has a hierarchical organisational structure with the Executive Secretary at its head:

(iii) The Executive Secretary, as the Principal Executive Officer of the Community, is responsible for co-ordination and overall supervision of policy matters in the Community and all its institutions, within the framework of decisions and directives of the Authority or the Council of Ministers:

. . . . .

(ix) With effect from 1 May 1978, the salaries of the statutory appointees of the community shall be as follows:
Executive Secretary – 40,000 dollars per annum gross.
Managing Director – 36,000 dollars per annum gross.
Deputy Executive Secretary and Deputy Managing Director – 30,000 dollars per annum gross
Financial Controller – 30,000 dollars per annum gross.

. . . . .

(xi) In between sessions of the Council of Ministers or the Board of Directors, all the powers of the Council or the Board shall vest in the Chairman of the Council or the Board as the case may be.

Secondly, can this authoritative interpretation offered by the Authority be regarded as a revision of the treaty? Since it was also regarded as a decision, it could be regarded as such provided the two secretariats apply them, and particularly because Article 5, paragraph 3 states that all decisions and directives of the Authority shall be binding on all institutions of the Community. But if we examine the Authority's decision critically, we cannot say that it was a revision because it was regarded *prima facie* as an 'authoritative interpretation of the provisions of the Treaty and the Protocols . . .'[83] and could therefore not have any force of law because it was a *modus vivendi* established for functional purposes only. Furthermore the treaty provides an imprecise procedure for a revision in Article 63 by which a proposal must be submitted by a member-state for eventual consideration by the Authority after member-states must have been given one month's notice. This procedure neither suggests how a decision is to be arrived at nor does it indicate a method of entry into force of a revision of an amendment. From the above reasoning we may say that the decision of the Authority was arrived at through consensus, with Liberia again expressing a dissenting opinion; otherwise, a revision of the treaty could immediately have been the logical decision of the Authority instead of the authoritative interpretation given. All these interpretations given as to the true intentions of the Founding Fathers of the Treaty would still not solve the problems of legal responsibilities of the two Great Executives because of the conflict of personalities that have crept into their relationship and the politicisation of this conflict by some member-countries. Although the provision of Article 28, paragraphs 7–8 of the Fund (that its Managing Director shall be its legal representative) has not been legally amended it must be seen as falling within the scope of the authoritative interpretation of the Authority which has not been given proper functional legal effect. However, if one day this interpretation becomes fully operative on a cumulative basis, then a proposal for revision will become successful. The main cause of the fragility and instability of the ECOWAS institution can therefore be attributed directly to the personality conflicts of the two Great Executives who have not been able to develop a Secretariat-Diplomacy within the institutions. The recruitment exercise, which was postponed twice, is another case in point to the ineffectiveness of their leadership because of state politics. All these go to show that there is an urgent need to formalise the interpretation of the Authority into a revision, and in fact the whole treaty and its protocols call for immediate and general revision in order to remove all the ambiguities that tend to hinder the proper functioning of the institutions. This view is the more necessary because the time has come for a re-assessment of all thorny issues that could prevent the proper functioning of the institutions. If we continue to tolerate different interpretations to the texts of the treaty and protocols whose chief executives are recalcitrant in the application of decisions, they are bound to put a brake to the proper functioning of these very important institutions. The ECOWAS texts must therefore be given very honest and workable provisions in order to provide continuity within an economic community of contractual interests where recognised criteria for the choice of personalities heading it is a *sine qua non* for its eventual success.

Thirdly, there is the problem of evolving an adequate voting system that would reflect to some extent the financial contributions of member-states. If the treaty is silent on a definite voting procedure it is because of sovereignty considerations which ought to be played down in an economic community where solidarity among contractual interests is supposed to grow. There are two approaches by which a solution could be found to this problem. *The first approach* would be for every member-state to make equal financial contribution to the budget so as to justify the voting equality practised. Since this proposal is bound to be difficult to implement because of the inequality in the financial strengths among member-states, some small group of states could come together to cast one vote commensurate with equal financial contribution (see Table). This would then justify equality in the voting system. *The second*

TABLE 10.2 Contributions from ECOWAS member-states as at 30 September 1978
(expressed in units of account (1.31 US dollars = 1 unit of account))

	Contributions				
Country	*Ratio*	*Capital*	*1977 budget*	*1978 budget*	*Total contribution*
Benin	3·0	1,500,001	26,150	33,011	1,559,162
Gambia	2·6	1,300,000	22,664	28,610	1,351,274
Ghana	12·9	6,449,979	112,443	141,949	6,704,371
Guinea	2·9	1,450,097	25,278	31,911	1,507,288
Guinea-Bissau	1·5	750,000	13,075	10,506	779,581
Ivory Coast	13·0	6,499,978	113,315	143,049	6,756,342
Liberia	6·7	3,350,000	58,401	73,725	3,482,126
Mali	1·9	950,000	16,561	20,907	987,468
Mauritania	3·6	1,800,000	31,380	39,614	1,870,994
Niger	2·1	1,050,000	18,304	23,108	1,091,412
Nigeria	32·8	16,399,945	285,903	360,924	17,046,772
Senegal	5·4	2,700,000	47,069	59,420	2,806,489
Sierra Leone	4·4	2,200,000	38,353	48,417	2,286,770
Togo	3·6	1,800,000	31,380	39,614	1,870,974
Upper Volta	2·6	1,300,000	22,664	28,610	1,351,274
Cape Verde	1·0	500,000	8,717	11,003	519,720
	100·0	50,000,000	871,657	1,100,378	51,972,035

Source: Report of the Financial Controller, Doc. ECW/CM/IV/3, November 1978.

approach would be for those states which cannot pay equal contributions to do so in both money and exportable product. For instance a state that decides to pay the balance of the contributions of another state should receive payment in needed raw materials. *The third approach* would be the acceptance without reservation of a two-thirds non-qualified majority, since a weighted voting would not be acceptable to contractual members. This would facilitate application of decisions.

The reasons for suggesting these approaches is the veto element in the unanimity rule which has made the Authority's decision dis-functional. This type of veto becomes less irritating if everyone pays equally to the budget. Added to this was the difficulty in interpreting the notion of equity expressed in Article 8, paragraph 7 of the treaty on the desirability to maintain 'an equitable distribution of appointments' to offices in the Executive Secretariat. This notion, construed by some states as equality in the distribution of posts, did paralyse for some time the progress of work of the Appointments Committee until it was resolved in favour of the strength of financial contributions.

Finally it is interesting to note that African economic institutions tend to apply the unanimity rule which, if can be operated successfully, might become a new contribution to African diplomatic law.

(II) Power relationship between the Secretary-General of the CEAO and the Director of its Fund (FOSIDEC) in comparison with ECOWAS

A careful study of the CEAO Treaty on the status of its Fund (FOSIDEC), shows, that the Secretary-General acting as Chairman of the Management Committee is responsible to the Board of Directors. He could participate in their meetings to which he presents the accounts of the Fund and its annual budget made by the Director of the Fund who is legally his subordinate (Article 32 of the protocol 'M' of the Fund). No provision exists in this text for eventual ratification by states according to their respective constitutional methods. This is because the ACTS of the Conference of Heads of State has immediate force of law fifteen days after it has been published in the *Official Journal* of the community. The force of unanimity rule as a voting procedure provided in all the texts of the CEAO, Articles 31 and 32 of the treaty, for the heads of state and Council of Ministers respectively and Articles 30 and 31 for its Fund, is greatly helped by the serious sense of solidarity and quality of work produced by their meeting of experts which normally precedes the meetings of ministers and heads of state. The successes registered at this level are due to the closer solidarity existing within the group and the dexterity with which the Secretary-General, Mr M. N'Gom, and his staff approach problem-solving in the application of their Secretariat diplomacy. Nevertheless, it must be understood that the CEAO ministers who are themselves members of the ECOWAS have no doubt benefited tremendously or learnt very useful lessons from the vagaries and contradictions in the ECOWAS treaty in relation to its protocols as regards the functions and powers of the Executive Secretary of the ECOWAS Secretariat and the Managing Director of the Fund, and from all the personality conflicts that have arisen under cover of these texts. These are reasons why the Secretary-General of the CEAO is the overall administrative head of both its Secretariat and Fund, since he is not only the Chairman of the Management Committee of the Fund but also responsible for proposing the names of possible candidates to the Board of Directors, from among whom the Director of the Fund is chosen and appointed (Article 33 of the Fund). In this way, crisis of authority will not arise between the Secretary-General of the CEAO and the Director of the Fund (FOSIDEC). The ECOWAS experience has been due mainly to the parallelism of authority existing in the Treaty and its protocol's Fund, the differences in the age and previously acquired practical experiences between the two Great Executives.[84] For instance in reference to the texts, where Article 8, paragraph 9 of the ECOWAS treaty says that Executive Secretary shall be responsible for the daily administration of the community and all its institutions, Article 4, paragraph 1, which enumerates the institutions of the community, excludes the Fund as an integral part of the community although reference is made to it in Articles 50–52 of Chapter XI of the treaty. Secondly, while the CEAO Fund stipulates that its Director shall be appointed by the Board of Directors made up of the Council of Ministers, through the proposal of the Secretary-General, the ECOWAS Fund stipulates in Article 28, paragraph 1 that the Managing Director of the Fund shall be appointed by the Council of Ministers which also constitutes the Board of Directors. This follows that while the appointment of the Fund's Managing Director is strictly political, that of the CEAO is first administrative before being sanctioned politically because it has a four-year term subject to renewal (Article 33 of the protocol 'M' of the Fund). This therefore makes the CEAO Fund a subordinate institution of its community.[85]

(III) Diplomatic privileges and immunities: implications for host governments

The privileges and immunities granted to officials of the ECOWAS at its headquarters and in member states are spelt out in Articles 60, paragraph 4 of the treaty and 42 of the protocol relating to the Fund. These immunities and privileges are the same as those accorded to diplomatic missions at the headquarters of the community and in member states. They are again buttressed by paragraph 2 of Article 60, which states that the community shall have in each member state the legal capacity required for the performance of its functions. That is to say, the community can contract, acquire, hold or dispose of immovable property and institute legal proceedings.

These provisions imply that the ECOWAS has been granted quite generously and exceptionally two types of diplomatic privileges, the one emanating from the Vienna Convention on Diplomatic Relations adopted on 16 April 1961 by the UN Conference on Diplomatic Intercourse and Immunities,[86] and the other, on institutions emanating from the Convention on Privileges and Immunities of the UN adopted by its General Assembly on 13 February 1946.[87] These two types of 'mixed-grill' privileges and immunities are not without problems and implications for host governments, particularly with respect to the financial institution – the Fund for co-operation and compensation which has to borrow from international capital markets.

First, in traditional international public law, a big difference exists between privileges and immunities granted to diplomatic missions which in essence represent sending states in the receiving states (Article 3 of the 1961 Vienna Convention) and international institutions whose functions are those of international functionaries granted immunities not for their personal benefit but for the purpose of safeguarding the independent exercise of their functions.[88] Consequently, those granted to diplomatic missions arise from international customary practice, while those granted to international institutions arise from international legislative acts. This is to say that while immunities from international institutions are granted for the proper exercise of their functions, those of diplomatic missions enjoy plenipotentiary privileges.

Secondly, Article 60, paragraph 4 of the ECOWAS treaty does not make any reference to the nature of the institution as an international organisation except in paragraph 1, which refers to it in terms of its legal personality. It rather grants it and its officials diplomatic status normally reserved to foreign missions of states. We could then conclude that it is rather a reflection of the Vienna Convention (1961) on Diplomatic Relations than that of the UN Convention on International Institutions (1946) which has less privileges than that of diplomatic missions.

In the Rome Treaty, Article 218 stipulates that the community shall 'enjoy in the territories of the member states the privileges and immunities necessary for the achievement of its aims' and specifically adds that a separate protocol shall define these privileges. If we have to go by the above analysis of Article 60, paragraph 4 without taking into consideration the international character of the ECOWAS as an international organisation, the headquarters governments, and in respect of the General Convention, member states, shall have great difficulty in solving thorny diplomatic problems likely to be posed to them on the level of persons attending meetings as experts, or to the personnel of the secretariat carrying out official assignments in member states. This was why the General Convention on Privileges and Immunities of the community, signed at Lagos on 22 April 1978 by the sixteen heads of state of the community,[89] recognised the diplomatic status of representatives of member-states in its dual form as diplomatic persons and as delegates to meetings of an international institution in Article 6, paragraphs 1a–b and 4. While Article 6, paragraph 1 of the convention grants privileges and immunities to representatives of member states attending meetings or travelling to and from place of meeting, paragraph (a) grants 'immunity from personal arrest or detention . . .' and (b) 'from legal process of every kind in respect of word spoken, written or acts done by them . . .'. In respect of officials of the community, Article 7, paragraph 1 makes it mandatory for the Executive Secretary to specify the categories of officials whose names shall be communicated to the governments of member states. It goes further in paragraph 2 to state that community officials shall have the same privileges and immunities as diplomatic persons at the headquarters of the community. If we consider the last lines of paragraph 4 of Article 60: 'other privileges and immunities to be recognised and granted by member states in connection with the community shall be determined by the Council of Ministers', we begin to wonder what these other privileges are? Are they those of international organisations for which the CEAO treaty does not even provide because it leaves the onus of granting immunities to the conference of heads of state (Article 43 of Chapter 1: Legal Personality – Immunities)? Certainly they are, since the ECOWAS is an international organisation.

Thirdly, Article 60, paragraph 4 did not take cognisance of the protocol relating to the Fund for co-operation, compensation and development of the ECOWAS, since it is omitted in the treaty among the institutions of the community although reference is made to it in the protocol that the 'Fund is an international financial institution' (Article 37, paragraph 1). While this protocol relating to the Fund makes its Managing Director a legal representative (Article 28, paragraph 7) and recognises it as an international financial institution, Article 42 still considers the Fund as falling under the requirements of Article 60, paragraph 4 of the treaty by stating 'that the immunities and privileges will be those provided under Article 60, paragraph 4 of the Treaty'. This means that, legally speaking, while the Lagos Secretariat has only diplomatic status similar to those of diplomatic missions (although reference made to it as an international organisation was simply with respect to legal personality, that is ability to contract, acquire or dispose of property and institute legal proceedings), the Lomé Fund is recognised both as an international institution of a financial character and a diplomatic mission. Hence it is provided in Article 39, paragraph 2 of the Fund that 'action may be brought against the Fund in the territories of member-states only in a court of competent jurisdiction in a member state in which the Fund has an office, has appointed an agent for the purpose of accepting service or notice of process or has issued or guaranteed securities'. This provision is perfectly in order if only to grant it credibility in the international capital market from which it has to seek loans, and if it had to be able to carry out its banking operations accordingly. On a further examination, this provision denies it of its diplomatic status commensurate with that of diplomatic missions, since action can be brought against it in a court, for Article 22 of the Vienna Convention (1961) states that 'the premises of the mission shall be inviolable. The agents of the receiving state may not enter them, except with the consent of the head of the mission.'

This also means that the premises of the Fund shall not be immune from requisition, attachment or execution. Thus while the Lagos Secretariat is considered a diplomatic mission whose agents 'shall enjoy immunity from criminal jurisdiction of the receiving state' (Article 31, paragraph 1 of the Vienna Convention), the Lomé situation is still confused because of its financial character compounded with the fact that while its agent cannot be sued because it is considered a Diplomatic Mission in practice, the Institution is vulnerable. This latter factor therefore distinguishes the legal immunities of the Fund from those of the Lagos secretariat which is free from any legal process since in conformity with its full diplomatic status except a waiver is granted by its Executive Secretary[90] who is considered the same as the head of a diplomatic mission as well as the Managing Director of the Fund (Article 7 of the ECOWAS General Convention).

A problem here arises as to whether Nigerians and Togolese professional international civil servants resident in Lagos and Lomé are entitled to the immunities of persons in diplomatic missions? If we go by Article 7, paragraph 4 of the General Convention and staff rules and regulations (which includes these nationals provided they are in the professional class), we may conclude that they are entitled to all the immunities, much more so that Article 7, paragraph 3(f) exempts all community officials, which includes nationals of the professional class in the headquarters, from taxation on their salaries and emoluments paid to them by the community. This follows *ipso facto* that the Headquarters Agreement must reflect the provisions of the General Convention. Furthermore if the Executive Secretary or the Managing Director of the Fund is a Nigerian or a Togolese, he must be covered by full diplomatic status as provided in Article 60, paragraph 4 of the treaty. Here lies the problem as to whether nationals of the host government can be immune from the laws of their land. The answer appears positive, but when one considers also that the Executive Secretary has the right of a waiver, while sending states also have this right according to the Vienna Convention (Article 32, paragraph 1) of 1961, it would be in the proper interest of the host national not to abuse these privileges. The dual nature of the diplomatic immunities accorded by Article 60, paragraph 4 of the Treaty and the provisions of the ECOWAS General Convention lend themselves to the above positions. Nevertheless in diplomatic practice a Headquarters Agreement is a bilateral issue which is negotiable with the host government and normally does not accord full privileges to its nationals except in the performance of its duties, but ECOWAS has modified this practice.

The ECOWAS General Convention, made up of eleven Articles adopted and signed on 22 April 1978, gave its blessings to the issuing of a *laissez-passer* to the staff of the community[91] (Article 9) and provides for Preamble, Definitions (Article 1); Juridical Personality (Article 2); Property, Funds and Assets (Article 3); Tax Exemptions (Article 4); Facilities in Respect of Communications (Article 5); Representatives of Member-States (Article 6); Officials of the Community (Article 7); Experts on Mission for the Community (Article 8); Community *Laissez-passer* (Article 9); Settlement of Disputes (Article 10); Entry into Force and Accession (Article 11).

(C) Has the ECOWAS any prospects?

From the above analysis it is crystal clear that this young institution is beset with problems which are nevertheless surmountable if the community leaders are willing to tackle them objectively. This is to say that when the advantages of maintaining the institution are thoroughly weighed against the disadvantages, the community is bound to emerge an important sub-region to reckon with internationally.

The first problem we have seen so far is that of leadership at the level of community institutions whose resolution is a very critical factor for its eventual success; this is also dependent on the extent to which the component units within the community are ready to concede national sovereignty after a thorough revision of the treaty. In the absence of this revision, a considerable amount of political will, not merely issue from declarations but from concrete actions, shall be a condition *sine qua non* for the continued existence of the community. So far, mere declarations of political will have characterised the community diplomacy. For instance:

1. For the 1977 budgetary contributions the position as at 30 September 1978 showed that seven countries have yet to pay fully.[92] This was why the Report of the Financial Controller stressed the need at a very high level to bring subtle pressure to bear on member states for the payment of amounts outstanding in favour of the two institutions. It went further to state that because of this delay one of the institutions, in reference to the Fund, had to resort to overdraft facilities in order to prosecute its budgetary commitments.[93]
2. The special *ad hoc* committee which was set up by the Council of Ministers to handle recruitment exercise for the two institutions could not for more than a year carry out this assignment because of state politics and the reservations made by Liberia. We cannot underestimate the adverse effect this delay has caused to the smooth running of the institutions and in the employment of high-quality manpower for such an important institution. The absolute desire of certain states to be represented on the level of Directorship of Divisions at all costs, even when their candidates are not sufficiently experienced, appears unhealthy for the effectiveness of the Secretariats. It becomes more disturbing when it is realised that some of these states have not even completely paid up their budgetary and capital contributions for the first operative year 1977 as at 30 September 1978.

Secondly, in spite of the above problems the community leaders are however cognisant of the fact that the ECOWAS region is a potentially large market to which they could look forward for the promotion of their trade in goods and services and the free movement of persons and capital. The reasons are obvious. The sub-region is highly endowed with all sorts of mineral wealth and food beverages such as tin, lead, zinc, bauxite, gold, diamonds, fruits, coffee, cocoa, etc. These had hitherto been exploited as raw materials and exported principally to the USA and Western Europe. ECOWAS therefore intends to find ways of collectively exploiting these potentials. Apart from Nigeria, which is the sixth-largest producer of crude oil in the world (2.1 million barrels per day), many petroleum refineries in the sub-region rely heavily on imported crude oil, which bites deeply into their budgetary provisions. This was why bilateral arrangements between Nigeria and Ivory Coast had gone a long way to reducing her reliance on outside sources. For instance Ivory Coast's importation of crude oil from Nigeria was valued at 11,898 million francs CFA in 1975, and although there was a decline in 1976 (7,979 million CFA), a considerable increase was recorded after the 1977 Agreement.[94] It is therefore the policy of ECOWAS to harness all energy resources, including coal, groundnut, kernel shells and hydroelectric power from their rivers. Already the dams on the major rivers within the community cater for more than just the countries in which they are located. For instance, while the Volta Dam Project in Ghana extends its hydroelectric power to Togo, the Kainji Dam in Nigeria provides electricity to Niger.

Thirdly, in spite of ideological and linguistic differences within the community there must be a meeting point for the establishment of common policies and strategies within new institutions required to transform domestic markets and train manpower needs. This was why the political reconciliation between the Republic of Guinea on the one hand, and the Republics of Ivory Coast and Senegal on the other in March 1978, will go a long way to harmonise policies and strategies and promote trade relations up to now inexistent, if we go by the IMF (*Direction of Trade, 1968–72*). See Matrix of West African Trade 1972 (Table 10.3), expressed in millions of US dollars. Since Nigeria, Ivory Coast and Senegal are potentially the richest, they would automatically have the role of giving primacy to the least-developed countries in respect of project implementation or development programmes for the first few years of the operation of the treaty. This would tend to eliminate the fears of domination for which Senegal had insisted in the admission of Zaire as a *contre-poids* to Nigeria. Nigeria, like the USA to the Latin American sub-region, has a greater share of such responsibility vis-à-vis the community, with some proviso however that the decision-making processes are modified to sustain the community.

Fourthly, the report of a trade mission from Ivory Coast led by Mr Amuah David, a Director at the CICE (Ivory Coast Centre for Foreign Trade) to Lagos in 1977, revealed that in spite of Nigeria's April 1977 Decrees banning and increasing customs duties of certain commodity items, Nigeria remained a potential market for their goods. Although they lost an order for the supply of Ivorian commodities worth about 3·6 milliard CFA francs which was to cover a period of three months,

TABLE 10.3 1972 Matrix of West African trade 1972 (in million of US dollars)

	Benin	*Gambia*	*Ghana*	*Guinea-Bissau*	*Guinea Republic*	*Ivory Coast*	*Liberia*	*Mali*	*Mauri-tania*	*Niger*	*Nigeria*	*Senegal*	*Sierra Leone*	*Togo*	*Upper Volta*	*Total West Africa*
Benin			0·169	–	–	–	0·003	–	–	0·370	0·309	1·596	–	0·707	–	3·15
Gambia			0·039	–	–	–	–	–	–	–	0·019	0·097	0·079	–	–	0·23
Ghana	0·018	0·047	–	–	–	0·300	0·058	0·058	–	–	4·674	–	0·66	3·622	0·176	9·00
Guinea-Bissau	–	–	–	–	–	–	–	–	–	–	–	–	–	–	–	–
Guinea Republic	–	–	–	–	–	–	0·182	–	–	–	0·073	–	0·038	–	–	0·29
Ivory Coast	–	–	–	–	–	–	–	7·650	–	–	0·180	10·011	0·093	–	7·130	28·62
Liberia	0·001	–	–	–	–	–	–	0·632	1·744	–	–	–	1·148	–	–	4·51
Mali	–	–	2·762	–	–	–	0·077	–	–	0·024	–	1·872	–	–	2·405	7·14
Mauritania	–	–	–	–	–	–	–	–	–	–	–	0·060	–	–	–	0·06
Niger	2·542	–	1·332	–	–	0·302	–	0·069	–	–	–	–	–	0·260	–	4·51
Nigeria	0·51	0·033	30·85	–	–	14·21	–	0·06	0·04	2·18	–	4·36	6·87	0·43	0·03	60·15
Senegal	4·530	0·978	0·422	–	2·078	16·978	1·010	10·864	15·516	0·666	1·866	1·866	0·719	0·719	0·354	0·530
Sierra Leone	–	0·558	0·047	–	0·177	0·095	0·492	0·040	–	–	0·083	0·058	–	–	–	1·55
Togo	0·411	–	0·387	–	–	0·258	0·007	–	–	0·212	0·314	–	–	–	–	1·59
Upper Volta	0·053	–	1·417	–	–	6·050	–	0·683	–	0·205	–	0·023	–	–	–	8·43
Total West Africa	8·07	1·61	37·43	–	3·77	38·19	1·83	20·06	17·35	6·58	7·52	18·68	9·01	5·37	10·27	
Total EEC	58·00	11·00	116·00	6·00	53·00	331·00	376·00	41·00	49·00	41·00	886·00	204·00	57·00	55·00	9·00	
World	89·00	25·00	373·00	30·00	77·00	466·00	766·00	69·00	82·00	66·00	1584·00	339·00	120·00	63·00	13·00	
% West Africa/World	9	6	10	–	5	8	0	29	21	10	0	6	8	9	79	
% EEC/World	65	44	31	20	69	71	49	59	60	62	58	60	48	87	69	

and 10 milliard CFA francs for a period of 12 months, they discovered that Nigeria's production would still not cover her domestic demands. For instance, to take two examples alone: (a) in *textiles* their trade mission report mentioned that Nigeria needed about 230,000,000 yards while her industrial output or capacity was 180,000,000 yards, that is a deficit of 50,000,000 yards which was just about the equivalent of the industrial output of Ivory Coast; (b) for *footwear*, for which Nigeria's production capacity was 27·7 million pairs[95] for a market of about 80 million people, here was another area where they could have provided the needs of Nigerians. The areas of Ivorian commodities hit by the Nigerian Decrees of 1 April 1977 among others were: textiles, fruits and fresh vegetables, fruit juices, plastics materials, canned fruits and vegetables represent the prohibited goods; while confectioneries, furniture, footwear, soluble coffee, dried fruits and conserved fruits had their customs duties increased.[96] This case-study proves beyond doubt the importance of the ECOWAS to its members in spite of the political problems plaguing them. Hitherto Ivory Coast direction of trade in Africa was principally to the countries of the CEAO Treaty to which she also belongs. The value of her exports/imports with the CEAO represent the following: exports/imports to and from the five CEAO countries:

Exports: 1974 20,145 million CFA francs
1975–26,572 million CFA francs
1976–26,541 million CFA francs
1977–35,041 million CFA francs

Imports: 1974–4983 million CFA francs
1975–5106 million CFA francs
1976–6202 million CFA francs
1977–6601 million CFA francs

Nigeria's list of prohibited items and the new customs tariffs of 1 April 1978, call for some comments in the light of the ECOWAS treaty provisions. Article 13, paragraph 2 of this treaty specifically states that:

> Within a period of two (2) years from the definitive entry into force of this treaty, a member state may not be required to reduce or eliminate import duties. During this two-year period, member states shall not impose any new duties and taxes or increase existing ones and shall transmit to the Executive Secretariat all information on import duties for study by the relevant institutions of the commodity.

From this provision, Nigeria has *prima facie* flouted the provisions of the treaty without recognising that the treaty had already come into force. A rectification of the decrees cannot be effected by bilateral negotiations since Article 13, paragraph 2 had established a procedure. Therefore a matter of this dimension affecting the trade flow of contractual member states must be made known immediately by the affected states to the Executive Secretariat of the ECOWAS who would take it up with the defaulting government. There is no doubt that this was an oversight by the Nigerian Federal Ministry of Trade and an indication of a communication gap between it and the Federal Ministry of Economic Development responsible for ECOWAS matters.[97] This is why the Trade Ministry should be kept in charge of the ECOWAS, since there is need for its thorough understanding of the intricacies involved within the community trade which is its full responsibility. Probably it might be better to create an entirely new Ministry for Foreign Trade and International Development Relations in order to establish better involvement and understanding of the intentions of the treaty. It is unfortunate that in none of these ECOWAS meetings have the Ministry of Trade officials been represented.

Finally the eventual success of this community would depend upon several factors: development of a secretariat diplomacy, resolution of the personality conflicts, recruitment of competent and well-qualified staff, enormous political will matched with proper action and a revision or amendment of the treaty. The CEAO treaty, to which six francophone member states of the ECOWAS belong and which has so far registered quantifiable successes, can only disappear if ECOWAS proves its mettle.

11 Commodity Agreements under a Quasi-United Nations System

SECTION I. THE COCOA DIPLOMACY

Attempts at negotiating an international cocoa agreement with the consumers started as early as 1957 and for about fifteen years no success was registered. The difficulties lay not only in the erratic nature of the cocoa market, in that it is very speculative, but also in the fact that the negotiating parties have always found it difficult to strike at an acceptable price range and the functioning principles of the buffer stock. The fall in prices in 1970/71 cocoa year could be attributed to the fact that there were expectations in many market circles that the 1970/71 cocoa production would be higher than the estimated consumption for 1971. Hypothetically, cocoa production was expected to be 1,720,000 metric tons if world estimated stocks, at approximately 256,000 tons, were added to 1,464,000 tons when the estimates of consumption were put at 1,418,000 tons. From 1965 to 1970 market prices were relatively

TABLE 11.1 World production of cocoa beans by regions, 1000 metric tons 1968–71

Region	*1968–69*	*1969–70*	*1970–71*
North and Central America	76.2	87.0	68.2
South America	255.6	285.2	276.7
Asia	9.8	9.8	10.1
Africa	840.9	1008.3	1076.4
WORLD TOTAL	1214.0[a]	1416.0	1464.0

[a] Excludes shipment from Dahomey.

Source: Report of the Meeting of the Sales Executives of the member governments of the Alliance held in Accra, Ghana, 19–21 April 1971.

high because consumer demands were higher than production. But between 1970 and 1971 there was a sudden fall in prices within six months from £360 sterling per ton in September 1970, to £230 per ton in March 1971 (see Table 11.1), this being the sharpest drop in recent years. Another notable period of price degradation was during the 1964–65 season when world production was at 1·5 million tons. This fluctuation tendency in the world cocoa market, and the importance of this product to some national economies, have kept the minds of the producing countries alert as to possible solutions to the problem of its stabilisation. Unfortunately some very important consumers do not seem to have enough political will to wish to conclude an agreement; moreover some producer countries even

> allowed themselves to become victims of the diverse manoeuvres of traders and of international brokers, victims also of insidious rumours destined, on the one hand to sow seeds of distrust and of discord among member-countries' sales directors, and on the other hand, to destroy their solidarity and to neutralise their efforts to harmonise their sales policies in the common interest of our states.[1]

Besides, cocoa is a very difficult product to stock in the form of beans because of humidity and hot climate, although it can now be stocked in the form of cocoa-butter in producing countries. In the final analysis, these problems go to show that producers' salvation lies in their own hands, because any international organisation which they form cannot succeed in bargaining with the world of consumers without a united force capable of obliging purchasers to pay a fair price for their commodities.

Nevertheless, in order to understand the conflicts and co-operation between these two divergent interest groups, it would be necessary to examine them in the light of institutions to which they belong and/or in which these attitudes arise. Thus we shall examine, in the first instance, the politics of co-operation within the Cocoa Producers Alliance, and secondly conflicts with the consumers in Cocoa Conferences under the auspices of UNCTAD.

(1) THE POLITICS OF CO-OPERATION WITHIN THE COCOA PRODUCERS ALLIANCE

The Cocoa Producers Alliance was born in Abidjan after its Charter was negotiated, adopted and initialled on 19 and 20 January 1962. This 'Abidjan Charter' has become the legal document which regulates the activities of the Alliance. Its objective is 'to ensure adequate supplies to the market at remunerative prices'. The question therefore arises as to whether the Alliance has pursued this objective with enough dynamism. The answer could be negative because its members have not sufficiently played their roles of supporting the Alliance, as would be seen from Ghana's attitude towards a collective decision taken in Accra in February 1971 during an Emergency Meeting. The decision taken was that no forward sales would be made of the 1971–72 crops before the April 1971 Meeting of the Alliance, and before a decision on a sales quota system had been taken. But before this, Ghana's sales representative in New York had negated the decision by making an open offer of cocoa of the main crop. Although the Ghanaian government later apologised to the Alliance, she was of the opinion 'that the whole incident was inadvertent and arose from a misunderstanding on the part of the Agents who were then newly appointed'.[2] The government then promised to be dedicated to co-operating with the other member-governments in supporting decisions taken by the Alliance.[3] This raised a constitutional issue as to the legal status of the sales executive as a decision-making body, although it was observed that 'an international organisation derived its force not only from its legal aspect but also from the moral support given by its members'. The 16th General Meeting of the Alliance, held in Abidjan from 21 to 28 May 1971, provided a testing ground for members as to their capability to co-ordinate their policies. This was at the 4th Session of the Committee when delegates had to re-examine a number of basic issues in preparation for the informal discussions between producers and the Secretary-General of UNCTAD, fixed for 31 May–1 June 1971. Decisions had to be taken on several operational matters leading to the formulation of a common strategy. Some of the items on which decisions had to be taken were the following:

(a) International Cocoa Agreement.
(b) Proposal for the establishment of an International Producer Cocoa Agreement and a Fund.
(c) Mission to Eastern Europe, membership drive and Cocoa Annual Dinners as instruments of co-operation.

(A) International Cocoa Agreement

The decisions taken here covered a wide variety of areas, viz. quota mechanism; price; buffer stock mechanism; processed cocoa; and removal of obstacles to trade.

(a) Quota mechanism and prices

On quota mechanism, the Executive Committee decided to withdraw its previous position for a sales quota system in preference for an 'export quota system in regulating the market under an international cocoa agreement'. On the price issue which had plagued several negotiations, the delegates held the view that a price range should no more figure in the Cocoa Agreement since the Cocoa Council would be empowered to fix the price range to be defended, from year to year. However, there should be guidelines on the general level below which prices must not fall, which level must not be below an average of prices for the past five years. There must be provisions for correcting the effects of devaluation and changes in the real values of currencies. Perhaps it would be informative to examine this new strategy against the causes of conflict at the 1968 Cocoa Consultations in Geneva in order to understand this new policy of the Alliance. Article 33, paragraph 7 of the Draft Agreement[4] in the Memorandum of Agreement negotiated in October 1967, provided for a further quota cut if the indicator price was below 20 cents per pound. It also provided that the total cuts, which should not be more than 9 per cent of the stipulated annual quotas, should be made by simple majority after the Director General had advanced reasons for the failure of the previous cuts. If, one month after such a maxi-cut had been operated, the price still remained below 20 cents, a further report and recommendation will be submitted by the Executive Director. Decisions as to a further cut by the Council shall then be made by a special vote. This action could be repeated as long as the price remained below 20 cents.

The cause of conflict here between the producers and the consumers arose from an additional clause to Article 33, paragraph 7A which was not in the original draft. It was surprisingly included for proposal at the instigation of the United States delegation. It provided for an automatic restoration of annual sales quota within two working days if the price is at 20 cents per pound – the minimum price to be defended. When this additional clause was first discussed in a plenary session[5] all the producers, and a good following of the consumers, did ask the USA to accept 21 cents as the point of restoration of quota cuts made at 20 cents and below, since this was the level to be defended in the agreement. The next day, 21 June 1968, it was interesting to note a sudden change of attitude among certain producers when the USA delegation confirmed that her delegation had refused 21 cents, when only on the previous day she had expressed pessimism as to whether her government would reply to her telex message even in the next week. But the dice had changed (in spite of the common strategy that had been made by producers to withhold the previous position), when Ghana accepted 20 cents because she wanted an agreement at all cost. The USA then held fast to this new Ghanaian position and, in spite of disapproval from France and the Ivory Coast, she refused to be shaken. 'After all', her delegation maintained, 'there is no reason why France and the Ivory Coast should insist bitterly on what a majority of producers had accepted.' It was with frustration that the Cameroun delegate said, *inter alia*,'. . . we have lost the war and there is no need to continue a discussion on this point'. These discussions revealed a number of weak points on the producer side.

1. A lack of precise method of approach and calculations of probability in commodity negotiations.
2. Producers tended to play a defensive game all the time when the international conjunctural position was favourable to producer interest. An opponent usually takes advantage of such an opportunity.
3. There was a tendency for producers to put forward too much of sentimental political considerations in a negotiation of a highly technical nature which require the expression of national interest with a certain amount of political will. Producers have therefore not been able to define their collective interests correctly. In fact, some individual negotiators seem to put their own selfish interests before those of their nations.

This brief case-study shows the basis of the collapse of the previous Draft Agreement under consideration.

(b) Buffer stock mechanism, processed cocoa and removal of obstacles to trade

The Executive Committee accepted that there should be a built-in buffer stock mechanism in a Cocoa Agreement which should be internationally controlled. The finances of the buffer stock should be obtained from the IMF but it must operate by buying from the producers' surplus cocoa at the end of each season instead of the traditional method of direct intervention on the market. On the industrialisation of cocoa, it was agreed in principle to incorporate a clause on processed cocoa on condition that, to the developing countries is recognised the right of processing and exporting the resultant products, and that only cocoa products for exports should be charged against export quotas on the basis of their bean equivalent using FAO conversion figures: cocoa butter 2·15; cocoa powder 0·30 and cocoa paste 1·23.

It was finally accepted that for the purpose of removing obstacles to trade, measures must be taken to eliminate barriers in the internal legislations of consuming countries, and that a common stand must be taken to pressurise the latter into accepting such a policy.

(B) Proposal for the Establishment of an International Cocoa Agreement and Fund Among Producers

The integration of the Fund into the Producer Agreement proposed by the Ivory Coast was accepted in principle during the 17th Meeting of the Alliance in Lagos[6] because it could be 'a most important instrument for exercising control over the market'. This proposed draft agreement was considered by the said Lagos Meeting as consistent 'with the spirit and key objective of the Alliance'. Its purpose was to 'fill the vacuum pending the possible conclusion of an International Cocoa Agreement between producers and consumers'. But as they did not want to give the impression to consumers, with whom a co-operation was also necessary, that the Alliance might be abandoning efforts to conclude an agreement, it was agreed that the preamble should read 'concerned about the failures so far to conclude an International Cocoa Agreement between producers and consumers for the stabilization of cocoa prices'.[7]

At the 17th Lagos Meeting the old strategy formulated at the 16th Meeting of the Alliance in Abidjan had to be modified when the revised economic Articles of the proposed draft International Cocoa Agreement prepared by the UNCTAD Secretariat was submitted for consideration. The draft was considered in the light of the fact that it would give them the opportunity of testing once more the political will of the consumers at the multilateral consultations on cocoa convened by the Secretary-General of UNCTAD for 22 September to 6 October

1971, in Geneva. A number of new decisions were arrived at during this 17th Lagos Meeting, modifying the strategies of the 16th General Meeting in Abidjan. Three major economic Articles of the draft agreement were examined, viz. Articles 27(bis) on the price range; 36 on the compliance with the export quotas, and 39 on purchase by the buffer stock.

On Article 27(bis), the Executive Committee decided that its previous decision in Abidjan (that there should be no definite price range), should be abandoned and renewed support given to the principle of a definite price range of 25 US cents to 34 US cents. Although it was believed that this new policy strategy might create an element of rigidity, the complementary provision of Article 41 of the draft dealing with 'changes in the par values of currencies' should adequately compensate the interests of the producers.

On Article 36, the delegates noted that provision was made for the distribution of annual export quotas and so decided that 'the maximum proportion of its annual export quota which an exporting member may export during the first two quarters should be raised from 80 to 85 per cent'. It was thus decided that member-governments of the Alliance should negotiate this revision under Article 36, paragraph 2.

On Article 39, paragraph 4, the delegates observed that the buffer stock would buy only cocoa beans from exporters and that cocoa products were excluded for four reasons:

1. cocoa butter may not be easily marketable;
2. its long storage might adversely affect the quality;
3. the relationship between the price of beans and butter does not follow a consistent pattern;
4. buffer stock price for cocoa butter poses a problem.

(C) Mission to Eastern Europe, membership drive and cocoa Annual Dinners as instruments of co-operation

While the proposal to send a mission of information to Eastern Europe was ultimately rejected at the 17th Lagos Meeting of the Alliance, because of the psychological effect it would have on the traditional cocoa market in respect of future cocoa negotiations and prevailing prices, and the fact that Eastern European governments operate a bilateral trade policy based on barter, the Conference did not hesitate to consider the possibility of attracting countries with annual cocoa production of about 10,000 tons in order to effect a more global co-operation. It was then decided to open up avenues to the Dominican Republic, Mexico, Ecuador, Venezuela and Equatorial Guinea who could in future attend meetings on observer status. While Nigeria undertook to bring Brazil into the Alliance, the Secretariat was commissioned to invite Equatorial Guinea. Although a proposal made, to use Annual Cocoa Dinners as a technique for achieving some co-operation among member-countries, met with the support of delegates, a decision on this was carried forward to the 18th General Meeting, after reactions to this proposal must have been gathered from member-governments.

(II) CONFLICTS WITHIN UNCTAD CONFERENCES ON COCOA BETWEEN THE PRODUCERS AND CONSUMERS

Under the auspices of UNCTAD, producers and consumers have met several times to find adequate answers to the problems posed by the need for an International Cocoa Agreement. Every attempt had met with failure until recently. Reasons for these failures, and the various conflicting positions of the negotiators, form the object of our study here. The conflict which arose from the restoration of quotas as proposed by the USA at the 1968 consultations in Geneva has been seen.[8] We have also already referred to the 'petit-negre' episode on p. 178 of this book. It is therefore sufficient to say that the conflicting positions of the negotiators, in all the conferences so far, have arisen from price-level problems and the role of the buffer stock. In attempting to find conciliatory positions, a committee of both producers and consumers has always been split into sub-group committees of both consumers and producers with whom a joint chairman negotiates separately. This technique was adopted in the June 1968 cocoa consultations in Geneva by Mr Osman Ali, the Pakistani Ambassador in Brussels, and Mr Gamani Corea of Ceylon, the Chairman of the 1972 Cocoa Conference, because a joint committee of conflicting interests never arrives at a conclusion easily. We have already seen the conflicting positions of the interest groups and how they led to a breakdown.[9] The 1972 Conference seems to present a slightly different picture although the USA had not changed radically, for she still asked for a minimum of 20 cents while some producers asked for 25 cents because of the relative changes in price structure since the 1968 draft was rejected. To achieve a minimum co-operation, Ghana and Great Britain did ask for a minimum price range between 21 and 25 cents per pound of beans. The only point of agreement at that time was that both the producers and the consumers had accepted a 9 cents difference between the maximum and minimum prices. In the 1968 consultations, the buffer stock was not allowed by the USA to buy at 20 cents. Rather she proposed restoration of quotas at this point. The 1972 UNCTAD negotiations, which accepted 20 cents as a purchasing level by the buffer stock, was an improvement on previous positions. Allowing for insurance and freight, this price level equivalent becomes 25 cents per pound. Perhaps the arrival at certain basic agreements in the 13-nation 1972 negotiations can be attributed to the secretarial competence of UNCTAD who, in fact, was responsible for the draft.

SECTION II. THE TIN DIPLOMACY

Conflict and co-operation in the tin diplomacy are determined by three main factors: national interest, international co-operation and appurtenance to the Tin Council. These three factors are within the grips of national policies. The national policies both of producer and consumer countries are not only expressions of their respective national interests, but also of political pressures from private commercial companies, as in the case of the USA whose national interests had been responsible for her non-membership of the Tin Council. Nonetheless, the principal producers and consumers of tin (except the USA and the People's Republic of China) who are signatory to the Tin Agreement have their interests mainly dictated by their common appurtenance to the Tin Council. For example, the export control policy imposed on signatory members during the period of over-production (1957–60) and the sales policy of surplus non-commercial stock materials in London and France did follow a set quota system dictated by the desire for co-operation within an identifiable community of interests. Also the Malaysian example shows another case of co-operation arising from the fact of her appurtenance to the Tin Council. In 1965 when Malaysia expressed the desire that she would not sign the 3rd Tin Agreement because it contained certain restrictive measures that militated against her (the producer of two-thirds of world tin supply), a Tin Council delegation led by Mr H. W. Allen, Chairman of the Council, left for Malaysia on 25 December, 1965, before the expiry date of the deferred signature (31 December 1965). It was during this meeting that he was able to convince the Prime Minister of Malaysia, Mr Tunku Abdul Rahman, to sign the Agreement 'in the interest of International co-operation and good will'[10] when on the previous, day, 24 December, his Finance Minister had declared:

> we said it was not in Malaysia's best interests to join the Agreement. We made it clear we could not accept, even for compromise or if modifications were made. The Cabinet had reached a firm decision after very careful consideration of all aspects of the case. We will stick to that decision.[11]

The refusal of Malaysia to sign the agreement could have been detrimental to the organisation of the Tin Market, since she is the greatest world producer.[12]

In the final analysis therefore, the amount of co-operation a country offers depends on his belonging to the Council rather than the simple expression of his foreign-policy ideals. With the USA, who is not a member of the Tin Council, conflicts have often arisen from her stock disposal policy; if co-operation is sometimes achieved this is because she does not perpetually wish to be accused by the poor nations of the world of sabotaging their economy. Nevertheless her non-appurtenance to the Tin Council is a source of great anxiety to the poor nations since she is the greatest consumer. The USA practises a policy which we might call 'policy of Private Interest Groups and of co-operation', because the conflicts which arise between her and the producers of tin stem from the pressures exercised on her government by private commercial companies and on the other hand from her expressed intention to accumulate strategic raw materials that she does not produce. Percy Bidwell, in his study of American policy on raw materials, affirms that the USA as an importer nation would lose more than profit from the membership of any arrangements meant to stabilise prices because of the possibility of high prices.[13] This factor, coupled with the desire to stockpile tin for strategic reasons, led to the enactment of the Stockpiling Act of 1946. This was motivated principally by the development of nuclear weapons and the emergence of Russia as a world power. These factors drastically changed American conceptions on defence policies, thus the constitution of stocks became a policy as well as an objective. However her policy of limited co-operation with the Tin Council has been a temporary solution to the problems which her non-appurtenance to the Tin Agreement has caused the world of producers. The principles on which her policy is axed, are often formulated by the

General Services Administration. They consist in reducing or suspending liquidations of strategic stocks into the world market when there is a fall in world prices of tin. Unfortunately these principles have not often been respected because of the strong pressure exercised by American commercial interest groups on the government. For instance towards the end of March 1966, the USA practised a policy described as 'aggressive' because she sold tin at prices lower than those of the world market. The American balance of payments was suffering a decline, and popular commercial opinion favoured any measures that would prevent her dollars being transferred outside the USA. The American commercial interests therefore found it more convenient to buy tin in New York as their industries were generally situated in the north. But as from 1966 the USA did not only sell tin from their southern warehouses of Louisiana, Georgia, Mississippi and Alabama at prices inferior to those of the world market, but also undertook to reimburse the cost of transportation from these warehouses to New York if it turned out to be more than that paid from New York to the overseas buyer. Thus American buyers found it cheaper to patronise the General Services Administration (GSA).

As the USA are not producers of tin, as they are of other products, there is an absence of a counter-pressure from national producers so that if the USA government had cause to discard these pressures, it was because of the incessant consultation which the International Tin Council has with her. At this juncture it would be necessary to examine her stockpile policy, and how she translates it in terms of multilateral co-operation through discussions with the Tin Council.

(A) BILATERAL DISCUSSIONS AND THE BASIS FOR AMERICAN STRATEGIC STOCKPILE POLICY

In pursuance of her policy, the American government stockpiles tin for strategic purposes from two main sources: the Reconstruction Finance Corporation and the GSA. Although her desire to stockpile tin dates back to 1934, it was not until 1946 that a new law, a 'Strategic and Critical Materials Stockpiling Act', was passed. It stipulated that, because the USA badly needed certain strategic materials for industrial, military and naval purposes, to build up a national defence policy, the US government could stockpile such materials in order to prevent her dependence on foreign nations in the period of national urgency. This led to the formation of the European Recovery Programme in which certain clauses of an Act of 1948 made it compulsory for all countries with whom the USA had established bilateral agreements to furnish her with strategic raw materials either through sales or barter arrangements. For example, there was an agreement between the USA and Great Britain in July 1948 which required that Great Britain should furnish her with the surplus of her strategic raw materials. This policy also included the two other countries (Belgium and Netherlands) which received the Marshall Aid Plan. Their total tin production at this period was established at 95,000 tons. This policy led to a further formal agreement with their dependencies of Burma and Indonesia. For instance, only this Act would permit the withdrawal of tin from the strategic stockpile, in time of acute national need. Only the President of the USA could permit a release of tin in time of war or immediate national needs. Through this stockpile policy, the USA has been able to determine the course of the tin market. In spite of the conflict which the USA policy creates, it is even noteworthy that this Economic Co-operation Agreement between the USA and the UK governments contained, in its Article V, a procedure of consultation in accordance with the principles enunciated in Article 32 of the Havana Charter for liquidation of stocks. The result of her bilateral policy was that, up to 1954, American industries signed a lot of buying contracts with Bolivia.

(B) MULTILATERAL DISCUSSIONS AS SEEN THROUGH THE AMERICAN STOCKPILE POLICY

In examining her multilateral co-operation aspects we must not overlook the importance of the 'gentleman's agreement' of Washington in 1964 between consumers and producers in which no official document was signed but which was meant to guarantee a favourable price level at 1·30 dollars per pound in order to safeguard the economies of the six producer countries. Other multilateral methods used are promoted by the Tin Council through negotiations with the US government. As from 1961, the price of tin became so high (£950 sterling in June, at a time when the buffer stock was already exhausted), that the Tin Council requested the American government to release 3920 tons held by the Texas City smelter.[14] This created a problem because of the stipulations of the 'Strategic and Critical Materials Stockpiling Act' of 1946, in which the Congress enumerated the conditions under which tin could be released outside the period of immediate national needs. The conditions were:

1. from the procedural point of view, the American Congress must be informed of the intention to release strategic stocks;
2. from the point of view of method, this notification of the Congress must be published six months before the date of the liquidations.

In this notification must figure the reasons and method of liquidations, including the intervals at which they would be carried out. The American 'Defence Mobilisation Order of 1959' also puts American interests in the forefront without, however, neglecting the repercussions which such a selfish policy could have on third parties. What strikes the observer most, in this Order of 1959, is the importance given to *a priori* negotiation with American industries before any attempt at liquidation is carried out. Despite these stipulations the American Administration asked the Congress to permit the release of 50,000 tons stretched out in several months from their strategic stockpile, including another 10,000 tons as a matter of urgency without calling for the application of the 1946 law. This did not however materialise before the Congress went on adjournment. The Tin Council then met again from 10 to 12 July 1962 after the House of Representatives and the Senate had approved the sales of the 50,000 tons requested, during this period it formulated recommendations to the US government on the method of liquidations. A Tin Council Delegation was then sent to Washington from 23 to 26 July 1962 to discuss this problem of release covering a period of six months. Although this meeting was a failure as regards the quantity and method of disposals, the American Administration re-affirmed not only its desire to dispose of them according to market conditions, but also to undertake consultations with the Tin Council and interested governments when the need arose, before sales. In the execution of her sales policy the GSA would not dispose of tin whenever this could bring a fall in prices. Thus only 1400 tons, out of 3000 tons, were sold for the period of 12 weeks (12 September to 19 December 1962) at the rate of 200 tons per week maximum. Another discussion was held in London on 12 to 13 June 1963 (when the USA had sold a total of 2430 tons at a time when prices were rising to producer advantage) between the Tin Council and the US government representatives. The negotiation[15] was based on the following points:

1. that the USA put her strategic stockpiles at the disposal of the buffer stock;
2. that scarcity as indicated by statistical figures be palliated by an increase of 200 tons weekly;

3. that the Council would accept a maximum offer of 300 tons subject to reduction to 200 tons per week if prices were below the upper sector structure of price margins (£910) but she could sell whenever the price reached the ceiling price.

These negotiations did not produce any positive result as the American authorities eventually did not transfer any surplus to the Tin Council. When in September 1963 the USA announced new sales of a maximum of 400 tons per week for a period of six months (October 1963 to March 1964) under the condition that the total sales would not be more than 9000 tons, the Tin Council did not hesitate to react violently against this new American policy. It expressed publicly that those sales must not be more than three months so that they would in a concerted action study their effect on the world market. It also added that sales be made only when world prices had reached the ceiling price. But when prices were soaring high, at a level unknown before the Korean War, the Tin Council had to send another delegation[16] to the USA after the price structures of the agreement had been revised on 3 December 1963. The result of this meeting was that the Council would ask the USA to dispose of tin whenever the price reached the ceiling. The Council could still grant in supplementary sales if the price went above £965, with the proviso that market conditions were favourable.

We can continue to multiply areas of conflict and co-operation in the tin diplomacy but we think that the foregoing negotiations are sufficient to illustrate that the USA uses her non-appurtenance to the Tin Council and her disposal policy as weapons of diplomacy calculated at holding the world of producers to ransom and at protecting her national interests.

Nevertheless, it could be said of her that her *periodical* concessions were dictated by the limitations of international co-operation.

12 Final Remarks

SECTION I. THE PLIGHT OF POOR NATIONS

International conflicts do not just occur in a vacuum. They emanate from divergent interests of a world divided into poor and rich zones, where the rich (the north of the globe), representing one-third of the total world population hold the majority of the wealth of the world while the poor suffering masses of the southern hemisphere 'eat from the crumbs that fall from the masters' table'. In a situation like this, there is not bound to be perpetual peace in the world, particularly when the concept of co-operation in Article 55 of the UN Charter is deliberately ignored by the developed nations because of permanent interests, growing nationalisms and suspicions still existent within the international community. In fact the developed world still appears to perpetuate, in a fox-like manner, classical diplomacy where the stronger took all to himself, including his own, and only made slight concessions to appease. Raw materials to the poor nations form the lifeline of their existence. For instance, the Cocoa Producers' Alliance countries are responsible for about 80 per cent of world production of cocoa, which suffers from the vicissitudes of market fluctuations and which has been a subject for international diplomacy for the past twenty-five years. It is therefore a very important commodity to certain national economies like Ghana, who is a mono-producer, and the Camerouns who depend much on cocoa for her foreign-exchange earnings.

The changes of government in Ghana could be traced primarily to price fluctuation in the international cocoa market. To Bolivia, tin forms about 74 per cent of her export earnings while over 90 per cent of Nigeria's export earnings come from her crude oil in recent years. In these circumstances, we cannot underrate the importance of price stabilisation of raw materials in the international market. Presently, the commodities provided with international agreements are: tin, wheat, cocoa, sugar, and coffee; the only ones provided with buffer stocks are cocoa and tin. The Sugar Agreement concluded in 1968 entered into force provisionally on 1 January 1969 and definitely on 17 January 1969.

It regulates a 'free' sugar market representing about 40 per cent of the total, and makes use of export quotas, minimum and maximum prices and commitments on national stocks[1] to regularise the market. The USA and the EEC countries, which admit sugar importation on a preferential basis, are not contracting parties to the agreement. The USA and Germany are also not contracting members of the Tin Agreement. This non-membership of major consumers to international agreements is a source of perpetual anxiety and conflict to the poor nations. But if the purpose of an agreement is to secure 'stable, equitable and remunerative prices', in the light of the present situations, for instance with the reservations of certain very important trading partners during the last 1974 Raw Materials Conference in New York as we have already seen, developing countries will continue to be poorer, and richer nations richer, unless the producer countries begin to find alternative measures of disposing of and treating their surpluses. Alternative measures are the more necessary because the demand for raw materials is inelastic in developed countries where, in the event of an increase in incomes, there is a shift of emphasis from food consumption to manufactures and services. These tendencies are the more aggravated by the development of synthetics and the protectionist agricultural policies in developed countries. They consequently lead to overproduction in developing countries, particularly with the increasing tendencies of the developed countries themselves becoming producers of certain agricultural products such as milk, for instance.

For the above reasons, the producer countries must begin to promote alternative juridical arrangements (for example, that of the Cocoa Producers Alliance) for the regulation of their surpluses, particularly as they are bound to industrialise and may themselves become consumers. African countries in particular must continue to intensify their efforts to conclude a continental economic community. They must also find alternative non-traditional markets for their products, reduce existing production in too-sensitive areas, diversify production in more marketable areas, encourage consumption of locally produced materials and food at home and the processing of raw materials into finished products. A dynamic approach in this direction will induce the rich nations, in need of raw materials, into willingness to co-operate on the establishment of international agreements and their participation therein can be assured. The Cocoa Producers Alliance countries must look forward in this direction for salvation, and must try to reconcile their various interests and problems to their Abidjan Charter objectives in dealing with surpluses whenever they arise. An international organisation cannot succeed in bargaining without a uniting force to press its opponents into accepting co-operative terms. 'With the requisite good will, the creakiest of international machinery will operate fairly satisfactorily; without good will, the best machinery will fail to produce the desired results.'[2]

SECTION II. FOR A FLEXIBLE TRADE POLICY

Most developing countries still find themselves polarised commercially to former colonial masters. The direct implication of this is a perpetual subjugation of their entire trade policy in one direction, so that as soon as the prices of raw materials fall drastically, they find themselves at the mercy of the richer countries, 'hats in hand', for preferential considerations. This factor of absolute dependence is a great source of political weakness of the developing world. The type of trade policy which developing countries need is that which will enable them to sell their products to whoever needs them, particularly if they are blessed with many products. Even with mono-producers, this is most desirable because at a period of low prices they could decide to divert their attention to another zone where trade by barter terms exists in respect of the purchases of capital equipment. This will solve partially the problem of having to look for foreign currencies for payment on capital equipment when prices of commodities fall.

Most developing countries do not seem to pay sufficient attention to the formulation of a dynamic external trade policy because most of their administrators are most concerned with internal development processes. The direct implication of this is that university curricula, geared to the requirements of these administrators, pay little attention to processes of international development and affairs. They argue that their immediate needs are not within the domain of international affairs but forget that, to the developing world, the process of development is both internal and external. These limitations affect quite adversely the formulation of a dynamic external trade policy which could look at external transactions from a critically international political angle. This is a defect which has to be corrected with the utmost rapidity even for those administrators who are in regional or 'state' trade or economic development ministries, because the growing but unfortunate practice is that foreign entrepreneurs and envoys often make direct contacts with such regional administrations, where certain products are grown, before they make direct contacts with central authorities.

SECTION III. THE NEED TO RESTRUCTURE THE INTERNAL POLITICAL ORDER OF DEVELOPING COUNTRIES AS A PREREQUISITE FOR ATTAINING THE DESIRED INTERNATIONAL ECONOMIC ORDER

Since the 6th and 7th special sessions of the UN, the 4th UNCTAD Conference, the North/South dialogue, Mexico and Manila Conferences on Economic Co-operation among the Developing Countries of the Group of 77, there have been no structural changes in the societies of the third world. Nevertheless, these meetings indicate the growing concern of the international society to find solutions to their problems. Even if there have been some limited successes in the developing countries, the lack of structural changes in their socio-political life make their economic development efforts a child's play. Professor Adebayo Adedeji, the Executive Secretary of the Economic Commission for Africa, enumerates two important structural dimensional changes,[3] if the developing countries must achieve a meaningful international economic order. They are national and regional economic orders to which I shall add what I consider the most important prerequisite for both national and international economic orders. This is the national political order which most developing countries have ignored so much that little conscious attempt has been made to pay attention to national political development either as a deliberate administrative or university policy, since the faculties of political sciences are often looked upon with suspicion and fear, that they breed agitators. All the great powers of the world have at one time or the other in their histories given primacy to processes of national political development before treating *in extenso* with the outside world. The examples of the USA with her Monroe Doctrine in 1823, the USSR after their 1917 Revolution, and China's forced isolation, gave them the unbridled opportunities to restructure their societies politically by giving themselves political thoughts and systems which permeated their entire societal structure while however not neglecting the importance of international trade to their economies. Except for Great Britain, who for a long time was master of the seas and a colonial master, all other now-advanced societies have used national political development processes as a factor for socioeconomic development.

Developing countries must therefore be told, or made to be awakened to the need to realise, that the new international economic order which they cherish so much will fail to produce the desired results without an incumbent internal political order within their national boundaries.

They have experienced, since independence, frequent changes of government which in themselves have not in any way created the adequate atmosphere for socioeconomic development of their societies. Rather the political fragility to which they have been exposed over the years, through frequent changes of governments by unconstitutional means, have lent so much indiscipline to the administration of their external debt and financial aid burdens which they now call upon the rich world to underwrite. The direct consequence of this is that, no matter how much aid they receive, the quality of their political leadership, the newness of the types of systems they have been called upon to operate, which in themselves have not learnt respect to the rules of the political game, are all factors which militate against their national development programmes.

If we examine the main features of the African economy over a period of 15 years (1960–75) and compare them with those of other developing areas she appears worse off. *First*, there is a generalised external debt burden in all developing countries, particularly Africa whose burden rose from 7 billion US dollars in 1965 to more than 28 billion US dollars in 1974 and in spite of the series of negotiations already undertaken under the UNCTAD no substantial progress appears on the horizon. What has worsened these debt burdens over the years has been the inflationary tendencies imported from industrialised countries because of cyclical fluctuations in their economies. This is particularly so in the OECD countries which are the major export markets for African commodities. *Secondly*, between 1960 and 1975 Africa only achieved a 4.5 per cent growth rate out of the target of 5 per cent fixed for the first development decade, while the average growth rate in the Latin Americas, the Middle East, East and South-East Asia and the Pacific are higher except in Burma and South-East Asia (the Indian subcontinent and Burma) where the growth rates were lower.[4] *Thirdly*, the third-world countries have in the process of encouraging the plantation of agricultural export commodities alone become great importers of exotic foodstuffs with the result that there is a great shortage of local foodstuffs. These countries are therefore obliged to import exotic ones at great costs to their foreign-exchange reserves.

Fourthly, there is a great disparity in economic performance among African countries with the attendant consequence that only nine countries have achieved a relative increase in real per capita income from 1960 to 1975. The annual average growth in real GDP % is shown in Table 12.1. The disparities in the per capita income of the African countries can be categorised into three groups.[5] These are so low compared with the developed countries whose lowest is about 4000 US

TABLE 12.1 Average annual growth in GDP % of African countries (US dollars)

	1960–70	*1970–75*	*1962–75*
Major oil exporters	6.9	7.0	6.9
Non-oil-exporting countries per capita in US dollars			
300–40	6.5	4.3	5.8
200–300	3.5	5.0	4.1
100–200	4.3	3.8	4.1
Below 100 US dollars	2.5	2.8	2.6
Average for non-oil-exporting countries	4.9	3.6	4.0
Average for developing America	5.0	4.5	4.9

dollars. This low situation of the African per capita income can best be traced to their political instability, about which we have already written above. It becomes more evident that the world has not achieved the desired international co-operation, but interdependence where the developing countries must supply raw materials in exchange for manufactured goods.

Without this desired internal political order any attempt to institutionalise a common market as an instrument of regional co-operation will meet with grave difficulties and challenges. Yet they have no option than to seek alternative ways of trade co-operation, since the concept of international co-operation as articulated by the original authors of Article 55 of the UN Charter has not found respect in international economic relations between the poor and the rich nations. This is because of ideological commitments and the politics of self-preservation of great powers, as we have witnessed from all the debates and negotiations undertaken within the four UNCTAD Conferences and in the 6th and 7th special sessions on the New International Economic Order in 1974. Consequently, the regional organisations of the developing world must begin to look inwards among themselves, on what they can produce, and to work out methods not only of diversifying their economies but also of establishing methods of industrial locations for the collective transformation of their raw materials. These otherwise are termed surpluses, because alternative marketing systems have not been sought vis-à-vis traditional ones, nor have they exploited the possibilities of internally consuming their local production.

This situation affects quite adversely their desire to have technology transferred to them. I believe that, like other developed societies, the developing countries must begin to develop research centres, encourage talented nationals and create a political and material atmosphere conducive to the return of the 'brain-drains', who themselves constitute a type of aid and asset to the growth of other advanced societies. Unless there is an adequate internal political order within the component units of a regional economic grouping, acquired technology cannot be translated into meaningful gains. Technology is not transferred but acquired from manpower training abroad, contractual arrangements for technical assistance at home for determined periods, for the purpose of on-the-job training, and from espionage. Most developing countries already possess the rudimentary elements required for the development of an indigenous technology; what they have not paid sufficient attention to is political development which is a condition *sine qua non* for the transformation of technology and the attainment of an eventual national, regional and international economic order.

SECTION IV. LEGAL AND DIPLOMATIC DIMENSIONS

This book has attempted to show the interdependence between law and diplomacy in the area of international economic transactions, be it of a common market type or a relationship between consumers and producers of raw materials. In the process of examining this relationship we have found that law and diplomacy in this area are still in evolution, although certain characteristic features have started to emerge as distinct from traditional law and diplomacy. These characteristic features have evolved gradually because of the need for solidarity and rapidity required in the execution of agreements and in the stabilisation of the raw materials market. In this way, a gradual birth has been given to a modern international law and diplomacy in the areas of community and international economic transactions. As an improvement on traditional international law, international economic and community law and diplomacy have brought in flexibility in treaty-making processes, and this has made it less formal in the many ways that we have already examined in this book. However, its continuous use of terminological imprecisions can not only be attributed to the ruse of classical diplomacy but also to the anxiety for flexibility in the accession of new members, although its long-term results could be disadvantageous as we have already examined in this book. Therefore a deliberate attempt should be made by international economic jurists to eliminate imprecise vocabularies and terminologies in the process of treaty drafting.

The general adoption of economic draft agreements, text resolutions, recommendations and in some processes of decision-making, by consensus often couched with reservations, is an expression of the use of compromise techniques among states whose legal systems are still different. Perhaps with gradual improvements in this discipline, and because of the nature of the gradual evolution of a binding force in economic agreements on both physical and corporate persons, it might one day produce a generally acceptable legal system within national boundaries. But this is still a long way off, because of the political and localised military conflicts which tend to increase the gulf of already inherent suspicions among nations of the world. For these reasons, international economic law and diplomacy still uses some of those techniques of traditional law and diplomacy characteristic of an era of sordid diplomacy of distrust. In spite of these, however, the executives of economic institutions have been strengthened, because the actors in international diplomacy lack the moral strength to regulate the forces of the international society. This is also because of the need for international co-operation which, however, is not forthcoming; the fast rate of growth of international relations since the Treaty of Versailles put an end to secret diplomacy. Furthermore, within the legal provisions of economic agreements, 'acceptance' and 'accession' have become devices whereby those states which did not originally participate in the negotiation, drafting and adoption of an agreement could be attracted to join after conclusion.

Finally, the reader of this book must bear in mind that we are not here dealing with a study of political economy, yet politics and economics have been useful tools of analysis of the conflict and co-operation which characterise this law and diplomacy in commodity economics. This book therefore is written out of the inspiration, hope and anxiety to give the rich and poor nations food for thought and a philosophy of co-operation, knowing full well that 'our world is too small for anything but truth and too dangerous for anything but brotherhood'. This book, which has also used the descriptive method of analysis among others, because of dearth of information in developing countries, is yet an introduction and contribution to the discipline of International Economic and Community Law and Diplomacy, which cries for improvement which only research students can further provide.

Notes

PRELIMINARY CONSIDERATIONS

1. Created by a General Assembly resolution of the UN (No. 1995 XIX), of 30 December 1964. In December 1962 the General Assembly endorsed a decision taken in August 1962 by the Economic and Social Council to convene a UNCTAD meeting held in Geneva 23 March–6 June 1964. It was attended by 120 states for the purpose of finding solutions to the problems of world trade.
2. S. O. Babalola, *The Emergent African Nations and Economic Progress* (published by the Sketch Publishing Company Limited, Ibadan). The above observation was also true for Cocoa.
3. Ibid.

1 CHARACTERISTICS

1. 'Arrangements' refers to conventions whether general or particular. It may not be regarded as imprecise because it is meaningful.
2. Adopted by the United Nations Monetary and Financial Conference at Bretton Woods (1–22 July 1944).
3. Adopted at Washington on 25 May 1955.
4. See UNCTAD Report for 1966.
5. Pierre Vellas, *Droit International Public et Institution International* (Toulouse, 1967) pp. 22–39.
6. Article 67 of the International Coffee Agreement (1968). See also Marcel Merle, *La Vie Internationale*. Collection V (Librairie Armand Collin).
7. Ibid.
8. Convention creating OECD in its Article 3 'The Members agree to consult in a continuous manner . . .', p. 5.
9. Metzger, 'Settlement of International Disputes by Non-Judicial Methods', in *American Journal of International Law*, XLVIII (1954), pp. 408, 416–17.
10. The problems of the unanimity rule and the notion of equity espoused by the ECOWAS Treaty will be discussed in Chapter X, Section III (II B): The ECOWAS (vi) 1: Decision-making Processes.
11. Robert Rosenthal and Ralph L. Rosnow, *Primer of Methods for The Behavioral Sciences* (London: Wiley, 1975), p. 1.
12. This experience arises from the personal participation of the author at the 1968 June Cocoa Conference in Geneva.
13. See Article 37 of the EEC for exception. Accession to EEC is by unanimity vote of the council.

14. See J. G. Starke, *An Introduction to International Law*, 6th edn (London: Butterworths, 1967), pp. 30–1.
15. See G. Schwarzenberger, *The Frontiers of International Law*, p. 218. These may include protectionist or free exchange policies, right of pavilion, open-gate policy, free zone, law of telecommunication.
16. Article 3, para. 20. The 1963 and 1965 Protocols of Extension of the International Sugar Agreement (1958) provides for immediate entry into effect from signature. It requires formal statement as to whether the signature of a signatory government 'is or not subject to ratification, acceptance or approval'.
17. For instance the Munich Agreement of 29 September 1938 ceding the Sudeten Territory to Germany, and the Yalta Agreement of 1945 consecrating the division of the world into zones of influence. These are all political agreements executed on signature.
18. This is a bilateral treaty. For details see J. G. Starke, *An Introduction to International Law*, p. 353.
19. Friedman, *The Changing Structure of International Law*, p. 88. For details see the two case studies in Chapters 7 and 8 of this book. For conflict between USA and Brazil regarding Coffee see AFDI (*Annuaire Français du Droit International*), pp. 620–1.

2 DIPLOMATIC TECHNIQUES

1. The Tin Council, on 12 March 1959, invited the Secretary General of UNO to convene an International Conference on Tin. UNO also convened that of Olive Oil in 1956 and 1963.
2. The Cocoa Draft Agreement of 28 November 1967 contains the text of Articles as at the time of suspension of the UN Conference, 1967. At the request of the Chairman of the Executive Committee, the secretariat prepared this draft. Each Article is adopted in the Executive Committee and reviewed in the Legal and Drafting Committee.
3. All trade ministries should maintain a permanent group of ministry experts for all products, as is the practice of Brazil and France.
4. This practice is not exclusive to Nigeria. It is exemplified by the type of delegations of other countries to the Preparatory Conferences on International Agreement on Olive Oil (1953); Wheat (1962); Sugar (1956), Cocoa (1968). The author was a technical adviser to the Nigerian Delegation to the 1968 Cocoa Conference in Geneva.
5. This is when a conference is being called for the first time.
6. This technique was largely used by Mr Osman Ali, the Pakistani Ambassador in Brussels, who was the Chairman of the June 1968 Cocoa Consultations in Geneva.
7. See 'Reciprocate Concessions', in *How Nations Negotiate*, by Fred Charles Ikle, pp. 104–5.
8. See Ikle, op. cit. for more details on fear of domestic interference.
9. OECD uses weighted voting, and the 4th International Tin Agreement was adopted on 15 May, 1970.
10. See page 37 of Doc. ADB/OAU/CONFMIN/SC/WP/1, Abidjan, 9–13 May

1973. African Ministerial Conference on Trade, Development and Monetary problems.
11. In 1969 the sugar deficit was 800,000 tons. When it increased to 820,000 tons in 1970 only 45,000 tons were redistributed among exporters.
12. See doctoral thesis, 'Nigeria and the International Agreement on Tin' in French, University of Toulouse, France, December 1967 by Emiko Atimomo. Available in the University of Ibadan Library. See also L. T. Galloway, 'The International Coffee Agreement', *Journal of International Trade Law*, vol. 7, no. 3 (May June 1973).
13. See UNCTAD IV. The World Commodity Situation and Outlook. Doc. TD 184, Suppl. 1, Table 15, p. 6.
14. For a more detailed study see Professor Pierre Vellas, 'Les Accords de longue durée et les relations internationales agricoles', *Annuaire Français de Droit International* (1957) p. 134. See also *Droit International Economique* by the same author, pp. 118–22 and 446–9 (Université de Toulouse, France).
15. The meeting was attended by the following countries: Burundi, Dahomey, Ivory Coast, Mali, Nigeria, Senegal, Sudan, Gambia, Chad, Zaire and Upper Volta.
16. *States who were parties to the convention*: Algeria, Benin, Cameroon, Central African Empire, Republic of Chad, Gabon, The Gambia, Guinea, Kenya, Liberia, Libya, Niger, Nigeria, Senegal, Sierra Leone, Somalia, Sudan, Tanzania, Togo and Zaire.
17. See Doc.AGC/CM/7/92ECC of the African Groundnut Council for details.
18. It also meets in extraordinary session.
19. M. P. Cracknel, 'Fats and Oils: The Legal Framework of the World Market', *JWTL*, vol. 2, no. 4 (July–August) 1968), pp. 401–44.
20. Figures as orally given by the Deputy-Director AGC during the discussions held with him by the author.

3 DIPLOMATIC PREREQUISITES FOR LEGAL TECHNIQUES

1. Sir Ernest Macon Satow: *A Guide to Diplomatic Practice*, 4th ed. (Neville Bland, 1957) p. 120.
2. International Coffee Agreement, 1968, p. 59. The ECOWAS Treaty, which is a package type of a regional Commodity arrangement (arrangement being used in a general sense), signed by heads of states, reads as follows: 'In witness whereof, we the Heads of State and Government in West Africa, have signed this Treaty Done at Lagos this 28th Day of May 1975 in single original in the English and French Languages both texts being equally authentic.'
3. This Conference was represented by the following delegates:
   (a) *Representatives*: Algeria, Argentina, France, Greece, Israel, Italy, Lebanon, Portugal, Spain, Tunisia, Turkey, UAR, United Kingdom of Great Britain and Northern Ireland.
   (b) *Observers*: Australia, Austria, Brazil, Dominican Republic, Republic of Germany, Finland, Iraq, Republic of Vietnam, South Africa, Switzerland, USA, Yugoslavia.
   (c) *Specialised agencies*: ILO; FAO; IMF; GATT.

4. In the Tin and Wheat Agreements there are provisions made for Credentials Committee in their Councils. For instance Rule 30 of Article 28 of the International Wheat Agreement, 1962, states that the Credentials Committee in its report to the Council shall list:
   (a) any exporting country which has authorised another exporting country to exercise its votes at any meetings at the Session;
   (b) any importing country which has authorised another importing country to exercise its votes at any meeting or meetings at that Session;
   (c) any member country which has been deprived of its votes under Article 20 of the Agreement or has forfeited them under Article 33 of the Agreement.
5. Chairman of the Tin Council Mr Peter (France); Mr Brook (Australia); Mr Mac Mahon (UK); Sir Padovon and Sir Vincent de Tufo (Malaysia).
6. The Committee of Jurists and Experts was made up of the following countries: Dahomey, The Gambia, Ghana, Guinea, Guinea-Bissau, Liberia, Mali, Nigeria, Sierra Leone and Togo. Mauritania, Niger, Senegal, Upper Volta and Ivory Coast, who were also members, did not attend the meeting. At the invitation of General Yakubu Gowon, the Nigerian Military Head of State, and President Etienne Eyadema of Togo, a Ministerial Conference of 15 countries of the West African Sub-Region was held in Lomé, Togo, from 10 to 15 December 1973 to study the draft proposals on ECOWAS submitted by Nigeria and Togo. The Accra Meeting, which took place from 11 to 15 February 1974, had the responsibility to draft into law the above proposal. *For the 1962 Coffee Agreement*, a 10 nation coordinating and Drafting Committee was set up to prepare the draft. The Chairman was Mr W. Mitchell Blumenthal of the USA. This Committe then chose three representatives in a personal and expert capacity to prepare the draft with the assistance of the Coffee Study Group Secretariat. By 1961, the draft had been distributed to fifteen additional countries, members of the Coffee Study Group.
7. The details of this conflict situation will be discussed in Part II of this book dealing with the Cocoa diplomacy. The draft Article involved, and the various price ranges being negotiated, will be discussed therein.
8. Richard B. Bilder in *Law and Contemporary Problems*, vol. 28. See also Bilder in *AJIL* (1962), 'The office of the legal adviser. The State Department Lawyer and Foreign Affairs', pp. 648–54.
9. R. B. Bilder in *AJIL* (1962), p. 653.
10. This is a conservative view in a fast-moving international society. It is an opinion which stems from a desire not to accept the supranationality of international institutions, although this argument could be valid to some extent from the viewpoint of the need to eliminate conflicts between national and international policies. In this case the distinct study of International Law with International Relations could be blended with Constitutional and Administrative Laws in order to close this lacuna. For the dissenting opinion see R. Bilder in *Law and Contemporary Problems*, vol. 28, p. 367.
11. To the Third Tin Conference in 1965 for the 1966 Agreement her delegation, which was the largest, was made up of the following: Mr George R. Jacobs, Deputy Director of the State Department, 16 alternates, 12 of whom were representing private commercial interests and 5 the State Administration.

This importance in private representation is indicative of the enormous influence which private American commercial companies have over her national tin policy. The Nigerian delegation to this Tin Conference was made up of His Excellency Chief Adebo, Ambassador Extraordinary and Plenipotentiary to the Permanent Mission; two alternates; S. O. Soyode, Commercial Attaché of the Nigerian High Commission in London: London; E. A. Ifaturoti, Chief Inspector of Mines; and Mr. M. E. Whitefield, Chairman of the Nigerian Chamber of Commerce.

12. For the general United States position as set forth by Mr Blumenthal in a statement to the Conference on 10 July 1962, see 47 *Department of State Bulletin* 234 (1963). For general US Commodity Policy at this time, see Blumenthal: 'International Commodity Problems' 46 *Department of State Bulletin*, 997 (1962).
13. In the draft which the study group submitted, it was evident that the obligations therein limiting consumer countries from importing from non-participating countries would create difficulties for the US position. Nevertheless, paragraph 204 of the Agricultural Act of 1956 as amended did not allow such limitation, but it advised new legislation in order to be able to accomplish this objective. Some of the legal questions raised were the following:
    (1) authority to import coffee into the USA accompanied by certificates of origin;
    (2) to grant diplomatic immunities to the international coffee organisation if it went commercial in its transactions;
    (3) how consistent was the quota provision in consonance with the US anti-trust law and policy?
    (4) its relevance to the provisions of Public Law No. 495, 82nd Congress, 2nd Session (10 July 1952) which prohibits US representatives, in international organisations to which she is not a member, from making any commitment requiring appropriation of funds for a contribution by the US in excess of $33\frac{1}{3}$ % of the budget of such organisations.
14. This is in consonance with the Department of States 'Circular 175' procedure. In fact in the US practice, the 'Circular 175' procedure, which is a normal or regular departmental procedure, provides that the 'Secretary or Under Secretary or his delegate must specifically approve: (1) the institution of every negotiation which might lead to an international commitment on the part of the United States, and (2) the signature of any agreement resulting from such negotiations.' Thus the Office of the legal Adviser is a guardian and overseer of the 'Circular 175' procedure. For more details see Bilder, 'The Office of the Legal Adviser; the State Department Lawyer and Foreign Affairs', 56 *American Journal of International Law*, (1962), pp. 633, 651–2.
15. Ibid., p. 652.
16. The initials of delegates and dates of the conference in the prototype are arbitrarily my choice for illustration purposes only.
17. See News Release No. 1021 of 15 September 1975 of the Federal Ministry of Information. This signature took place during a Nigerian Trade Mission to the 31st Bulgarian Trade Fair in Plovdiv in September 1975.

4 LEGAL TECHNIQUES: CONCLUSION AND ENTRY INTO FORCE

1. See *Droit International et Science Politique* (Receuil de textes). Paris: Librairie Générale de Droit et de Jurisprudence, p. 51 by Professor Pierre Vellas, Toulouse, France.
2. This agreement was signed by an Assistant Secretary to the Ministry of Food on behalf of the United Kingdom Food Minister and the Norwegian Director of Fisheries. For further details see Lord McNair, *The Law of Treaties*.
3. See *Bulletin on Foreign Affairs*, Vol. 2, Nos 1 and 2 April–December 1972 published by the Nigerian Institute of International Affairs. Other examples are:
   (i) Ethyl Alcohol Agreement between the Federal Military Government of Nigeria and Erven Lucas Bols N. V. of Holland on the 12 January 1973 for the distillation of Ethyl Alcohol in Nigeria (Source: Nigerian Bulletin of Foreign Affairs Vol. 3 Nos 1–4 January – December 1973 pp 11–12)
   (ii) Agreement for the Manufacture of Edible Salt signed on Monday 19 March 1973 in Lagos between the Federal Military Government of Nigeria and two Technical Partners (Atlantic Salt and Allied Chemical Industry Ltd). Salt consumption in 1964 was about 129,297 tons at a cost of over ₦4 million. It rose to 297,000 tons in 1971 at a cost of over ₦8 million. The Federal Military Government thereafter earmarked ₦924,000 in the Four Year Development Plan. The Federal Military Government has 55 % equity shares as in each of the two companies (Source: Nigeria Bulletin on Foreign Affairs Vol. 3 Nos. 1–4. Jan–Dec. 1973, pages 54–55).
4. Lord McNair, *The Law of Treaties*, p. 123.
5. West Africa of 1 January 1966. See also my PhD thesis, Toulouse, 1967.
6. Notes on Tin (January – February 1966), extract from *Comtet–Reuter* 24 December 1965.
7. The *Mining Journal* of 24 December 1965 declared, 'How this attitude can be compatible with its membership of the UNCTAD is difficult to understand, particularly as Malaysia is a member of the Committee on Commodities.' Does her membership of this Committee mean that she would have to accept any agreement even if detrimental to her interests?
8. 'The Agreement shall be open for signature at the United Nations Headquarters until and including 31 March 1968 by any Government which is a contracting Party to the International Coffee Agreement 1962.' The 4th Tin Agreement was open for signature in London from 1 July 1970 until 29 January 1971. As at 29 January 1971 all countries represented at the conference had signed the Agreement with the exception of the USA and the Philippines. Notable additions were the USSR, Federal Republic of Germany adhering for the first time. (Source JWTL, vol. 5, no. 3, May/June 1971, p. 357).
9. The headquarters for Olive Oil is in Madrid while those for Coffee and Cocoa are in London.

10. The 4th International Tin Agreement, in its Article 47(a) (i), states the following:

    . . . this Agreement shall, for the Governments which have deposited instruments of ratification, approval or acceptance or have given notification of intention to ratify, approve or accept, enter into force provisionally on the day following the date of termination of the Third Agreement provided that such instruments or notifications have been deposited with the depository Government. . .

11. Such dates and conditions are always provided in texts. For example, in Article XXIV of the 3rd Tin Agreement para 4a(i): that such instruments or notifications are deposited with the United Kingdom Government by 30 June 1966 or if the 2nd Agreement is extended by the date of the termination of the said Agreement.

    Para 4a(ii): that such instruments or notifications are deposited by at least 9 consuming countries together holding at least 400 votes and at least 6 producing countries together holding at least 950 votes set out in Annexes A and B of the Agreement. In the 4th Tin Agreement, while 9 consuming countries are expected to hold at least 300 votes, the 6 producing countries should hold at least 950 votes. Since in the 2nd Agreement, the consuming countries were expected to hold at least 500 votes, it is clear that the consumer countries are finding it increasingly difficult to ratify the Tin Agreements.
12. *Droit International Economique et Social*, by Professor Pierre Vellas, p. 20. Refer also to my PhD Thesis, 1967: Le Nigéria et L'Accord International sur l'étain, Toulouse, France.
13. See Article XXIV, para 5 of the 3rd Tin Agreement and Article 47(b) of the 4th Tin Agreement.
14. Article 64 of the 1972 International Cocoa Agreement states the following in its paragraph 1: 'This Agreement shall be subject to ratification, acceptance or approval by the signatory Governments in accordance with their respective constitutional procedures'. (Cocoa Agreement as adopted on 20 October 1972.)
15. Under the French Constitution of the 5th Republic, only the Parliament is competent to ratify treaties of peace, commerce, agreements relative to international organisation, those which commit state finances, those that modify legislative texts, etc. The diplomatic competence of the French Parliament and President of the Republic are however kept in check by the Constitutional Council to which treaties considered contrary to the Constitution are referred. If this body declares the treaty contrary to the Constitution, then a need occurs for a constitutional amendment. Treaties which can only be done by consent of the population are: cession, exchange, annexation of territory.
16. Article 64, paragraph 1 of the International Cocoa Agreement as adopted on 20 October 1972 states: 'This Agreement shall be subject to ratification, acceptance or approval by the signatory governments in accordance with their respective constitutional procedures.' The ideas expressed here are therefore the same as in all commodity agreements.
17. The Joint Ratification of Congress requires a simple majority in each House and this presupposes a similar action from the other party to the Treaty. For

details see Marcel Merle, *La Vie Internationale*, Collection U, Librairie Armand Collin, Paris, p. 33.

18. Political agreements are more easily abrogated by evoking the clause 'sic rebus stantibus' while economic agreements, because of the solidarity which they produce among signatory members, are not easily abrogated; rather there is a desire to employ the procedure of amendment (which all commodity agreements contain) if the interests of a contracting member of an agreement are jeopardised.
19. For example the UNCTAD in 1964 recommended that 'less formal arrangements' or 'different types of arrangements' could be adopted in legal texts so that the objectives of stabilising the market of raw materials could be attained. The term 'arrangements' has no precise meaning in international law, although it refers to conventions, whether general or particular.
20. Some documents expressly refuse the right to make reservations e.g. International Cocoa Agreement 1972, Article 64: 'Reservations may not be made with respect to any of the provisions of the Agreement'.
21. Reservations are not allowed in bilateral economic agreements generally.
22. Louis Delbez, *Les Principes Généraux du Droit International Public*, p. 333. 'Imperfect Treaties' are therefore Treaties which accept the right to express reservations. By this definition, the 1972 International Cocoa Agreement is a perfect Treaty' since it forbids the right to make reservations (Article 64 mentioned in Note 20).
23. Ibid.
24. Article 44 of the 4th Tin Agreement on signature specifically states the depository government as the government of the United Kingdom of Great Britain and Northern Ireland. This is also true of all the three previous Tin Agreements.
25. The areas of this notification are signatures; ratifications; approvals or acceptances; intention to ratify, approve or accept; entry into force; accessions and notification of separate participation; amendments and dates of their entry into force, withdrawal and of cessation of participation; termination of the agreement.
26. Notification here includes: group membership (Article 5); a dependent territory to which the agreement has been extended under paragraph 1, Article 65; entry into force (Article 62, paragraph 1); voluntary withdrawal (Article 66); compulsory withdrawal (Article 67); date to which the Agreement is extended or terminated (Article 69); date on which an Amendment becomes effective (Article 70).

5 LEGAL TECHNIQUES: THE SCOPE OF APPLICATION OF THE LEGAL OBLIGATIONS IN COMMODITY AGREEMENTS

1. The 1972 International Cocoa Agreement as adopted on 20 October 1972 is for three years, from 1 October to 30 September inclusive of each quota year to the end of the third full year after its entry into force (Article 74, paragraph 1). The 1968 Coffee Agreement 'shall remain in force until 30 September 1973' (Article 69(1)). The Agreement Revising and Renewing the In-

ternational Wheat Agreement of 13 April 1953 remained in force until and including 31 July 1956.

2. Article 65 of the Havana Charter. However note that the 3rd Tin Agreement and other Agreements after 1964 have been inspired by UNCTAD principles.
3. See Chapter VIII: Coffee in International Agricultural Diplomacy: Case Study Two.
4. Article 53, paragraph d (ii) of the 4th Tin Agreement, and Article 69, paragraph 3 of the 1968 Coffee Agreement.
5. Article 69, paragraph 2 of the 1968 Coffee Agreement provides for renegotiation, otherwise called renewal, after 30 September 1972; that is, one year before its normal expiry date. The 1972 Cocoa Agreement also provides for renegotiation 'before the end of the third quota year' (Article 74, paragraph 2).
6. Ibid.
7. For details of the procedure of this Committee see Chapter III: Diplomatic Prerequisites of Legal Techniques, Section II: Drafting and the Jurist in International Economic Negotiations.
8. See case-studies on Coffee and Tin in Chapters VII and VIII for the roles of preparatory conferences.
9. Prolongation of the 1962 Wheat Agreement: *1963/67 Annual Report of the International Wheat Council*, p. 17.
10. The previous 3rd Tin Agreement provides that as soon as the agreement is ratified by 9 consuming countries holding 400 votes and 6 producing countries holding 950 of the 1000 votes for each contracting side of the agreement, it could enter into force definitively for them. In the 2nd Agreement, the number of votes required of consumer countries was 500 of the 1000 stipulated in Article XXI, paragraphs 3a and 5. Similar provisions exist in other agreements; e.g. Article 67, paragraph 1 of the 1972 Cocoa Agreement and Article 62 paragraph 1 of the 1968 Coffee Agreement.
11. This provision also existed in the Agreement Revising and Renewing the International Wheat Agreement, Washington, 13 April 1953, Article XX, paragraph 3: 'Provided that Governments of countries listed in Annex A to Article III responsible for not less than 50 per cent of the guaranteed purchases and the governments of countries listed in Annex B to Article III responsible for not less than 50 per cent of the guaranteed sales have accepted this Agreement by July 15, 1953, Parts 1, 3, 4 & 5 of the Agreement shall enter into force on July 15, 1953 and Part 2 on August 1, 1953, for those governments which have accepted the Agreement.'
12. For further discussions see PhD Thesis of the author, Toulouse, France 1967: 'Le Nigeria et l'accord international sur l'étain'.
13. *International Legal Materials*, vol. XIII, no. 5 (September 1974) published by the American Society of International Law. Panama notified that her constitutional procedures have been completed on 21 July 1974 while acceptances were deposited by the USA on 30 November 1973; Denmark (9 August 1973); Guinea (6 August 1973); Kenya (15 August 1973); Columbia (4 September 1973). The Protocol modifying and extending the Wheat Trade Convention (Part of the International Wheat Agreement) 1971, done at Washington on 2 April 1974 entered into force on 19 June 1974 with

respect to others. Declaration of provisional application was made by Nigeria on 20 June 1974; Egypt (7 May 1974); Brazil (30 May 1974).

14. Article 67, paragraph 1 states the conditions for definitive entry into force thus: If by 30 April or by 30 June 1973, five exporting governments with at least 80 per cent of the basic quotas and government representing at least 70 per cent of total imports as set out in Annexes A and D respectively, ratify, approve or accept, then the Agreement will enter into force definitively. Since this Article does not consider the number of importers as a factor for its condition of entry into force, it shows it is cognisant of the difficulties that could arise if number was considered so important. However, the Agreement will also enter into force definitively if all these conditions were met after a provisional entry into effect.
15. See Chapter IV, Section I, paragraph 2: Provisional Effects of Signature, for a detailed analysis.
16. They were for the consumers: Australia, Austria, Belgium, Canada, Denmark, France, India, Italy, Japan, Mexico, Netherlands, Spain, Turkey and the United Kingdom, that is 14. Producers were the following: Bolivia, Zaire (at the time Congo Kinshasa), Indonesia, Federation of Malaysia, Nigeria and Thailand, that is, 6. This was for the 2nd Tin Agreement. For the 3rd Agreement of 1966, it entered into force provisionally on 1 July 1966 for the 15 consumer countries, this time including Republic of Korea and the six producers already cited above.
17. A signatory state of an agreement never accedes to it. It ratifies the agreement under normal constitutional procedures.
18. The exceptions were China and the USSR in the Tin Agreements. The reasons for their non-admission was political, made to satisfy the USA who was against communist entry. The USSR has, since the 4th Tin Agreement, been admitted. China is still out in spite of her increasing western imports e.g. 3500 tons in 1959, 4600 tons in 1960 and 6500 tons in 1962.
19. See *The American Metal Market* of 29 December 1965 in which the USA advanced reasons why she could not join the Tin Agreement. One of the reasons adduced by her was that she disapproved of the stock disposal policy of the 2nd International Tin Agreement. Although the 3rd Tin Agreement and subsequent ones did put this position into consideration, the USA has not deemed it proper to join the agreement.
20. This notice is effective after a given period. In the 1968 Coffee Agreement, as well as in the 1972 Cocoa Agreement, withdrawal becomes effective 90 days after the notice is received by the depository authority, that is, by the Secretary General of the United Nations or a depository government. The Tin Agreement provides that a country can withdraw only after one year of entry into effect of the Agreement by giving 12 months notice (Article 52, paragraph ii of the 4th Tin Agreement). Those which withdraw earlier than 12 months will not be entitled to sharing in the proceeds of the buffer stock on termination of the agreement. This includes other assets established under the terms of Article 53 on the termination of the agreement.
21. See Paragraph I-A(iii) above: States acceding to an Agreement.
22. This is a distributed two-thirds majority vote of consumers and producers of the commodity agreement, counted separately. There is no compulsory withdrawal or exclusion clause in the tin agreements which only provides for

unilateral withdrawal and suspension. Coffee and Cocoa do not provide for suspension.

23. Article 8, paragraph M (i–ii) of 4th Tin Agreement. Other Agreements make similar provisions; e.g. the International Wheat Agreement (Article XVIII, paragraph 1 of the 1953 Agreement, Revising and Renewing it); Article 21 of the 1968 Coffee Agreement; Article 13 of the 1972 International Cocoa Agreement which adds FAO, cocoa producers, traders and manufacturers to those institutions with which there should be 'effective contact'.
24. See Chapter VII: Tin in International Metallic Diplomacy.
25. Idem: Russian exports were limited to 13,500 tons in 1959.
26. By private persons, we mean physical (nationals) or moral persons (private commercial or extracting companies).
27. For further details on the eventual supremacy of Commodity Law on private and public persons, see Chapter I: Characteristics.
28. For 'Separate Participation' see Article 70, paragraph 1 of the 1972 Cocoa Agreement; Article 4 of the 1968 Coffee Agreement; Article 49 of the 4th Tin Agreement.

6 LEGAL TECHNIQUES: CONFLICT RESOLUTION AND HEADQUARTERS AGREEMENT

1. F. C. Ikle, *How Nations Negotiate* (New York, Evanston and London, 1964), pp. 3–4.
2. See Itsejuwa Sagay, *The Legal Aspects of the Namibian Dispute* p. xxix. For details see ICJ Reports (1966), p. 51.
3. See Chapter 1.
4. F. S. Northedge and M. D. Donelan: *International Disputes. The Political Aspects*, p. 321. For more details of state behaviour towards the ICJ and International Adjudication see pp. 321–30. It is interesting to note how Great Britain and the USA amended the optional clause of the ICJ to soothe their interests, thus paving the way for other states to follow their examples. For package-deal type of examples see pp. 291–3. This section brilliantly discusses the advantages and disadvantages in political negotiations. The author discusses the differences between the 'tie in' and 'package deal'. 'In deciding between "package deal" or "tie-in" and the "single issues" techniques of negotiation much will depend upon the general characters of the states concerned and the state of existing relations between them', p. 293. Although this refers to disputes of political nature, it is also true of economic disputes.
5. *Journal of Conflict Resolution*, vol. 2 (1958), Conflict Resolution in the UN: A Review of three studies by Brookings Institute by Robert. H. Cory Jr. (Denison University), pp. 184–7.
6. For details see Havana Charter, Article 46, introductory provision on restrictive business practices resulting from international trade transactions among governments rather than among private individuals. They are regarded as 'species of cartel' since they restrain competition and limit

access to markets. See also *Law and Contemporary Problems*, vol. 28 (1963). Quarterly Journal of the Duke University School of Law.

7. For waiver granted from 1947 to 1961 see GATT. *Basic Instruments and Selected Documents*, pp. 284–7 (10th Supp., 1962).
8. The non-committed Final Act authenticating the text was signed by representatives of 53 countries, comprising most of the then members of the UNO with the noticeable absence of the USSR.
9. The main reason for its non-entry into force was due to the US Congress' refusal to ratify it. Other countries therefore thought it unnecessary to ratify unless the USA did so.
10. *JWTL*, vol. 2 (1968) pp. 445–62.
11. This recommendation was accepted in the General Assembly of the UN as Resolution 1995 (XIX) establishing the UNCTAD. For the full text of this Resolution, see pp. 463–466 of *JWTL*, vol. 2, pp. 445–62, for paragraph 25 of the said Resolution.
12. The conference is convened at intervals of three years.
13. This was in recognition of the anxiety experienced by many countries during the first conference for the adoption of a record system for the views and votes of participants. However, this is in conformity with the UN practice of keeping records of participation and decisions reached in subsidiary bodies.
14. Conciliation Procedures in UNCTAD: an explanatory note in *JWTL*, vol. 2 (1968), pp. 453–4.
15. *Institutions Internationales*: Claude-Albert Colliard, 3rd ed., p. 570. *Article 9* of the Headquarters Agreement between the Government of the Republic of Upper Volta and the Economic Community of West Africa, which groups only Francophones, stipulates that 'privileges and immunities are granted in the interest of the community and not in the interest of any individual'.
16. Article 17, paragraph 2, of the Cocoa Producers Alliance, Draft Headquarters Agreement as negotiated between the Cocoa Producers Alliance and the Government of the Federal Republic of Nigeria. Signed on 15 January 1976 by Mr Fadiga for the Alliance and Major-General Mohammed Shuwa for the Federal Military Government, the Alliance was represented by member-governments of the Alliance who were observers at the signing ceremony. The headquarters agreement was inspired from Article 11, paragraph 4 of the Charter of the Cocoa Producers Alliance.
17. Article 21, paragraph 1 of the 1972 International Cocoa Agreement; Article 14b of the 4th Tin Agreement; and Article 22, paragraph 1 of the 1968 International Cocoa Agreement refer.
18. Draft Headquarters Agreement between the Cocoa Producers Alliance and the Federal Government of Nigeria as negotiated between the Parties.

    Article 11 of the Headquarters Agreement between the Government of the Republic of Upper Volta and the Economic Community of West Africa, whose headquarters is situated in Ouagadougou, stipulates that this agreement enters into force on the date when the Upper Volta Government notifies the Community that it has been approved through the constitutional procedures of the Republic of Upper Volta. Furthermore, it states that all provisions of the agreement not contrary to international agreements and practice, or not against the legislation and practice of the Upper Volta Republic, could enter into force before approval. The treaty establishing the Economic Community of West Africa was signed in Abidjan (Ivory Coast) on 17 April 1973 by six member states: Ivory Coast, Niger, Mali, Mauritania, Senegal and Upper Volta. It entered into force on 1 January 1974.

19. Article IV, paragraph 28 of the 3rd International Tin Agreement and Article 14(c) of its 4th. These exemptions are from taxations on assets, income and other property of the Council as may be necessary for the discharge of its functions under this agreement. This provision also exists in other commodity agreements.
20. This is subject however to the approval of the council in matters relating to the privileges and immunities as may be necessary for the proper functioning of the agreement. See also Articles 22, paragraph 5 and 21 paragraph 5 of the 1968 Coffee Agreement and 1972 Cocoa Agreement respectively.
21. Refer to Article II, Section 18(a) of the UN Convention on Privileges and Immunities adopted by the General Assembly on 13 February 1946, which says that officials of the UN shall be 'exempt from taxation on salaries and emoluments paid to them by the United Nations'. Source, UN Treaty series, Vol. 1–2 of 1946–47.
22. See Claude-Albert Colliard, *Institutions Internationales*, p. 5 and Philippe Cahier, *Etude des Accords des sièges conclus entre les Organisations Internationales et les Etats ou elles resident*. See also Agreement Establishing the African Development Bank in its Article 57, paragraph 2, which exempts its 'directors, alternates, officers and other professional staff of Bank' from any tax on their salaries and emoluments. All these benefits are thus enjoyed by their functionaries of the host government of Ivory Coast.
23. For detailed list of Conventions on Privileges and Immunities of International Organisations see P. Cahier: *Etudes des Accords des sièges conclus entre les Organisations Internationales et les Etats ou elles resident*. See also *Accords et Conventions de l'OCAM*, Articles 24–27, pp. 86–88.
24. P. Cahier, *Le Droit Diplomatique Contemporaine*, p. 44.
25. The 6th Session of the UN Assembly, in Paris in 1951, led to this type of specialised agreement between France and UNO. International agreements on tin and cocoa do specify the need for this type of specialised agreement.
26. Article 15, paragraph 3. This is also the practice in all other similar headquarters agreements.
27. Article 9, paragraphs 2–6 of the headquarters agreement between France and UNESCO, signed on 2 July 1954 and which entered into force on 23 November 1955.
28. Article 17, paragraph e of the Cocoa Headquarters Agreement between Nigeria and the Cocoa Producers Alliance.
29. Article 5, paragraph 3 of the Cocoa Headquarters Agreements.
30. Louis-Lucas, 'L'Affaire de la Legation de Rumanie à Berne', AFD 1 (1955) pp. 175–82.
31. Ibid.
32. This is similar to Article 9(a) of the Ouagadougou Headquarters Agreement already referred to above, but adds that the action must not also be prejudicial to the interests of the Community.
33. This is also expressly provided for in Article 24 of the OCAM Agreement (Common Organisation for African and Malagasy States).

34. Philippe Cahier, *Le Droit Diplomatique Contemporaine*, p. 432.
35. Article 26 (a-c) of the Accords et Conventions de L'Organisation Commune Africaine et Malagache (OCAM), September 1961–May 1967. This Article refers to the Headquarters Agreement between the Federal Republic of the Cameroon and the OCAM countries whose signatories were the following: Cameroon, Central African Republic; Democratic Republic of Congo; Ivory Coast; Dahomey; Gabon; Upper Volta; Republic of Malagasy; Republic of Niger; Republic of Rwanda; Republic of Senegal; Republic of Chad and the Republic of Togo.
36. See Article 60, paragraph 4 of the Treaty of ECOWAS.

7 TIN IN INTERNATIONAL METALLIC DIPLOMACY

1. This part of the book is an aspect of my doctoral thesis at,Toulouse, France (December 1967). This is therefore a highly improved piece on the original in view of the non-static nature of the subject-matter. It is here used because it is the only known metal with an international agreement.
2. Patterns of World Tin Consumption 1957–58, by Mr Laspada (statistician to the International Tin Council).
3. 'In North Africa, in 1964, out of a total of 3,246 million dollars imports, only 435 million dollars were for machinery and equipment. The remaining 2,811 million dollars were consumer goods. Reserves dropped by 60 million dollars between 1960 and 1964 despite the fact that five North African countries export crude petroleum. . . . In West Africa only 526 million dollars out of total imports of 2,434 million dollars in 1964 was for machinery and equipment. Reserves dropped by nearly 300 million dollars between 1960 and 1964.' Source: *The Emergent African Nations and Economic Progress*, by S. O. Babalola, p. 249.
4. *Democracy and Totalitarianism*, by Ramond Aron, p. 4 (translated from French).
5. For example, the preparatory work to the 1956 and 1963 agreements on olive oil followed this same pattern.
6. There were 35 delegations, out of which 23 were representatives and 12 observers.
7. *Droit International et Science Politique*, Prof. Pierre Vellas (Recueil des Textes), p. 30.
8. There is a redistribution of votes on accession or withdrawal of consuming members.
9. For criticism of a simple distributed majority calculated on the weighted system, see section (D) Administrative and Financial Competencies of the Council.
10. The financial year runs from 1 July to 30 June of the following year.
11. At a period when contributions are determined.
12. Decisions of the Council are normally taken on simple distributed majority unless the Council thinks otherwise (Article IV, paragraph 18). Refer also to Legal Techniques (Amendments and Suspension).
13. Vide page 80 of 'The Doctrine of Equality of States as Applied in

International Organisations', by Bengt Broms (Doctoral thesis in the University of Helsinki, 1959). Refer also to the principle of equal rights as contained in Article 55 of the UNO Charter.

14. Mr. Wirjopranoto was Vice-Chairman of this session. Note however that this procedure of simple distributed majority was maintained in the 1961 and 1966 Agreements.
15. For the 1961 Agreement, the date of the first contribution was 3 July 1961, although its date of entry into effect was 1 July 1961.
16. Unless he finds it impossible to intervene because his funds are exhausted.
17. For the financial year 1957–8, the six producer countries of the agreement contributed £7,300,000 which was the equivalent of 10,000 tons of tin metal calculated at the floor price of £730 per ton. These figures include 240 tons of tin metal at £730 per ton. For 1956–7, contributions were £9,600,000, i.e. an equivalent of 15,000 tons of tin metal calculated at the floor price of £640 per ton. The total income of the stock for 1957–8 was £17,142,122.
18. Note that the contribution for the 3rd Agreement was fixed at 20,000 tons.
19. The contribution in cash is calculated on the basis of the floor price on the entry into force of the agreement. If in metal, it is included in total permissible exports of the country for the control period for which the contribution is made.
20. 'Special exports' are meant to be part of government stock and will probably not be used for industrial or commercial purposes during the life of the Agreement.
21. The Council could make alternative arrangements to borrow for the buffer stock on condition that a two-thirds distributed majority vote is obtained, and in which case no country will be under any obligation without its consent.
22. See Report on UNCTAD Conference: 'Creation and Activities'. Basic Document. Sale No. 66.1.14.
23. This excludes emergency meetings referred to in Article XII, paragraph 1, which can be convened in less than 7 days.
24. This was 21 days before the 2nd Agreement of 1961.
25. Claude-Albert Colliard, *Institution Internationales*, 3rd., ed., p. 570.
26. This was the 1st International Agreement on Tin (1956).
27. Note the word 'approval' has not been employed.
28. These two paragraphs are 29 and 30 in the 3rd Agreement.
29. See Formal Provisions: Amendments and suspension.
30. They are those who are not nationals of the host country, London.
31. See p. 570, *Institutions Internationales,* by Claude-Albert Colliard. See also *Etude des Accords de Siège entre les organisations Internationales et les Etats oū elles resident*, by Philippe Cahier.
32. From the draft text of the International Tin Agreement as adopted at the final plenary meeting of the Preparatory Conference, on 15 May 1970. Ditto for the 3rd Agreement. (UNCTAD Doc. TD/TIN.4/7 of 15 May 1970.)
33. See pp. 58–64, *Etude de L'UNCTAD sur les Produits de Base 1966* (UNCTAD Report 1966).
34. *Trade Prospects for Developing Countries*, by Bela Belassa (The Economic Growth Centre Yale University), pp. 62–63.

8 COFFEE IN INTERNATIONAL AGRICULTURAL DIPLOMACY

1. The following international agricultural agreements are each of a three-year duration: (1) the 1972 Cocoa Agreement (1972 to the third full quota year 1975 according to Article 72, paragraph 1); the 1962 Wheat Agreement (1962 to 31 July 1965); however the Olive Oil Agreement is a four-year one (Article 37, paragraph 1). This means that the variations in the normal duration of an agreement depends on its cycles of production, planting and harvesting periods of commodity.
2. For the study of the Olive Oil Agreement see P. Vellas, '*Droit International Economique et Social*, Tome I, and *Law and Contemporary Problems*, 28 (1963) contain a number of very well-informed studies on commodity agreements. See also 'Commodities in Search of Stability,' in *The Economist*, 12 January 1963, p. 130. The proposals to include bananas, tea, lead and zinc as basic agreements are yet under study because of their growing importance in world economy and trade. The EEC concern is noticeable because of their growing ties with African, Caribbean and Pacific countries.
3. See *Law and Contemporary Problems*, 48 (1963), p. 331. This importance hails from the fact that coffee is chiefly consumed in areas that do not produce it, like the USA and EEC countries. There are 43 exporting countries and 24 importing countries listed in the 1968 Agreement.
4. Coffee is in the US Tariff Free List (71 Stat. 516 (1957)).
5. These restrictions formed one of the main points of the 1962 negotiation of the agreement.
6. Colombia 71, Togo (1959) 41, Guatemala 60, Angola (1960) 35, El Salvador 59, Uganda 34, Ethiopia 51, Nicaragua 27, Brazil 51, Cameroun 21, Costa Rica 49, Malagasy 20, Ivory Coast 46, Haiti 41. (Expressed in percentages of world production.) *Source*: *Law and Contemporary Problems*, Vol. 28, p. 333.
7. For details on background attempts at international coffee stabilisation see Part IV of the Coffee Study Group's findings, 17–48.
8. This agreement, which was signed on 28 November 1940 in Washington, entered into force on 16 April 1941. The quota arrangements were terminated in 1945 and the agreement expired in September 1948. For details see 'The Inter-American Coffee Agreement' in 8 *Law and Contemporary Problems* (1941) by Paul. C. Daniels, pp. 708–20.
9. This agreement was extended further to 1961 and 1962 in anticipation of a new long-term contractual arrangement.
10. 'Fifth, the US is ready to co-operate in a serious case-by-case examination of commodity market problems. Frequent violent changes in commodity prices seriously injure the economies of many Latin American nations, draining their resources and stultifying their growth. Together we must find practical methods of bringing an end to this pattern' (Sources: *Department of State Bulletin*, 471, 473 (1961). Although the previous US Administration also accepted the case-by-case approach, it was President Kennedy's statement that reinforced and amplified the US real change of policy.

11. For full text see *Department of State Bulletin*, 355, 359–60 (1961). This statement was made on 7 August 1961.
12. Title IV of the Charter of Punta del Este establishing the Alliance for Progress deals with the subject of 'Basic Export Commodities'; paragraph 6 of Chapter II specifically endorses commodity agreements as a means of solution to commodity problems. See *Department of State Bulletin*, 459, 469 (1961).
13. The ECOSOC Resolutions 296(XI), 373(XIII) and 557F (XVIII) authorised the UNO to convene commodity conferences the rules of which are stipulated, e.g. nature of states to be invited, provisional agenda, etc. This practice is similar to that already described in the Tin Conferences.
14. 'The selection of any Chairman is vital to any Commodity Conference. He should naturally be of international stature, impartial, not identified with any particular interest group, have leadership ability and have some experience with commodity or other economic conferences. Another qualification for any chairman of a commodity conference is considerable physical stamina. In crucial moments of the Conference, the Chairman's personal morale may be all that stands in the way of failure.' Richard B. Bilder in *Law and Contemporary Problems*, vol. 28, pp. 328.
15. See UN Coffee Conference Press Release EC/2149 of 25 August 1962. The international organisations represented as observers were: FAO, IBRD and IMF.
16. The issues were: (1) establishment of quotas and the manner of their adjustment; (2) prices and their relationship to quotas; (3) problems of production and stocks; (4) scope and powers of the organisation to be formed; (5) problems of consumption and trade obstacles; (6) attitude to non-members; (7) method of application of the agreement.
17. For details of international conference procedures see Vladimir D. Pastuhov: *A Guide to the Practice of International Conferences* (1945). Also see Sir Ernest Mason Satow; *A Guide to Diplomatic Practice*, (4th ed., Sir Neville Bland, 1957) pp. 303–23.
18. This was the position during the Preparatory Conference on Cocoa (1968) in which the author participated as technical adviser to the Nigerian delegation in Geneva.
19. Portuguese was used at this Coffee Conference for the first time because of Brazil and Portugal's Angola. Although Chinese is a UN working and official language, it was not used at this Conference since its delegate had an observer status.
20. This example arises from the personal experience of the author who was adviser to the Nigerian delegation.
21. In most commodity conferences, consensus rather than a formal vote is usually the technique used for decision-making by the chairman. Where procedural questions pose problems, a formal vote or even roll-call vote may be resorted to. For instance at this Coffee Conference when Italy proposed to invite the EEC, it unexpectedly turned into a political issue, and so other countries were proposed. The whole squabbles ended only after a number of votes including roll-call had been taken, with the EEC, OAS and the Arab League being invited to participate.
22. At the plenary, Mr Mitchell Sharp, a Canadian, was unanimously elected

Chairman while the heads of delegations of Brazil, the USA, the Malagasy Republic and Italy were elected 1st, 2nd, 3rd and 4th Vice-Chairmen respectively.

23. The Executive Committee establishes the main Committees and it is also responsible for executing the principal items on the agenda. The provisional agenda prepared by the ICCICA for this Conference consisted of the following items: (1) opening of the Conference; (2) adoption of the agenda; (3) adoption of rules of procedures; (4) election of chairman and two vice-chairmen; (5) credentials of representatives to the UN Coffee Conference, 1962; (a) appointments of credentials committee (b) report of the credentials committee; (6) discussion of international measures designed to meet the special difficulties which exist or are expected to arise concerning coffee; (7) establishment of an Executive Committee and other committees as required; (8) preparation of an international agreement embodying international measures considered desirable; (9) consideration and adoption of resolutions, final Act and so on; (10) any other business.
24. Usually these reports are debated in the Executive Committee of the plenary before a decision is taken. They could be modified or accepted, or further instructions given as to the study of relevant areas. This appears to be a recurrent practice as most debated reports are returned to the appropriate committee for further reconsideration before formal decisions are taken. This is a common feature in all commodity negotiations. However the committee has three opportunities to comment on each article of the proposed agreement before it is sent to the Executive Committee for adoption.
25. The legal consequences of adoption and the variation in systems of adoptions have been discussed in the general theoretical chapter of this book. The Conference reconvened on 28 September 1962 and after the usual laudatory orations the text as submitted was formally approved and opened for signature. 23 States signed on this day. The act of signature ended on 20 November 1962.
26. It was made up of Legal Adviser (Mr Gurdon Wattles of the UN legal staff) and jurists from the UK, USA, Germany, Brazilian, Colombian and Ethiopian delegations. The working language mainly used was English. This is also the practice in the tin agreements where any speech in any of the official languages in committees are translated into the working language, however, only after the Secretary has consulted with the interested delegation.
27. The 54 governments which signed the Coffee Agreement are listed in United Nations Press Release L/1041 of 4 December 1962. The UN General Assembly's Economic and Financial Committee approved the Agreement by a resolution of 82 to 1.
28. See pp. 237–240 of *International Legal Materials*, vol. I, no. 2, October 1962. This document, published by the American Society of International Law, also contains the full text of the 1962 Agreement.
29. These conditions are contained in paragraphs 4 and 5 of Article 45, paragraph 4: 'If the Council's estimate of world imports adopted under Article 30 for any coffee year is less than its estimate of world imports for the first full coffee year after the Agreement enters into force, the quantity which

each Member may import from non-member countries as a group under the provisions of para. 2 shall be reduced by the same proportion.' Paragraph 5: 'The Council may annually recommend additional limitations necessary in order to further the purposes of the Agreement.'

30. According to the provisions of Article 31 paragraph 1, the following exporting countries did not have a basic export quota and therefore received, in the coffee year 1968–9, the following export quotas: Bolivia 50,000 bags; Congo (Brazzaville) 25,000 bags; Cuba 50,000 bags; Dahomey 33,000 bags; Gabon 25,000 bags; Ghana 51,000 bags; Jamaica 25,000 bags; Liberia 60,000 bags; Nigeria 52,000 bags; Panama 25,000 bags; Paraguay 70,000 bags; Sierra Leone 82,000 bags; Trinidad and Tobago 69,000 bags. According to Annex A from which these figures were culled, Burundi, Congo (Democratic Republic), Cuba, Rwanda and Venezuela, after presentation to the Executive Board of acceptable evidence of an exportable production larger than 233,000; 1,000,000; 50,000; 150,000 and 325,00 bags respectively shall each be granted an annual export entitlement not exceeding the annual export entitlement it would receive with a basic quota of 350,000; 1,300,000; 200,000; 260,000 and 475,000 bags respectively. In no event, however, shall the increases allowed to these countries be taken into account for the purpose of calculating the distribution of votes. (*Source*: International Coffee Agreement, 1968 Annex A, Basic Export Quotas.)
31. *Paragraph 3*: not later than 31 July of each year each member in question must notify the Executive Director for the ultimate information of the Council, of the likely quantity of coffee available to it for export under quota in the next coffee year. This will represent its exportable quota for this season.
32. These special markets are contained in Annex B of the 1968 Agreement: Bahrain, Botswana, Ceylon, China (Taiwan), China (Mainland), Hungary, Iran, Iraq, Japan, Republic of Korea, Kuwait, Lesotho, Malawi, Muscat and Oman, North Korea, Poland, Qatar, Romania, Saudi Arabia, Somalia, Republic of South Africa, Southern Rhodesia, South-West Africa, Sudan, Swaziland, Thailand, Trucial Oman, USSR, Zambia.
33. For the list of Meetings of the Executive Board see page 35 of the Report of the ICO (1 July 1963–30 September 1966). This regular attendance showed that the signatories of the agreement were willing to make it work. Mr Joao Oliveira Santos, who was appointed Executive Director at the first session of the Council, became the Chief Administrator of the ICO entrusted with the responsibility of creating the permanent Secretariat with headquarters in London.
34. This refers to Annex B of the Agreement – the non-quota countries referred to in Article 40, Chapter VII. The countries are: Bahrain, Botswana, Sri Lanka (Ceylon), China (Taiwan), China (Mainland), Hungary, Iran, Iraq, Japan, Republic of Korea, Kuwait, Lesotho, Malawi, Muscat and Oman, North Korea, Poland, Quatar, Romania, Saudi Arabia, Somalia, South Africa, Sudan, Switzerland, Thailand, Trucial Oman, USSR, Zambia.
35. For the purposes of the Resolution, four groups of coffee were used with the following floor and ceiling prices:
    (1) Colombian Milds (43.50–47.50 US cents per lb)
    (2) Other Milds (40.50–44.50)

(3) Unwashed Arabicas (37.50–41.50)
(4) Robustas (30.50–34.50)
Therefore the selective system replaced the pro-rata adjustment method provided for under Resolution No. 67 which ceased to have effect as of 30 September 1966.

36. '1972 Geneva Agreement' by Ursula Wassermann in *Journal of World Trade Law*, vol. 6, no. 5 (September/October 1972).
37. This group, which met on 8 April 1972, actually comprises 14 exporting countries representing 90 per cent of the world's coffee exporters, signed the Geneva Document. Observers feared that this document would preclude the renewal of a coffee agreement.
38. For 1972 average prices for all types of coffee under the Coffee Council rose by more than 13 per cent over prices in 1971, particularly for unwashed and Colombian mild Arabicas (16–17 per cent) than for robusta's (7 per cent) *Source: International Trade 1972*, p. 41, GATT.
39. See *Journal of World Trade Law*, vol. 7, No. 3 (May-June 1973.) p. 375.
40. See Section III(A): General Provisions of the Agreement, where total distributable votes are discussed for the 1962 Agreement. There has been no change in the 1968 Agreement so that the total distributable votes remain 1,000 for each contracting group of interests (exporting and importing members) according to Article 12, paragraph 1. Paragraph 6 of Article 12: 'The Council shall provide for the distribution of votes in accordance with this Article whenever there is a change in the Membership of the Organisation, or if the voting rights of a Member are suspended or regained under the provisions of Articles 25, 38, 45, 48 or 59.
41. In accordance with Article 12, paragraph 2, this means that the votes of the member will be calculated on the basis of the total membership exceeding 30. Its initial votes will then be distributed as we have already discussed in Section III(A) in accordance with the strength of its financial contributions.
42. The conditions for suspension under the above Articles are the following: *Article 38: Compliance with Export Quotas*: If a member exceeds its quarterly quota for more than twice, its voting rights will be suspended until the Council decides to implement the provision on withdrawal (Article 67). The Council is however also competent to deduct from one or more of its subsequent quotas a total amount equal to twice that excess.
Article 45: Regulation on Imports: To prevent excessive importation of coffee from non-member countries of the agreement, members are expected to limit their annual imports to a quantity not in excess of their average imports during the three years (1960–62). By a two-thirds majority, the Council could vary or suspend this quantity if it was in the interest of the agreement. Paragraph 4 stipulates that if conflicting obligations arise from a member's previous bilateral or multilateral obligations, the Council must be duly informed of attempts to reduce these conflicts and must make efforts to reduce them.
Article 48: Production Policy and Controls. Producer goals are either established by the Council or the producer. If the producer, it must conform to a level not exceeding the need for domestic consumption, permitted exports and stocks. If the Council finds that a member has fallen short of expectation, such a member shall not enjoy any subsequent increase in its

annual exports and shall have its voting rights suspended until it fulfils its obligations under the agreement. Persistent failure to comply could lead to withdrawal.

Article 54: Diversification Fund. Any exporting member who fails to carry out the obligations concerning this Fund, which we have already examined in Section III, shall have its voting rights suspended by a two-thirds distributed majority vote.

Article 59: Disputes and Complaints: If a member commits a breach of the agreement, the Council could by a two-thirds distributed majority vote suspend that member's voting rights both in the Council or in the Board or may require by the same voting system, its compulsory withdrawal if failure to carry out its obligations significantly impairs the operations of the agreement.

9 GENERAL ECONOMIC SCOPE OF THE PROBLEM

1. For details see H. M. Onitiri, 'Major Issues in Stabilization of Primary Commodity Prices and their Implications for Domestic Marketing Arrangements', Paper presented at the International Conference on the Marketing Board System 29 March–3 April 1971.
2. UNCTAD TD/B/C.1.131 Add. 16 of 6/2/73 (Committee on Commodities).
3. For details see note 2 above. There are also preference treatments for 18 associated states to the EEC under the Yaoundé Convention, thus they have a free duty access to the EEC market. Also produce from Turkey enjoys a reduction of the external tariff of 40 per cent for oranges and 50 per cent for lemons and tangerines, satsumas. Citrus imports from Somalia and Libya enjoy free duty into Italy.
4. Idem.
5. See Doc. TD/188/Supp. 1, Chapter 11 and Doc TD/184 Supp. 1 of UNCTAD IV, item 8, p. 13.
6. See PhD thesis of the author on 'Nigeria and the International Agreements on Tin, 1967' (December), Université de Toulouse France, in French, for recommendations. Since a copy of this thesis was submitted to the Tin Council in 1968, by the author, subsequent provisions of the Tin Agreements have contained the need for voluntary contributions of the consumers, which is a step further but still inadequate. See also section IIIB of Chapter VI of this book on the weakness of the buffer stock.
7. Costa Rica, Honduras, Panama, Colombia and Guatemala. The five countries accounted for 42 per cent of exports of bananas.
8. For details see extracts of the agreement, and Ursula Wassermann in *JWTL* vol. 11, no.3 (May–June 1977) pp. 287–90.
9. UNCTAD: Elements of an International Agreement on Rubber, in Doc. TD/B/IPC/ Rubber/L.2 Geneva, 17 December 1976.
10. Ursula Wassermann, in *JWTL*, vol. 11, no. 3 (May–June 1977) p. 287.
11. Australia, Guinea, Guyana, Jamaica, Sierra Leone, Surinam and Yugo-

slavia were the original members who were subsequently joined by Dominican Republic, Ghana, Haiti and Indonesia.
12. This group has now increased to 117 developing countries.
13. See Proceedings of the UNCTAD, Geneva 23 April 1964–16 June 1964, Vol. I, Final Act and Report, UN Public Sales No. 64.11. B.11 page 3, paragraph 1.
14. For a continued discussion refer to pp. 67–70. The group system in New Delhi in International Conciliation published by the Carnegie Endowment for International Peace, May 1968, No. 568.
15. All previous tin agreements and the 4th one, the coffee agreement of 1968, etc. contain this requirement. Refer to Articles 8(i–ii) of the 4th Tin Agreement and 21 of the 1968 Coffee Agreement: 'The Council may take whatever arrangements are desirable for consultation and co-operation with the UN and its specialised agencies and with other appropriate inter-governmental organisations. The Council may invite these organisations and organisations concerned with Coffee to send observers to its meetings.'
16. Manila Declaration and Programme of Action (Note by the Secretary General of UNCTAD) in Doc. TD/195 of 12 February 1976.
17. Doc. TD/184/Supp. 1 of the 4th UNCTAD Conference.
18. Fabio R. Fiallo: 'The Negotiation Strategy of Developing Countries in the Field of Trade Liberalization', *JWTL*, vol. 11, no. 3 (May–June 1977).
19. Ibid.
20. Ibid., p. 210.

10 COMMODITY DIPLOMACY WITHIN THE UNITED NATIONS SYSTEM

1. The UNCTAD officially started in January 1965 with Dr Raul Prebisch as first Secretary-General after the 1328th plenary meeting on 10 January 1965 when the Assembly of the UNO confirmed his appointment under section II, paragraph 27 of the General Assembly Resolution 1995 XIX of 30 December 1964. Gamani Corea is the current Secretary-General.
2. Proceedings of the UNCTAD, General 23 April–16 June 1964. Vol. I, Final Act and Report, UN Publications Series No. 64. 11. B. 11, p. 3.
3. See *International Conciliation*, May 1968, No. 568, p. 46 published by the Carnegie Foundation for International Peace.
4. It seemed actually that the developed countries did not come to because after the conference it was common talk that two conflicting telegrams were sent to home governments. 'Conference success. We gave away nothing.' 'Conference failure. We got nothing' (Ref. see Note 3 above).
5. See Report of UNCTAD 2nd Session in New Delhi (1 February–29 March 1968) in Doc. TD/L. 37 Add. 3 of 6 May 1968.
6. Of the four primary commodity agreements on wheat (mainly a developed-country export), sugar, coffee and tin, only the latter is provided with a Buffer Stock. These commodities together form one-fifth of the commodity exports of the developing countries.
7. Consumers under the 4th Tin Agreement have refused voluntary contributions except Netherlands.

8. The 1968 Coffee Agreement, Article 54, paragraph 2 stipulates that participation in the 'Diversification Fund' shall be compulsory only to producers. It also provides for the possibility of voluntary participation 'from other sources under such conditions that may be agreed upon between the Fund and the parties concerned'.
9. In fact in July 1969 the World Bank and IMF promised to consider loans to developing countries for the buffer stock financing.
10. This agreement provides for compulsory contributions for producers and voluntary ones for consumers (Article X, paragraph 1). The scope of contributions has been widened in the 4th Agreement since the invitees to the 1970 UN Tin Conference can also make contributions. Its purpose is far more a desire to facilitate the future accession of those countries which participated in the adoption and signature of the agreement but who might fail to ratify it, than a desire to increase the coffers of the buffer stock.
11. *International Conciliation*, published by the Carnegie Endowment for International Peace, September 1971, No. 584.
12. It is a committee of the whole house open to all member states of the conferences and to some inter-governmental bodies. For details see *Multilateral Trade Negotiations under GATT*, September 1973–75.
13. The recommendations were on the need to increase financial support for the International Trade Centre by the developed countries and the creation of export promotion centres in developed countries.
14. For details also refer to Resolution 73(x): commodity problems and policies: pricing policy and liberalisation of trade (Agenda Item 7a of the Trade and Development Board. Official Records 12th Session 26 August–27 September 1970. Doc. TD/B/331 of 18 September 1970, pp. 3–4.
15. Reference Doc. TD/B/L. 301. Inter-governmental consultations on commodities in connection with access to markets and pricing policy. The draft resolution was submitted by the following developing countries: India, Indonesia, Iran, Iraq, Jordan, Malaysia, Pakistan, Philippines, Sri Lanka, Syria, Arab Republic, Thailand and Yugoslavia. 'With a view to initiating the effective implementation of Resolution 83(iii) the following programme and time-table of action is proposed: (1) During the period October 1972 to February 1973, the Secretary-General should carry out, on a continuing basis until informal agreement is reached, consultations with the representatives of interested member governments concerning the commodities which should be the subject of intensive consultations starting in February 1973 and the procedures to be followed therein. (2) The commodities to be the subject of intensive consultations should include: (a) On the basis of Conference Resolution 16(ii): oil seeds, oils and fats, natural rubber, hard fibres, jute, bananas, citrus fruits, cotton, tungsten, tea, wine, iron ore, pepper, mica, shellac, phosphates. (b) On the basis of developments since the adoption of Resolution 16(ii): rice, maize, tapioca, meat, dried fruits, nickel, hides and skins including leather, copper, vegetables. (c) Other commodities which may be agreed upon at the consultations envisaged in paragraph 1.'
16. Official Records of the General Assembly 13th Session, Supplement No. 15 (A/10015/Rev. 1), part III, Annex II.
17. See Doc. TD/195 and Add. I.

18. Foreword by the Commonwealth Secretary-General in *Towards a New International Economic Order: A Final Report by a Commonwealth Expert Group.*
19. Item 9 of the Agenda: manufactures and semi-manufactures, item 12: transfer of technology: For details of other items of the agenda other than those mentioned in this text, refer to UNCTAD Doc. TD/217 of 12 July 1976, pp. 147–9. See also Note 20 below, for contents of items 8–16.
20. *Negotiating Group I*: item 8 on commodities.
    Negotiating Group II: item 9 on manufactures; item 10 on review and evaluation of progress made in the multilateral trade negotiations etc; item 12 on transfer of technology.
    Negotiating Group III: item 11 on money and finance etc; item 10 on review developments in the international field.
    Negotiating Group IV: item 13 on least developing among developing countries, developing island countries and developing land-locked countries; item 14 on economic co-operation among developing countries.
    Negotiating Group V: item 15 on trade relations among countries having different economic and social systems; item 16 on institutional issues.
21. Manila Declaration and Programme of Action (Doc. TD/195).
22. Group B position paper on commodities (Doc. TD/B/607 Annex v).
23. UNCTAD Secretariat Papers: The World Commodity Situation and Outlook (Doc. TD/184, Supp. 1); Preservation of the purchasing power of developing countries' exports (Doc. TD/184, Supp. 2 and Corr. 1); proportion between export prices and consumer prices of selected commodities exported by developing countries (Doc. TD/184, Supp. 3 and Corr. 1); ways and means of normalising the development of World Commodity Markets (Doc. TD(iv) GC/1) was also submitted by Bulgaria, Byelorussian Soviet Socialist Republic, Czechoslovakia, German Democratic Republic, Hungary, Mongolia, Poland, Ukrainian Soviet Socialist Republic and the USSR.
24. Doc. TD/217: Report of the United Nations Conference and Development on its 4th Session held in the Kenyatta Conference Centre, Nairobi, from 5 to 13 May 1976, pp. 4–8. See also this programme discussed in Section VII, Chapter IX of Part Two of this book.
25. For details see Doc. TD/217, pp. 6–8.
26. Indexation simply means measures designed to maintain the purchasing power of the prices received by developing countries for their exports in relation to the cost of the products they import. It is not designed to increase prices in real terms but to place their purchasing power in such a way that the advantages which accrue to a rising volume of exports will not be lost.
27. Ursula Wasserman: 'The Common Fund', *JWTC*, vol. II, no. 4 (July–August 1977) p. 378.
28. Ibid., p. 377.
29. Ibid., p. 378–379.
30. General Assembly Resolutions 3201 (S-VI) and 3202 (S-VI) of 1 May, 1974.
31. General Assembly Resolution 32081 (XXIX) of 12 December, 1974. Article 13, paragraphs 1–4 of the Charter.
32. Doc. TD/195.
33. UNCTAD/ST/ECDC/WP/CRP.2 Add 1 of 17 April 1978. The author

represented the Economic Community of West African States at this meeting which took place 10–18 April 1978.

34. For details, refer to Doc.A/9556, Part 1 of 30 April 1974, it deals with Fertilizer Pool Resolution by New Zealand and Sri Lanka; call for Central Economic Observatory by France and USA Resolution for Emergency Relief (2 Draft Resolutions); an expert group of 20 on non-renewable resources to make recommendations on an early warning system to foreshadow impending surpluses and scarcities; and a call for contributions to the new UN Revolving Fund for National Resources Exploration by 8 Nations (Bolivia, France, Indonesia, Japan, Kenya, Malaysia, the Philippines and Zaire).
35. For details see UN Doc.OPI/CESI Features ESA/133 of 8 May 1974.
36. UN Commission on Permanent Sovereignty over Natural Resources (A/AC.97/SR.1–30 meetings) GAOR, 17th Session, 2nd Commission (A/C.2/SR 758–877 meetings (i) and ESCOR 32 Session (E.S.R. 1177–1179, 1181 meetings).
37. 'UNCTAD: Permanent Sovereignty over Natural Resources', *JWTL*, vol. 7, no. 3 (May/June 1973) pp 376–83.
38. See Resolution 88 of 19 October 1972 of the Trade and Development Board at its 335th Meeting.
39. As the court did not carry out proper enquiry before granting an *arrêt de saisie* on 30 October 1972; it further ruled on 29 November 1972 that Codelco be paid for the cargo but should not use the money until after the Court would have made a final judgement on the dispute with Kennecott. See pp. 376–82 of op. cit. above, for details.
40. A Transitional Article 17(c) of the political constitution of the state created the tribunal to which the state and the affected parties could appeal within 15 days of the decision determining the compensation. Its decision is final.
41. Doc. TD/B/SR.330. The declaration appears in TD/B/421, Annex III.
42. Paragraph 3(b) of the General Assembly Resolution 1995 (XIX) which established the UNCTAD as an organ of the General Assembly.
43. Doc. TD/B/S.R.336. The text of the Resolution appears in TD/B/42, Annex 1. Those who voted in favour of the Resolution were: Argentina, Bolivia, Brazil, Bulgaria, Chile, China, Colombia, Czechoslovakia, Ecuador, Ethiopia, Ghana, Guatemala, Guinea, Hungary, India, Indonesia, Iran, Iraq, Kenya, Libya Arab Republic, Madagascar, Malaysia, Mauritius, Mexico, Pakistan, Peru, Philippines, Poland, Romania, Sudan, Syria Arab Republic, Thailand, Uganda, Ukrainian Soviet Republic, U.S.S.R., *Abstentions*: Austria, Australia, Belgium, Canada, Denmark, Federal Republic of Germany, Finland, Gabon, Ireland, Italy, Japan, Netherlands, New Zealand, Norway, Rwanda, Senegal, Spain, Sri Lanka, Sweden, Switzerland, Turkey, United Kingdom of Great Britain and Ireland, Zaire. *Against*: Greece, U.S.A.
44. See (1) Jenks, 'Unanimity, the veto, weighted voting, special and simplified majority and consensus as modes of decision in international law' in *Cambridge Essays on International Law*: in honour of Lord McNair (1965). (2) Lacharière, Consensus et Nations-Unies (1968) in *Annuaire Français de Droit International Public*. (3) See also the text of the Charter in *United Nations Monthly Chronicle*, January 1975, vol. XII, no. 1.

45. 'Lima Declaration and Plan of Action on Industrial Development and Cooperation', *United Nations Chronicle*, April 1975, vol. XII, no. 4, pp. 28–30.
46. Pierre-Marie Martin, 'Le Nouvel Ordre Economique International' in *Revue Générale de Droit International Publique*, April–June 1976, no. 2.
47. Bangladesh, Central African Republic, Chad, Dahomey (Republic of Benin), Democratic Yemen, El Salvador, Ghana, Guinea, Guyana, Haiti, Honduras, India, Ivory Coast, Kenya, Lesotho, Madagascar, Mali, Mauritania, Niger, Pakistan, Senegal, Sierra Leone, Somalia, Sri Lanka, Sudan, Camerouns, Tanzania, Upper Volta and Yemen. (Source: *United Nations Monthly Chronicle*, vol. XI, no. 10 (1974) p. 60.)
48. Ibid.
49. *United Nations Monthly Chronicle*, January 1975 (French edition) pp. 64–5, Algeria, Iran, Iceland, Norway, Venezuela were some of the first contributors to the Fund. See also Pierre-Marie Martin, 'Le Nouvel Ordre Economique International' in *Revue Générale de Droit International Public*, p. 517.
50. For its detailed report see UNCTAD Doc. TD/AC.1/4.
51. See paragraph 142 of Doc. TD/217, p. 125 for details of the opinion of the Group of 77.
52. For Group B position ibid., p. 125, paragraph 139.
53. They had noted at the 4th UNCTAD Conference (Nairobi) that most of the information available to governments was developed by private enterprises (see Doc. TD/217, p. 124, paragraph 136).
54. A. F. Ewing, 'UNCTAD and the Transfer of Technology', *JWTL*, vol. 10, no. 3 (May–June 1976) p. 201.
55. R. Solow, 'Technological Change and the Aggregate Production', *Review of Economics and Statistics*, vol. 39 (1957).
56. A. F. Ewing, 'Transfer and Development of Technology – the Problems of Developing Countries in Perspective', *JWTL*, vol. II, no. 1 (January–February 1977) pp. 7–10.
57. Edward McWhinney, 'The International Law-Making Process and the International Economic Order' in *Canadian Year Book of International Law*, vol. XIV (1974) pp. 67–8. The most affected countries of the third world, Asian, African and the smaller Latin American countries now called the 4th world, were greatly hit by the economic recession of the West, and their fertiliser price increases.
58. Ibid., p. 71.
59. Pierre-Marie Martin, 'Le Nouvel Ordre Economique International', *Revue Générale de Droit International Public*, April–June 1976, no. 2, p. 534.
60. Emiko Atimomo: 'Natural Resources and the United Nations', *JWTL*, vol. 10, no. 3 (May/June 1976).
61. See *West Africa* of 11 December 1978, p. 2477. The negotiations broke down without reaching any substantial agreements although the negotiations were expected to continue in 1979. The difficulties that arose, according to *West Africa*, are identifiable with: (1) the initial contributions to the Common Fund which the developed countries had proposed as 100 million dollars while the developing countries proposed 800 million dollars; (2) the proportion of the amount to be contributed by commodity institutions in

relation to the amount to be borrowed (the developing countries had suggested 25 per cent as against 75 per cent proposed by the developed countries); (3) the amount of the Fund that the developing countries shall use for research development and diversification as opposed to mere pricing. Should it be voluntary (developed countries) or partially mandatory (developing countries)? (4) the minimum equal contribution to be paid by the rich and the poor nations.

62. The author represented the ECOWAS at this Meeting of the Working Party on Trade Expansion and Regional Economic Integration among Developing Countries. It was opened by Mr Gamani Corea, the UNCTAD Secretary-General. At its first meeting on 10 April 1978, Mr Ahmed Minai, the Secretary-General of the Regional Co-operation for Development (Iran) was elected Chairman while Mr J. A. Fernandez Jiminez (Coordinator, Board of the Cartegena Agreement) and Mr S. Moutia (Secretary-General of the African and Mauritian Common Organisation) were Vice-Chairmen. *The Groupings present were*: Association Latinamericana de Libre Comercio (ALALC) Uruguay; ECOWAS (Lagos); Communauté Economique des Pays des Grands Lacs (CEPGL) Rwanda; Junta del Acuerdo de Cartegena (JUNCA) Lima (Peru); Conseil de l'Entente (Abidjan Ivory Coast); Council of Arab Economic Unity (CAEU) Cairo (Egypt); East Caribbean Common Market, Antigua (Antilles); League of Arab States (Cairo); Organisation Africaine et Mauricienne (OCAM) Bangui, Central African Empire; Regional Co-operation for Development RCD Tehran (Iran), OAU (Ethiopia), ECA (Addis Ababa); Secretaria Permanente del Tratado de Integracion Economica Centra Americana (SIECA) Guatemala (Venezuela); Mano River Union Sierra Leone (Freetown). *United Nations Agencies*: FAO: GATT/UNCTAD: UNDP; UNIDO.
63. TD/B/628/Add. 1. of 8 October 1976, Report of the Conference on Economic Co-operation among Developing Countries (Mexico City, 13–22 September 1976); Annexed Note by the UNCTAD Secretariat.
64. See Doc.AGC/CM/7/85. This report of the African Groundnut Council dealt with the world situation of oil seed market in which the possible re-entry of India on the European market was mentioned, including an allegation that the USA plans also to penetrate the same European market with subsidised groundnuts. It was also alleged that the EEC intended to impose duties on oilseed meals which would equally affect groundnut cakes.
65. Doc. E/CN./14/CEC/1/Rev. 2 of the UN Economic Commission for Africa 1976 (Directory of Intergovernmental Co-operation Organisations in Africa).
66. Ibid.
67. For West Africa: ECOWAS, CEAO; East Africa (defunct East African Community); North Africa (the Arab Economic Unity Council) and the Afro-Asian Organisation for economic co-operation; Central Africa (UDEAC); for details see ECA Document as above.
68. François Durand: Organisations Internationales, un supplement de Jeune Afrique (CEAO) des Pays en Symbiose.
69. Doc. ECW/CM/111/Res. 17 of April 1978.
70. Benin, Cape Verde Islands, The Gambia, Ghana, Guinea, Guinea-Bissau,

Ivory Coast, Liberia, Niger, Nigeria, Sierra Leone, Togo, Upper Volta, Mali, Mauritania, Senegal. Cape Verde acceded later.

71. The treaty uses the word 'direction' instead of 'directive' as contained in the French text, which in the opinion of the author has more relevance with giving orders than the notion of a course to be taken which has already been expressed in paragraph (1–2) of Article 5. This may have been an error in translation, because directives have a legal effect which directions do not have.
72. For the year 1977–78 its Chairman was the Nigerian head of state, Lt General Olusegun Obasanjo.
73. ECOWAS Doc. A/DEC 7/4/78: Procedure for the Dissemination of Decisions and Directions of the Authority and the Council of Ministers.
74. Its first chairman for 1977–78 was the Nigerian Commissioner for Economic Development, Dr Omoniyi Adewoye. The Chairmanship is rotational on a yearly basis. The chairman also presides over the Board of Directors of the Fund.
75. See Doc. C/DEC 14/11/77: Functioning of the Institutions of the Community and Doc. A/DEC 6/4/78: Decisions of the Authority.
76. J. Eghagha (Director of Administration); E. Atimomo (Legal and Socio-Economic Affairs); Mr Adetovi (Legal); Mr Jemiyo (Legal); Mr Mensah (Economic); Mr Dzogbleklo and F. Ofei (Economic); and Mr Fadjara (Customs); Mr Ennison (Legal); Dr Vanlare (Social).
77. Doc. o1/EXP(11)/3/Rev.1.
78. At the time of writing the meeting has not yet been convened. However what is important to us here for examination is the nature of decisions reached. Organisations represented were the following:
    (i) *Intergovernmental*: ECOWAS, Niger-Nigeria Mixed Commission (Niamey); CEAO; CIEH (Inter African Committee on Hydraulic Studies, Ouagadougou); West African Clearing House, Freetown; Niger River Commission (Nigmey); CEBV (Meat and Cattle Interstate Committee, Ouagadougou); BOAD (West African Development Bank); Association of African Universities (Accra); WARDA (West African Rice Development Agency); OCAM (Bangui).
    (ii) *United Nations Agencies*: FAO, UNIDO.
    (iii) *Continental Organisations*: ADB, OAU.
79. The CEAO represented by its Chief Executive, Mr M. Ngom, disapproved of the ECA recommendation that the ECOWAS Council of Ministers be made a policy organ for all intergovernmental organisations in the sub-region, because of institutional and operational problems, since the CEAO exists in reality with its own policy organs, not forgetting the fact that they are all members of the ECOWAS.
80. Doc. ECW/CM/(2)/11: Report of the Council of Ministers during its 2nd Meeting in Lagos, 18–19 November 1977. *Those in camera by Heads of Delegations were*: Report of the Executive Secretary; ECOWAS Fund and other documents; Recruitment and Salary Review. *Those in the plenary were*: Rules of Procedure of the Council of Ministers; Staff Regulations; Financial Regulations; Study of the Accounting Manual; Insurance scheme; Draft Provident Fund; Resolution on the Assistance and Technical Co-operation with International Organisations; Resolution on Access to

Information and Documents on Member States; Draft Non-Aggression Treaty.

81. Doc. C/DEC 5/7/77.
82. See Doc. A/DEC 6/4/78: Interpretation of the Treaty and Protocol for all the twelve declarations.
83. Ibid.
84. *The ECOWAS Executive Secretary*: Dr A. Diaby Ouattara, born 25 December 1938, was a graduate of the Ecole des Hautes Etudes Commerciales in Paris. He holds a Masters degree in Business Administration from Syracuse University in New York and a Doctorate degree in the same discipline from Harvard University. He joined the Internationational Bank of West Africa (BIAO) in 1965 where he later became its Managing Director. With a group of BIAO officials from Senegal, Mali, Cameroon and Ivory Coast, he founded the African Centre for Cultural and Technical Research (CARECT).
Managing Director of the ECOWAS Fund: Dr A. Romeo Horton born in 1924 holds a Masters degree in Business Administration from the Wharton School of Finance and Commerce of the University of Pennsylvania. He was awarded an LLD degree from Morehouse. Dr Horton promoted the founding of the Bank of Liberia in 1953 and has since been its President. He was Liberia's first assistant economic adviser to the Liberian President, the first Secretary of Commerce, Industry and Transportation, the first Dean of the College of Business and Public Administration of the University of Liberia. He was Chairman of the committee of nine African countries that negotiated, planned and drafted the Charter that led to the founding of the African Development Bank.
85. The author was an observer representing ECOWAS, at the 7th Meeting of the Council of Ministers of the CEAO which took place in Bamako, Mali (18–19 January 1978) during which the main features of the Draft Protocol 'M' on the status of the Fund (FOSIDEC), were examined both at the Experts and Council of Ministers Levels.
86. For full texts see Ian Brownlie: *Basic Documents in International Law* (2nd ed) pp. 123–39.
87. See UN Treaty Series, vol. 1–2 (1946–47) pp. 16–33 and also UN Charter Article 105, paragraphs 1–2.
88. For details see Article IV, Section 14 of the UN Treaty Series, vol. 1–2 (1946–47).
89. Doc. A/DEC 3/4/78: Convention on Privileges and Immunities.
90. The right of a waiver in the convention is granted only to the Executive Secretary in respect of all community officials. Article 7, paragraph 3 (i).
91. Doc. A/DEC 3/4/78. A '*laissez-passer*' is a type of diplomatic passport granted for travel purposes, which in this case is valid only among ECOWAS states.
92. Benin ($104,494); Mali ($68,462); Mauritania ($13,669); Senegal ($190,972); Sierra Leone ($154,940); Upper Volta ($90,081); Guinea-Buissau ($54,409). However Cape Verde and Guinea-Buissau were exempted later for two years.
93. As at 30 September 1978, the Fund's account was overdrawn to the tune of

CFA 243,426,484 or US $1,159,173. *Source*: Doc. ECW/CM.IV/3 of November 1978.

94. Central Bank of Nigeria Annual Report 30 December 1977, p. 80. The value of oil exports to Ivory Coast increased to a provisional figure of 39.8 million naira for 1977, that is about 8,000 million CFA Francs calculated approximately at 1N = 200 CFA. From 1975 to 1977 the value of Nigerian exports of oil to Ivory Coast yearly was as follows: 28.7 million naira (1975); 24.9 million naira (1976) and 39.8 million naira (1977). To Ghana it was 33.1 (1975); 58.00 (1976) and 79.8 million naira respectively while for Senegal it was 14.2 (1975), 20.2 (1976) and 15.9 million naira in 1977. Others in West Africa: 11.6 (1975), 11.8 (1976) and 23.9 million naira respectively in 1977.
95. Annual Report of the Central Bank of Nigeria 31 December 1977, p. 23. Total Domestic Production in 1976 was 28.8 million pairs plus 7.1 million imports, and in 1977 the total was 27.7 million plus 6.3 million imports. The Ivorian Trade Mission report mentioned Nigeria's production capacity at 10 million pairs.
96. *Federal Republic of Nigeria Official Gazette*, No. 16, Lagos; 1 April 1978, vol. 65.
97. An Inter-Ministerial Council has now been set up at the Nigerian Cabinet Office to coordinate ECOWAS matters. Member states grumbled at Nigeria's economic measures which did not, however, produce too much displeasure because the Institution took off late.

    However, a decision was taken at the last Dakar Meeting of the Authority (28–29 May 1979) on Consolidations of Import Duties and Non-Tariff Barriers for two years beginning on 28 May 1979, during which period a 'Member State may not be required to reduce or eliminate Import duties; however, Member States shall not impose any new duties and taxes nor increase existing ones' (Article 2 par. (i), and 'There shall be no creation of new Non-Tariff Barriers and those in existence shall not be increased' (par. ii). *Source: Official Journal of the ECOWAS*, June 1979, vol. 1 (English edition, p. 11).

11 COMMODITY AGREEMENTS UNDER A QUASI-UNITED NATIONS SYSTEM

1. His Excellency Mr Leonard-Claud Mpouma at the first plenary session of the General Meeting of the Cocoa Producers Alliance, in Abidjan, Republic of Ivory Coast, 21 May 1971.
2. Letter Ref. No. SC: 8006/SF.24 dated 14 May 1971 from the Ghanaian Ministry of Trade and Industries (Trade Division). Taken from the minutes of the 16th General Meeting of the Alliance held in Abidjan 21–28 May 1971. This letter was written to the Secretary General of the Cocoa Producers Alliance and copied to the Chief Executive, Ghana Cocoa Marketing Board, Accra.
3. Ibid.
4. This draft was later rejected by the producers as inequitable in preference for a complete new one drafted by the UNCTAD. The Draft under consideration here was Doc. TD/Cocoa.2/EX/R.9.

5. The author was technical adviser to the Nigerian delegation at this conference.
6. The author participated at this meeting.
7. Doc. CPA–AC351 (Appendix XI) of the Cocoa Producers Alliance Meeting, Lagos 10–17 September 1971. A representative of the Secretary-General of the UNCTAD Mr G. N. O. Sefia addressed this meeting on behalf of the Secretary-General.
8. See the Politics of Co-operation within the Cocoa Alliance: (A) International Cocoa Agreement.
9. For fuller discussion see Section I(1) above: The Politics of co-operation within the Cocoa Producers Alliance.
10. West Africa of 1 January 1966.
11. *Notes on Tin* (January–February 1966) extracts from Committees – Reuter 24 December 1965.
12. The *Mining Journal* of 24 December 1965 declared: 'How this attitude can be compatible with its membership of the UNCTAD is difficult to understand, particularly as Malaysia is a member of the Committee on Commodities.' Does her membership of this Committee mean that she would have to accept any Agreement even if detrimental to her interests?
13. *Raw Materials: A Study of American Policy*, by Percy Bidwell.
14. Although this smelter belonged to the US government, the tonnage did not belong to the strategic stockpile.
15. This delegation consisted of the following personalities from the Tin Council: the Chairman and Secretary, Vice-Chairman of Consumers, Indonesia, Malaysia and United Kingdom delegates and the Chairman of the Statistical Committee.
16. Delegations: Chairman (Mr Allen); 2 Vice-Chairman (Mr Coppietes 't Wallant and Mr Adnalu), and the delegates of Bolivia, Canada, Congo Leopoldville (Zaire Republic), France, Japan, Malaysia, Federation of Nigeria, Thailand and UK, Chairman of the Statistical Committee (Mr Brooke) and the Secretary of the Council.

12 FINAL REMARKS

1. IMF/IBRD: the problem of stabilisation of prices of primary products, as staff study Part I (Washington, 1968) p. 84.
2. Economic and Social Council Officials Records, 36th Session, 1963, Annexes Agenda item 5e/3756, paragraph 136a.
3. Adebayo Adedeji: 'Africa – The Crisis of Development and the Challenge of a New Economic Order', address delivered to the 4th Meeting of the Conference of Ministers and the 13th Session of the ECA Kinshasa, 28 February–3 March 1977, p. 4.
4. Ibid., p. 7. See also P.B. Okoh, *Nature and Character of Contemporary International Conflicts* (Seminar Series NIIA, Lagos, No. 1 p. 10). Dr Okoh contends that the low income countries (below 200 dollars per capita) with a billion people are expected to increase their average GNP from 410 to 540 dollars and the OECD countries from $3,100 to $4,000. In other words for

an entire decade the poor nations might increase their income by $3 annually while the rich will get $900 increase.

5. (a) *Major oil exporters*: Algeria, Gabon, the Libyan Arab Republic and Nigeria; that is four countries.

(b) *41 non-oil exporting countries are in four groups*

300–400 US dollars:	the Congo; Ivory Coast; Sao Tome and Principe; Tunisia and Zambia, i.e. 4 countries.
200–300 US dollars:	Cape Verde; Egypt; Equatorial Guinea; Ghana; Guinea-Bissau; Liberia; Mauritius; Morocco; Mozambique; Senegal and Swaziland, i.e. 11 countries.
100–200 US dollars:	Botswana, Central African Empire; the Gambia; Kenya; Madagascar; Mauritania; Sierra Leone; Sudan; Togo; Uganda and United Republic of Cameroon, i.e. 11 countries.
(c) *Below 100 US dollars*:	Benin; Burundi; Chad; Ethiopia; Guinea; Lesotho, Malawi; Mali; the Niger; Rwanda; Somalia; United Republic of Tanzania; Upper Volta and Zaire, i.e. 14 countries.

Source: ECA Estimates.

Further Reading

I. AGREEMENTS AND TREATIES

Accords et Conventions de l'Organisation Commune Africaine et Malgache, Septembre–Mai 1967.
Accord portant création de la Banque Africaine de Développement.
Accord de Siège entre la République Togolaise et le Comité International de la Croix-Rouge (CICR).
Cocoa Producers Alliance: Draft Headquarters Agreement between the Cocoa Producers Alliance and the Government of the Federal Republic of Nigeria signed on 15 January 1976.
Communauté Economique de l'Afrique de l'Ouest (Traité et Protocoles instituant la CEAO).
International Tin Agreements up to 1975.
International Wheat Agreements (1962, 1968) and Rules of Procedure.
International Agreements on Olive Oil (1963) and its Protocols of Extension.
International Sugar Agreement (1958) and its Rules of Procedure and the 1965 Protocol Extending the 1958 Agreement.
International Cocoa Agreement (1972).
International Coffee Agreements.
Projet d'Accord de Siège entre le Gouvernement de la République de Haute Volta et la Communauté Economique de l'Afrique de l'Ouest.
The Treaty of the Economic Community of West African States and its Protocols (ECOWAS).
The Treaties establishing the European Communities.

II. BOOKS

Adedeji Adebayo, *Collective Self-reliance in Developing Africa: Scope, Prospects and Problems* (Lecture series No. 17, Lagos: NIIA).
Akiwumi, A. M., 'Judicial Aspects of Economic Integration Treaties in

Africa' (Extract from the *Colloquium*, vol. I, 1972 (Hague: Academy of International Law).

Atimomo, Emiko, 'Le Nigeria et l'Accord International sur l'Etain' (Doctorate thesis, Toulouse, December 1967).

Babalola, S. O., *The Emergent African Nations and Economic Progress* (Ibadan: Sketch Publishing Ltd, 1967).

Bala, Balassa, *Trade Prospects for Developing Countries* (Homewood Ill.: R. D. Irwin, 1964).

Bengt, Broms, 'The Doctrine of Equality of States as applied in International Organisations' (Doctorate thesis for the University of Helsinki; English translation, 1959).

Bowett, D. W., *The Law of International Institutions*, 2nd edn (London: Stevens and Sons, 1970).

Brownlie, Ian, *Basic Documents in International Law*, 2nd edn (Oxford: Clarendon Press, 1972).

Cable, J., *Gunboat Diplomacy: Political Applications of Limited Naval Force* (New York: Praeger, 1971).

Cahier, P., *Le Droit Diplomatique Contemporaine* (Genève: Librairie Droz; Paris: Librairie Minard, 1962).

Campbell, A., *Common Market Law*, vols I and II (London: Longman and Oceana, 1969).

Colliard, Claude-Albert, *Institutions Internationales* (Paris: Dalloz, 1965).

Dam, K. W., *The GATT Law and International Economic Organisation* (Chicago: University of Chicago Press, 1970).

David, V. Edwards, *International Political Analysis* (New York: Holt, Rinehart & Winston, 1969).

Delbez, Louis, *Les Principes Généraux du Droit International Public*, 3rd edn (Paris: Librairie Générale de Droit et de Jurisprudence, 1964).

Delupis, Ingrid, Doimi di (née Detter), *The East African Community and Common Market* (London: Longman, 1970).

Donelan, M. D. and Grieve, M. J., *International Disputes: Case Histories 1945–1970* (London: Europa Publications, 1973).

Donelan, M. D. and Northege, F. S., *International Disputes: The Political Aspects* (London: Europa Publications, 1971).

Elias, T. O., *Modern Law of Treaties* (Dobbs Ferry: Oceana, 1974).

Eze, Osita, *The Legal Status of Foreign Investments in the East African Common Market* (Leiden: Sijthoff Genève, 1975).

Fenwick, Charles G., *International Law*, 4th edn (New York: Appleton, 1965).

Flory, Thiebaut, 'Le GATT – Droit International et Commerce

Mondial' (Doctorate thesis, Paris, December 1966).
Forgac, Albert A., *New Diplomacy and the United Nations* (New York: Pageant Press, 1965).
Friedmann, Wolfgang Gaston, *The Changing Structure of International Law* (London: Stevens, 1964).
Hedges, E. S., *Tin in Social and Economic theory* (London: Arnold, 1964).
Holloway, Kaye, *Modern Trends in Treaty Law; Constitutional Law, Reservations and Three Modes of Legislation* (London: Stevens; Dobbs Ferry: Oceana Publications, 1967).
Ijalaye, D. A., *The Extension of Corporate Personality in International Law* (New York: Oceana, 1978).
Ikle, F. C., *How Nations Negotiate*, (New York: Evanston, 1976).
International Disputes; The Legal Aspects (Report of a study group of the Davies Memorial Institute of International Studies – Europe Publications).
Khurshid, Hyder (Hassan), *Equality of Treatment and Trade Discrimination in International Law* (The Hague: Martinus Nijhoff, 1968).
McNair, Lord, *The Law of Treaties* (Oxford: University Press, 1961).
Marcel, Merle, *La Vie Internationale* (Paris: Collection du Librairie Armand Collin, 1963).
Mario, Amadio, 'Le Contentieux International de l'Investissement Privé et la Convention de la Banque Mondiale du 18 Mars 1965' (Doctorate thesis, Toulouse, 1966).
Mathijsen, P. S. R. F., *A Guide to European Community Law*, 2nd edn (London: Sweet & Maxwell/Mathew Bender, 1975).
Nkrumah, Kwame, *Neocolonialism – The Last Stage of Imperialism* (New York: International Publications, 1965, 1966).
O'Connell, D. P., *International Law*, vols I and II (London: Stevens, 1970).
Ogene, Chidozie, F., *The Politics of Scarcity: African Resources and International Politics*. Seminar series, No. 4 (Lagos: NIIA).
Okoh, Bushel P., *Nature and Character of Contemporary International Conflicts*. Seminar series, No. 4 (Lagos: NIIA).
Osagie, Eghosa, *Elements of Economic Principles, Policies and Essays* (Scholars Press) (Ibadan: Ogiso Publishers, 1978).
Pope Paul, 'Populorum Progessio' Encyclique, 26 March 1967.
Rosenthal, Robert and Rosnow, Ralph, *Primer of Methods for the Behavioural Sciences* (New York: John Wiley & Sons Inc, 1975).
Sagay, Itsejuwa, *The Legal Aspects of the Namibian Dispute* (Ile Ife (Nigeria): University of the Ife Press, 1975).

Sanu, Olu E., *The Lome Convention and the New International Order*. Lecture series, No. 18 (Lagos: NIIA).

Starke, J. G., *An Introduction to International Law*, 6th edn (London: Butterworth & Co. Ltd, 1967).

Temu, P. E., *Marketing Board Pricing and Storage Policy: The Case of Maize in Tanzania* (Nairobi: East African Literature Bureau, 1977).

Uche, U. U., *The Law and the New International Economic Order: Reflections on Nigeria*. Lecture series, No. 20 (Lagos: NIIA).

Vellas, Pierre, *Droit International Economique et Social*, Tome I (Toulouse: Sirey-Paris, 1965).

Vellas, Pierre, *Droit International Public*

Vellas, Pierre, *Droit International et Science Politique*. Recueil de textes. (Paris: Librairie Générale de Droit et de Jurisprudence, 1967).

Vellas, Pierre, Arthur Karasz and V. Z. Tabona, *Coopération Economique et Social et Droit International Public*. Recueil Sirey Publications, No. 5 de l'Institut d'Etudes Internationales et des Pays en voie de Développement.

III. PERIODICALS AND JOURNALS

L'Affaire du Conflit du Café entre le Brézil et les U.S.A. (Annuaire Français du Droit International), pp. 620–1.

African Declaration on Cooperation, Development and Economic Independance (Abidjan, 12 May 1973)

Buchan, A., 'The Irony of Kissinger', *Journal of International Affairs*, vol. 50, No. 3 (July 1974), pp. 367–79.

Bilder, Richard B., 'The Office of the Legal Adviser, The State Department Lawyer and Foreign Affairs', *American Journal of International Law* (1962), vol. 56, pp. 633–84.

Chile, 'Decree Law Approving Settlement with Kennecott (October 24)', *International Legal Materials*, vol. XIV, No. 1 (January 1975), pp. 135–7.

Cocoa Producers Alliance Reports.

Comprehensive Report on the Technical Studies on Trade, Development and Monetary Problems presented by the African Experts of the Drafting Committee appointed by OAU, ADB and ECA.

Cory, Robert, H. (Jr.), 'Conflict Resolution in the United Nations: a Review of Three Studies by the Brooking Institute', *Journal of Conflict Resolution*, vol. 2 (1958).

Eze, Osita. C., 'Patents and Transfer of Technology with special reference to the East African Community, East African Law Review', *A Journal of Law and Development*, vol. 5, No. 1 and 2 (1972).

Fisher, V., 'Le Mode Règlement des Différends Adopté par l'Accord International sur le Blé', *Annuaire Français du Droit International* (1955), p. 208.

Francisco Orrego Vicuma, 'Some International Law Problems posed by the Nationalisation of the Copper Industry by Chile', *American Journal of International Law*, vol. 67 (1973), pp. 711–27.

GATT, Tokyo Declaration on Multinational Trade Negotiations, 14 September 1973. *International Legal Materials*, vol. 12 (November 1973), pp. 1533–6 (Ministerial Meeting, Tokyo, 12–14 September 1973 Declaration).

Hugo, J. Hahn, 'International and Supranational Public Authorities', *Law and Contemporary Problems*, vol. 26 (1961), p. 638.

International Coffee Agreement 1962, *International Legal Materials*, vol. 1, No. 2 (October 1962), published by the American Society of International Law, pp. 237–40.

International Tin Council, Annual Reports.

Martin, Pierre-Marie, 'Le Nouvel Ordre Economique International', *Revue Générale de Droit International Public*, No. 2 (Avril–Juin 1972).

Metzger, S. D., 'Settlement of International Disputes by non Juridical Methods', *American Journal of International Law*, vol. 48 (1954), pp. 408, 416–17.

Mining Journal, 27 December 1965.

Multilateral Trade Negotiations on GATT, September 1973–75.

'Notes On Tin' (January–February 1966). Extracts from Committee Reuter, 24 December 1965.

Report of the Meeting of the Sales Executives of the Member Government of the Cocoa Producers Alliance held in Accra, Ghana, 19–24 April 1971.

Turner, Louis, 'The Politics of Energy Crises', *Journal of International Affairs*, vol. 50 (July 1974), pp. 404–15.

IV. JOURNAL OF WORLD TRADE LAW (*JWTL*)

Akiwumi, A. M., 'The East African Community', *JWTL*, vol. 6, No. 1 (March/April 1972).

Alnasrawi, Abbas, 'Collective Bargaining Power in OPEC', *JWTL*, vol. 7, No. 2 (March/April 1973), p. 188.

Atimomo, Emiko, 'Natural Resources and the United Nations', *JWTL*, vol. 10, No. 3 (May/June 1976).

Burnett, Robbin, 'Negotiation of International Agreements in the Field of Commerce and Investment Problems of Relevance to Newly Independent States', *JWTL*, vol. 9, No. 3 (May/June 1975).

Cracknell, M. P., 'Fats and Oils', *JWTL*, vol. 2, No. 4 (July/August 1968), pp. 401–44.

Dam, K. W., 'The GATT as an International Organisation', *JWTL*, vol. 3, No. 4 (May/June 1969).

Edwards, J., 'The International Tin Agreement', *JWTL*, vol. 3, No. 3 (June/August 1969).

Elias, T. O., 'The Association Agreement between the E.E.C. and the Federal Republic of Nigeria', *JWTL*, vol. 2, No. 2 (March/April 1968).

Erb, G. F., 'The Second Session of UNCTAD', *JWTL*, vol. 2, No. 3 (May/June 1968), pp. 345–59.

Horowitz, David, 'After the UNCTAD', *JWTL*, vol. 2, No. 5 (September/October 1968), pp. 489–94.

'International Coffee Agreement', *JWTL*, vol. 2, No. 3 (May/June 1968), pp. 359–62 (Notes).

'International Grains Arrangement', *JWTL*, vol. 2, No. 2 (March/April 1968); vol. 2, No. 5 (September/October 1968), pp. 544–65.

'International Sugar Agreements', *JWTL*, vol. 3, No. 2 (March/April 1969), p. 467 (Notes).

'The 4th International Tin Agreement', *JWTL*, vol. 5, No. 3 (May/June 1971), p. 355.

'The International Wheat Agreement', *JWTL*, vol. 5, No. 3 (May/June 1971), p. 360.

'1972 Geneva Coffee Agreement', *JWTL*, vol. 6, No. 5 (September/October 1972).

'International Olive Oil Agreement', *JWTL*, vol. 7, No. 4 (July/August 1973).

'The Energy Crisis', *JWTL*, vol. 8, No. 4 (July/August 1974).

'Interview with Gamani Corea, Secretary General of UNCTAD on the Problem of Production of Primary Commodities', *JWTL*, vol. 9, No. 1 (January/February 1975).

'African Trade and Commodity Price Boom', *JWTL*, vol. 9, No. 2 (March/April 1975), p. 224.

Vellas, Pierre, 'Development of the Franc Area and the Franco-African Monetary Cooperation', *JWTL*, vol. 2, No. 1 (January/February 1968).

Wassermann, Ursula, 'UNCTAD Cocoa Negotiations', *JWTL*, vol. 3, No. 6 (November/December 1969).

IV. UNITED NATIONS PUBLICATIONS

Adedeji, Adebayo, 'The Crisis of Development and the Challenge of a New Economic Order' (Address delivered to the 4th Meeting of the Conference of Ministers at the 13th Session of Economic Commission for Africa, Kinshasa, 28 February–31 March 1977).

'New Directions and New Structures for Trade and Development' (Report by the Secretary General of UNCTAD to the 4th UNCTAD Conference (Doc. 183/Rev. 1).

Zalmani, Haquani, 'UNCTAD for a New Economic Order'.

Doc. TD (iv)/GC/L. I: Draft Report of the General Committee.

Doc. TD (iv)/GC/RIL: Report by the Chairman of Negotiating Group I on the position as of Saturday 22 May 1976.

Doc. TD (iv)/GC/R. 6 'Strengthening the Technological Capacity of Developing Countries'.

Doc. TD (iv)/GC/ 1–4.

Doc. TD/207: Statement made by the International Wheat Council (IWC): Note by the UNCTAD Secretariat.

Doc. TD/202: Statement made by the Secretary General of UNO at the 120th Plenary Meeting on 5 May 1976.

Doc. TD/199 and Add/I: Pre-Conference Meeting held at the Kenyatta Conference Centre, Nairobi, Kenya, on 4 May 1976. Report by the Chairman.

Doc. TD/192: 'Economic Cooperation among Developing Countries', Report by the UNCTAD Secretariat.

Doc. TD/195: Manila Declaration and Programme of Action.

Doc. TD/L/37 Add. 3: Report of UNCTAD 2nd Session.

Doc. TD/B/628 Add. 1: Reort of the Conference on Economic Cooperation among Developing Countries (Mexico City, 13–22 September 1976) Annexes Note by the UNCTAD Secretariat.

E/CN/14/CEC/1 Rev. 2: Directory of Intergovernmental Cooperation Organisations in Africa (ECA 1976).

Commerce de Produits de Base (1965).

UNCTAD: Creation and Activities (Basic Documents).

Etude de l'UNCTAD sur les Produits de Base (1966). Conference des Nations Unies sur l'Etain, 1960. Résumé des débats. Proceedings of the UNCTAD, Geneva, 23 April and 4–16 June 1964, vol. 1: Final

Act and Report (UN Public Sales no. 64.11. B. 11, p. 3, para. 1).

The Group System in New Delhi in International Conciliation. Published by the Carnegie Endowment for International Peace, May 1968, No 568.

Report of UNCTAD Second Session in New Delhi, 1 February–29 March 1968, in Doc. TD/L. 37 Add. 3 of 6 May 1968.

IMF/IBRD: The problem of Stabilization of prices of Primary Products, as staff study Part I (Washington) p. 84. Economic and Social Council Official records, 36th Session 1963, Annexes Agenda item 5 E/3756 para. 136a.

Year Book of International Trade Statistics 1953 (United Nations). Reports of the UNCTAD on its 3rd Session held at Santiago, Chile, from 13 April to 21 May 1972.

Report of the Secretary-General on the Multilateral Trade Negotiations under the Auspices of GATT.

Study of the problems of Raw Materials and Development. Report of the *Ad Hoc* Committee of the 6th Special Session. Doc. A/9556 Part II, of 1 May 1974 United Nations General Assembly.

Study of the Problems of Raw Materials and Development. Text submitted by the Chairman, 'Declaration on the Establishment of a New International Order'. Doc/A/AC. 166/L.50 of 30 April 1974 of UNO.

'Six Proposals for Action on Problems of Raw Materials and Development introduced in *Ad Hoc* Committee', Press Release GA/5012 of 29 April 1974, 6th Special General Assembly, *Ad Hoc* Committee, 19th Meeting.

Principles for a New International Economic Order adopted by the 6th Special Session of the General Assembly. Doc. DPI/CESI, Features ESA/133 of 8 May 1974.

6th Special Session of the General Assembly on Problems of Raw Materials and Development Ends.

(a) Adopts Principles of a New International Order.
(b) 7 Draft Resolutions on Emergency Measures for Developing Countries Referred to ECOSOC Doc. OPI/CESI, Features ESA/134 of May 1974.

UNCTAD: Trade and Development Board Official Records, 12th Session Resolutions, Agreed Conclusions and Decision, Supplement No. 1 of 3–25 October 1972.

UNCTAD Doc. TD/B/C. 1/131 Add. 18 of 16 February 1973. 'Intensive Inter-Governmental Consultations on Commodities in Connection with Access to Markets on Pricing Policy'.

United Nations General Assembly Doc. A/9544/Add. 1 of 4 April 1974 'The Significance of Basic Commodities in World Trade in 1970', 6th Special Session, item 7 of the Provisional Agenda, pp. 1–3.

Resolution 73 (x): Commodity Problems and Policies Pricing Policy and Liberalisation of Trade (Agenda item 7a, Doc. TD/B/331 of 18 September 1970; Trade and Development Board Official Records, 12th Session, 26 August–24 September 1970.

UNCTAD Doc. TD/B/C.1/131 Add. 16 of 6 February 1973 on Committee on Commodities.

Index

Note: Names of individual commodity agreements will be found under the name of that commodity (e.g.: Olive oil, 1st International Agreement (1956)).